THE INDONESIAN RURAL ECONOMY

The **Institute of Southeast Asian Studies (ISEAS)** was established as an autonomous organization in 1968. It is a regional research centre for scholars and other specialists concerned with modern Southeast Asia, particularly the many-faceted problems of stability and security, economic development, and political and social change.

The Institute's research programmes are the Regional Economic Studies (RES, including ASEAN and APEC), Regional Strategic and Political Studies (RSPS), and Regional Social and Cultural Studies (RSCS).

ISEAS has an active publishing programme and has issued more than 1,000 scholarly books and journals on Southeast Asia.

THE INDONESIAN RURAL ECONOMY
Mobility, Work and Enterprise

Edited by

Thomas R. Leinbach

Institute of Southeast Asian Studies
Singapore

First published in Singapore 2004 by
Institute of Southeast Asian Studies
30 Heng Mui Keng Terrace
Pasir Panjang
Singapore 119614
E-mail: publish@iseas.edu.sg
Website: http://bookshop.iseas.edu.sg

All rights reserved.
No part of this publication may be reproduced, stored in a retrieval system, or transmitted in any form or by any means, electronic, mechanical, photocopying, recording or otherwise, without the prior permission of the Institute of Southeast Asian Studies.

© 2004 Institute of Southeast Asian Studies, Singapore

The responsibility for facts and opinions expressed in this publication rests exclusively with the editor and authors and their interpretations do not necessarily reflect the views or the policy of the Institute.

ISEAS Library Cataloguing-in-Publication Data

The Indonesian rural economy: mobility, work and enterprise/edited by Thomas R. Leinbach.
1. Indonesia—Rural conditions.
2. Small business—Indonesia.
3. Rural industries—Indonesia.
I. Leinbach, Thomas R. (Thomas Raymond), 1941–
HN710 Z9C6I42   2004   sls2003015543

ISBN 981-230-214-X (soft cover)

Typeset by Superskill Graphics Pte Ltd
Printed in Singapore on acid-free paper ∞ by Seng Lee Press Pte. Ltd.

CONTENTS

List of Tables	vii
List of Figures	ix
Contributors	xi
Acknowledgements	xiii
Glossary	xiv
Foreword by Hal Hill	xvii

Part I **The Development Context**

Chapter 1 The Indonesian Rural Economy 3
Thomas R. Leinbach

Chapter 2 The Changing Importance of Off-Farm Income for Agricultural Households in Indonesia 15
Anne Booth

Chapter 3 The Economic Policy Environment for Small Rural Enterprises in Indonesia 38
Peter van Diermen

Chapter 4 The Contribution of Household and Small Manufacturing Establishments to the Rural Economy 61
Robert Rice

Part II **Entrepreneurship, Gender and Mobility Issues**

Chapter 5 International Labour Migration and Rural Dynamics: A Study of Flores, East Nusa Tenggara 103
Graeme Hugo

Chapter 6	Gender, Socio-Spatial Networks, and Rural Non-Farm Work Among Migrants in West Java *Rachel Silvey*	134
Chapter 7	Micro and Small-Scale Enterprises in Java: A Gender-Based Comparative Analysis of Entrepreneurial Behaviour and Performance of Enterprises *Surendhra P. Singh, Harsha N. Mookherjee and Safdar Muhammad*	152
Chapter 8	Migrant Entrepreneurs in East Indonesia *Marthen L. nDoen, Cees Gorter, Peter Nijkamp and Piet Rietveld*	182
Part III	**Indonesia's Rural Non-Farm Economy: Case Studies and Policy Development**	
Chapter 9	Small Enterprises, Fungibility and South Sumatran Transmigration Livelihood Strategies *Thomas R. Leinbach*	209
Chapter 10	Transitions to Non-Farm Employment and the Growth of the Rattan Industry: The Example of Desa Buyut, Cirebon *Social Monitoring and Qualitative Analysis Team, The SMERU Institute*	244
Chapter 11	Policy Implications for RNFEs: Lessons from the PARUL Project in Indonesia *Hugh Emrys Evans*	267
Chapter 12	The Indonesian Rural Economy: Insights and Prospects *Thomas R. Leinbach*	293
Index		307

LIST OF TABLES

2.1	Percentage Breakdown of the Increase in the Labour Force: 1990–95	16
2.2	Rural Households by Income Sources and Region, Indonesia: 1995	17
2.3	Income Accruing to Agricultural Households by Income Sources, 1984 and 1993	20
2.4	Total Annual Farm Household Income and Percentage from the Farm Holding by Province, 1984 and 1993	21
2.5	Breakdown of Agricultural Households by Size of Holding and Main Income Source	23
2.6	Sources of Non-Agricultural Income for Agricultural Households, 1993	23
2.7	Percentage Breakdown of Agricultural Household Income by Agricultural Income Source and Income Size, 1993	25
2.8	Percentage Breakdown of Agricultural Household Income by Non-Agricultural Income Source and Income Size, 1993	26
2.9	Linkage Ratios and the Percentage of Total Farm Income Accruing from Off-Farm Employment	28
2.10	Breakdown of Agricultural Households by Sources of Income	32
3.1	Policy Design Criteria	51
4.1	The Rural-Urban Distribution and Change in Indonesian Household and Cottage Manufacturing Industries 1987–96	66
4.2	Comparison of Household Manufacturing Establishments in Urban and Rural Areas 1987–96	68
4.3	Small Establishment Manufacturing Sector in Urban and Rural Areas in 1996	69
4.4	Value-added of Household, Small and Medium/Large Manufacturing Establishments in 1996	72

4.5	Employment of Household, Small and Medium/Large Manufacturing Establishments in 1996	74
4.6	Household Manufacturing Establishments 1996, 1998, 2000	76
4.7	Small Manufacturing Establishments 1996, 1998, 2000	77
4.8	Household and Small Manufacturing Establishments 1996, 1998, 2000	79
5.1	Number of Indonesian Overseas Workers Processed by the Ministry of Manpower, 1969–2001	106
5.2	Main Southeast Asian Labour Exporting Countries: Workers' Remittances Relative to Exports and Imports, 1980–99	107
5.3	East Nusatenggara and East Flores: Major Demographic and Economic Characteristics	111
5.4	East Nusatenggara and East Flores: Fertility, 1976–97	116
5.5	*Desa* Nelereren, East Flores: Major Use Made of Remittances in the Origin Area	122
6.1	Rural-Urban Resource Exchange; Network Density	138
7.1	Distribution of Selected Enterprises by Gender of the Owner/of Operator, Enterprise Type, and Average Number of Years in Operation	160
7.2	Selected Organizational and Performance Indicators of Selected Enterprises in Java, Indonesia	162
7.3	Selected Characteristics of Entrepreneurs by Gender	166
7.4	Lack of Knowledge in Marketing and Basic Enterprise Management Skills Perceived to be Problems by Selected Entrepreneurs	170
7.5	Differences in Attitudes/Perceptions (Entrepreneurial Behaviour) of Selected Entrepreneurs by Gender of Entrepreneur	171
7.6	Differences in Responses to Statements Regarding Leadership Qualities and Behaviour by Gender of Entrepreneur	173
7.7	Regression Results of Factors Affecting Performance of Female-Operated Enterprises in Java, Indonesia	175
8.1	Means and Standard Deviations of Characteristic Variables by Place of Origin	185
8.2	Migrants' Characteristics by Occupational Status, Parents' Occupation and Reason to Migrate to East Nusatenggara	187

8.3	Cross-Tabulation of Reason for Migration in Relation to Migrant's Occupation in Place of Origin	189
8.4	Regression Results for Migrants' Propensity to Stay at Their Current Place as a Function of Socio-economic Factors	191
8.5	Proportion of Migrants' Responses to Core Variables	193
8.6	Proportion of Migrants with and without Employees by Place of Origin	196
8.7	The Relationship of Employee to Migrants' Employers by Place of Origin	196
9.1	Transmigration Study Sites: South Sumatra	219
9.2	Home Industries: Head and Spouse-Operated	225
9.3	Logistic Regression Results: Head-Owned Business	227
9.4	Logistic Regression Results: Spouse-Owned Business	229
10.1	The Pattern of Rice Farming in Buyut	247
10.2	Growth in the Number of Rattan Enterprises in Kabupaten Cirebon and the Volume of Exports	250
11.1	Selected Clusters by Region	277
11.2	Impact on Incomes from Diversification of Coconut Production	283
11.3	Impact on Incomes from Processing Cashews	286
11.4	Impact on Incomes from Shrimp Fishing	288

LIST OF FIGURES

5.1	East Flores: Main Areas of Origin of Labour Migrants to Sabah	108
5.2	East Flores: Population Growth by *Kecamatan*, 1990–97	113
5.3	East Flores: Sex Ratios by *Kecamatan*, 1997	114
5.4	East Flores: Age-Sex Structure, 1990	117
6.1	Locations of Jowo and Sunda Villages	139
7.1	Primary Motivation to Start a Business as Indicated by the Selected Entrepreneurs by Gender	167
7.2a	Important Problems as Perceived by Enterpreneurs by Gender at the Time of Start-up	168
7.2b	Important Problems as Perceived by Enterpreneurs by Gender at the Time of Survey (Currently)	169
9.1	Location of South Sumatran Transmigration Sample Sites	219
9.2	Head-Operated Businesses	222
9.3	Spouse-Operated Businesses	223
9.4	Family- (both Head and Spouse) Operated Businesses	224
10.1	Map of Kecamatan Cirebon Utara	246
11.1	North Sulawesi	282

CONTRIBUTORS

Thomas R. Leinbach, Department of Geography, University of Kentucky

Anne Booth, School of Oriental and African Studies, University of London

Hugh Emrys Evans, School of Policy, Planning and Development, University of Southern California

Cees Gorter, Department of Spatial Economics, Vrije University, Amsterdam

Graeme Hugo, Department of Geography, University of Adelaide

Harsha N. Mookherjee, Tennessee Technological University, Cookeville

Safdar Muhammad, Department of Agricultural Economics, Tennessee State University, Nashville

Marthen L. nDoen, Department of Economics, Satya Wacana Christian University, Salatiga, Indonesia

Peter Nijkamp, Department of Spatial Economics, Vrije University, Amsterdam

Robert Rice, Department of Economics, Monash University, Melbourne

Piet Rietveld, Department of Spatial Economics, Vrije University, Amsterdam

Rachel Silvey, Department of Geography, University of Colorado

Surendhra P. Singh, Department of Agricultural Economics, Tennessee State University, Nashville

Social Monitoring and Qualitative Analysis Team, The SMERU Research Institute, Jakarta

Peter van Diermen, Geographical Sciences, School of Resources, Environment and Society, The Australian National University, Canberra

ACKNOWLEDGEMENTS

The idea for a book comprised of essays on the Indonesian rural non-farm economy has emerged over the last ten years as a result of my research on transmigration livelihood strategies in South Sumatra and the Moluccas. But the opportunity to invite authors and to produce this work was made possible by a sabbatical leave from the University of Kentucky and the generous support provided by the Institute of Southeast Asian Studies (ISEAS) through a Senior Visiting Research Fellowship in 2001. I am very grateful to ISEAS and its stimulating research environment which it has provided me over the years. In addition I gratefully acknowledge a University of Kentucky Research Professorship for the year 2002–03.

For my earlier work on off-farm employment in the transmigration areas of South Sumatra and the Moluccas I must mention the U.S. National Science Foundation for their awards and a Fulbright-Hays Senior Faculty Research Award to Sriwijaya University, Palembang in 1994.

In addition, I wish to acknowledge funding from the U.S.–Indonesia Society and a generous grant from the Committee for Research and Exploration, National Geographic Society. These awards contributed to the overall effort to produce the current volume but most importantly they have provided support for my current and on-going research on this theme.

Richard Gilbreath, Director of the University of Kentucky's Geo-Informatics and Cartographic Laboratory once again has produced magnificent graphics from my crude drafts.

Finally, my greatest thanks go with love to Marge, my life long partner, who has shared my Indonesian experiences and many of the editing chores associated with the research products. Her advice and insights, as well as cautions, have provided wonderful guidance for my academic efforts over the years.

GLOSSARY

ADB	Asian Development Bank
AKAN	Antar Kerja Antar Negara
AKATIGA	Yayasan Akatiga i.e., Foundation for Social Analysis, Bandung
Bappenas	National Planning and Development Board
BILC	Bank Indonesia Liquidity Credits
BIPIK	Bimbingan dan Pengembangan Industri Kecil i.e., Small-Scale Industries Guidance and Development
BKD	Badan Kredit Desa i.e., village credit units
BPR	Bank Perkreditan Rakyat i.e., People's Credit Bank
BPS	Central Bureau of Statistics
BRI	Bank Rakyat Indonesia i.e., People's Bank of Indonesia
CEFE/AMT	entrepreneurship training
DEPKOP	Department Koperasi i.e., Department of Cooperatives
DPE	Dewan Penunjang Ekspor i.e., Export Support Board of Indonesia
DPR	House of Representatives, Indonesia
EF	extended fungibility
FDI	foreign direct investment
FMP	family mode of production
FNS	West German Assistance Institute
GBHN	State Policy Guidelines
GDP	gross domestic product
GNP	gross national product
GOI	Government of Indonesia
GONGO	government sponsored non-government organization
HE	household establishment
HME	household/cottage manufacturing establishment
HMI	household manufacturing industry
IMF	International Monetary Fund

Glossary

KIK	Likungan Industri Kecil i.e., small-scale industrial areas
KKB	Klinik Konsultasi Bisnis i.e., small business consultancy clinics
KKN	corruption, collusion and nepotism
KKPA	Koperasi Kredit Primer Anggota i.e., cooperative credits
KMKP	Credit for Fixed Capital programme
KOPINKRA	Koperasi Industri Kecil i.e., Cooperatives of Small-Scale Industries
KPEL	Kemitraan bagi Pengembangan Ekonomi Lokal i.e., Partnerships for Local Economic Development
KSP	Koperasi Simpan Pinjam i.e., Savings and Loan Cooperative
KUD	Koperasi Unit Desa i.e., loan facility
KUK	Credit for Small Enterprises
KUPEDES	micro-credit programme
LDCs	less developed countries
LIK	Lingkungan Industri Kecil i.e., small-scale industrial estates
LIPI	Indonesian Institute of Sciences
LLPM	Research and Community Development Institute
LP3ES	Institute of Research, Education, and Economic and Social Information
MENNEGKOP	Kantor Menteri Negara Urusan Koperasi dan Usaha Kecil dan Menengah Republik Indonesia i.e., GOI Office of the State Minister for Cooperatives and Small and Medium Enterprises
MOPS	Mid Oil Platts Singapore
MOT	Ministry of Transmigration
MS/MUK	management training
MSE	micro and small enterprises
MSMEs	micro, small and medium-sized establishments
NGO	non-government organization
NTT	Nusatenggara Timur
OCWs	overseas contract workers
OFE	off-farm employment
PARUL	Poverty Alleviation through Rural-Urban Linkages
PHE	peasant household enterprise

PMT/GKM	Total Quality Control programme
PPK	Permohonan Pemeriksaan Karatina
PPPAs	policies, programmes, projects and activities
RGDP	regional gross domestic product
RNFE	rural non-farm enterprises
SAMS	social accounting matrices
SIC	Standard Industrial Classification
SME	small and medium enterprise
SMERU	Social Monitoring and Early Response Unit
SMI	small manufacturing industry
SNI	Standard Nasional Indonesia i.e., National Management Quality System
TFR	total fertility rate
TKI	Tenaga Kerja Indonesia i.e., overseas labour
UNCDF	United Nations Capital Development Fund
UNCHS	United Nations Centre for Human Settlements
UNDP	United Nations Development Program
UNSRI	Sriwijaya University, Palembang
UPT	Unit Pelayanan Teknis i.e., Technical Service Centres
USP	unit usaha simpan pinjam i.e., enterprise unit
WARSI	Warung Informasi Konservasi i.e., Conservation Information Forum

FOREWORD

This is an important volume. Featuring the work of leading scholars from five countries, it addresses an important dimension of the development challenges facing Indonesia, the world's fourth most populous nation.

It is also a very timely volume. There has been a rich tradition of scholarship on Indonesia's rural economy, stretching back to the colonial period. It is no exaggeration to state that, in this field, the country has been a "social laboratory" for the international research community. Indonesia was the intellectual breeding ground for Boeke's famous but now discredited theory of dualistic development. Thirty years ago, there was the landmark Penny/Singarimbun study of rural Yogyakarta, with its Malthusian subtext. There has been a long-running debate about the socio-economic impacts of technological change in rural areas, particularly centred on the introduction of new high yielding rice varieties and associated agricultural mechanization from the late 1960s onwards. There were thirty years of very rapid economic growth during the Soeharto era, accompanied by unparalleled structural change, infrastructure expansion, an oil boom and bust, and much else. All this transformed the rural economy, as never before. Finally, Indonesia's social, economic, and demographic database is one of the richest in the developing world, and its research environment one of the most open, enabling scholars to undertake very detailed research to test their favourite theories and to interact with a lively domestic community.

A fresh look at these issues in the Indonesian context is also timely in the wake of Indonesia's deep economic crisis of 1997–98, and the significant political and institutional changes triggered by the collapse of the Soeharto regime. In this new era of *reformasi*, much of the post-crisis literature on Indonesia has been dominated by urban-centred macroeconomics and finance — fiscal deficits and growing public debt, corporate collapse and reform, exchange rate volatility, and the like. Yet, rural and agricultural resilience has been a key factor ameliorating the socio-economic impacts of the crisis. In the long sweep of development agriculture, and the rural economy more generally, may be a shrinking share of the economy. But, as Thomas Leinbach reminds us, in important respects "Southeast Asia remains a land of farmers".

The volume's sub-title provides the key connecting analytical themes: mobility, work, and enterprise. Organizationally, there are four chapters in each of three parts. The scene is set in Part I with an overview of the development context. The focus then shifts to entrepreneurship, gender, and mobility issues. Finally, in Part III, there are case studies and policy analyses of a sub-set of the broader issue, looking specifically at the rural non-farm economy.

As is appropriate in this sort of volume, the contributions are diverse in their methodologies and disciplinary backgrounds. An attractive feature is that demographers, economists, geographers, planners, and regional scientists happily co-exist in these pages. Some chapters "let the data speak" as it were, drawing on intensive analysis of census and survey data. Notable here are the chapters by Anne Booth and Robert Rice. Others draw on intensive and localized field research, in locations as diverse as transmigration settlements in South Sumatra, and Kupang, East Nusatenggara. There are also thematic studies which for example paint an interesting picture of gender networks and crisis impacts on Java, and explore the growing international migration from Flores, East Nusatenggara in search of employment.

There is no "party line" permeating this volume. But there are clear messages for both the research and policy communities. The contributions on SMEs draw attention to past policy failures, in spite of much official rhetoric about their importance. "Specific programs should be avoided", cautions Peter van Diermen. There is also evidence of resilience in the SME sector, nicely illustrated by SMERU's careful analysis of the rattan industry in Cirebon. Marthen nDoen and colleagues highlight the important role of migrant entrepreneurs, especially in local environments characterized by "social tolerance".

Several writers argue that policy-makers need to pay more attention to on-the-ground realities. Graeme Hugo, for example, underlines the importance of international migration as a poverty alleviation strategy, and advocates a policy framework which supports and facilitates these migration flows, of the sort which now occurs in the Philippines. The two chapters on gender call for greater recognition of the fact that women manage the majority of micro and household enterprises, while still suffering numerous official, legal, and social handicaps. The importance of education permeates Anne Booth's analysis. Robert Rice worries that poorly developed collateral markets are a barrier to financing the development of SMEs.

Tom Leinbach and his team, together with ISEAS, are to be congratulated for preparing and publishing a stimulating, varied and interdisciplinary collection, rich in empirical and analytical insights, and constructive in its policy advice. This volume advances our understanding not just of Indonesia's rural economy but of broader development issues. It deserves to be widely read.

HAL HILL
H.W. Arndt Professor of Southeast Asian Economics
The Australian National University

PART I
The Development Context

1
THE INDONESIAN RURAL ECONOMY

Thomas R. Leinbach

The last two decades have seen unprecedented change in the economic, political and social fabric of most of Southeast Asia. Traditional patterns of livelihood have been dramatically transformed, and the sum of the influences has gradually had a deep impact over an even longer span of time. While urban centres have been the subject of much attention, the rural areas in Asia are equally critical as we attempt to understand and assess developmental change against the backdrop of the increasingly globalized economy. The transformation of these rural situations continues as a result of the processes of urbanization, industrialization, trade and technological change. While in many ways agriculture remains the heart of development in rural areas, the viability of such places must increasingly be viewed in terms of non-agricultural developments because of the need for increased employment and the impact on and linkages to the broader global economy.

The mutually reinforcing dynamisms of commerce and demography especially have had a tremendous impact on the traditional social fabric of the region—the rural population. Development has in some ways ushered in a cultural crisis where local identities have been lost. There are indeed some arguments suggesting that the end of the peasantry has come to Southeast Asia even though there is an enduring existence of rural production and of the social and economic circuits of life and livelihood which accompany it. "But the rural producers of today are productive and enduring only insofar as they have moved from being peasants into new and different worlds of production, and consequently, of social and economic life. In fact the rural labour force has been radically reconstituted through its own agency and that of the broader forces of change" (Elson 1997, p. 240).

Despite the rapid industrial growth of the last two decades, it is true that Southeast Asia remains a land of farmers. While there is considerable regional variation, nearly 60 percent of the labour force is found in agriculture and roughly 70 percent of the people live in rural areas (Rigg 1997). Yet it is clear that village economies are undergoing dramatic change and can no longer be uniformly characterized as isolated, inward looking and self-sufficient based solely on agriculture. This is especially true of villages situated on the fringes of urban areas. Even for those more remote villages, transport improvements have provided stronger linkages to production and export centres. As the forces of globalization continue to expand and isolation is broken down, new opportunities and forms of employment have become more and more accessible to rural populations. The quest for new employment may be driven by a dream to own consumer goods, to obtain necessary funds for children's education or simply the need to ensure family survival in a precarious agricultural environment. It is almost a truism that the livelihood patterns and strategies of families increasingly assume non-agricultural or non-farm employment.

Although there is a growing literature on the non-farm economy and its associated employment, there is much we do not know about its characteristics and potential. In addition, while governments in some countries are implementing projects to support small-scale and rural enterprises, more commonly the rural non-farm sector operates in a policy environment that is biased against it. Evidence continues to show that the rural non-farm sector can promote growth and welfare by slowing rural-urban migration, using more appropriate technologies, providing seasonal or alternative employment, and improving household security through diversification. Thus the neglect of the sector does not seem warranted given available information (Lanjouw and Lanjouw 1995).

Within Southeast Asia Indonesia remains the important focus for examining rural economy. With a human capital resource of nearly 140 million people residing in rural areas and nearly 3 million persons entering the labour force annually, there is both a tremendous potential for development change as well as an urgency to better understand the non-farm aspects of rural areas. Indonesia has a long history of programmes and policies, which have been directed, to the rural areas (Daly and Fane

2002). Examples are those dealing with transmigration, intensified agricultural production, infrastructure development, provincial, regency, sub-regency and village development and employment creation. New and ongoing programmes alike will benefit from a deeper understanding of the 'other' side of rural development—the non-farm dimension. The theme is also important because while non-farm employment creation is critical, basic food needs of the still rapidly growing population must be met in decades to come. While rice self sufficiency was achieved for the 1980s and 1990s, it is likely that demand will surpass supply in the years ahead. Thus, it is crucial to understand the interactions between agricultural production and other rural non-farm activities in order to better understand the rural sector's changing capacity to satisfy the rapidly growing population's nutritional needs.

The Current Development Context

The considerable economic success that Indonesia enjoyed through the Suharto period was dramatically altered by the economic crisis that began in July 1997. Attention first shifted to the strength of the Indonesian rupiah and subsequently was followed by an extraordinary depreciation of the currency prompted in part by speculators. Compounding this was the experience of severe drought, fires (the Asian Development Bank revealed that in 1998 Indonesian fires destroyed $4.5 billion worth of forest), low world petroleum production prices, regional financial instability, domestic social unrest, and ultimately a change of government. The weakness of the rupiah means that existing foreign debt is repaid at an unfavourable exchange rate. But on the positive side, the undervalued currency clearly gives Indonesia a competitive edge in connection with labour-intensive production. In 2002 while the weak banking sector and a huge amount of foreign commercial debt remained as major problems, there were positive changes. One of the most significant adjustments under the IMF-guided restructuring has been the gradual reduction in the fuel subsidy.

As part of the 2002 budget approval process at the end of 2001, the DPR and the government agreed that the fuel subsidy would be reduced to Rp. 30.4 trillion and that this would require an average price increase of 30 percent. In January the Government of Indonesia did not simply announce new fuel prices, it announced a radical change in the way in which prices for fuels sold to the public will be set in the future. In addition to raising prices by an average of 22 percent, the government announced that prices for all fuels other than kerosene would be adjusted monthly based on changes in the Mid Oil Platts Singapore (MOPS) price.[1] Thus the price of premium gasoline was to be set at 100 percent of the MOPS price for similar fuel plus a 5 percent margin for administration, a 10 percent VAT charge, and a 5 percent tax on motor vehicle fuels.[2] Prices for automotive diesel, fuel oil, and industrial diesel were to be set at 75 percent of their respective MOPS prices, adjusted for appropriate taxes. Having begun to implement this pricing plan, in late January 2003, the government backtracked on price increases of industrial-use kerosene and auto diesel in a concession to two weeks of street protests across major cities in the archipelago. The IMF, which has made the reduction of subsidies a condition of further loans, essentially supported the government's defence of the backtracking recognizing that social unrest was not conducive to continued development progress after the financial crisis.

Other remedies to address macroeconomic imbalances, financial weaknesses, real sector inefficiencies, and the loss of private sector confidence continue. Of course stimulation of foreign direct investment has a high priority and in this regard the government now has a plan to overhaul the tax structure by 2005. Theoretically such improvements should lower prices for legitimate domestically produced items and induce firms to locate production and jobs in Indonesia.

Now well into its second year of implementation, Indonesia's ambitious decentralization programme has made uneven progress and some would argue has even democratized corruption (Borsuk 2003). While some employees have been transferred to regional government payrolls, considerable work needs to be made in establishing the necessary fiscal, legal, and administrative framework for successful decentralization (Alm, Aten and Bahl 2001). Lack of political consensus has prevented the national inter-agency decentralization coordinating team from making progress in designing and implementing a plan for strengthening the regions' institutions and capacities (Athukorala 2002, p. 145).

Another key goal of economic reform is the privatization of state-owned enterprises. While public sector stakes have been sold, the revenue generated has been less than previously forecasted. In the case of PT Indonesian Satellite Corporation (Indosat) the sales price was diminished by foreign companies' marginal interest which was in turn due to the government's lack of clarity on the future of the sector. The small stakes divested also seem to indicate the government's ambivalent attitude to the broad notion of privatization. Coupled with this, corruption remains a severe problem and the remedial steps have thus far not convinced the public (and more importantly, outside investors) of the government's commitment to decisively attack cronyism and corruption (Athukorala 2002, p. 143). Over the medium term the country faces the daunting challenge to improve tax and customs administration, to contain the proliferation of regulations in the regions, to speed up the sale of assets, to improve labour policies, and to improve the regulatory framework for investment, especially in infrastructure (Alisjahbana and Manning 2002, p. 302).

Although the above picture paints a gloomy portrait of economic health, in fact the rural areas of Indonesia were least affected by the 1997–98 financial crisis. In truth, economic activities and behaviours change much more slowly than media reports suggest. Thus the sharp changes in employment patterns that arose from the crisis only affected about 10 percent of the workforce. While this is huge in respect to year-to-year changes, essentially 90 percent of the workforce kept doing what they had been doing before the crisis (Molyneaux, email communication, 28 February 2001). Perhaps a more interesting set of issues and questions emphasizes the impact of restructuring measures and the turns of the decentralization effort on the rural areas (Alm, Aten and Bahl 2001; Holtzappel, Sanders and Titus, eds, 2002).

On a more significant matter, while the income inequality gap shrank between 1970 and 1990, the boom years of the 1990s suggest another trend. The share of national wealth held by the lowest 40 percent of the population has been contracting. In this light the role of non-farm employment as a means of reducing unemployment and commencing a redistribution of wealth is seen as critical. Thus the current period in Indonesian economic history, characterized by a struggling economy, favourable attitudes toward liberalization, and the development of decentralized decision-making and local autonomy, represents a ripe venue for a study of employment and the non-farm economy.

The Theme of Rural Non-farm Activities

The topic of the rural non-farm sector is not, of course, a new theme. There are at least two volumes, now a bit dated, which deal with this topic in the Asian context (Mukhoopadhyay and Chee 1985; Shand 1986). This literature essentially underscores the importance of off-farm employment in a variety of dimensions in Asia. In addition, a general treatment of the rural non-farm sector has been produced by Saith (1992). This volume notes that the major policy issue is not how to increase the size of the sector, but rather to identify and establish the economic conditions and institutional environment within which specific policy interventions might enable this sector to perform its ascribed developmental and poverty alleviating functions. One major value of the work is its attempt to develop an analytical framework within which strategic and policy issues can be located. It attempts to establish patterns within the existing array of differing forms and types of rural non-farm activities. Necessarily the author also focuses on the relationship between the development of the RNFE, rural inequality and agrarian differentiation. Using this framework, the second part of the volume then introduces key issues concerning the choice of appropriate strategies and policies.

In a more theoretical vein, Ranis and Stewart (1993) model rural non-farm activity by relaxing restrictive assumptions and introduce the notion of a dynamic agricultural and general goods sector. They show for Taiwan and the Philippines how a dynamic labour-intensive agriculture combined with an appropriately functioning modern goods sector can lead to a broad spread of employment and income with resulting rapid growth, egalitarian distribution and an early elimination of rural underemployment.

In regards to works on Indonesian development, there are several excellent treatments of the economy in general (Booth 1992, Hill 2000), the gradual industrial transformation (Hill 1997) and more recently the crisis (Hill 1999), as well as agricultural development (Booth 1988; Hart, Turton and White 1988). There are in addition several studies of development in regional context (e.g., Mac Andrews and Hardjono 1995; Dick, Mackie and Fox 1993) and two volumes on small industries in Indonesia (van Diermen 1997 and Tambunan 2000).

But despite the huge importance of this activity there is a dearth of works dealing specifically with the rural non-farm aspects of Indonesian development. It is, however, important to recognize the value of various Indonesian case studies in Shand (1986), and the excellent historical analyses of non-farm activities in the Javanese economy by Breman and Wiradi (2002), Huisman and Kragten (1997) and especially the monograph by Alexander, Boomgard and White (1991). A very rich essay in this volume is that by Ben White (pp. 41–69) which examines Javanese rural economic diversification in historical context. A particularly valuable aspect of this piece is the emphasis on the analytical implications of rural sector economic activities in examining rural change more broadly. For example the conclusions note that:

> The role of non-farm incomes and investments can help us to understand why land concentration and agricultural polarization have not proceeded faster in Java, although agrarian surpluses available to finance further acquisition of land by wealthy households are increasing. For land-rich households, many other avenues of profitable investment compete with the alternative of land concentration; for the millions of marginal farm households unable to survive on their meager agricultural incomes, access to non-farm incomes provides an alternative to the liquidation of their inadequate holdings. A focus on patterns of part-time farming at all levels of the agrarian structure is therefore an important tool in the empirical analysis and interpretation of agrarian differentiation processes. (White 1991, p. 65)

The topic of agrarian differentiation in Southeast Asia is also the theme of an earlier work (Hart et al. 1989) and its impact on income distributions analyzed for rural Java by Rietveld (1986). This theme segues nicely into the broader subject of household strategies and rural livelihood diversification (see e.g., Ellis 1998; Ellis 2000). Off-farm employment is critical in many contexts including the transmigration effort in Indonesia. Using a sample of schemes in South Sumatra, researchers show the importance and intensity of off-farm activities in livelihood strategies and the ways in which off-farm employment is influenced by land holdings/ purchases and family life cycle stages (Leinbach et al. 1992; Leinbach and Smith 1994). Finally a study of rural investment patterns and rural non-farm employment in West Java is very useful (Braadbaart and Wolters 1992).

The canvas for this contemporary picture of Indonesian rural non-farm economy is quite broad. Included are all non-agricultural activities whether they take place on-farm or off-farm. The rural industrial sector constitutes one part of the set of rural non-agricultural activities. But also included are service enterprises (especially important in rural Java), household based petty production activities and non-agricultural labour including work on infrastructure and public works programmes. The locational aspect of this theme of course is that the primary criterion of an RNFE activity is one which is performed within a designated rural area.[3] The second, and equally important one, is the linkage approach. Here the test is whether an industrial enterprise or other non-agricultural activity generates significant developmental linkages, both direct and indirect, with the rural population. Each of these approaches, which are not mutually exclusive, would probably yield very different profiles of the rural industry. Bearing in mind the important goal of generating non-agricultural employment and incomes for rural populations, it is important to include any economic activity which displays strong rural linkages, irrespective of whether it is located in rural areas or not. Thus, following Saith (1992), rural located-rural linked, rural located-urban linked, urban located-rural linked, and urban located-urban linked comprise the full set of possibilities. The first three will be the focus of this volume. An especially under-studied aspect of the non-farm economy has been the roles of population and mobility. Specifically, there has been very little research on the implications of widespread circulation and out-migration, changing rural dependence ratios, increasing age at marriage, or declining fertility rates for rural economies in Indonesia.

Structure of the Book

The book is divided into three broad themes. The first of these is the development context. In addition to the introductory essay, Anne Booth provides important evidence from recent census data that focuses on the changing importance of off-farm income for agricultural households. In addition, Peter van Diermen writes about the economic environment for small enterprises. In the final chapter of this section, Robert Rice examines the contribution of household and small manufacturing establishments to the rural economy.

The following section examines entrepreneurship, gender, and mobility issues in the rural economy. The lead essay by Graeme Hugo discusses the international labour dynamics of rural Indonesia through a case study in Flores and assesses the potential of export labour issues in terms of policy and regional economic development. Following from this, Rachel Silvey examines the gender-differentiated nature of low-income migrants' socio-spatial network in West Java during the recent economic retrenchment. Specifically, the chapter investigates the ways in which the gendered operation of these networks has affected rural non-farm work among circular migrant communities. The final two chapters in this section examine entrepreneurship in Java and East Nusa Tenggara. Singh and Mookherjee look at micro-scale enterprises and the perceptions and performance of entrepreneurs with special attention to women. Marthen nDoen et al. note that the Outer Islands in Indonesia are often seen as the main source of migrants to the island of Java, being the core region of the country, while only a few studies look the other way round. This chapter then addresses a variety of socio-economic factors that play a key role in the migrants' propensity to stay in the province of East Nusa Tenggara. Their results give further credence to the 'middlemen minority' theory.

In order to bring additional evidence and examples to the theme, the final section of the book emphasizes case studies and policy aspects of the rural economy from a variety of perspectives. Leinbach examines small enterprises and off-farm employment in South Sumatra within the context of the transmigration programme. Case studies from the transmigration schemes show the relevance of the concept of fungibility, the conversion of resources into higher revenue earning activities, in household decision-making toward income production for survival and accumulation. Using the example of Desa Buyut in Kabupaten Cirebon, a team of SMERU researchers examines the gradual shift to non-farm employment through the development of the rattan industry. Following this Evans suggests that RNFEs perform a valuable role in the rural economy, but efforts to design and implement programmes to support them and other small-scale economic activities face numerous difficulties, both administrative and pragmatic. This chapter looks at one approach adopted by the PARUL (Poverty Alleviation through Rural-Urban Linkages) programme in Indonesia, and presents three case studies. These have to do with diversifying production from coconuts in North Sulawesi, processing cashews in villages in South Sulawesi, and expanding markets for fishermen in remote locations of Papua. Experience shows that while external factors play a dominant role in determining success or failure, appropriately designed programmes can make a difference. The concluding chapter attempts to draw together the findings and themes discussed throughout and suggests several additional topics which would benefit from additional research.

Notes

1. While the final figures are not in, it is expected that the 22 percent average price increase combined with the new pricing formula will result in a fuel subsidy bill, if oil prices remain in the $19/bbl range, of well less than Rp. 30.4 trillion.
2. The government has stated that at this price regular gasoline is no longer

subsidized. This would seem unlikely as the price charged should not be sufficient to provide Pertamina and the gasoline stations with a sufficient wholesale to retail margin to cover the cost of distributing fuel throughout Indonesia. Retail margins in Thailand on gasoline are about 40 percent of the ex-refinery price (Thai National Energy Policy Office web site) while a GTZ study from 1999 assumed that wholesale plus retail margins for gasoline amounted to 70 percent or more of the landed price of imported gasoline.
3. The distinction between rural and urban in Indonesia is a functionality-based definition. The 1980 and 1990 population censuses defined a locality as 'urban' when it complied with the three following requirements: (1) having a population density of 5,000 people or more per square kilometre; (2) having 25 percent or less of the households working in the agricultural sector; (3) having 8 or more kinds of urban facilities. These included primary and high schools, hospital, cinema, health centre, telephone/postal agency; market infrastructure, shopping centre, bank, factory, restaurants and public electricity. Biro Pusat Statistik (BPS) uses a more technical scoring system to distinguish between urban and rural but this has been criticized because of its arbitrariness. Further, it is increasingly clear that the distinction between urban and rural (especially in Java) is blurred and this further reduces the relevance of the above criteria (see McGee 1991).

References

Alexander, Paul, Peter Boomgaard and Ben White (eds.). *In the Shadow of Agriculture: Non-Farm Activities in the Javanese Economy, Past and Present*. Amsterdam: Royal Tropical Institute, 1991.

Alisjahbana, Armida and Chris Manning. "Survey of Recent Developments". *Bulletin of Indonesian Economic Studies* 38, no. 3 (December, 2002): 277–305.

Alm, James, Robert H. Aten, and Roy Bahl. "Can Indonesia Decentralize Successfully? Plans, Problems, and Prospects". *Bulletin of Indonesian Economic Studies* 37, no. 1 (April 2001): 83–102.

Athukorala, Prema-chandra. "Survey of Recent Developments". *Bulletin of Indonesian Economic Studies* 38, no. 2 (August, 2002): 141–62.

Booth, Anne (ed.). *The Oil Boom and After: Indonesian Economic Policy and Performance in the Soeharto Era*. Singapore: Oxford University Press, 1992.

Booth, Anne. *Agricultural Development in Indonesia*. Sydney: Allen and Unwin, 1988.

Borsuk, Richard "Corruption, Decentralized". *Asian Wall Street Journal*, 28 January 2003, p. A-4.

Braadbaart, Okke and Willem G. Wolters. *Rural Investment Patterns and Rural*

Non-farm Employment in West Java. West Java Rural Non-farm Sector Research Project, Project Report Series No. RB-5, Hague: Institute of Social Studies, March 1992.

Breman, Jan and Gunawan Wiradi. *Good Times and Bad Times in Rural Java: case study of socio-economic dynamics in two villages toward the end of the twentieth century*. Singapore: Institute of Southeast Asian Studies, 2002.

Bangladesh: The Non-Farm Sector in a Diversifying Rural Economy. Washington, D.C.: World Bank, Report No. 16740-BD, June 23, 1997.

Daly, Anne and George Fane. "Anti-Poverty Programs in Indonesia". *Bulletin of Indonesian Economic Studies* 38, no. 3 (December, 2002): 309–29.

Dick, H. James J. Fox and Jamie Mackie. *Balanced Development: East Java in the New Order*. Singapore: Oxford University Press, 1993.

Ellis, Frank. "Household Strategies and Rural Livelihood Diversification". *The Journal of Development Studies* 35, no. 1 (October 1998): 1–38.

Ellis, Frank. "The Determinants of Rural Livelihood Diversification in Developing Countries". *Journal of Agricultural Economics* 51, no. 2 (May 2000): 289–302.

Elson, R.E. *The End of the Peasantry in Southeast Asia: a Social and Economic History of Peasant Livelihood, 1800–1990s*. Canberra: St. Martin's Press, 1997.

Hart, Gillian, Andrew Turton, and Benjamin White (eds.). *Agrarian Transformations: Local Processes and the State in Southeast Asia*. Berkeley and Los Angeles: University of California Press. 1989.

Hill, Hal. *The Indonesian Economy*. 2nd edition. Cambridge: University Press, 2000.

Hill, Hal. *The Indonesian Economy in Crisis: Causes, Consequences and Lessons*. Singapore: Institute of Southeast Asian Studies, 1999.

Holtzappel, Coen, Martin Sanders, and Milan Titus (eds.). *Riding a Tiger: Dilemmas of Integration and Decentralization in Indonesia*. Amsterdam: Rozenberg Publishers, 2002.

Huisman, Henk and Marieke Kragten. "Development of the Rural Non-Farm Economy on Java: A Search for Roots and Determinative Factors". *The Indonesian Journal of Geography* 29, no. 74 (December, 1997): 1–27.

Lanjouw, Jean O. and Peter Lanjouw. *Rural Non-farm Employment: A Survey*. Policy Research Working Paper 1463. Washington: World Bank, May 1995.

Leinbach, T.R., John Watkins and John Bowen. "Employment Behavior and the Family in Indonesian Transmigration". *Annals, Association of American Geographers* 82, no. 1 (March 1992): 23–47.

Leinbach, T.R. and Adrian Smith. "Off-Farm Employment, Land and Lifecycle: Transmigrant Households in South Sumatra, Indonesia". *Economic Geography* 70, no. 3 (July 1994): 273–96.

MacAndrews, Colin and Joan Hardjono (eds.). *Development in Eastern Indonesia*.

Singapore: Institute of Southeast Asian Studies and Canberra: Research School of Pacific Studies, 1996.

McGee, T.G. "The Emergence of Desakota Regions in Asia: Expanding a Hypothesis". In *The Extended Metropolis: Settlement Transition in Asia*, edited by N. Ginsburg, B. Koppel and T.G. McGee, pp. 3–25. University of Hawaii Press, Honolulu, 1991.

Mukhopadhay, Swapna and Chee Peng Lim (eds.). *The Rural Non-Farm Sector in Asia*. Kuala Lumpur: Asian and Pacific Development Centre, 1985.

Ranis, Gustav and Frances Stewart. "Rural Nonagricultural Activities in Development: Theory and Application". *Journal of Development Economics* 40 (1993): 75–101.

Rietveld, P. "Non-Agricultural Activities and Income Distribution in Rural Java". *Bulletin of Indonesian Economic Studies* 22, no. 3 (1986): 106–19.

Rigg, Jonathan. *Southeast Asia: The Human Landscape of Modernization and Development*. London: Routledge, 1997.

Saith, Ashwani. *The Rural Non-Farm Economy: Processes and Policies*. Geneva: ILO, 1992.

Shand, R.T. (ed.) *Off-Farm Employment in the Development of Rural Asia* Volumes I and II. Canberra: National Centre for Development Studies, Australian National University, 1986.

Tambunan, Tulus. *Development of Small Scale Industries During the New Order Government in Indonesia*. Sydney: Ashgate, 2000.

van Diermen, Peter. *Small Business in Indonesia*. Sydney: Ashgate, 1997.

White, Benjamin. "Economic Diversification and Agrarian Change in Rural Java, 1900–1990" in *In the Shadow of Agriculture: Non-Farm Activities in the Javanese Economy, Past and Present*, edited by Alexander, Paul, Peter Boomgaard and Ben White. Amsterdam: Royal Tropical Institute, 1991, 41–69.

2
THE CHANGING IMPORTANCE OF OFF-FARM INCOME FOR AGRICULTURAL HOUSEHOLDS IN INDONESIA

Anne Booth

Rural Households, Agricultural Households and Landowning Households in Rural Indonesia

The twenty-five years from 1970 to 1995 witnessed dramatic changes in the role of agriculture in the Indonesian economy. There was a marked decline in the proportion of total national output (GDP) accruing from the agricultural sector, and the proportion of the labour force employed in agriculture also fell. By 1990, just under half the employed labour force was working in agriculture (in the sense that agriculture was the main source of income), according to the Population Census of that year. Between 1990 and 1995 the absolute size of the agricultural labour force declined, and by 1995 only 44 percent of the employed labour force was reported as "working in agriculture". This percentage was lower for the densely populated inner islands of Java and Bali where the process of structural change and diversification away from agriculture was especially rapid. If the absolute increase in the employed labour force between 1990 and 1995 is distributed between urban and rural areas, and between economic sectors, it is clear that much of the increase in the non-agricultural labour force occurred in urban areas. In rural areas, which accounted for about one third of the total increase in employment over these five years, much of the growth occurred in the trade and service sector (Table 2.1).[1]

In 1995, the Intercensal Survey (*Supas*) reported that there were 45.7 million households in Indonesia, of which only about 32 percent were wholly dependent on agriculture for their income, and a further 9.5 percent were largely dependent on agriculture with some non-agricultural income sources. Less than half of the households located in rural areas, which comprised 65 percent of all households, were earning all their income from agriculture in 1995. On the other hand, of those rural households earning at least part of their income from agriculture (over 70 percent of all rural households), the great majority reported that agriculture was either the sole or the main source of their income (Table 2.2). Clearly it would be wrong to argue that the agricultural sector, even before the crisis of 1997, was not an important source of income for many millions of rural households in Indonesia.[2]

The 1995 *Supas* also made it clear that only 63 percent of all rural households owned agricultural land (Table 2.2). The number of rural

TABLE 2.1
Percentage Breakdown of the Increase in the Labour Force: 1990–95

Sector	West Java/ Jakarta (urban)	Other (urban)	Rural	All Indonesia
Manufacturing	5.6	10.5	6.7	22.8
Trade	7.9	19.2	12.0	39.1
Transport	1.7	3.4	4.8	9.9
Construction	1.3	3.2	5.3	9.8
Other services	7.3	14.3	11.0	32.6
Other[a]	–0.6	–1.3	–6.3	–8.2
Non-agriculture	23.2	49.3	33.5	106.0
Agriculture	1.1	4.8	–11.9	–6.0
Total	24.3	54.1	21.6	100.0

[a] Other includes sectors such as mining, utilities and financial services as well as activities that were not stated in the 1990 census.

Source: Central Bureau of Statistics (1992), Tables 41.1–41.9; Central Bureau of Statistics (1996), Tables 41.1–41.9

TABLE 2.2
Rural Households by Income Sources and Region, Indonesia: 1995
(millions)

Region	All rural[a]	Agriculture main source[b]	minor source	Non-agri-cultural	Land owning
Indonesia	29.690 (63)	17.675 (60)	3.885	8.128	18.618
Java/Bali	17.308 (56)	9.123 (53)	2.804	5.381	9.637
West Java	5.627 (47)	2.595 (46)	0.855	2.177	2.620
Central Java	4.918 (61)	2.700 (55)	0.810	1.408	2.980
Yogyakarta	0.321 (77)	0.163 (51)	0.083	0.075	0.246
East Java	5.989 (59)	3.425 (57)	0.968	1.596	3.515
Bali	0.453 (61)	0.240 (53)	0.088	0.125	0.276
Sumatra	6.342 (71)	4.385 (69)	0.514	1.443	4.482
Kalimantan	1.653 (73)	1.099 (66)	0.154	0.400	1.199
Sulawesi	2.263 (75)	1.541 (68)	0.235	0.487	1.689
Eastern Islands	2.124 (76)	1.526 (72)	0.179	0.419	1.612

[a] Figures in brackets refer to landowning households as a percentage of all rural households.
[b] Figures in brackets refer to households with agriculture as their main source of income as a percentage of all rural households.

Source: Central Bureau of Statistics (1996), Table 59.2

households reported as owning land for the country as a whole slightly exceeded the number giving agriculture as the sole or main source of household income. Although it is probable that the great majority of landowning households did rely on cultivation of land for the bulk of their income, there might have been a number of households which rented or sharecropped out their land in order to pursue non-agricultural activities. In addition households owning only small parcels of land would have been forced to rely on other sources of income. Thus not all landowning households would have been classified as relying on agriculture for most of their income, and not all rural households classified in this way would have owned agricultural land.

As would be expected, there was considerable variation across the regions of Indonesia in the percentage of rural households reporting agriculture as the main source of their income, and also in the proportion of landowning to total rural households. In West Java, the most populous province in the country in 1995, only 46 percent of rural households reported agriculture as their main source of income, and only 47 percent owned agricultural land. This can be contrasted with what were, in 1995, the five provinces of Eastern Indonesia (West and East Nusatenggara, East Timor, Maluku and Irian Jaya), where 72 percent of rural households relied on agriculture for most of their income and 76 percent owned some agricultural land. Reliance on agriculture was also considerably higher than the national average in Sumatra, Sulawesi and Kalimantan (Table 2.2).

Thus in spite of the relative decline in the role of agriculture which had occurred in Indonesia over the three decades up to 1995, it is clear that the agricultural sector remained the most important source of income and employment for many millions of Indonesians even before the severe crisis of 1997/98. But the broad trends described in Tables 2.1 and 2.2 provoke a number of questions. To what extent do the regional differences in the role of agriculture in total household income reflect different income earning opportunities outside agriculture and to what extent do they reflect "push" factors, especially those related to lack of access to agricultural land? To the extent that agricultural activities have become a less important income source for many millions of rural households in Indonesia in recent decades than off-farm earnings, how have these changes varied by household income group and by household asset status? Have the richer households been able to diversify their sources of income more rapidly than the poorer households? The answers to these questions have obvious implications for changes in the distribution of income in rural areas of Indonesia since the 1970s. A further set of questions relates to how the Indonesian experience compares with that of other rapidly industrializing parts of Asia. How do the trends discerned in economies such as Taiwan's since the 1950s compare with Indonesia's more recent experience?

The purpose of this chapter is to cast some light on these questions, making particular use of the data collected in the two sample surveys of agricultural household incomes carried out as part of the 1983 and 1993 Agricultural Censuses.[3] The focus of the chapter is thus on that subset of rural households which still have at least a toehold in the agricultural sector, in the sense that at least one family member is engaged in agricultural work.[4] I begin with a discussion of what these surveys show regarding changes in sources of agricultural household income in Indonesia between 1984 and 1993, both at the national level and by province.

Where Do Agricultural Households Earn Their Income?

In 1984, the average annual agricultural household income in Indonesia was Rp. 664,000; nine years later this had increased to Rp. 1,760,000 in nominal terms (Table 2.3). Although this also implied a substantial increase in real terms, these nine years witnessed rapid growth in the non-agricultural economy and the real growth in farm household incomes was rather slower than real growth in total household expenditures as given in the national income statistics, which indicates that farm incomes on average were falling behind those in other parts of the economy. This was indeed confirmed by the data from the Social Accounting Matrices (SAMS) which show that all categories of agricultural household (except those operating very small holdings) experienced some decline in their incomes relative to the national average between 1985 and 1993 (Booth 2000, Table 2.7). Between 1984 and 1993, the proportion of total farm household income which came from operating the farm holding *(usaha pertanian)* fell from 55 to 50 percent. The proportion derived from wage labour (both agricultural and non-agricultural) also fell while that from other non-agricultural activities stayed roughly constant. The most rapid growth was in income derived from "other" sources which included income from remittances, and pensions (Table 2.3).

We can also examine the changes in total income accruing to farm households, and in the percentage derived from the farm holding, by province. By 1993, when on average 50 percent of total farm household income was being derived from the farm holding itself, seven provinces were deriving less than 50 percent and two (West Java and Yogyakarta) were deriving less than 40 percent (Table 2.4). At the other end of the provincial distribution, farm households in eight provinces were still depending on the farm holding for over 60 percent of their income, and in three of these (Jambi, South Sumatra and South Sulawesi) the proportion had increased between 1984 and 1993.

Neither in 1984 nor in 1993 was there any correlation between total farm household income from all sources by province and the proportion derived from the farm holding. It is clear from Table 2.4 that there were several provinces (Jambi, Riau, South Sumatra) where total farm household income from all sources was well above the national average and where there was a relatively high dependence on income from the farm holding itself. But there were also provinces (Yogyakarta, Bali, North Sulawesi)

TABLE 2.3
Income Accruing to Agricultural Households by Income Sources, 1984 and 1993
(Rp. '000)

Income source	1984	1993	% Increase
Foodcrop	193	399	107
Other crops	92	264	187
Livestock	57	115	102
Fisheries	17	79	365
Forestry	6	23	283
Total from agricultural holding	365	880	141
Wages and salaries	166	387	133
Agriculture	n.a	129	
Non-agriculture	n.a	258	
Non-agricultural activities	73	189	159
Other	60	304	407
Total			
Nominal	664	1760	165
1993 prices[a]	1313	1760	34

[a] Deflated by the household consumption component of the GDP deflator

Source: Central Bureau of Statistics (1987), Table 9; Central Bureau of Statistics (1995), Tables 1–5

where total farm household income was above the national average but where the reliance on income from the farm holding was much less. Similarly if we look at the provinces where the total farm household income was well below the national average, some such as Central Java had a high reliance on off-farm income while others such as East Nusatenggara and East Timor derived over 60 percent of their total income from the holding itself. It is possible that in a province such as Jambi, most farm households can make a reasonable living from agriculture and feel less need to seek extra income elsewhere, while in a province such as East Nusatenggara, farm households would like to supplement their relatively meager incomes from the farm holding but have little opportunity to do so.[5]

TABLE 2.4
Total Annual Farm Household Income and Percentage from the Farm Holding by Province, 1984 and 1993

Province	Total farm household income (Rp. '000)		Percentage from farm holding		Percentage of the total farm population 10+, 1993
	1984	1993	1984	1993	
West Java	640	1744	41.6	35.2	14.3
Yogyakarta	750	1884	42.5	36.5	1.5
Central Java	609	1635	50.4	40.7	14.1
West Sumatra	735	1752	51.8	42.4	2.8
Bali	847	2733	58.9	44.7	1.6
South Kalimantan	574	1714	50.0	45.4	2.1
North Sulawesi	907	1956	56.3	46.1	1.7
East Java	593	1585	58.0	51.3	18.4
West Nusatenggara	523	1578	62.7	52.0	1.8
West Kalimantan	655	1938	63.7	52.4	2.4
Central Sulawesi	836	1879	57.5	52.4	1.4
Maluku	909	1687	66.8	52.6	1.6
East Kalimantan	702	2439	61.3	54.4	1.0
North Sumatra	735	1871	55.2	55.8	4.7
Lampung	590	1418	63.1	57.8	5.7
Central Kalimantan	853	2123	60.4	58.6	1.4
Bengkulu	821	1614	69.1	58.8	1.1
Southeast Sulawesi	659	1975	60.8	59.1	1.0
Aceh	791	1987	60.3	60.0	2.9
East Nusatenggara	621	1573	72.6	61.2	3.7
Riau	1086	2594	57.1	62.7	2.0
Irian Jaya	770	1653	73.8	63.0	1.7
East Timor	676	1438	71.2	63.3	0.8
South Sulawesi	634	1781	65.3	66.3	4.4
South Sumatra	878	2056	66.7	69.4	4.9
Jambi	724	2407	69.2	69.8	1.1
Indonesia	664	1760	55.0	50.0	100.0

Total farm household income from all sources correlated with percentage of income from farm holding:
r =
1984   0.069
1993   0.108

Source: Central Bureau of Statistics (1987), Central Bureau of Statistics (1995)

Variations in Sources of Agricultural Household Income by Size of Holding and by Income Class

While income from the farm holding (*usaha pertanian*) accounts for a diminishing percentage of total household income in many parts of Indonesia, it was still the case in the mid-1990s that the great majority of households which were involved in agricultural activities claimed that agriculture was the "main" source of household income. (This of course does not mean that it accounted for a large part of total household income; simply that it was more important than any other single source). In 1984, almost 82 percent of farm households claimed that agriculture was the main source of their income; by 1993 this percentage had dropped only slightly (Table 2.5). In both years, there was a marked tendency for the percentage of households reporting agriculture as their main activity to increase by holding size. In 1993, only about 56 percent of those households cultivating less than 0.1 hectares reported that agriculture was the main source of household income, compared with over 90 percent of those cultivating more than 2.5 hectares (Table 2.5).

Of those agricultural households who reported that agricultural activities (including agricultural wage employment) were not the main source of household income in 1993, the majority gave services as the main source. Fewer than 2 percent of all agricultural households gave remittances and other earnings as their main income source. Manufacturing (both agricultural processing and other forms of manufacturing) was the main source of income of only 4 percent of all agricultural households. There was a very pronounced inverse relationship between holding size and the percentage of households reporting trade and other service sector activity as the main source of household income (Table 2.6). This inverse relationship was also clear for households reporting manufacturing as the main income source.

The presence of this inverse relationship could be used to support the view that off-farm activities in the manufacturing and especially in the service sector in Indonesia have had an equalising effect on incomes accruing to agricultural households, in the sense that those households with fewer agricultural assets (as represented by size of operated holding) are more reliant on these activities for the bulk of their income. Thus it could be hypothesized that the asset-poor agricultural households compensate for their low earning potential in agriculture by earning most of their income from other activities. But the evidence does not really

The Changing Importance of Off-Farm Income

TABLE 2.5
Breakdown of Agricultural Households by Size of Holding and Main Income Source

Size of cultivated holding (hectares)	1984		1993	
	Percentage breakdown of holdings by holding size	Percentage of households with main income from agriculture	Percentage breakdown of holdings by holding size	Percentage of households with main income from agriculture
Under 0.1	8.5	62.6	7.0	56.4
0.1-0.249	16.4	69.7	18.4	66.5
0.25-0.49	21.3	79.8	22.3	75.5
0.50-0.99	24.1	87.0	22.4	83.1
1.00-2.49	23.4	90.5	24.2	89.5
over 2.5	6.3	92.2	5.7	92.1
Indonesia	100.0	81.7	100.0	78.5

Source: Central Bureau of Statistics (1987), Table 5; Central Bureau of Statistics (1995), Table 5

TABLE 2.6
Sources of Non-Agricultural Income for Agricultural Households, 1993

Size of cultivated holding (hectares)	Percentage of households Other with main income from non-agricultural activities	Main source of household income				
		Manufacturing		Trade	Other Services	Other
		Agri-processing	Other			
Under 0.05	45.8	1.6	6.3	12.8	20.2	4.9
0.05–0.099	42.4	2.0	6.5	12.6	17.8	3.5
0.10–0.249	33.5	2.0	4.9	10.8	13.6	2.2
0.25–0.499	24.5	1.6	2.9	8.3	10.3	1.4
0.5–0.999	16.9	1.1	1.9	5.5	7.5	1.0
1.0–2.499	10.5	0.7	1.1	3.1	5.0	0.7
2.5–4.999	7.6	0.6	0.7	2.2	3.7	0.4
5.0–9.999	8.7	0.8	0.5	2.0	4.7	0.7
Over 10 hectares	15.6	..	2.0	5.4	6.4	1.8
Average	21.5	1.3	2.7	6.8	9.2	1.4

Source: Central Bureau of Statistics (1995), Table 19

support such an argument. The data in Table 2.6 does not tell us whether the asset-poor households are in fact earning sufficient from their off-farm activities to compensate for lower incomes from their farm holding. Rather they simply indicate that the households with smaller operated holdings tend to rely more on non-farm activities for their "main" source of income.

To explore the impact of off-farm earnings on the overall distribution of income between agricultural households, we need to examine the breakdown of income accruing to agricultural households from different sources by total household income class. Fortunately relevant data from the 1993 Survey of Agricultural Household Incomes was available (Table 2.7). There was no strong evidence of an inverse relationship between the income size group and the percentage of income derived from non-agricultural sources. Quite the reverse in fact. With the exception of the smallest and the largest income size group, there was a steady tendency for the percentage of total household income derived from the farm holding, and from all agricultural activities including wage labour, to fall as household income increased (Table 2.7). There was a significant degree of positive correlation between income from the farm holding (by total income class) and the proportion of total income derived from non-agricultural sources ($r = 0.53$).

As total agricultural household income from all sources grew, non-agricultural wage earnings and income from self-employment activities (manufacturing, trade and other services) both accounted for a growing percentage of total household income (Table 2.8). There was some sign of an "inverted U" relationship for non-agricultural wage income, and of a "U" relationship for other income (which includes pensions and remittances), although other income only accounted for more than 30 percent of total household income in the top income class. The top income class in turn accounted for a very small percentage of all agricultural households (Table 2.7). The top four income classes, all of which derived less than half of their total income from agricultural activities, only accounted for about 4.5 percent of all agricultural households.

This apparently paradoxical combination, of a rising percentage of on-farm to total income as holding size increases and a falling percentage of on-farm to total income as income size increases, has in fact been found in a number of Latin American case studies (Reardon, Berdegue and Escobar 2001, p. 404). On the one hand it seems reasonable to expect that those agricultural households operating larger than average holdings have less need to seek off-farm work. But how can we explain the fact that the richer

TABLE 2.7
Percentage Breakdown of Agricultural Household Income by Agricultural Income Source and Income Size, 1993

Income per month (Rp. '000) income group	Percentage of agricultural households in	As percentage of total household income		
		Farm holding[a]	Agricultural wages	All agricultural income[b]
under 20	2.0	48.3 (71.2)	7.4	62.5
20–24	1.4	55.6 (73.2)	10.5	73.3
25–29	2.1	53.3 (71.2)	11.5	72.2
30–39	5.2	54.4 (68.6)	13.0	74.4
40–49	6.2	54.1 (64.5)	13.9	74.4
50–74	17.0	54.2 (60.5)	14.2	74.3
75–99	15.6	54.1 (57.3)	13.1	72.3
100–149	21.5	54.2 (52.5)	10.7	69.8
150–199	11.2	52.3 (47.7)	8.3	64.1
200–299	9.7	48.5 (43.5)	5.8	57.1
300–399	3.8	45.1 (39.7)	3.4	50.6
400–499	1.8	44.2 (38.1)	2.7	49.0
500–749	1.6	44.1 (33.7)	2.1	47.9
750–899	0.4	39.7 (23.9)	1.4	42.4
over 900	0.7	46.7 (12.4)	0.4	48.0
Indonesia	100.0	50.0 (45.4)	7.4	60.7

[a] Figures in brackets show the percentage of farm holding income which is derived from foodcrop agriculture.

[b] Total agricultural income is the sum of income from the farm holding, agricultural wages and "other sources", not shown here. Typically they would include hiring out of agricultural equipment and land.

Source: Central Bureau of Statistics (1995), Tables 8–12

agricultural households (ranked by income, rather than by operated land holding) are more dependent on off-farm income than the poorer ones? The direction of causality is clearly more complex when we examine rankings by income size, and it appears that in Indonesia, as in a number of Latin American economies, households which have managed to diversify their economic activities away from agriculture, and especially those households which have managed to gain access to non-agricultural employment opportunities, have been the most successful in increasing their total incomes. These are sometimes, but by no means always, those

TABLE 2.8
Percentage Breakdown of Agricultural Household Income by Non-Agricultural Income Source and Income Size, 1993

Income per month (Rp. '000)	As percentage of total agricultural household income[a]					
	Non-agricultural wages	Manu-facturing	Trade	Other services	Other income	All non-agricultural income
Under 20	3.2	1.3	1.1	0.3	31.7	37.5
20–24	1.7	1.1	1.4	0.4	22.1	26.7
25–29	2.4	1.6	2.1	1.1	20.7	27.8
30–39	3.4	1.6	1.8	0.7	18.2	25.8
40–49	4.1	1.7	2.4	1.0	16.5	25.6
50–74	5.8	1.8	3.1	1.2	13.7	25.7
75–99	8.3	1.9	3.9	1.6	12.0	27.7
100–149	10.7	1.9	5.2	2.0	11.0	30.7
150–199	14.3	1.9	6.9	2.2	10.6	35.9
200–299	19.5	1.8	8.1	2.4	11.0	42.9
300–399	25.3	2.0	8.1	2.4	11.5	49.4
400–499	28.3	2.1	8.2	2.4	10.0	51.0
500–749	25.3	3.4	7.4	3.3	12.6	52.1
750–899	21.0	3.6	10.1	5.5	17.4	57.6
Over 900	5.7	3.1	7.0	3.4	32.9	52.0
Average	14.6	2.1	6.3	2.3	13.4	39.3

[a] Manufacturing includes both agri-processing and other forms of manufacturing. Other sources of income include pensions and remittances and also sources not elsewhere included.

Source: Central Bureau of Statistics (1995), Tables 8–11

households which control relatively large amounts of agricultural land. But control over other assets, including educated labour, permit households to diversify successfully into non-agricultural activities, and are thus important determinants of total household income.

Linkage Between Growth of On-Farm and Off-Farm Incomes

Over the last two decades in many parts of the world, much research has been carried out which examines the nature of linkages between the agricultural and non-agricultural sectors of rural economies.[6] There seems to be little doubt that interactions between different sectors of the rural economy have varied greatly both between countries and over time. Some authors have put forward an "Asian example" where the combination of a "relatively egalitarian distribution of income, well-functioning factor markets, and a strong emphasis on educational expansion" has produced rapid growth of non-agricultural employment in rural areas, which benefits most rural households (Deininger and Olinto 2001, p. 464). This benign outcome is then contrasted with the much less egalitarian outcomes which have occurred in many parts of Africa and Latin America. But in fact the so-called "Asian" result seems to be based on the recent history of just one country, Taiwan, and there is growing evidence that the Taiwanese experience is far from typical of other Asian countries, let alone other parts of the developing world.[7]

Ranis, Stewart and Angeles-Reyes (1990) and Ranis and Stewart (1993) have investigated differences in urban-rural linkages between the Philippines and Taiwan. They have argued that the more skewed distribution of land and income in the Philippines, combined with the more capital-intensive, urban-biased nature of the industrialization process, have led to a much slower growth of non-agricultural employment and incomes in rural areas in the Philippines compared with Taiwan. This in turn has meant that a given amount of agricultural income growth created fewer non-agricultural employment opportunities in rural areas compared with Taiwan. Thus the ratio of growth in non-agricultural incomes to growth in agricultural incomes was much lower in rural areas in the Philippines; in fact over the two decades from 1965 to 1985 they estimate that rural non-agricultural incomes grew more slowly than agricultural incomes (Ranis and Stewart 1993, Table 14).

The agricultural household income surveys in Indonesia can be used to estimate linkage ratios for Indonesia over the years from 1984 to 1993. For Indonesia as a whole, the growth of off-farm income of agricultural households was only about 24 percent faster than the growth in income from the agricultural holdings (Table 2.9). As would be expected, the average for the country as a whole masked considerable inter-provincial variations. In the five provinces where the proportion of total agricultural household income derived from the farm holding was lowest in 1993, the linkage ratios were higher than the national average. But even in Bali, the linkage ratio, although higher than the average for Indonesia, was much below that found in Taiwan between 1962 and 1972. The evidence

TABLE 2.9
Linkage Ratios and the Percentage of Total Farm Income Accruing from Off-Farm Employment

Country/Years	Linkage Ratio[a]	Per Capita GDP (Initial Year)[b]	Percentage of Farm Income from Off-farm Sources	
			Initial Year	Final Year
Taiwan (1962–80)	3.55	1364	25	60
Philippines (1965–85)	0.94	1248	45	56
Taiwan (1962–72)	2.99	1364	40	60
Thailand (1971/2–1982/83)	1.38	1507	46	59
Indonesia (1984–93)	1.24	1602	45	50
West Java	1.34		58	65
Yogyakarta	1.35		58	64
Central Java	1.54		50	59
West Sumatra	1.60		48	58
Bali	1.70		41	55

[a] Growth in off-farm incomes over the period shown divided by growth in farm incomes.
[b] ICP dollars in 1985 prices adjusted for changes in the terms of trade. Data taken from Penn World Tables (Version 5.6)

Source: Taiwan (1962–80) and the Philippines: Ranis and Stewart (1993), Tables 9 and 14. Taiwan (1962–72): Ho (1986), Table 4.2. Thailand: Onchan (1990), Table 2.13; Indonesia: Central Bureau of Statistics (1987), (1995).

suggests that Indonesia, like Thailand, was an "intermediate case" between Taiwan on the one hand and the Philippines on the other. Faster overall rates of economic growth over the 1980s and the first part of the 1990s in both Thailand and Indonesia compared with the Philippines must have played an important role in generating faster growth in off-farm earning opportunities even if the result was hardly as impressive as in Taiwan.

Conclusions

The evidence reviewed above shows that the off-farm, and non-agricultural incomes of agricultural households grew rapidly in Indonesia over the years from 1984 to 1993, and that by 1993 incomes from all off-holding sources accounted for 50 percent of total incomes of agricultural households. This in itself is hardly surprising; a large body of literature now exists which demonstrates that agricultural households throughout Asia, Africa and Latin America are deriving significant and increasing shares of their total incomes from off-holding activities.[8] Indeed it has been argued that rural households "increasingly come to resemble miniature highly diversified conglomerates, many of them with a foothold in the urban sector" (Cain and McNicoll 1988, p. 105). While this is true to an increasing extent of at least some parts of Indonesia, we should not overlook the fact that the great majority of those households classified as agricultural still claim that agriculture is their 'main' source of income. To the extent that income diversification is taking place, agriculture is still the core activity for most agricultural households. At the same time, by the mid-1990s, a significant minority of rural households (around 27 percent according to the 1995 Intercensal Survey) had no involvement with agriculture at all.

In the two surveys of agricultural household incomes carried out as part of the 1983 and 1993 Agricultural Censuses, total incomes from all sources are broken down into agricultural wages, other income from agricultural activities (such as hiring out equipment etc.), non-agricultural wages, and various types of self-employment activities in manufacturing and services. In addition many households receive income from remittances, pensions etc. In 1993, wages and salary earnings were the largest single source of off-farm earnings, and non-agricultural wage earnings were greater than those from agriculture (Table 2.3). There is evidence of an inverted "U" relationship, in that both agricultural and non-agricultural wages account for a higher proportion of total agricultural household incomes for the middle income groups (Tables 2.7 and 2.8).

But it is also clear that dependence on non-agricultural wages and salaries is more skewed towards the upper income groups. When all sources of non-agricultural income are added together, the result is a steady increase in the proportion of total income derived from non-agricultural activities by income group, with the exception of the very lowest and the highest income groups (Table 2.8). In this sense Indonesia would appear to contradict what Reardon et al. (2000, p. 271) term the "conventional wisdom" that there is a strong negative relationship between the non-agricultural share and total household income, although, as these authors demonstrate, evidence from a number of other countries or regions also tends to refute the conventional wisdom.[9]

Numerous authors over the years have pointed out that rural households try to take a longer term view of income security than "merely taking advantage of currently available income earning opportunities" (Ellis 2000, p. 296). Investment in a variety of income yielding assets is obviously of crucial importance to rural households seeking to secure their income over the longer term. Traditionally households with some surplus would invest in acquiring extra land, in improving the quality of existing land, in purchasing agricultural implements and vehicles for own use and for hire, and in purchasing livestock, or gold and jewelry. Over the past two decades, investment in the education of children and other family members has also become a very important part of rural household asset diversification (Ellis 2000, pp. 296–97). Increasingly many rural households appreciate that access to the more lucrative and secure non-agricultural occupations requires education, and investment in the education of family members is thus viewed as an even more important part of the household investment strategy than the acquisition of land or equipment.

Although many rural households now appreciate the value of educational investment, there are significant up-front costs associated with education in Indonesia, especially at the secondary and tertiary levels (Booth 2000, p. 93). Thus it is the more affluent households which can afford to keep their children in school long enough to gain the entry-level qualifications needed for the better paid and more secure jobs in the manufacturing and the service sector. Over time it is likely that the effect of growing access to non-agricultural wage employment will aggravate income inequalities in many parts of rural Indonesia, as indeed appears to be the case in other parts of the world.[10] Reardon, Berdegue and Escobar (2001, p. 404) report that both ownership of land and access to education position households to undertake well-paid non-agricultural activity in many parts of Central and South America, and that in some countries the "educated landless" may be earning as much as households operating large agricultural holdings.

Even so, access to off-farm and non-agricultural employment permits even the poorest households to increase their total income and also, in many cases, to reduce the insecurity inherent in exclusive reliance on agriculture (including agricultural labour) as the only source of income. There seems to be little doubt that income diversification has been an important reason for the decline in the headcount measure of poverty which has occurred in many parts of rural Indonesia since the 1970s. In this respect it is important to note the importance of trade and other services in providing the "main source of income" for a significant number of those households cultivating very small amounts of agricultural land (Table 2.6). Typically in many parts of Indonesia trade and services provide employment for large numbers of women workers. In 1995, the trade sector provided more employment for both male and female workers than manufacturing in rural areas. In the Latin American context, Reardon, Berdegue and Escobar (2001, p. 404) point out that many non-farm employment programmes in rural areas focus on the manufacturing sector in spite of the evidence that employment in trade and other services is more important.[11] This point would also seem to be highly relevant in Indonesia. Given the importance of rural trade as a means of employment and income in many parts of the country, especially for land-poor households, it is perhaps surprising that so little research had been carried out in this sector.[12]

There are considerable regional variations in the extent to which agricultural households in Indonesia have been able (or been compelled) to diversify their incomes away from exclusive reliance on the farm holding. While the proportion of on-farm to total income has fallen in some of the more isolated and agriculturally less productive parts of the country between 1984 and 1993, it is clear from the 1993 data that many households in East Nusatenggara, East Timor and Irian Jaya were unable fully to compensate for low on-farm earnings by earning more from off-farm employment. This is unlikely to change in the immediate future. There seems to be a persuasive case for continued emphasis on increasing agricultural productivity in Eastern Indonesia, and on improving rural infrastructure (roads, irrigation etc.) and rural credit facilities. Government investment in these programmes will be needed, both to increase on-farm incomes and to expand access to off-farm employment.

For Indonesia as a whole, off-farm income grew more rapidly than on-farm income over the nine years from 1984 to 1993, but the difference in growth rates was certainly much less than in Taiwan during the 1960s and 1970s. Indeed a higher proportion of agricultural households in Indonesia were wholly dependent on farming for their income in 1993 than was the case in Taiwan in 1960 (Table 2.10), in spite of the fact that per capita GDP was lower in Taiwan in 1960 than in Indonesia three decades later.[13] Even in Java and Bali, the proportion was higher. Exploring the reasons for these differences is beyond the scope of this paper, although they are

TABLE 2.10
Breakdown of Agricultural Households by Sources of Income

	Only agriculture	Mixed: mainly agriculture	Mixed: mainly other	Total
Indonesia: 1995				
Sumatra	75.3	11.7	13.0	100.0
Java/Bali	52.4	20.9	26.7	100.0
Kalimantan	66.6	18.8	14.6	100.0
Sulawesi	67.1	17.1	15.8	100.0
Eastern Islands	73.3	14.7	12.0	100.0
All Indonesia	61.0	18.0	21.0	100.0
Taiwan				
1960	47.6	29.8	22.5	100.0
1970	30.2	40.6	29.2	100.0
1980	9.0	35.5	55.5	100.0
1990	13.2	17.3	69.5	100.0
Thailand: 1993				
Northeast	45.6	40.0	14.4	100.0
North	47.0	37.3	15.7	100.0
Central	46.5	38.2	15.3	100.0
South	44.8	32.8	22.4	100.0
All Thailand	46.0	38.0	16.0	100.0

Source: Kingdom of Thailand (1995), Table 10.1; Republic of China (1995), pp. 64–65; Central Bureau of Statistics (1996), Table 59.3

probably related both to the unusually egalitarian distribution of land in Taiwan after the reforms of the 1950s, and to greater access to education.

Notes

1. The employment data from the 1990 Population Census reported a considerable number of employed workers, especially in rural areas, whose sector of employment was "not stated". If, as seems probable, most were in fact employed in agriculture, then the decline in the agricultural labour force would have been much larger. On the other hand if they were earning most of their income from non-agricultural jobs then the share of the rural non-

agricultural sector in overall employment growth between 1990 and 1995 shown in Table 2.1 is overstated.
2. Since 1997 there has been a rapid growth in the size of the agricultural labour force and almost all the new jobs created between 1997 and 2000 have been in the agricultural sector.
3. The survey carried out as part of the 1983 Agricultural Census in fact took place during calendar year 1984. The survey carried out as part of the 1993 Agricultural Census was conducted over the calendar year 1993. The main findings are summarised in Central Bureau of Statistics (1987) and Central Bureau of Statistics (1995) respectively.
4. The definition of an agricultural household used in the 1983 Agricultural Census is one where at least one household member carries out agricultural activities, including foodcrops, treecrops, fisheries, livestock or forestry. In 1993 this definition was qualified with the additional clause that an agricultural household is one where at least one member produces agricultural output with the aim of sale or profit or exchange, at his or her own risk. It should be noted that this definition was probably rather more restrictive than the definition used in the 1995 Intercensal Survey, with the result that the number of households reported as deriving all or part of their income from agriculture in 1995 (24.1 million) was considerably larger than the number of agricultural households reported in the 1993 Agricultural Census (20.3 million).
5. Booth (2002), Table 11, examines the correlates of agricultural household dependency on income from the farm holding by province with a range of geographic and economic indicators. Significant negative correlations were found with population densities, road densities, and the percentage of rural households not owning land. An OLS regression analysis indicates that around two thirds of the inter-provincial variation in dependency on income from the farm holding (as shown in Table 2.4) can be accounted for by rural poverty, and some agricultural variables including area per farm, and value added in smallholder agriculture per hectare.
6. See Lanjouw and Lanjouw (1995, pp. 19–23) and Ellis (1998, pp. 19–23) for a discussion of the literature.
7. Ho (1979) in an early examination of the Taiwanese success with decentralized industrialization stressed the difference between Taiwan and South Korea. In the latter country, a labour force survey carried out in 1974 showed that less than 30 percent of total employment in commerce and services was located in rural areas.
8. The literature on off-farm employment is now substantial. Oshima (1984) and the papers in Shand (1986) review the evidence up until the early 1980s in the context of Asia. Saith (1992) draws on work in both Asia and other parts of the developing world, as do Lanjouw and Lanjouw (1995), and

FAO (1998). Ellis (1998) gives a comprehensive survey, albeit with a focus on sub-Saharan Africa. There is also a body of literature for Indonesia based on colonial censuses and surveys which demonstrates the importance of non-agricultural employment in the early decades of the twentieth century in Java, especially for women. See White (1991) for a discussion of these sources.

9. White (1991, Table 2.10), contrasts data from Japan with those from a survey of over one thousand agricultural households in rice-growing areas of Java in 1981. The Javanese data showed that the larger landholding households earned more in absolute terms from off-farm activities, although such income accounted for a smaller share of total household income than for the households controlling less land.

10. One detailed field study, carried out in West Java, found, perhaps surprisingly, that no relationship existed between mean earnings from non-agricultural labour and access to land. Construction work and becak driving were the two most common sources of non-agricultural wage employment pursued by men, and earnings from these were spread evenly by landholding class (Pincus 1996, pp. 69–70).

11. It is indeed striking that several studies of off-farm employment in Asia continue this focus on rural industries, in spite of the evidence that the service sector is more important in generating employment and incomes. See for example Mukhopadhay and Chee (1985), Islam (1987) and Hayami (1998). The historical evidence from Japan and even Taiwan would also appear to suggest that income from self-employment in industrial activities was a very small part of total farm household income until the 1960s. Income from wage labour was much more important. See Oshima (1984), Appendix Tables 1 and 2.

12. An important exception is the work of Jennifer Alexander. See Alexander (1998) and the literature cited there. Women have been heavily involved in rural trading activities in Java at least since the early decades of the twentieth century, as White (1991) and Alexander and Alexander (1991) have shown. This trend has continued into the 1990s.

13. According to the Penn World Tables (PWT) data (Version 5.6), per capita GDP in Taiwan (constant 1985 international dollars) was 1,256. Per capita GDP in Indonesia in 1992 was 2,102 dollars and 3,942 dollars in Thailand.

References

Alexander, Jennifer. "Women Traders in Javanese Marketplace: Ethnicity, Gender and the Entrepreneurial Spirit". In *Market Cultures: Society and Morality in the New Asian Capitalisms*, Robert W. Hefner (ed.), pp. 203–23. Boulder: Westview Press, 1998.

Alexander, Jennifer and Paul Alexander. "Trade and Petty Commodity Production in Early Twentieth Century Kebumen". In *In the Shadow of Agriculture: Non-Farm Activities in the Javanese Economy, Past and Present*, Paul Alexander, Peter Boomgaard and Ben White (eds), pp. 70–91. Amsterdam: Royal Tropical Institute, 1991.

Booth, Anne. "Poverty and Inequality in the Soeharto Era: An Assessment". *Bulletin of Indonesian Economic Studies* 36, no. 1 (April 2000): 73–104.

Booth, Anne. "The Changing Role of Non-farm Activities in Agricultural Households in Indonesia: Some Insights from the Agricultural Censuses". *Bulletin of Indonesian Economic Studies* 38, no. 2 (August 2002): 167–88.

Central Bureau of Statistics. "Pendapatan Rumahtangga Pertanian dan Indikator Sosial Ekonomi". *Sensus Pertanian 1993*. ("Agricultural Household Incomes and Socioeconomic Indicators". *Agricultural Census 1993*) Series D1. Jakarta: Central Bureau of Statistics, 1995.

Central Bureau of Statistics. "Penduduk Indonesia: Hasil Sensus Penduduk 1990" ("Results of the 1990 Population Census") Series S2. Jakarta: Central Bureau of Statistics, 1992.

Central Bureau of Statistics. "Penduduk Indonesia: Hasil Survei Penduduk Antar Sensus 1995" ("Indonesian Population: Results of the 1995 Intercensal Population Survey") Series S2. Jakarta: Central Bureau of Statistics, September 1996.

Central Bureau of Statistics. "Sampel Pendapatan Petani". *Sensus Pertanian 1983* ("Sample Survey of Farm Incomes". *Agricultural Census 1983*) Series 1. Jakarta: Central Bureau of Statistics, August 1987.

Cain, Mead and Geoff McNicoll. "Population Growth and Agrarian Outcomes". In *Population, Food and Rural Development*, Ronald D. Lee et al. (eds), pp. 101–17. Oxford: Clarendon Press, 1988.

Deininger, Klaus and Pedro Olinto. "Rural Non-farm Employment and Income Diversification in Colombia". *World Development* 29, no. 3 (March 2001): 455–65.

Ellis, Frank. "Household Strategies and Rural Livelihood Diversifications". *Journal of Development Studies* 35, no. 1 (October 1998): 1–38.

Ellis, Frank. "The Determinants of Rural Livelihood Diversification in Developing Countries". *Journal of Agricultural Economics* 51, no. 2 (May 2000): 289–302.

FAO (Food and Agricultural Organization). "Rural Non-Farm Income in Developing Countries". In *The State of Food and Agriculture*. Rome: Food and Agricultural Organization, 1998.

Hayami, Y. (ed.). *Towards the Rural-Based Development of Commerce and Industry: Selected Experiences from East Asia*. Washington: Economic Development Institute, World Bank, 1998.

Ho, Samuel P.S. "Decentralized Industrialization and Rural Development: Evidence from Taiwan". *Economic Development and Cultural Change* 28, no. 1 (October, 1979): 77–96.

Ho, Samuel P.S. "Off-Farm Employment and Farm Households in Taiwan". In *Off-farm Employment in the Development of Rural Asia*, edited by R.T. Shand, pp. 95–128. Canberra: National Centre for Development Studies, Australian National University, 1986.

Islam, Rizwanul (ed.). *Rural Industrialisation and Employment in Asia*. New Delhi: ILO-ARTEP, 1987.

Lanjouw, Jean O. and Peter Lanjouw. *Rural Nonfarm Employment: A Survey*. Policy Research Working Paper 1463. Washington: World Bank, May 1995.

Mukhopadhyay, Swapna and Chee Peng Lim (eds). *Development and Diversification of Rural Industries in Asia*. Kuala Lumpur: Asian and Pacific Development Centre, 1985.

National Statistical Office, Kingdom of Thailand. *Report on the 1993 Agricultural Census*. Bangkok: National Statistical Office, 1995.

Onchan, Tongroj. *A Land Policy Study*. Research Monograph No. 3. Bangkok: The Thailand Development Research Institute Foundation, 1990.

Oshima, Harry T. "The Significance of Off-Farm Employment and Incomes in Post-War East Asian Growth". Asian Development Bank Economic Staff Paper No. 21. Manila: Asian Development Bank, 1984.

Pincus, Jonathan. *Class Power and Agrarian Change*. London: Macmillan Press, 1996.

Ranis, Gustav and Frances Stewart. "Rural Non-agricultural Activities in Development: Theory and Application". *Journal of Development Economics* 40, no. 1 (February 1993): 75–101.

Ranis, Gustav, Frances Stewart and Edna Angeles-Reyes. *Linkages in Developing Economies: A Philippine Study*. San Francisco: International Center for Economic Growth, 1990.

Reardon, Thomas, J. Edward Taylor, Kostas Stamoulis, Peter Lanjouw and Arsenio Balisacan. "Effects of Non-Farm Employment on Rural Income Inequality in Developing Countries: An Investment Perspective". *Journal of Agricultural Economics* 51, no. 2 (May 2000): 266–88.

Reardon, Thomas, Julio Berdegue and German Escobar. "Rural Non-farm Employment and Incomes in Latin America: Overview and Policy Implications". *World Development* 29, no. 3 (March 2001): 395–409.

Republic of China. *Statistical Abstract of the Agricultural Censuses, Taiwan, Republic of China*. Tapei: Statistics Office, Council of Agriculture, July, 1995.

Saith, Ashwani. *The Rural Non-farm Economy: Processes and Policies*. Geneva: International Labour Office, 1992.

Shand, Richard T. (ed.), *Off-farm Employment in the Development of Rural Asia*.

Canberra: National Centre for Development Studies, Australian National University, 1986.

White, Benjamin. "Economic diversification and agrarian change in rural Java, 1900–1990". In *In the Shadow of Agriculture: Non-farm Activities in the Javanese Economy, Past and Present*, Paul Alexander, Peter Boomgaard and Ben White (eds), pp. 41–69. Amsterdam: Royal Tropical Institute, 1991.

3
THE ECONOMIC POLICY ENVIRONMENT FOR SMALL RURAL ENTERPRISES IN INDONESIA

Peter van Diermen

Introduction

Indonesia's 1999–2004 State Policy Guidelines (GBHN) provide the broad policy and direction for the country's president. Under the current guidelines, which are used to draw up the annual development plans (*Repelita*) and the state budget, high priority is given for the development of small and medium enterprises (SMEs) and cooperatives within a free market framework. Furthermore, the current GBHN emphasizes a need to promote industry to support agriculture and to eliminate barriers to domestic and international trade. In respect to SMEs, the current Guidelines do not greatly depart from previous GBHN. Over the life of the New Order, almost all the five-year guidelines contained policies extolling the virtues of SMEs and directing the President to give them special attention. A reasonable person would assume that despite a certain amount of slippage between the Guidelines and their implementation, the policy environment in Indonesia should overwhelmingly favour rural SMEs. The reality, however, is quite the opposite. This chapter will argue that since the beginning of the New Order, the economic policy environment and outcomes for rural SMEs have been very mixed.

To add to the confusion, even the most casual observer can't help but notice Indonesia's current turmoil. Not since the mid-1960s has Indonesia undergone such dramatic changes. From late 1997, every analyst has pointed to tremendous financial, economic, political and social changes that are taking place. In relation to the rural SMEs policy environment, important changes include:

1. declining real incomes for public servants,
2. declining national and regional budgets, greater accountability required from public servants,
3. rapidly changing financial support programmes for SMEs,
4. a range of new policies focusing on reducing corruption and increasing competition and transparency,
5. local governments creating regional trade barriers, primarily through taxation,
6. the 1999 decentralization and fiscal devolution policies,
7. rapidly changing national subsidy and taxation policies for basic commodities and production inputs crucial for rural SMEs.

A history of mixed signals from progressive macro-planners and micro-policy implementers as well as recent changes in the policy environment has provided a mixed and confused policy picture for rural SMEs.

The above circumstances make it difficult to analyze the economic environment and, more specifically, the policy environment under which rural SMEs have developed and continue to operate. Nevertheless, it remains crucial that we have some means of understanding and analyzing the economic environment for SMEs. In doing so we provide information and tools for decisions makers and it is useful for policy makers, at all levels, as well as SMEs themselves, to understand the constraints under which rural SMEs operate. To make sense of both the overall economic environment and the specific policy environment, this chapter will separate the pre-crisis and crisis periods and analyze several policy elements within each of these periods. In doing so, the chapter will comment on each period and forecast what the future policy environment for rural SMEs might look like. Thus, we begin by examining the macro-policy environment faced by rural SMEs prior to the financial crisis of 1997. This provides a useful backdrop for the next section in which micro-policies (programmes) are examined in more detail. It is then possible, in the third section, to discuss how rural entrepreneurs of SMEs responded to these mixed policy signals. Finally, we study the crisis and how it changed the policy environment and the chapter concludes by looking at the future policy environment for rural SMEs.

Macro-Economic Policy Environment

Since 1966, Indonesian policy makers have applied a range of economic policies and achieved impressive economic growth rates. In the period from 1966-68, inflation was brought under control and the economy brought back from the brink of chaos. In the late 1960s and early 1970s the Indonesian economy made a remarkable recovery by following sound economic management policies instituted by the New Order. In particularly, Western-trained Indonesian economists were used to advise the government and manage policy. The New Order sought to bring certainty and stability to the Indonesian economy and re-establish ties with the Western world. For the entire period of the New Order, policy makers and politicians sought to achieve high rates of economic growth, both for its own sake and as a way of legitimizing its rule. In the end, it was the regime's failure to assure continued economic stability and growth that led to its rapid decline.

Despite strong economic recovery at the beginning of the New Order and the shift away from socialist ideals, Indonesia periodically changed its macro-policy direction in response to national and international circumstances. Several macro-policy periods can be identified. The first of these is from 1966 to 1973, and was marked by rapid economic liberalization and application of strong orthodox economic management. A second period, coinciding with the oil boom, started in 1973 and lasted till about 1986. During this time, state intervention increased and there was a move towards a more interventionist economic approach. By 1986, the decline in oil revenue had begun to affect the Indonesian economy and the international setting had become more focused on deregulation. This also marked the turning point to a more liberal approach in Indonesia. During the period between 1986 and 1997, Indonesia embarked on a series of deregulation packages and the creation of a more liberal economy.

1966 to 1973. During this initial phase, policy makers moved quickly to liberalize the economy. Because the period under Sukarno had seen a rapid shift to nationalization of key economic sectors, the reversal of policies by the New Order seemed all the more stark. In the late 1960s, the GBHN and *Repelita* focus was on rapid economic recovery and stabilization. In particular, policies focused on rehabilitating basic infrastructure. A key legislation passed early during the New Order was the 1967 Foreign Investment Law. This law reversed the earlier restriction on foreign investment and indicated to the international community a commitment by the new policy makers to a dramatic shift towards liberalization of the Indonesian economy. In Indonesia's first *Repelita* (1969/70 to 1973/74), as in most of the *Repelitas* that followed, emphasis was placed on promoting industries that saved foreign exchange. Emphasis was also placed on developing SMEs and the agricultural sector through backward and forward linkages (Hill 1988, p. 11). Despite lip service to the issue of SMEs, little was done in this first period of rapid liberalization.

1973 to 1986. The emphasis on policy documents, such as the GBHN and *Repelita*, as well as the actual implementation of policy, focused attention on the promotion of SMEs and developing *pribumi* (indigenous) entrepreneurs. Several factors explain the shift of the government towards a more interventionist policy regime. First, the massive windfall from oil revenue provided the government with a much greater range of options. Second, after the initial reforms of the late 1960s and early 1970s it became increasingly more difficult for policy reform to have an immediate and significant impact. Third, during the early 1970s, the rapid change in the economy and strong growth also added to the confidence of policy makers and increased their options available. Fourth, ideals of economic nationalism continued to exist within the government and those advocating it were able to push this line on the basis of large oil revenue and a strong economy. As a result, state owned enterprises grew in number and in size. Moreover, the regulatory framework became more interventionist and created distortions in economic incentives. In particular, monopoly power was handed to a number of well-connected conglomerates and individuals connected to the military and the president's family. Protection was also extended through non-trade barriers to several sectors of the economy.

In regards to rural situations, a large number of subsidized credit schemes were developed and implemented for cooperatives, SMEs, and *pribumi* entrepreneurs. These three are closely related. For example, many SMEs are *pribumi* and belong to cooperatives. Conglomerates, particularly, ethnic Chinese, were taxed in various ways to finance some of these schemes, while others were paid for out of government revenue. Most of the support schemes developed during this time were motivated by political and social rather than economic management concerns. These concerns stemmed from an economy dominated by a small group of large conglomerates owned by ethnic Chinese and the larger *pribumi* population resentment of the concentration of economic wealth in their hands. The significant number of SME/cooperative programmes was seen as a means of supporting what was commonly referred to as a 'weak economic group'. These programmes were primarily used as a means of wealth transfer with little consideration for the economic rational and viability of the programmes. On the whole, the programmes resulted in ineffective and costly policies that in some cases did more harm than good in terms of creating a dynamic and competitive SME sector.

1986 to 1997. By 1985, large revenues from oil had begun to taper off. Moreover, under an increasingly restrictive regulatory framework, international investment in the economy had also begun to wane. Thus, by 1985 the initiative was again with the rational economic managers. In early 1985, custom services were reformed and placed in the hands of a Swiss company. By early 1986, this was followed by several measures liberalizing the use of imported inputs in exports. In late 1986, this was followed by a more comprehensive reform package aimed at reducing tariff barriers. In the years following (1987, 1988, 1990 and 1991) several other reform packages were announced. In general the decade from 1986 saw a sustained attempt to reduce the high cost economy and move towards an export-orientated economy.

During this time, the decline in government revenue had an important impact on rural SMEs. While the government's broad policy statements continued to emphasize the importance of agriculture and SMEs, in practice, there was a decline in revenue for implementing the programmes. In 1990, the large KIK/KMKP credit programme was discontinued. This programme had been operating since 1973 providing SMEs with subsidized credit. In 1990 it was replaced with a non-subsidized credit scheme (KUK) which required banks to lend 20 percent of their loan portfolio to SMEs. While government ability to finance SME schemes declined between 1986 and 1997, its policy focus did not change, as indicated by the large number of programmes for SMEs and cooperatives that continued or were developed during this time. Of particular significance were programmes that required little government funds but placed social obligations on large conglomerates (i.e., the *kemitraan* programme). Furthermore, the reform packages brought down the high cost economy and created a more competitive business environment. The reduction in unnecessary regulatory requirements helped in improving the business environment, which benefited most enterprises, including SMEs. Many of the reform packages focused on removing barriers to exporters and foreign investors, while micro-reforms were not addressed. As a result, by the late 1990s SMEs still faced a large number of unnecessary regulatory requirements.

Notwithstanding the above mentioned economic policy swings, there have been a number of significant and constant features of the macro-economic policy environment. This included state ownership in key sectors of the economy. During the entire time of the New Order, there existed a large state enterprise sector. This included the key oil refinery sector. The issue of indigenous entrepreneurship was also a long and continuous policy concern of the New Order. This policy was often implemented by favouring the SMEs through concessionary loans and reserving economic sectors for SMEs. While these issues remained part of the New Order, the attention given to them fluctuated as domestic and international economic circumstances changed. As Hill (1994, p. 66) argues, these policy concerns indicated ambivalence by policy makers and particularly politicians towards a liberal economic system.

The considerable emphasis placed on developing the agricultural sector has also been a significant feature of the macro-economic policy environment. As a result, agricultural output increased rapidly. In particular there was a rapid increase in rice production to the point that Indonesia was self-sufficient. The emphasis on the agricultural sector had several consequences. It consolidated land holdings and created a significant landlord class (Booth 1988, p. 252). It also created a large bureaucratic structure and numerous cooperatives through which to channel inputs and farm outputs. The result was a significant release of labour to work in the rural non-farm sector. A further consequence was the rise in real income for agricultural workers and farmers. However, the rise in real income had been slower than that of other sectors (Manning 1998, p. 139). These changes have had a profound impact on rural SMEs, which were closely linked to the supply and demand of the agricultural sector. On the supply side the changes in the agriculture created a range of inputs for SMEs, including releasing labour to work in these enterprises. On the demand side, rising real incomes created greater purchasing power by the rural sector that was primarily met by the goods and services provided by rural based SMEs (Tambunan 2000, p. 71).

The system of political/economic patronage has been a further persistent feature of the New Order. For most large investments it was necessary to have someone from the military or the Suharto family connected with the project. Sound economic management of the macro-policy environment was plagued by what has been termed in the late 1990s as KKN, or corruption, collusion and nepotism. The system of KKN has meant several significant distortions remained in the Indonesian economy. In particular, large conglomerates with close connection to the military and the president's family enjoyed economic privileges which created market distortions and more importantly, created a lack of transparency in the regulatory environment which was exploited by a large number of elites. For rural based SMEs with little connection to a network of patronage, it translated into a high cost economy with a lack of transparency in the regulatory framework.

A final significant and constant feature of the policy environment was the macro-policy's urban bias. Despite the significance given to developing the agricultural sector, much of the policy framework was urban biased and Java centred. The New Order policy focus was often on the formal large-scale industrial sector at the cost of the rural non-farm sector. After the late 1990s, some of the distinction, however, between the rural-urban divide became more blurred. With the improvements in infrastructure, including telecommunications, the increased mobility of the population and the spread of urban sprawl, particularly in Java, the distinction between rural and urban is less well defined.

In general, it can be argued the New Order policy makers and politicians have focused on maximizing economic growth while simultaneously, looking towards the state playing an interventionist role. This generalization is somewhat simplistic given the large number of policy makers and politicians with a range of ideologies and vested interests, but, nevertheless, provides a useful description. At the macro-policy level, there has not necessarily been a significant focus on economic policies for rural SMEs. Rather the emphasis has been on improving agricultural output and on political and social policies for SMEs, cooperatives and *pribumi* entrepreneurs. The difference between political/social policies and economic ones is that the former does not necessarily create a strong SME sector but it does lead to resource transfers. In contrast, the latter, may not necessarily lead to resource transfers but does aim to create an economically viable and internationally competitive SME sector.

More than anything and like most enterprises, rural SMEs benefited from a strong economy where demand is high and inflation, interest rates and transaction costs are low. At the macro-economic level however,

SMEs have suffered from an economic bias which favours conglomerates and special interest groups. This has created a high cost and an overly regulated economy with weak institutions for policy implementation and regulatory compliance.

Micro-Policy Environment

At the micro-policy or programme level, there has been an abundance of programmes for rural SMEs in Indonesia. Consistent with the government's urban policy bias, most SME programmes have made little distinction between rural and urban. These micro-policies or programmes, in contrast to the macro-policy concerns, have been primarily motivated by social and political imperatives. Furthermore, SMEs and their mostly *pribumi* entrepreneurs were viewed by the state as a 'weak economic group' and as a result most programmes were heavily interventionist and paternalistic in nature. To complicate matters, almost all government departments have generally seen fit to use public servants to deliver programmes. As a result few if any of the wide range of programmes have been successful (Thee 1993, p. 14). Even under the best circumstances, when the underlying motivation is to create an efficient and dynamic SME sector and implementation is carried out using best practice, it should be noted that the likelihood for SME programme success is small. The experience of numerous developing countries indicates that on the whole there have been very few large-scale successful programmes for SMEs (Snodgrass and Biggs 1996, p. 243).

Several government departments such as the Ministry of Industrial Development and Trade and the Ministry of Cooperatives and Small Business have taken the lead in SME policies. These, as do other ministries, have regional offices for delivery of services. Regional offices are known as Kanwil or Kantor Wilayah. The Kanwil offices in all provinces deliver the ministries' SME services. In general, the Kanwil offices are poorly staffed and lack financial resources. For these local offices, rural SMEs often present a dilemma, as they are both a source of revenue and a target for development policies.

While it is impossible to itemize all government programmes, below is a list of some of the most significant SME programmes delivered by various ministries in the Indonesian government. As such it provides a useful overview of the government's extensive SME micro-policy concerns.

Kemitraan

Since 1978, a programme of Foster Parent/Child (*Bapak Angkat*) has been developed to encourage large enterprises to link with and assist SMEs in marketing their services. More recently this programme has been extended into a more general partnership programme for state owned as well as private enterprises. The Ministry of Industrial Development and Trade actively promotes this policy as does the Ministry of Cooperatives and Small Business. To a large degree, the development of mandatory partnerships relies on the requirement of state enterprises to set aside between 1 to 5 percent of their net after tax profit for helping 'weaker economic groups'.

KOPINKRA

Similar to other government ministries, and in line with its policy of promoting clusters of SMEs, The Ministry of Industrial Development & Trade encourages and assists in the setting up of Cooperatives of Small-scale Industries (*Koperasi Industri Kecil—KOPINKRA*). The agency has concentrated on cottage industries and small clusters of similar producers, and encouraged them to form into KOPINKRA. These are then further targeted for other forms of technical assistance (described below). From 1986, when this policy was first established, until 1990 over 1,100 KOPINKRA have been set up with the government's assistance.

LIK (small-scale industrial estates)

In a few cases the government has gone beyond setting up the cooperatives and built small-scale industrial estates (*Lingkungan Industri Kecil—LIK*). These are industrial estates specifically designed for SMEs to locate their economic activity. From 1980 to 1991, thirteen such estates were built.

Common Service Facilities (UPT)

A more comprehensive technical assistance programme has been the development of Technical Service Centres or sometimes called Common Service Facilities (*Unit Pelayanan Teknis—UPT*). These units provide extension and technical services and training courses. Government technical officers who have received special training staff the units. Originally these service centres were supplied with modern technological equipment.

However, over the years, budget constraints have prevented the replacement of the existing equipment. Today, much of the technical equipment is outdated. There are some 103 UPT units across 24 provinces and located in existing clusters of similar industries.

Small Business Consultancy Clinics (KKB)

A similar scheme, but one that focuses more on providing general business advice is the Small Business Consultancy Clinics (*Klinik Konsultasi Bisnis—KKB*). This programme is executed by the Ministry of Cooperatives and Small Business but has the involvement of the Ministry of Industrial Development and Trade. In 1994, the clinics were set up to provide consultancy services for SMEs. They provide advice on market conditions and legal and technical services related to SMEs. Currently there are 82 KKB units across 22 provinces. Regional Kanwil DEPKOP offices administer 26 KKB units and the remainder are joint ventures with large state owned enterprises, private domestic firms and universities and other institutions. Services are provided free of charge but there is some move to partial cost recovery. The clinics are aimed at responding to the needs of SMEs and providing professional services in response to specific needs.

A separate initiative started in 1996/97 under PPK and with the help of a Bappenas-GTZ project, has been the establishment of *Team Technis Daerah* (Local Technical Teams). Under this scheme, entrepreneurial field staff in the Kanwil offices of the Ministry of Cooperatives and Small Business were recruited to assist cooperatives to expand their business and start-up new businesses. So far, three units have been set up in East Java, South Sulawesi and West Nusa Tenggara. There has been some suggestion that these units could be housed in the KKB clinics, however the onset of the financial crises halted the expansion of this project.

KUD

This is a loan facility provided on the basis of Bank Indonesia Liquidity Credits (BILC). KUD is primarily targeted at small farmers and village cooperatives. The loans are made from banks to village cooperatives which then on-lend to individuals or groups of farmers. Loans are funded 75 percent by BILC and 25 percent by commercial banks. A similar loan scheme funded by BILC is the cooperative credits (KKPA) which can be used for any economic activity and are not restricted to agriculture. These schemes channel funds at subsidized interest rates.

Small Scale Credit (KUK)

Introduced in 1990, all banks, both domestic and foreign, are required to lend 20 percent of their loans to SMEs and cooperatives. While penalties exist for non compliance, this rule has rarely been fully complied with. Since the Asia Financial Crisis the 20 percent rule has been relaxed. Furthermore, the banks have often counted consumer lending as part of the 20 percent ratio. Of the outstanding KUK loans, approximately 22 percent are in arrears and an almost 10 percent are deemed unrecoverable. Some banks have also taken non-performing KUK loans off their books.

Credit for Village Units (KUPEDES)

KUPEDES is a self-sustaining micro-credit programme managed by Bank Rakyat Indonesia. Loans are targeted at the village level and secured by collateral or letters of support from local leaders. Loans are charged at 1.5 percent per month (equivalent to 33.2 percent per annum) and are usually for short durations of about two weeks. The programme has a 97 percent loan repayment rate and encourages local savings in the scheme.

Small Rural Development Banks

Across Indonesia there are approximately 9,000 Small Rural Development Banks. Of these, over 5,000 are owned by local regional governments (BKD) and the rest by cooperatives. Most of these banks make small, short-term loans at high interest rates and within their local community.

System ISO-9000

Through the use of independent private service providers, the Ministry of Industrial Development & Trade has contracted to train SMEs in management quality systems ISO-9000. The independent service providers are qualified in the delivery of ISO-9000 training and certified by the Ministry of Industrial Development and Trade. After the delivery of the services, the Ministry carries out quality control checks on the SME recipients to verify that the services have been successfully delivered. Since the beginning of the programme 4,000 SMEs have been appraised for their suitability to undertake the training, 250 have entered ISO-9000 instructions, 61 have successfully completed and implemented ISO-9000 standards and 120 have achieved Indonesia's National Management Quality System Standard (SNI).

Total Quality Control

The Ministry of Industrial Development and Trade has been providing quality control advice to SMEs since 1983. The Total Quality Control (PMT/GKM) programme has a similar focus as the ISO-9000. This programme, however, is implemented by an annual regional and national level conference promoting Total Quality Control (PMT). The programme also provides technical advice and assistance on specific quality control problems. In 1994, some 2,524 SMEs received advice on Total Quality Control. By 1997 the annual number of clients had grown to 4,200.

Human Resource Development

From its local Kanwil office in the 27 provinces, the Ministry of Industrial Development & Trade provides a range of seminars and workshops for development of human resources. These range from motivational and entrepreneurial training to more specific technical training and internship in other larger companies. Several specific programmes are: management training (MS/MUK); entrepreneurship training (CEFE, AMT); technology training in processing, design and packaging and internship and case studies.

WARSI

The WARSI programme has attempted to enlarge access to information by providing technology and especially Internet access to SMEs. The planning and development of this programme is still in the early stages but agreement has been reached between the Ministry of Industrial Development and Trade to locate the computer terminals in local post offices (PT Pos Indonesia). Already 28 post offices have set up the computer networks and 246 SMEs have registered on the WARSI programme.

Export Support Board of Indonesia

The Export Support Board of Indonesia (*Dewan Penunjang Ekspor—DPE*) is an autonomous body established in 1986 by the Ministry of Industry and Trade with the help of the World Bank. Its primary aim is to assist SMEs to export non-oil commodities. For this task, assistance is given in the form of financial and technical advice. The advice is provided free to clients that are considered suitable recipients. Finance is provided interest free except for a 3 percent levy to cover administrative costs. Between 1988 and 1998 the programme assisted 1,134 SME exporters with a total of 1,617 projects.

Incubator Systems for New Entrepreneurs

In conjunction with several other ministries, the Ministry of Cooperatives and Small Business has since 1994/95 implemented an incubator system for promoting the development of new entrepreneurs. During a maximum period of three years, it provides selected candidates with workshops, training and other assistance. It also uses this programme to promote mandatory partnership agreements. Regional government offices, state owned enterprises, universities and other local institutions provide the services. As of March 1998, there were 26 such incubator schemes.

Few if any of the above programmes have experienced 'real' success. For government departments, success is measured by the number of participants. Moreover, there is a tendency to collate little if any data beyond the simple numbers of participants. A more realistic measure of success would be to measure the net benefit to society of micro-policies (programmes). While programmes may provide significant benefits for SMEs, they also accrue costs. Programme benefits must be measured against the costs they incur. In a study on design principles for small business programmes and regulations, Lattimore et al. summarized the need for government programmes by stating:

> Governments should intervene where there are clear market failures and where intervention will bring net benefits to society: or to address equity or fairness objectives (Lattimore et al. 1998, p. 233).

In the same book the authors point out that market failure in itself does not necessarily require intervention (Lattimore et al. 1998, p. 97). Intervention needs to provide net benefits to society. For example, where SMEs face difficulty in accessing export markets, the use of export quotes to provide access may increase the cost of exporting, create administrative costs and lead to rent-seeking behaviour. This creates a net cost to society. Furthermore, when there is net benefit to society, there are several design criteria that should be considered, as set out in the table below. Programmes should be judged against these criteria and should as closely as possible address the criteria below.

Despite the lack of published data, applying the net benefit principle and the criteria set out in Table 3.1, it is obvious from a range of studies (van Diermen 1997, Thee 1993, Tambunan 2000, Sandee 1995, Klapwijk 1997, Kragten 2000) that few of the above programmes have been 'successful'. Moreover, in many cases the biases created by macro-policies in favour of large manufacturers have often outweighed the specific benefits for SMEs—an issue returned to in the next section of this chapter.

To summarize, three important influences can be seen at work in the policy environment for rural SMEs. First, at the macro-policy level, the improvements in economic conditions have greatly benefited rural SMEs. The sound economic management policies have been motivated by the government's desire for rapid development and a need to legitimize its regime. Second, counter to this, macro-policies favouring large conglomerates and vested interest groups have created distortions and increased costs that have been unfavourable to rural SMEs. Such policies have been motivated by nationalism as well as the system of patronage

TABLE 3.1
Policy Design Criteria

a.	Does the program target the problem effectively?
b.	Does it have acceptable take-up?
c.	Is it timely?
d.	Does it induce new activity?
e.	Are large transfers overseas avoided?
f.	Does the program have the right duration, scale and target group?
g.	Is it administratively efficient for government?
h.	Does it impose big compliance burdens on firms?
i.	Is it transparent and accountable?
j.	Is it financed in the least cost way?
k.	What are the risks posed by the program? e.g. • — Strategic behaviour by firms • — Unforeseen liabilities for government • — Adverse interaction with other policies
l.	Does it breach the country's International obligations?
m.	Does it impose a significant cost on any group?

Source: adapted from Lattimore et al. 1998

created by the New Order. Third, at the micro-policy level, the government has implemented numerous and significant SME programmes that have transferred resources from the state and conglomerates to rural SMEs. These transfers however, have not created a competitive and robust rural SME sector. It could be argued such transfers have created a dependency on government programmes and undermined rural SMEs' ability to compete nationally and more importantly, internationally. For example, easy access to highly subsidized credit distorts the cost structures of rural SMEs which leaves the entrepreneur unable to compete for export markets against more competitive foreign SMEs in the same sector. The micro-polices have not been motivated by economic imperatives but rather by social and political needs.

Responses to the Economic Environment

The above analysis of the macro- and micro-policy environments leads us to ask the obvious question of how entrepreneurs of small rural enterprises have reacted. On the one hand, given the diversity of the Indonesian archipelago and the rural industry sector, it is hard to generalize. On the other hand, the consistent reaction and behaviour by a significant number of small entrepreneurs makes it possible to identify some general trends. The five most significant trends that can be observed can be summarized as:

1. Few of the micro-policies implemented by the government have had a lasting impact on improving rural SMEs.
2. A significant number of macro- and micro-polices placed additional costs and burdens on rural SMEs' compliance and has led to most operating outside of the formal economy.
3. Macro-polices that created a favourable economic environment, as reflected by consistently high growth rates in GDP, provided the best stimulus for SMEs sector growth.
4. Growth in the agricultural sector, particularly rice, was closely connected to opportunities for and growth of rural SMEs.
5. Policy biases towards the urban sector have exacerbated existing patterns of rural-urban migration.

The first major trend elaborated here also picks up the theme from the previous section: how well have SME programmes done? As stated above, the evidence generally points towards few programmes having any lasting impact on improving rural SMEs. The three most significant are evaluated here. If measured by the above criteria (i.e., market failure; targeting the problem effectively; setting the right duration, scale and target group; being administratively efficient for government; and not imposing excessive compliance burdens on firms) most of the above programmes would score badly. There is no doubt that many SMEs have gained benefits under the micro-policies previously listed, some of which have been in operation for decades. But the more relevant question is at what cost were these benefits gained? The cost of programmes should be measured in terms of economy-wide loss in efficiency and the specific costs to other sectors of the economy. Almost all of the previously listed programmes were indiscriminately applied without consideration for targeting or overall efficiency gains.

One of the most widely-practised programmes, *kemitraan*, places immense compliance costs on large firms. They are required to set aside 1 to 5 percent of their net after tax profit for assisting 'weak economic groups'. SMEs who are recipients of these programmes may benefit in the direct transfer of funds or goods and services, but the cost in terms of economic efficiency is significant. Furthermore, in the medium to long term, the SMEs recipients may be disadvantaged by assistance that is given for social/political reasons rather than economic. Having been sheltered from market transactions, SMEs are left in a more vulnerable state when the benefits delivered by large enterprises come to an end.

While some of these agreements may have been commercially successful, the majority of these agreements are viewed by large enterprises and often by the SMEs, as a form of welfare transfer. Large enterprises undertake mandatory linkages programmes because of a need to comply with the regulatory framework and under pressure from the government. Few are undertaken purely for commercial reasons. This has two implications. First, a welfare transfer occurs. However, such welfare transfers are badly targeted and should not be regulated by commercial and financial law intended to promote economic growth. Second, commercially unsustainable linkages are formed often between highly unsuited partners and possibly displacing more viable networks. Unless both partners commercially benefit from the linkages, they are unlikely to survive or increase in number. International evidence shows dense patterns of linkages and partnerships are not formed through mandatory linkage requirements, but because they offer commercial benefits to all participants.

The UPT extension service programme provides another example of poor performance. It has failed to deliver efficient services, target appropriate recipients and address the important criteria of providing a net benefit to society and/or effectively addressing equity or fairness objectives. Even if success is measured solely by the number of clients served, the UPT programme has done poorly as indicated by declining use of their services (Thee 1994, p. 113). The UPT or Common Service facilities have several problems that are briefly listed here. First, the provision of services is highly supply orientated rather than demand driven. The delivery of services has more to do with government regulations and planning than responding to the demands of their clientele. Second, when the UPT were originally set up, they had modern equipment and access to the latest technology, however, years of under funding has resulted in most UPT working with outdated technology. Third, services have been delivered indiscriminately to clusters of SMEs or cooperatives. Fourth, the staff of the UPT has not had the appropriate training to respond to entrepreneurs' needs. In reviewing many government-run programmes, Harper (1984, p. 137) notes "government officials have no personal experience in trade or business" and that "decisions are inevitably centralized" making civil servants poor facilitators of technical assistance programmes. Finally, the structure of the UPT as part of the government meant that in most cases, there was not great enough flexibility in the system for responding to the changing needs of SMEs.

The KIK/KMKP subsidized credit programme provides a further example of poor performance. It was widely implemented and had significant impact on rural SMEs. In 1990 the KIK/KMKP subsidized credit programme was converted to KUK. Immediately after 1997, in an effort to kick-start the economy and win political office, numerous further subsidized and non-subsidized credit programmes were implemented. These numerous credit programmes were almost void of any real economic rationale other than to pump money into the economy and have now largely been scaled back. The now discontinued KIK/KMKP subsidized credit programme, while pumping significant amounts of money into the economy were, as Thee (1993, p. 12), Grizzell (1988, p. 18) and Kragten (2000, p. 53) note, very ineffective. The programme had default rates of around 27 percent caused by problems in collection, poorly trained staff, corruption and mismanagement (Thee 1993, p. 12). The KUK scheme (started in 1990 and suspended in 1998) requiring banks to allocate 20 percent of their loan portfolio to SMEs has also performed poorly against the criteria developed earlier in this chapter. While banks claim to have met the 20 percent target, many of the loans have been for consumption items and banks have tended to distort their statistics. Banks have tended to target a minority of SMEs which have experienced an oversupply of credit while the majority of rural SMEs have faced a scarcity of KUK credit (Teleki 2001, p. 72). The reason for this is threefold. First, because rural SMEs are traditionally poor record keepers; second because most Indonesian banks are inexperienced in lending to SMEs; and third because the regulatory framework for securing assets and debt recovery are inadequate. Without doubt the various credit programmes have consistently over many years pumped significantly large amounts of money into the rural SME sector. However, this has not addressed the real problem, which is not a lack of available credit or high interest rates, but rather a mismatch between bank requirements and rural SMEs' mode of operation (van Diermen 2001, p. 15).

The second major trend observed are most entrepreneurs of small rural enterprises operate outside of the formal economy. A significant number of macro- and micro-polices place additional compliance costs and burdens on rural SMEs. Therefore, most rural SMEs tend to avoid the formal economy. Studies by the World Bank (2002, p. 138) have shown the size of the informal sector rises with the number of procedures and licences required to start a business. In a study of rural SMEs in central Java, Kragten (2000, p. 55) noted half of all small industries are found in the rural sector and almost 90 percent of all the small rural industries observed operated outside the formal economy. Despite avoidance of the formal economy, a study of 800 small businesses by AKATIGA (1999, p. 54) found 80 percent of respondents were paying formal and informal levies imposed by local governments. In an earlier study by the same organization, it was recorded that it took 34 licences for a small business to operate in West Java. The system of licenses and fees at the district, regional and national level has become so ingrained into the civil service that it has been difficult to change, despite persistent efforts by the central government urged on by multi-lateral donors. Furthermore, local and regional authorities rely on these levies for supplementing their income and to a lessor degree for revenue.

An example of the impact of local market restrictions on rural entrepreneurs was the Decree No. 231 of 1990 from the Governor of East Nusa Tenggara concerning local cooperatives (KUD). This decree was in effect until at least early 1998. It stipulated small-scale farmers must sell their agricultural produce to the local cooperative, which then marketed the products through a 'Trading Body' largely in the control of local government officials. While the decree was ostensibly created to guarantee prices for farmers, its effect was to restrict efficient market operations and provide district officials with a source of revenue.

In contrast, the Gianyar District *(Kabupaten)* in Bali provides an example of what is possible when levies are lifted. In response to the local population's complaints about the uncertain and ambiguous regulatory framework, the regional head in 1994 set up an integrated service unit (UPT). The idea was to combine under one roof the many government services and requirements needed by SMEs. Staff were selected and trained to deal with the variety of client needs. Emphasis was placed on efficient and accurate delivery of services and information.

Service delivery was carried out in two ways. First, a regional office was set up and its services were advertised through local media. Second, in order to be more effective, a mobile unit was created such that services could be brought to clients. The mobile vehicle regularly tours the sub-districts. The public response to the service has been impressive. While all the individual government authorities for the services provided by the UPT continue to exist, the public in the Gianyar *Kabupaten* tends overwhelmingly to use the UPT service. Moreover, there has been demand by the public to expand UPT service in order to become a more complete 'one stop shop'. In delivering the UPT service and planning its future role, the regional government continues to place emphasis on the creation of a professional and dedicated staff. Thus, the two key elements for the success of the UPT are its policy design (meeting market demand) and efficient implementation by its staff. Recently (2001) the Gianyar District head, in contrast to other districts in the region, reported significant increases in revenue from compliance by mostly rural SMEs.

The third response by rural SMEs is somewhat more nebulous. Consistently high growth rates in the Indonesian economy have created a favourable economic environment providing a stimulus for rural SMEs sector growth. Rural SMEs have shared in the benefits of economic growth. Hill (1996, p. 168) found between 1975 and 1986 employment in SMEs grew at an annual estimated rate of 6 percent compared to 5.6 percent for large and medium size enterprises. In trying to explain the reason for this strong growth in the SME sector, van Diermen (1995, p. 198) dismissed the numerous micro-policies as an explanation. Kragten (2000, p. 56) advances the explanation further and identifies the macro economic setting. She notes (Kragten 2000, p. 56) the rapid growth in rice production; huge government investment in social and physical infrastructure and high growth primarily explained the prosperity in the non-farm rural sector. The high employment rate in SMEs between 1975 and 1986 can be explained by the fourth trend of rural incomes. Simply put, economic growth and particularly a prosperous rural sector increased household income, stimulating demand for goods and services, primarily produced by rural SMEs.

Finally, the fifth response by rural SMEs has been to exacerbate the existing pattern of rural-urban migration. Throughout the 1980s and 1990s urban wages rose faster than rural wages. Employment opportunities also expanded faster in the urban areas than in the rural sector. Coupled with this are the rich tradition in Java and other parts of Indonesia of young men going off to find work elsewhere before coming home to settle down. The combination of these factors has seen a large number of entrepreneurs of small rural enterprises move to urban areas to start their businesses. This is particularly the case when income elasticity of demand is lower for products closely linked to agricultural inputs than for products less reliant on agricultural inputs (Kragten 2000, p. 155).

The 1997 Crisis and Beyond: Policy Issues for Rural SMEs

The 1997 Financial Crisis in Indonesia and the political, social and economic upheaval that followed and continued in the early part of the new millennium, has had major and profound implications on the policy environment for rural SMEs. These changes, previously mentioned in the introduction of this chapter, are now more fully discussed as a prelude to sketching out the future policy environment in a post crisis Indonesia. While many changes have taken place in Indonesia since 1997, in line with the focus of this chapter, priority is given to the policy aspect in contrast to the wider social implications.

The 1997 crisis resulted in a decline in government revenue and an increase in its fiscal obligations. As a result the government was severely hampered in its ability to create new policies. Despite this, in the immediate aftermath, and during the political turmoil of the elections, large amounts of money were made available for micro-finance programmes, much of it funded by government deficits and donor money. These programmes were however short-lived and primarily motivated by election considerations. Few if any of the multitude of micro-finance programmes survived. By late 2001, the national budget and therefore the regional allocation of funds had been drastically reduced.

Real incomes of public servants declined partly because of the decline in government revenue. The fiscal difficulties of the government and a decline in informal levies have impacted on public servant incomes. Inflation has eroded salaries and pay raises have been difficult to secure through parliament as Abdurrahman Wahid found early in his presidency. In large urban centres the greater accountability required of public servants by donors in the use of their funds has also seen an unwillingness by many public servants to process such programmes due to less opportunities for income generation by them.

The decline in regional budgets and public servants pay has placed great pressure on regions to find new means to raise revenue. At the same time the decline in the authority of the centre and the 1999 decentralization legislation has empowered regions. The rapid succession of presidents from Suharto to Habibie, Abdurrahman Wahid and most recently, Megawati, has also seen a decline in the authority of the centre. The diverse archipelago was kept together by the strong rule of Suharto and the military. Much of this was based on Suharto's personal power and the military's allegiance to him. Each of the presidents that followed him have found it difficult to exert the same authority and have had to negotiate with different elements of the military and regional politicians who are often serving or retired military commanders. The weakening of the centre was assured by the 1999 decentralization legislation, which required the devolution of decision-making and revenue expenditure to the district level. While the decentralization measures were not fully implemented by early 2002, many districts and regions had begun to put in place their own version of decentralization. The most devastating impact of this for rural SMEs has been the creation of regional trade barriers in the form of taxes and levies.

What then, does the future hold for rural SMEs? The period following 1997 has seen a decline in the central government's ability to make and implement policy. Because of, and despite the decentralization legislation, policy decision-making will continue to shift to the region but more likely to the provincial level rather than the district (*Kabupaten*) level. The previously mentioned dichotomy of macro-policy and micro-policy programmes will, driven by provincial governments, continue to generate greater regional variations. These regional variations will be influenced by the regions' resource endowment and historical development. Most importantly, they will be influenced by regional governments' priorities, locally developed legislation and their capacity to implement them. These trends are reflected in the concerns of entrepreneurs. At a national workshop on SME policies, entrepreneurs indicated their primary concern was how decentralization might result in an increase in regional regulations (van Diermen 2001, p. 61).

If this, then, is the future, what should policy advocates focus on? It is essential for policy makers to provide rural SMEs, as for all businesses with a stable and predictable macro-economic environment. Regional policy makers have an especially important role to play to make sure prices accurately reflect market signals and are not unduly distorted. Access to inputs and markets are essential focus points for policy makers. This includes access to inputs from other regions, foreign exchange, regional and international markets and credit. The policy environment should also be stable and predictable. Business people must be reasonably assured policies are stable, developed through consultation and expedient and transparent in their implementation. Given rural SMEs' close link to the agricultural sector, it is also important to use market mechanisms and demand driven policies to facilitate linkages and networks between the two sectors and across regions (Liedholm and Mead 1999, p. 70). Finally, specific programmes should be avoided. This is based on Indonesia's past failures in micro-policies; international evidence suggesting it is difficult to develop and implement successful programmes in developing countries (Snodgrass and Biggs 1996, p. 243) and the high cost and low returns on programmes. Moreover even if institutions are well developed programme impacts are problematic (Revesz and Lattimore 2001, p. VIII).

To summarize, policy makers should learn from international experience, incorporate principles of best practice and without distorting underlying principles, and adjust polices to take account of national and local circumstances. Such an approach should be followed in the design, implementation and evaluation of rural SME policies. Finally, international and Indonesia's national and local experience indicate, wherever possible, policy emphasis should be given on getting the macro-economic settings 'right' as opposed to implementing specific programmes.

References

AKATIGA. *The Impact of Economic Crisis on Indonesian Small Medium Enterprise.* Jakarta: The Asia Foundation, 1999.

Booth. A. *Agricultural Development in Indonesia.* Asian Studies Association of Australia, Southeast Asia Publication Series, Sydney: Allen & Unwin, 1988.

Grizzell, S. "Promoting Small-scale Manufacturing in Indonesia: What Works?". Research Memo No. 17, Jakarta: Development Studies Project II, 1988.

Hill, H. (ed.) *Indonesia's New Order: The Dynamics of Socio-Economic Transformation.* Sydney: Allen & Unwin, 1994.

Hill, H. *Foreign Investment and Industrialization in Indonesia* . Singapore: OUP, 1988.

Hill, H. *The Indonesian Economy Since 1966: Southeast Asia's Emerging Giant.* Hong Kong: Cambridge University Press, 1996.

Klapwijk, M. *Rural Industry Clusters in Central Java, Indonesia: An Empirical Assessment of their Role in Rural Industrialization.* Tinbergen Institute Research Series No. 153, Amsterdam: Vrije Universiteit, 1997.

Lattimore, R., Madge, A. Martin, B. and Mills, J. "Design Principles for Small Business Programs and Regulations". Production Commission Staff Research Paper, Canberra: AusInfo, 1998.

Liedholm, C. and Mead, D.C. *Small Enterprises and Economic Development: The Dynamics of Micro and Small Enterprises.* London: Routledge, 1999.

Manning, C. *Indonesia Labour in Transition: An East Asia Success Story?* Hong Kong: Cambridge University Press, 1998.

Marieke, K. "Viable or marginal? Small-scale Industries in Rural Java (Bantul District)". Royal Dutch Academy of Sciences and Faculty of Geographical Sciences of Utrecht University, 2000.

Revesz, J. and Lattimore, R. "Statistical Analysis of the Use and Impact of Government Business Programs". Production Commission Staff Research Paper, Canberra: AusInfo, 2001.

Sandee, H. *Innovation Adoption in Rural Industry: Technological Change in Roof Tile Clusters in Central Java, Indonesia.* Amsterdam: Vrije Universiteit, 1995.

Snodgrass, D.R. and Biggs, T. *Industrialization and the Small Firm: Patterns and Policies.* San Francisco: International Centre for Economic Growth and the Harvard Institute for International Development, 1996.

Tambunan, T. *Development of Small-Scale Industries During the New Order Government in Indonesia.* London: Ashgate, 2000.

Thee, K.W. "Industrial Structure and Small and Medium Enterprise Development in Indonesia", EDI Working Paper. Washington: World Bank, 1993.

van Diermen (ed.). "SME Policy in Indonesia: Towards a New Agenda". Occasional Paper Series on SME Development no. 1, Manilla: Asian Development Bank, 2001.

van Diermen, P. *Small Business in Indonesia.* London: Ashgate, 1997.

van Diermen, P., Thee Kian Wie, Tambunan, M. and Tambunan, T. "The IMF 50-Point Program: Evaluating the Likely Impact on SMEs", A Report for The Asia Foundation, Jakarta: The Asia Foundation, 1998.

World Bank. *World Development Report 2002: Building Institutions for Market.* New York: World Bank and Oxford University Press, 2002.

4
THE CONTRIBUTION OF HOUSEHOLD AND SMALL MANUFACTURING ESTABLISHMENTS TO THE RURAL ECONOMY

Robert Rice

Introduction

The development of labour-intensive manufacturing is very important in Indonesia, especially in densely populated Java, as a means of increasing incomes partly through the productive utilization of the large amounts of available unemployed labour. In densely populated rural areas, manufacturing and agriculture can be considered the leading sectors, followed by the development of wholesale and retail trade and services. In contrast with large and to a lesser extent medium sized manufacturing enterprises that tend to be located in urban areas, household/cottage manufacturing establishments (HMEs) as well as small manufacturing establishments (SMEs) are widely dispersed in rural areas.[1] Therefore in rural areas the HMEs and SMEs are especially important in increasing incomes. The per capita incomes normally generated from HMEs are low. The vast majority of these enterprises fail, and those that do not realize little growth. Thus, they are more important in poverty alleviation than in contributing to economic growth. As a last resort, many individuals who are unable to find paid jobs establish HMEs and other household enterprises as a survival activity (Liedholm and Mead 1999). SMEs are important to the survival of the people because they create many jobs, and to economic growth because over time, many of them increase in size generating more and more income.

The emphasis in this chapter is on the nature and importance of the development of the household manufacturing industries (HMIs) and small manufacturing industries (SMIs) from 1986 to 1996 and from 1996 to 2000. The latter period encompasses the economic crisis in Indonesia. To date little analysis has been done on the HMIs at the two-digit industry level—as opposed to case studies of particular industries in particular localities, and of the comparison of the HMIs with the SMIs. This chapter also initiates some analysis on the impact of the crisis on these industries. Finally some recommendations are made specifically focusing on the HMIs, without duplicating the policy recommendations already made by many studies about facilitating the development of small and medium manufacturing industries, (e.g., see Center for Economic and Social Studies and Asia Foundation 1999, International Labour Organization 1999, Poot et al. 1990, Hill 2001, Rice et al. 2002, Asian Development Bank SME Development TA 2001/2002, Urata 2000, Berry et al. 2001, and van Dierman 2000.)

The Importance of Rural Industries

The average income of rural dwellers in Indonesia is substantially lower than that of urban dwellers, meaning that the incomes of rural people need to be increased if the disparity in income between rural and urban areas is to be diminished. For example, in 1996 and August 1999, 19.9 percent and 20.2 percent of the population in rural areas were below the poverty line whereas in urban areas it was only 13.6 percent and 15.1 percent (*Statistik Indonesia 2000*, Table 12.1.B). Various case studies suggest that in Java, rural incomes have risen more slowly than those in urban areas (Hill 2000, p. 200). Perhaps without excessively simplifying our analysis of the Indonesian situation, one could state that in the very densely populated areas of Java, Madura, Bali and Lombok, per farmer incomes from agriculture are low primarily because of overpopulation, whereas in the more sparsely populated areas of Indonesia incomes are low mainly because of insufficient factors of production (resources) which are complementary to land, such as rural infrastructure, irrigation and drainage systems, working capital and advanced production technologies. In these latter areas there remains a large potential for increasing per farmer incomes from agriculture without much out-migration and rural industrial development. The densely populated areas are different because rural industrialization and other sources of off-farm income are necessary. This is complemented by some out-migration that increases the amount of arable land per farmer in order to realize large increases in per capita incomes.

The percentages of persons recording their primary occupation in the agricultural and manufacturing sectors have been steadily decreasing and increasing respectively during the last forty years in rural Java and Madura. In 1995 only 52.1 and 51.3 percent of males and females there recorded their primary occupation in the agricultural sector, down from 64.6 percent and 58.0 percent in 1985, and 81.6 and 74.2 percent in 1961.[2] The number of male and female farmers also decreased from 11.782 million and 6.118 million in 1985 to 9.945 million and 5.322 million respectively in 1995. The percentages of males and females in rural Java and Madura recording their primary occupation in manufacturing in 1995 were 10.5 percent and 16.8 percent respectively, up from 7.3 and 12.8 percent in 1985 and 4.1 and 7.5 percent respectively in 1961. However, the second most important primary occupation was trade, hotels and restaurants with 11.1 percent of the males and 22.5 percent of the females recording this as their primary occupation in 1995 (White 1991, p. 58, and calculations using data in *Penduduk Indonesia* 1996, pp. 313–14). We can conclude that rural industrialization is an essential component for poverty alleviation and economic development in these densely populated rural areas and is a complementary source of income in the more sparsely populated areas.

In the densely populated areas there is extensive unemployment, mainly disguised, on the farms as well as in the many off-farm income generating activities of rural people such as petty trading, the provision of services including transportation services, fishing, woodcutting, etc.[3] Rural industrialization results in increases in output and incomes because of the increased application of capital and technologies as well as increased utilization of otherwise unemployed labour.

The contribution of household/cottage and small manufacturing establishments to increased living standards especially in the densely populated rural areas is also examined. It is relatively easy for small farmers and others to establish HMEs and leave agriculture completely or work at it on a part-time basis. In 1996 among HMEs, 69 percent worked 21 days or more a month with an average working day of 7 hours, while 25 percent worked 11–20 days per month and 6 percent only 1–10 days per month, both with average working hours of 6 hours per day (*Statistik Industri Kerajinan Rumahtangga* 1996, Table 6.1). This shows that some workers in HMEs are still spending considerable amounts of time in other economic activities such as farming. In addition there are many farm families where some members are engaged in household manufacturing but are not considered to be HMEs by the Central Agency of Statistics (BPS), and therefore are not included in the HME data.

An Employment-oriented Rural Development Framework Strategy

One employment-oriented development strategy very suitable to the densely populated regions of Indonesia has been cited widely in the literature (Mellor 1976, pp. 12–18). This strategy contains three elements. The first, agricultural development, is based on the increased productivity of land. This is accomplished through the introduction of high yield seed varieties, additional labour input, and better use of capital, fertilizers and improved pest management, and expanded supply and control of water. The second element, industrialization, is accomplished by establishing widely dispersed, small labour-intensive manufacturing enterprises. The widespread increases in farmers' incomes through this type of agricultural development are expected to increase the demand for the manufacturing industries, with the growth in the two sectors reinforcing each other. The third element, international trade, encourages the export of labour-intensive manufactures, agricultural products and other products (in which the country has a comparative advantage) that finance the importation of products (in which the country has a comparative disadvantage) especially capital-intensive goods (Mellor 1976). In this chapter the focus is on the industrial development element. Elsewhere an adjusted Mellor strategy is discussed for densely populated areas in Indonesia including the development of labour-intensive, concentrated large manufacturing establishments with use of imported intermediate inputs (Rice 2000).

The Importance of Household and Small Manufacturing Industries in Rural Areas

The employment generated by household and small manufacturing establishments is very important as sources of income for rural inhabitants, especially in the densely populated regions such as Java. It is therefore important to examine how employment and income (value-added) from household and small establishments have grown in recent years in predominately rural industries.

Value-added is the income generated from economic activities. It is defined as the value of gross output minus 1) the value of raw materials and other intermediate inputs used in the production process, 2) expenditure for industrial services, and 3) expenses for the rent of machinery, apparatus, and buildings. It is composed of income in the form of wages and salaries of workers and income of the owners, with the income of the owners being composed of interest and other payments, their own implicit salaries if they are working, and their profits.

According to the Standard Industrial Classification somewhat adapted to Indonesian conditions (*Klasifikasi Lapangan Usaha Indonesia Sektor Industri Pengolahan*) the SIC codes represent the following industries:

31	Manufacture of food, beverages and tobacco products;
32	Manufacture of textile, garments and leathers;
33	Manufacture of wood, bamboo, rattan, willow products and the like, including furniture;
34	Manufacture of paper and paper products, printing and publishing;
35	Manufacture of chemical, petroleum, coal, rubber and plastic products;
36	Manufacture of nonmetallic mineral products, except products of petroleum and coal;
37	Basic metal industries
38	Manufacture of fabricated metal products, machinery and equipment;
39	Other manufacturing industries.

Source: Biro Pusat Statistik, *Statistik Industri Besar dan Sedang, Kode Klasifikasi Industri*, 1996.

An important question is which industries are predominately rural in Indonesia. Table 4.1 shows the percentages of establishments, employees and value-added of household and cottage manufacturing industries (that we shorten to household manufacturing industries or HMIs) that were rural in 1996 and percentage change from 1987 to 1996. If 50 percent or more of establishments' employees or value-added is located in rural areas and this is used to define "rural based", then using employment as a measure, all of the industries were predominately rural except paper and paper products, printing and publishing (34). In terms of value-added, six of the nine industries were predominately rural. In decreasing order of

TABLE 4.1
The Rural-Urban Distribution and Change in Indonesian Household and Cottage Manufacturing Industries 1987–96

SIC	% of Establishments				% Δ Establishments[a]		% of Employees				% Δ Employees[a]		% V.A. 1996	
	Urban		Rural		Urban	Rural	Urban		Rural		Urban	Rural	Urban	Rural
	1987	1996	1987	1996			1987	1996	1987	1996				
(1)	(2)	(3)	(4)	(5)	(6)	(7)	(8)	(9)	(10)	(11)	(12)	(13)	(14)	(15)
31	14	18	86	82	159	90	15	18	85	82	12	74	26	74
32	19	26	81	74	233	120	24	30	76	70	144	85	51	49
33	6	8	94	92	147	82	8	10	92	90	114	67	24	76
34		77		23				79		21			88	12
35	47	19	53	81	108	82	50	20	50	80	84	91	43	57
36	9	17	91	83	321	105	10	17	90	83	265	95	23	77
37	na	31	na	69	na	na	na	32	na	68	na	na	30	70
38	28	31	72	69	73	50	28	33	72	67	60	26	41	59
39	12	31	88	69	−22	−77	12	32	88	68	−32	−79	58	42
Total	12	17	88	83	145	67	14	18	86	82	105	52	31	69

[a]The percentage change in number of establishments and number of employees from 1987 to 1996. We use the *Badan Pusat Statistik* definition of household and cottage manufacturing establishments, also labelled as micro or just household manufacturing establishments, which are establishments having one to four employees, including a working owner.

Source: The 1987 data is from *Biro Pusat Statistik, Statistik Industri/Kerajinan Rumah Tangga 1987*. The 1996 data is from a *Badan Pusat Statistik* CD ROM.

their ruralness these six are nonmetallic mineral products (36), wood (33), food (31) and metal (37) industries—all 70 percent or above value-added from rural areas—in addition to fabricated metal and chemical products (38 and 35).

Table 4.2 shows that industries 31, 33, 36 and 32 were important in rural areas in 1996 with 1.54, 1.33, 0.49 and 0.36 million employees respectively, making a total of 3,714,698 employees in these industries out of total of 3,908,596 in the nine industries together, i.e., 95 percent of the total manufacturing employment of HMEs in rural areas. They also accounted for 92 percent of the total manufacturing value-added of HMIs in rural areas.

Turning to the small manufacturing establishments, Table 4.3 shows that the percentages of establishments, employees, and value-added that are rural are substantially less than for the household establishments, i.e., only 61 percent, 59 percent, and 44 percent respectively, and are also less for each of the nine industries. Again it is industries 31, 36, 33 and 32 (food, nonmetallic minerals, wood and textiles) which account for most of the employment and value-added in rural areas, with these four industries accounting for 93 percent of the employment and 95 percent of the value-added of the nine industries in rural areas taken together. We should note that the percentages of employment and value-added of the small establishments in industry 32 (textiles) are much less than the equivalent percentages for the household establishments. However, unlike the other eight industries, the percentages of employment and value-added of the small establishments in industry 36 (nonmetallic mineral products) in rural areas are only slightly less than the equivalent percentages of the household establishments (80 and 75 percent of employment and value-added rural compared with 83 and 77 percent for the household establishments).

The SMEs in rural areas generate much less employment and value-added in rural areas than the HMEs. From Tables 4.2 and 4.3 we can observe that in 1996, employment in rural SMEs was only 28 percent that of employment in rural HMEs, while value-added in rural small establishments was 61 percent that of rural HMEs. The productivity per employee in the small rural establishments was Rp. 2.225 million per year while in the household rural establishments it was only Rp. 1.043 million per year. This higher productivity per employee in the small establishments is partly a result of a higher percentage of persons in the household establishments working part-time and as unpaid workers than in the small establishments.

TABLE 4.2
Comparison of Household Manufacturing Establishments in Urban and Rural Areas 1987-96

SIC	Number of Establishments				Number of Employees				Value-added 1996	
	Urban		Rural		Urban		Rural		Urban	Rural
	1987	1996	1987	1996	1987	1996	1987	1996	(Million Rp)	
31	63,384	163,872	402,894	766,393	154,928	328,952	885,749	1,537,757	549,135	1,593,249
32	29,845	99,495	126,295	277,222	63,151	154,177	196,811	363,183	291,391	278,525
33	30,811	76,034	458,036	832,469	65,764	140,596	796,947	1,328,200	407,812	1,275,011
34	8,305	13,275		3,917	20,460	29,720		7,712	96,859	13,727
35		4,015	9,410	17,156		7,844	20,100	30,763	24,465	33,051
36	10,025	42,156	100,982	207,514	26,273	96,015	249,404	485,558	178,551	586,882
37	na	347	na	757	na	819	na	1,727	2,480	5,855
38	10,211	17,696	25,762	38,551	25,198	40,274	64,167	80,933	131,512	191,857
39	25,336	19,736	190,040	43,332	49,497	33,888	351,487	72,763	139,240	99,376
TOTAL	177,917	436,625	1,313,419	2,187,310	405,271	832,285	2,564,665	3,908,596	1,821,447	4,077,534

Source: The 1987 data is from Biro Pusat Statistik, Statistik Industri Kerajinan Rumah Tangga 1987. The 1996 data is from a Badan Pusat Statistik CD ROM.

TABLE 4.3
Small Establishment Manufacturing Sector in Urban and Rural Areas in 1996

SIC	No. of Establishments			No. of Employees			Value-added		
	Urban	Rural	% Estab. Rural	Urban	Rural	% Empl. Rural	Urban (Million Rp)	Rural	% V.A. Rural
31	22,536	59,351	72	173,262	466,378	73	535,382	722,166	57
32	27,557	10,397	27	241,937	80,595	25	1,145,495	191,363	14
33	15,909	29,138	65	126,288	211,386	63	572,492	800,769	58
34	5,803	432	7	47,798	3,217	6	239,472	6,289	3
35	2,176	2,301	51	19,353	19,463	50	105,239	56,985	35
36	10,047	39,845	80	71,062	281,471	80	180,904	534,181	75
37	322	270	46	3,337	1,739	34	12,339	7,937	39
38	5,833	3,727	39	47,901	25,449	35	218,290	95,116	30
39	3,580	2,842	44	29,907	22,725	43	107,788	60,545	36
TOTAL	93,764	148,303	61	760,845	1,112,423	59	3,117,401	2,475,350	44

Source: CD ROM from *Badan Pusat Statistik*, Republic of Indonesia. Small establishments are defined as having 5 to 19 employees.

In 1996, 77 percent of the HMEs had no paid or unpaid workers, while 14 percent had paid workers and 9 percent had unpaid workers. In the textile (32) and wood (33) industries, the percentages of enterprises using paid workers were particularly low at 9 and 11 percent, and were much higher in the manufacturing of nonmetallic mineral products (36) at 30 percent. In contrast, 91 percent of the SMEs had paid workers. For small manufacturing establishments (SMEs), 72 percent were paid and 28 percent unpaid (*Statistik Industri Kerajinan Rumahtangga 1996*, Tables 19.1 and 18.1.1, and *Statistik Industri Kecil 1996*, Tables 19.1 and 18.1). The "unpaid" workers usually are given a share of the owner's income in an informal manner, such as a mother and daughter weaving using the same loom in their household and sharing the income.

Those establishments with no paid workers are qualitatively different from those with paid workers because the former establishments' income prospects are such that apparently it is not attractive for them to hire paid workers, whereas for the latter, the income of the owner presumably is increased by hiring workers at prevailing local market wage rates. The high percentage of HMEs with no paid employees is an indication that many of the owners themselves are not earning the equivalent of market wage rates, but rather have engaged in the business as a survival activity in lieu of less attractive alternative income-generating opportunities.

Following Bungaran Saragih (1998) and Tulus Tambunan (1999), we can distinguish between industries producing inputs such as fertilizers, pesticides and agricultural equipment for the agricultural sector—named agricultural-oriented industries by Tambunan, and industries downstream processing agricultural commodities—named agro-industries by Saragih and agricultural-based industries by Tambunan (Saragih 1998, p. 96, and Tambunan 1999, p. 90). If we define rural industries as those located in rural areas, many of the agricultural-oriented industries are not rural industries. Most of the industries included in SIC 31 and 33 (food and wood manufacturing) are agro-industries (including forestry and fisheries as part of agriculture) whereas in Indonesia many of the industries in SIC 32 (textiles) are not agro-industries in the sense that most of the fibres to which they add value are imported natural fibres (mainly cotton) and synthetic fibres. In addition there are a considerable number of rural industries which are not agro-industries, some of which use raw materials from rural areas (such as ceramics, brick and tile making in SIC category 36, simple agricultural implements and utensils made from fabricated metal (38), and miscellaneous items such as crudely made toys, sporting equipment, jewelry, and musical instruments (39)). All of these rural industries are important as sources of income for rural residents.

The distribution of workers in the food (31), wood (33) and nonmetallic mineral manufacturing (36) sectors in the household and small manufacturing industries was quite even between Java and the rest of Indonesia. Calculating the percentage of industry *a* employees in Java in 1996 (out of the total of all the industries together in Java) divided by the percentage of industry *a* employees in Indonesia (out of total of all the industries together in Indonesia) we obtain the location quotients for Java relative to Indonesia for industry *a*. For SMIs and HMIs together we obtain for Java relative to Indonesia for industries 31 (food), 32 (textiles), 33 (wood) and 36 (nonmetallic minerals) the location quotients 1.00, 1.02, 0.97, and 1.06 (See Blakely 1994, p. 93, for a definition of location quotient). For SMIs they are 1.02, 1.21, 0.86, and 0.87 respectively and for HMIs the equivalent figures are 0.99, 0.86, 1.02, and 1.16. Therefore in terms of employment only the nonmetallic minerals industry (36) is significantly disproportionately located in Java. The textile industry (32) is unusual because SMIs are disproportionately located in Java but HMIs in the rest of Indonesia, especially in Nusa Tenggara Timur, West Sumatra, and South Sulawesi (calculated from Table 2.2 in *Statistik Industri Kerajinan Rumahtanga 1996* and *Statistik Industri Kecil 1996*).

Household and Small Manufacturing Industries 1986–1996

In order to trace the growth of manufacturing in rural areas we need to pay special attention to industries 31 (food), 33 (wood), 36 (nonmetallic minerals) and 32 (textiles) for both the household and small establishments. Table 4.4 shows that the annual compound nominal rate of growth of value-added (columns 5–7) from 1986 to 1996 of household manufacturing establishments was 23 percent less than that of small establishments, which in turn was 15 percent less than that of the medium/large (M/L) establishments. However, there was much variation in the performance of household, small and M/L establishments by sector. In sectors 33 (wood) and 36 (nonmetallic mineral products), small establishment value-added grew fastest, while in all other sectors M/L establishment value-added grew the fastest. However, the performance of household establishments in sectors 31–33 and 36 (the sectors in which their value-added was the largest) the growth rates were greater than the growth rate for the total for

TABLE 4.4
Value-added of Household, Small and Medium/Large Manufacturing Establishments in 1996

SIC	Value-Added 1996 (Rp mill.)			% Rate of Growth 1986–1996 (annual compound rate)[a]			VA Household/ VA Total	VA Small/ VA Total
	Household	Small	Med./Large	Household	Small	Med./Large		
(1)	(2)	(3)	(4)	(5)	(6)	(7)	(8)	(9)
31	2,142,384	1,257,548	17,594,386	19.2	15.9	20.3	0.102	0.060
32	569,916	1,336,858	15,908,913	18.9	26.1	28.1	0.032	0.075
33	1,682,823	1,373,261	6,863,992	22.1	28.6	21.8	0.170	0.138
34	110,586	245,761	4,815,774	30.5	17.7	31.7	0.021	0.048
35	57,516	162,224	12,189,979	20.9	12.1	24.3	0.005	0.013
36	765,433	715,085	3,748,767	19.7	25.8	22.8	0.146	0.137
37	8,335	20,276	9,851,356	n.a.	n.a.	28.8	0.001	0.002
38	323,369	313,406	21,657,987	20.1	19.6	32.6	0.015	0.014
39	238,616	168,333	682,315	-4.1	23.3	33.0	0.219	0.155
Total	5,898,981	5,592,752	93,332,462	16.7	21.8	25.9	0.056	0.053

[a]These are the annual compound percentage rates of growth of value-added in current prices. From 1986 to 1996 the gross domestic product deflator for manufacturing industries without petroleum and gas increased from 100 in 1986 to 247.016 in 1996, which is an annual compound rate of inflation of 9.46%. Therefore if we assumed that this was the rate of inflation for all of the nine two-digit industries, their rates of growth in constant prices would be the nominal annual compound rates of growth shown in this table minus 9.46%. Even though the rates of inflation of the two-digit industries varied around this figure, we can draw the conclusion that the rates of growth of real value-added for all of the industries were quite high.

Source: The 1996 value-added figures for household and small establishments is calculated from a *Badan Pusat Statistik* CD ROM. These figures for household and small establishments are 2.9% and 3.3% respectively larger than the figures published in *Statistik Indonesia 1999* (Table 6.1.2). These difference have practically no effect on the annual compound growth rates from 1986 to 1996. The data for medium/large enterprises is from *Statistik Industri*. The 1986 figures for household and small establishments are based on the 1986 Economic Census as reported in *Statistik Indonesia 1990*, Table 6.1.2.

household establishments, and were close to the growth rate of the M/L establishments in sector 31 (food), the household sector with the highest percentage of value-added in rural areas.

Given that the rate of inflation measured by the gross domestic product deflator for manufacturing industries without petroleum and gas was 9.46 percent per annum, the rates of growth in real terms were also high—approximately 7.2, 12.3 and 16.4 percent per annum for the household, small and M/L establishments respectively. In spite of the likely substantial measurement error in these figures, we can safely conclude that their rates of growth were high from 1986 to 1996. Given that Indonesia's economic policies somewhat favoured M/L manufacturing enterprises during this period, we think that with improved policies towards household and small manufacturing establishments, their growth rates can continue to be high during the coming decade. This will continue to have a strong positive impact employment and incomes in rural areas.

Overall, household and small manufacturing establishments are not very important in terms of total value-added from manufacturing, but are much more important in employment generation. Table 4.4 shows that household and small manufacturing establishments in 1996 accounted for only 5.6 percent and 5.3 percent respectively of total value-added from manufacturing. Columns 8 and 9 indicate that much of this activity was concentrated in sectors 31 (food) for household establishments, 32 (textiles) for small establishments, 33, 36, and 39 (wood, nonmetallic minerals and other manufacturing industries). In terms of employment generation, household and small establishments were important accounting for 44 percent and 17 percent respectively of total manufacturing industry employment in 1996, with 39 percent accounted for by M/L establishments (Table 4.5). They were especially important in employment generation in sectors 31, 33, 36 and 39 and in sector 34 for the small establishments.

The rate of growth of employment from 1986 to 1996 by household manufacturing establishments at 5.7 percent per annum was only approximately 60 percent of that of the small and M/L establishments, but still about double the rate of population growth (see Table 4.5). This slower growth rate of HMEs' employment is somewhat detrimental to the development of rural areas because 82 percent of their employment in 1996 was in rural areas compared with only 59 percent for the small establishments. Employment generation by the household and small manufacturing establishments together was slightly greater than that generated by their M/L counterparts in the latter part of the 1986–1996 period.

TABLE 4.5
Employment of Household, Small and Medium/Large Manufacturing Establishments in 1996

SIC	Number of Employees in 1996			% Rate of Growth 1986–1996 (annual compound rate)[a]			Employ. Household/ Employment Total	Employ. Small/ Employ. Total
	Household	Small	Med./Large	Household	Small	Med./Large		
(1)	(2)	(3)	(4)	(5)	(6)	(7)	(8)	(9)
31	1,866,709	639,640	810,221	7.1	7.2	4.5	0.563	0.193
32	517,360	322,532	1,354,716	8.0	9.3	13.3	0.236	0.147
33	1,468,796	337,674	562,231	6.2	12.3	12.0	0.620	0.143
34	37,432	51,015	165,390	9.7	9.0	10.2	0.147	0.201
35	38,607	38,816	485,701	9.2	4.5	7.1	0.069	0.069
36	581,573	352,533	190,308	8.9	12.8	8.9	0.517	0.314
37	2,546	5,076	50,420	n.a.	n.a.	11.6	0.044	0.087
38	121,207	73,350	525,438	4.4	6.4	11.2	0.168	0.102
39	106,651	52,632	72,542	−11.8	9.8	18.4	0.460	0.227
Total	4,740,881	1,873,268	4,214,967	5.7	9.3	9.6	0.438	0.173

[a] These are the annual compound percentage rates of growth of persons employed including working owners.

Source: The 1996 employment figures for household and small establishments is calculated from a *Badan Pusat Statistik* CD ROM. The data for medium/large enterprises is from *Statistik Industri*. The 1986 figures for household and small establishments are from the 1986 Economic Census as published in *Statistik Indonesia 1990*, Table 6.1.1.

Clearly growth in both employment and labour productivity help to raise employment and income levels in Indonesia. In 1996 labour productivity (value-added per employee) of SMEs was Rp. 2.986 million compared with only Rp. 1.245 million for HMEs. A more rapid rate of growth of SMI employment than HMI employment should be encouraged because it would raise per capita incomes as well as employment. SMEs are still likely to be widely distributed around the country like HMEs, close to or in rural areas, unlike especially the large manufacturing enterprises.

In Java, rapid employment and income growth of all sizes of manufacturing establishments have a greater impact on people living in rural areas than outside of Java. Industrial development in urban areas has a greater effect on rural people because on average people in rural areas of Java live closer to urban areas than in other regions and in general the transportation infrastructure including rural roads is denser and more developed making it easier for rural people to commute to urban areas to work. These factors make it easier for rural people to commute to manufacturing industry jobs in urban areas (Berry et al. 2001, p. 375 state there are relatively high urban-rural linkages on Java). A rough indicator of the nearness of rural people to urban areas is the land area of a region divided by the number of municipalities in the region. For Java in 2000 this was 4554 square kilometres per municipality, in Sumatra 20,974 square kilometres, and outside of Java 39,890 square kilometres.

The Impact of the Economic Crisis

The household and small manufacturing establishments were hit very hard by the economic crisis which began in August 1997. Over the period from 1996 to 1998 the value-added in constant prices of SMEs decreased by a greater percentage than did HMEs.[4] Further these SMEs suffered about the same in terms of decreases in their number of employees decreasing about the same percentage as the HMEs (see Tables 4.6 and 4.7). Various case studies also support the view that they were hit very hard (Berry et al. 2001, pp. 375–77). The AKATIGA Foundation in 1999 found that with the economic crisis the majority of small establishments experienced a decrease in their performance, especially because of large increases in the prices of raw materials used by many of them which was in turn due to the depreciation of the rupiah, and because of weak demand in domestic markets (Tim Usaha Kecil 1999, p. 31). Participants at the second national conference on small business held in Jakarta on 7–8 October 1998 revealed

TABLE 4.6
Household Manufacturing Establishments 1996, 1998, 2000

SIC	Number of Establishments			% Change		Number of Employees			% Change		Value Added (Rp. Million)			% Change[a]	
	1996	1998	2000	96-98	98-00	1996	1998	2000	96-98	98-00	1996	1998	2000	96-98	98-00
31	930,265	719,668	828,140	-22.64%	15.07%	1,866,709	1,487,258	1,722,711	-20.33%	15.83%	2,142,384	3,291,015	3,605,015	-15.84%	-12.61%
32	376,717	259,397	312,438	-31.14%	20.45%	517,360	397,196	456,729	-23.23%	14.99%	569,916	808,496	852,560	-22.28%	-15.87%
33	908,503	733,315	781,348	-19.28%	6.55%	1,468,796	1,261,894	1,445,664	-14.09%	14.56%	1,682,823	2,550,695	3,035,312	-16.96%	-5.06%
34	17,192	10,865	16,297	-36.80%	50.00%	37,432	25,089	35,883	-32.97%	43.02%	110,586	125,928	135,234	-37.46%	-14.32%
35	21,171	15,042	25,545	-28.95%	69.82%	38,607	33,195	52,554	-14.02%	58.32%	57,516	81,300	80,358	-22.56%	-21.14%
36	249,670	166,559	224,251	-33.29%	34.64%	581,573	397,356	532,797	-31.68%	34.09%	765,433	1,028,799	1,351,380	-26.65%	4.79%
37	1,104	810	663	-26.63%	-18.15%	2,546	1,488	2,380	-41.56%	59.95%	8,335	5,801	160	-61.87%	-97.80%
38	56,247	49,579	58,734	-11.85%	18.47%	121,207	110,306	132,517	-8.99%	20.14%	323,369	465,038	563,105	-21.21%	-3.40%
39	63,068	47,100	72,806	-25.32%	54.58%	106,651	82,812	120,948	-22.35%	46.05%	238,616	324,647	338,272	-25.46%	-16.87%
TOTAL	2,623,937	2,002,335	2,320,222	-23.69%	15.88%	4,740,881	3,796,594	4,502,183	-19.92%	18.58%	5,898,981	8,681,719	9,961,396	-19.40%	-8.46%

[a] % change is annual compound rate of change of value-added in constant 1993 prices using the GDP deflator for manufacturing industries without petroleum and gas.

Source: *Badan Pusat Statistik, Statistik Indonesia 2000, Jakarta, 2001*

TABLE 4.7
Small Manufacturing Establishments 1996, 1998, 2000

SIC	Number of Establishments			% Change		Number of Employees			% Change		Value Added (Rp. Million)			% Change[a]	
	1996	1998	2000	96–98	98–00	1996	1998	2000	96–98	98–00	1996	1998	2000	96–98	98–00
31	81,887	52,524	82,430	−35.86%	56.94%	639,640	402,558	594,923	−37.06%	47.79%	1,257,548	1,701,668	2,203,783	−25.86%	3.32%
32	37,954	30,071	41,438	−20.77%	37.80%	322,532	261,643	370,218	−18.88%	41.50%	1,336,858	1,449,188	1,846,905	−40.61%	1.67%
33	45,047	50,472	53,921	12.04%	6.83%	337,674	383,506	424,937	13.57%	10.80%	1,373,261	2,026,434	2,260,766	−19.15%	−10.99%
34	6,235	2,889	5,306	−53.66%	83.66%	51,015	22,009	44,961	−56.86%	104.28%	245,761	123,999	172,507	−72.36%	10.99%
35	4,477	1,748	3,661	−60.96%	109.44%	38,816	13,437	31,116	−65.38%	131.57%	162,224	58,135	153,473	−80.37%	110.61%
36	49,892	41,538	50,467	−16.74%	21.50%	352,533	307,741	383,911	−12.71%	24.75%	715,085	928,083	1,059,103	−28.89%	−8.96%
37	592	96	631	−83.78%	557.29%	5,076	942	5,405	−81.44%	473.78%	20,276	6,393	20,089	−82.73%	150.70%
38	9,560	10,940	10,638	14.44%	−2.76%	73,350	81,926	78,198	11.69%	−4.55%	313,406	496,171	439,586	−13.26%	−29.32%
39	6,422	4,286	8,361	−33.26%	95.08%	52,632	31,842	71,021	−39.50%	123.04%	168,333	133,349	223,841	−56.60%	33.92%
TOTAL	242,066	194,564	256,853	−19.62%	32.01%	1,873,268	1,505,604	2,004,690	−19.63%	33.15%	5,592,752	6,923,420	8,380,053	−32.18%	−3.44%

[a] % change is annual compound rate of change of value-added in constant 1993 prices using the GDP deflator for manufacturing industries without petroleum and gas.

Source: Badan Pusat Statistik, Statistik Indonesia 2000, Jakarta, 2001

that small establishments in the textile, wood products, leather goods, and metal goods industries also experienced large increases in the prices of raw materials after the crisis and those selling in the domestic market commonly suffered from weak demand (Center for Economic and Social Studies and The Asia Foundation 1999, pp. 39, 40, 50, 75, 85, 87). Similar type cost-price squeezes were also found by Rice et al. to be serious in the jewellry, garments, leather goods and wooden furniture industries especially for smaller enterprises that were heavily dependent on domestic markets (Rice et al. 2002). For the household and small establishments together, there were 23 percent and 20 percent decreases respectively in the number of enterprises and employees from 1996 to 1998 and an approximately 26 percent decrease in real value-added as is shown in Table 4.8. They had almost recovered in terms of number of employees by 2000 but not in terms of number of establishments and real value-added.

Sectors 31 (food) and 36 (nonmetallic minerals) were somewhat more adversely affected in terms of employment while sector 33 (wood) suffered only a 9 percent decrease in employment and fully recovered in terms of employment by 2000. Sectors 32 (textiles) and 36 had almost recovered in terms of employment by 2000 but employment in the most important sector 31 was still down 7.5 percent in 2000 compared with 1996.

The better performance of sector 33 (wood) is not surprising because many of these manufacturing establishments produce components for larger wooden furniture factories producing for export. These furniture exporters benefited from the huge depreciation of the rupiah which resulted in a gigantic percentage increase in their rupiah export prices with a much smaller percentage increase in the rupiah cost of their locally assessed inputs made out of wood (Rice et al. 2002, and Berry et al. 2001, p. 377). Other manufacturing industries (36), in which the household and small establishments produce mainly clay tiles and bricks, were badly affected by the collapse of the construction industry with the economic crisis (Berry et al. 2001, p. 377). From 1998 to 2000 the H/S establishments seemed to be recovering better than the M/L establishments, especially in terms of real value-added.

Both in terms of employment and value-added, the H/S establishments in industry 31 (food) performed poorly compared with the M/L establishments. The former suffered a decrease in employment from 1996 to 1998 of 25 percent while employment of the M/L establishments increased 4 percent. In the same period nominal value-added of the H/S establishments increased 47 percent while that of the M/L establishments

TABLE 4.8
Household and Small Manufacturing Establishments 1996, 1998, 2000

SIC	Number of Establishments			% Change		Number of Employees			% Change		Value Added (Rp. Million)			% Change[a]	
	1996	1998	2000	96-98	98-00	1996	1998	2000	96-98	98-00	1996	1998	2000	96-98	98-00
31	1,012,152	772,192	910,570	-23.71%	17.92%	2,506,349	1,889,816	2,317,634	-24.60%	22.64%	3,399,932	4,992,683	5,808,798	-19.55%	-7.18%
32	414,671	289,468	353,876	-30.19%	22.25%	839,892	658,839	826,947	-21.56%	25.52%	1,906,774	2,257,684	2,699,465	-35.13%	-4.61%
33	953,550	783,787	835,269	-17.80%	6.57%	1,806,470	1,645,400	1,870,601	-8.92%	13.69%	3,056,084	4,577,129	5,296,078	-17.94%	-7.69%
34	23,427	13,754	21,603	-41.29%	57.07%	88,447	47,098	80,844	-46.75%	71.65%	356,077	249,927	307,741	-61.54%	-1.77%
35	25,648	16,790	29,206	-34.54%	73.95%	77,423	46,632	83,670	-39.77%	79.43%	219,740	139,435	233,831	-65.23%	33.79%
36	299,562	208,097	274,718	-30.53%	32.01%	934,106	705,097	916,708	-24.52%	30.01%	1,483,518	1,956,882	2,410,483	-27.73%	-1.73%
37	1,696	906	1,294[a]	-46.58%	42.83%	7,622	2,430	7,785	-68.12%	220.37%	28,611	12,194	20,249	-76.65%	32.48%
38	65,807	60,519	69,372	-8.04%	14.63%	194,557	192,232	210,715	-1.20%	9.61%	636,775	961,209	1,002,691	-17.30%	-16.78%
39	69,490	51,386	81,167	-26.05%	57.96%	159,283	114,654	191,969	-28.02%	67.43%	406,949	457,996	562,113	-38.34%	-2.08%
TOTAL	2,866,003	2,196,899	2,577,075	-23.35%	17.31%	6,614,149	5,302,198	6,506,873	-19.84%	22.72%	11,494,460	15,605,139	18,341,449	-25.62%	-6.23%

[a] % change is annual compound rate of change of value-added in constant 1993 prices using the GDP deflator for manufacturing industries without petroleum and gas.

Source: Badan Pusat Statistik, Statistik Indonesia 2000, Jakarta, 2001

increased by 102 percent. From 1998 to 2000 nominal value-added of the H/S establishments increased a further 16 percent while that of the M/L establishments increased a further 26 percent. The small establishments in industry 31 were especially hard hit both in terms of employment and value-added compared with the household establishments as shown in Tables 4.6 and 4.7. This made the adverse impact in rural areas somewhat less because the household establishments are more concentrated in the rural areas than the small establishments. Two sub-sectors hard hit in industry 31 were soybean curd (*tahu*) in West Java and small clove cigarette (*kretek*) producers in Central Java, "with both cases due to a steep rise in the price of inputs" (Berry et al. 2001, p. 375).

Hindrakusuma (1996) has argued that in 1995 the growth of the traditional food processing industry was growing slowly and that generally it was not yet able to provide satisfactory incomes for entrepreneurs and workers. Although this was not satisfactory for the entrepreneurs, they continued because of a lack of alternative opportunities or did it as a sideline. Important factors inhibiting their competitiveness are the absence of brand-name products, generally low product quality which varied from producer to producer, inability to advertise on TV, competition from multinational food processors, the government's greater response to the needs of large processors, and little opportunity to utilize the low cost distribution network of super-wholesalers supplying supermarkets. Because of these limitations, their cost of distribution is high (Hindrakusuma 1996, pp. 192–95). Presumably most of these problems would be greater for HMEs supplying other than local markets.

Policy Objectives of Household Manufacturing Industries

Before addressing the matter of policy recommendations for HMIs, we must first discuss the objectives of the current policies. Two commonly adopted objectives are poverty alleviation and economic growth, sometimes with particular localities and groups targeted, such as left-behind villages (*desa tertinggal*), youth, a particularly isolated traditional ethnic group, etc. We assume in this discussion that the objectives are poverty alleviation and economic growth. HMIs can be important in achieving both.

Liedholm and Meade (1999) classify micro (household using my terminology) and small enterprises into four major categories: 1) New starts, or enterprises just getting under way; 2) Non-growing enterprises, or enterprises that have survived start-up but have not added to their employment since they were first established; 3) Small growers, or "enterprises that have been in existence for some time and have added to their work force since starting, but have grown only in small amounts"; and 4) Graduates, "enterprises that started from a very small base and have made a transition to reach at least the middle ranges of the small enterprise spectrum" (Mead and Lindholm 1999, p. 84).

In Indonesia, as in most low-income countries with extensive unemployment, there are large numbers of persons choosing to become self-employed "entrepreneurs" as a means of survival. The business failure rate in their business activity is usually high among these new "entrepreneurs" because they find that their incomes and returns are too low or negative, they are able to obtain employment which gives them a greater return to their labour and capital than continuing in this business, or they retire or become unemployed. A small percentage of them are successful and increase in size, generating economic growth and productive employment for others. One important opinion is that there is little need to assist persons to establish businesses because there is no shortage of start-ups (Mead and Liedholm 1999). However, they argue that assistance to very small establishments during their first two years of existence can be effective if poverty alleviation is the objective, even though most of them will not turn out to be graduates. One of the most effective types of assistance is to provide them with information on saving and loan acquisition. This is useful because most of them now rely largely on their own savings and those of friends and relatives for capital (Mead and Liedholm 1998, pp. 70–71). The details on the supply of credit and various institutions delivering credit are taken up in the next section of the chapter.

Supply of Credit to Household Establishments

There is a huge potential for increasing institution based loans for HME and SME activities. In 1996 only 13 percent of HMEs used loan facilities, and out of this 13 percent, only 11.3 percent, 3.7 percent and 1.7 percent respectively borrowed from banks, cooperatives, and non-bank financial institutions, with the remaining 83.3 percent borrowing from other sources. The percentage of HMEs using loan facilities in Java was slightly higher than in the rest of Indonesia: 15 percent compared with 11 percent (calculated from *Statistik Industri Kerajinan Rumahtangga 1996*, Table 22.2). The percentage of textile (32) HMEs using loan facilities was the highest at 24 percent and products made out of wood (33) the lowest at 8 percent. The percentage of SMEs using loan facilities in 1996 was the highest at 27 percent, with 42.1 percent of them borrowing from banks, 3.7 from cooperatives, 2.3 percent from non-bank financial institutions, and 51.9 percent from others (calculated using data from Table 22.2 in *Statistik Industri Kecil 1996*). The percentage of HMEs and SMEs together using loan facilities decreased from 14.3 percent in 1996 to 12.8 percent in 1998 (calculated using data from Table 17.1 of *Profil Usaha Kecil dan Menengah Tidak Berbadan Hukum: Sektor Industri Kecil dan Kerajinan Rumahtangga Indonesia, Survei Usaha Terintegrasi 1998*). Clearly, the Indonesian Government recognizes the importance of facilitating the development of all forms of institutions extending credit to household and small establishments to all villages in the nation. The key here is facilitating the development of all forms of financial institutions.

Facilitation of financial services helps to alleviate poverty both by making their businesses more successful as well as helping to free them from borrowing from the informal credit providers commonly at very high interest rates. However, in some industries the market is already so fully saturated with suppliers, such as bamboo weaving in parts of Indonesia, that benefiting some producers through improved financial services damages other producers by lowering their returns. This includes driving some of them out of the market (Weijland 1999, p. 1523). Frequently this is the case when the markets for the HMEs are fully saturated and growing very slowly.

For many years the government and Bank Indonesia have supported micro, small- and medium-sized establishments (MSMEs) through subsidized direct programme credits, the so-called "channelling system". These reached a peak in 1999 with 17 different kinds of credit directed at MSMEs, commonly through cooperatives. Most of these directed programme credits were managed by Bank Indonesia, but as a result of Act No. 23/1999 on Bank Indonesia they have now been transferred to the state enterprises Bank Rakyat Indonesia, PT. Permodalan Nasional Madani (PNM) and PT. Bank Tabungan Negara (State Savings Bank) (Timberg 2000). There has been widespread criticism of these credit programmes because of large credit arrears, considerable amounts of the funds never reaching the targeted borrowers because of corruption and mismanagement, adverse effects on commercially operated credit programmes targeted at MSMEs, and their allocative inefficiency (Cole and Slade 1996, p. 354, and Ravicz 1998, p. 2). The latter is caused by many borrowers with the higher social rates of return on their investments not being able to access rationed credit at subsidized interest rates while some with low social rates of return have accessed it. Since 1999 the number of subsidized credit programmes and their funding have been greatly decreased and the government seems committed to moving away from the "channelling system" to the so-called "executing system", which relies on the sustainable delivery of credit to MSMEs through formal credit institutions at market interest rates.

Indonesia has a rich and largely successful history with microfinance that has resulted in a large number of highly diverse microfinance institutions and programmes providing credit and savings facilities for household establishments (Ravicz 1998, p. 2) The largest facilities are those provided by the Bank Rakyat Indonesia (People's Bank of Indonesia), a government owned bank. It provides banking services for small-scale entrepreneurs through 323 branch offices, 3,694 BRI unit desa (village units) and 313 service units (http://www.sme-center.com). This was almost one BRI unit desa for each of the 4,049 sub-districts (*kecamatan*) in Indonesia but only one unit for an average of 18.69 villages in 2000 given Indonesia's total of 69,050 villages) (*Statistik Indonesia 2000*, Table 1.1). It has loan programmes for three categories of businesses: Level l) below the poverty line, Level 2) above the poverty line—mainly for micro and small-scale entrepreneurs and Level 3) up to Rp. 350 million loans for small-scale businesses. Loans for household establishments are mainly Level 2, which is the *kupedes* programme with a maximum ceiling on loans of Rp. 50 million. At the end of 2000 outstanding *kupedes* loans were Rp. 7,733.2 billion, up from Rp. 4,076.2 billion at the end of 1996, serving 2,646,752 borrowers (http://www.bri.co.id/micro/dream2/main.htm). The *kupedes* programme has been extremely profitable for Bank Rakyat Indonesia and is not limited by budget funds (Timberg 2000, p. 5). However, the BRI unit desa programme is still far from adequate to fulfill the credit needs of household establishments given it has branches in only about 5 percent of Indonesia's villages and it tends to cater to borrowers larger than household establishments.

The second largest source of institutional finance for household establishments is from Bank Perkreditan Rakyat (People's Credit Banks or BPRs). At the end of 2000 and 2001 the BPRs extended credit totalling Rp. 3,619 and 4,496 billion respectively, through 7,764 and 7,703 BPRs (Bank Indonesia 2001). At the end of 1999 there were 2,855 thousand borrowers from the BPRs and 5,255 thousand savers with the average loan size from BRI unit desa being Rp. 2.4 million and from BPRs Rp. 828,000 (Timberg 2000, Table II). The BPR lending has also generally been self-sustaining and profitable. The smaller sized BPR loans are more suitable for household establishments, but BPR branches were located in only about 11 percent of the villages in 2000. Thus BRI and the BPRs together are still far from being able to fulfill the credit needs of household establishments, and additional smaller more village level financial institutions are needed.

The third largest institutional provider of credit for household establishments is the savings and loan (*simpan pinjam*) cooperatives and enterprise units (that are affiliated with cooperatives) which are overseen by Kantor Menteri Negara Urusan Koperasi dan Usaha Kecil dan Menengah Republik Indonesia (MENNEGKOP) (GOI Office of the State Minister for Cooperatives and Small and Medium Enterprises). At the end of 1998 there were reported to be 1,164 savings and loan cooperatives (*koperasi simpan pinjam* or KSP) and 35,741 enterprise units (*unit usaha simpan pinjam* or USP) with 655,411 and 10,040,372 customers. In 1998 the KSPs and USPs gave loans worth Rp. 527.4838 million and Rp. 3,529.3042 million respectively (Departemen Koperasi, Pengusaha Kecil dan Menengah Republic Indonesia 1999, Tables 7.1, 7.2, 7.3, 7.4, 7.11 and 7.12).[5] Their loans are usually substantially smaller than BPR loans and more suitable for the smaller household establishments. In addition there are Lembaga Keuangan Masyarakat (Community Financial Institutions) and credit unions with especially the former being widespread in rural areas. Finally, there are many NGOs, especially government sponsored ones (GONGOs as they are called) who are serving the smallest borrowers. "The total volume of their lending is unclear except that thousands of organizations and trillions of rupiah are involved. The government supported programmes have channeled a fair amount of money through the years through there is some doubt about how much as been repaid and thus about the sustainability of the different credit programmes and their impact" (Timberg 2000, p. 13). The shortage of formal financial institutions in rural areas is especially acute in the more isolated areas outside of Java.

With the "executing system" that entails the sustainable delivery of credit through formal credit institutions usually at commercial interest rates, efforts are now underway to change the mentality of both borrowers and lenders. The micro/small borrowers must learn to realize that if they default on loans without very strong reasons, they should expect to face great difficulty obtaining further loans in the future. The various financial institutions need to more fully comprehend and be more sympathetic with the needs of micro/small borrowers and keep their administrative and collateral requirements to a minimum. The channelling system was dependent on ongoing government subsidies. Through the "executing system" it is hoped that the private sector financial system will eventually become sustainable in meeting fully the needs of micro and small establishments with minimal government support. With millions of micro and small establishments needing credit, the only way that these needs can be adequately met is through the thousands of private, including cooperative, financial institution providers, although it is expected that Bank Rakyat Indonesia will continue to also have an important role. These improvements associated with the "executing system" deserve to be supported.

An important factor hindering the lending to HMEs is the high transaction cost of making very small loans to hundreds of borrowers. In theory channelling credit to household establishments through cooperatives and business groups can cut transactions costs. However, in practice often there have been large credit arrears. Sometimes heads of business groups were required to be personally responsible for the repayment of the loans of the members of their group, such that they did not dare to sign any loan contracts. "This problem could be partly overcome through the formal cooperative status, while the creation of a guarantee fund also facilitated borrowing considerably" (Weijland 1999, p. 1526). In addition, Islamic (Shariah) financial institutions are a new and rapidly expanding category of institutions serving all levels of MSME borrowers. "They range from Bank Muamalat and the new syariah branches of the major commercial banks, to syariah BPR, to Syariah Baitul Mal Wa Tamwil (BMT) cooperatives" (Timberg 2000, p. 12).

Despite the above-described development of financial institutions serving household and small establishments, there are still many localities where the dearth of formal financial services is hindering the operations of household establishments. Operational costs become inflated as HMEs are forced to rely on informal sources of credit which provide loans at very high interest rates. The expansion of various financial institutions serving micro and small businesses into areas where they are underserved should be strongly supported. Because of these needs and underdeveloped rural infrastructure the Asian Development Bank is about to provide a loan and technical assistance grant for the "Community Empowerment for Rural Development Project" in six provinces in Kalimantan and Sulawesi (Asian Development Bank 2000). This project includes assistance to communities to establish and operate community-based savings and loan organizations (ADB 2000, p. 4). The ADB also has two ongoing micro-finance projects in Indonesia: the Microcredit Project extending credit to five regional development banks (Bank Pembangunan Daerah) in West, Central and East Java, South Kalimantan, and West Nusa Tenggara) which lend to small financial institutions and group organizations; and the Rural Income Generation Project that emphasizes the provision of micro-finance services by Bank Rakyat Indonesia to poor people living below the poverty line. (ADB 2000, p. 8).

In some villages local saving is not sufficient to fund the villagers' borrowing requirements. Commercial banks including the regional development banks have a very important function receiving deposits from some small financial institutions and re-lending to others—a function which needs to be facilitated. Previously the Government required that 22 to 25 percent of all loans from commercial lending banks go to small and medium enterprises. Since 1998 this is no longer required but commercial banks are strongly encouraged by the Government and Bank Indonesia to continue this practice—a policy which we support. Commercial banks can count lending to BPRs as part of their lending to small and medium enterprises (Timberg 2000, p. 7).

Many, especially rural, household establishments have difficulty providing lending institutions suitable forms of collateral. This is so because much of the land owned by them is not officially registered with a land certificate but is only registered in the local village office. This makes it difficult for their land to be used as collateral for a loan. In addition, business inventories are usually not acceptable as collateral. It is important that the present government policy of speeding up the formal registration of land be further accelerated and increasingly alternative kinds of collateral become acceptable to lending institutions. "In Indonesia only 7 percent of land has a clear owner. A lack of recognized property rights ties small businesses to the informal sector and restricts their access to formal services..." (Asian Development Bank, "Best Practice in Creating a Conducive Environment for SME", June 2001, p. 12).

There are several other ways to help to overcome the shortage and unsuitability of the collateral problem. Government owned pawnshops are helping to solve this problem. The encouragement of privately owned pawnshops needs to be considered by the Government. Companies leasing equipment to household establishments can greatly decrease their need to purchase their own machinery and equipment, and also need to be encouraged. The profit-sharing approach of Islamic banking usually directly involves the lender/partner in monitoring the operation of the establishment. It does not require collateral because the lender/partner is an owner of the equipment. However, frequently the high transaction costs for very small investments of this method do not make it feasible. A commonly used alternative method is for the Islamic financial institution to sell the HE a capital good with a mark-up and fixed repayment period; with the lender having the option of taking back the capital good in case of repayment default.

Efforts are now underway to expand the opportunities for lenders to micro and small establishments to have their loans partially guaranteed by a loan guarantee fund. This should somewhat alleviate the lending institutions' strict requirements for collateral. Indonesia has had considerable experience with credit guarantees through the state owned enterprises Perum PKK and PT ASKRINDO.

Business Services to and Policies Directly Affecting HMEs

Supporting policies and other assistance to small grower and graduate household establishments can enhance their major contribution to growth both in terms of increased value-added and productive employment generation. This can be achieved by helping the small growers to become graduates and the graduates to grow faster. By productive employment we mean employment that is productive in terms of the whole society, not just the establishment. Examples of privately productive and socially unproductive employment generation include those in which the social cost of increased pollution from manufacturing outweighs the social benefits, where greater capabilities of the fishing fleet result in overfishing and smaller catches, and where external diseconomies of increased logging in watershed areas, flooding and soil erosion outweigh the gains from the log production.

Liedholm and Mead point out that assistance programmes to small growers and graduates include taking the form of: 1) good macroeconomic policies; 2) education and training programmes to strengthen the human capital of the establishments' workforce; 3) a subsector focus; and 4) a market-based orientation (Liedholm and Mead 1999, p. 101). There is no question that good macroeconomic policies are a very important part of creating a favourable business climate for HMEs and SMEs. This occurs by avoiding frequent unnecessary changes in government policies and relations, keeping the rate of inflation low, smoothening out fluctuations in the exchange rate, decreasing the levels of corruption and unnecessary bureaucratic procedures, ensuring that prices reflect social costs and values, stopping government favouritism towards medium and large enterprises relative to smaller ones, and ensuring a smooth efficient functioning of the legal system including the protection of property rights and the enforcement of business contracts in order to lower transaction costs. Rapidly growing incomes from agriculture of millions of ordinary farmers will provide demand for HMI and SMI products. Continuing improvements and expansion in the rural road network and rural electrification lower the production and transaction costs of rural-based industries and make them more competitive.

Currently some Indonesian laws make it more difficult for females to operate and development businesses than males. For example the Indonesian Marriage Law (No. 1/1974) determines that the husband, as the head of the family, is responsible for supporting his wife. This law supports the practices prioritizing men in formal actions such as the formal organization in business associations, access to credit and training services, as well as the registration of property certificates and business licenses under the name of the husband (Asian Development Bank, "SME Constraints and Needs with Special Focus on Gender Issues", June 2001, p. 9). This law and other laws and regulations hindering the participation of females in business need to be reviewed and improved. It is especially important for the HMIs where females head 45 percent of the establishments. This includes 82 percent of the textile establishments (32) in 1996.

It is more difficult for the Government to supply technical assistance directly to HMEs than to farmers. This is so because there are a greater variety of products. Production processes vary greatly and often the establishments are widely scattered in location. Primary and secondary education, including training in areas such as bookkeeping and marketing, has been shown to be positively related to the productivity of household and small establishments, and deserve continuing emphasis. The Department of Industry and Trade has provided extension type technical services to small manufacturers for many years including the BIPIK programme. Although there have been some success stories, commonly they have not been successful especially when evaluated using a benefit-cost approach. With the decentralization begun in 2002 which transfers the main responsibility for facilitating local industrial development to district level governments (*kabupaten* and *kotamadya*), the capabilities of these local governments to formulate and implement policies and programmes to facilitate the development of HMIs and SMIs need to be increased.

Technical assistance and training can be divided into two types: 1) sub-sector specific and 2) generalized and useful to most types of HMEs. There will probably be few instances where local government delivery of the first type of assistance can be economically justified. This is so because of the wide variety of manufacturing activities with varying needs from those requiring the same type of sub-sector specific technical assistance. However, there will likely be some cases where partial and temporary local government subsidization of some privately delivered services of this type can be economically justified. Some local government subsidization of training in areas such as bookkeeping, marketing, management, and numeracy will be economically justified although it is likely the training will be more efficiently delivered by private and public sector training providers. In the past, government-provided training to small businesses has usually been provided free, often with some financial allowance for participants. This has commonly resulted in a misallocation of the training. It is very important that in most circumstances a fee be charged in order to ensure that those receiving the training value it enough to invest their time and money.

With decentralization the responsibility for delivering public education has also been transferred to district governments, including the establishment and operation of technical schools. The central government is considering transferring some education functions affecting more than one district—such as some technical schools and universities—up to the provincial government level. It is very important that publicly funded primary, secondary, and technical educational services be expanded and improved, because solid educational backgrounds of micro-entrepreneurs contribute to their competence, innovativeness, and flexibility—so important when operating under rapidly changing conditions. Policies on financial services and business services to household and small businesses are gradually emphasizing a market-based orientation. In this way they are more likely to be self-sustaining and efficiently provided and utilized.

There are differing views about the effect of allowing foreign direct investment (FDI) to be directed to small domestic manufacturing establishments. Hill argues that restrictions on FDI by small foreign investors impeded the development of FDI-Small/Medium Enterprise linkages and through this effect hindered the development of domestic enterprises. Until 1994 with Government Regulation 20/1994, foreign investments below one million dollars were either prohibited or denied facilities and this is still true for foreign investments under $250,000 (Hill 2001, p. 254). In contrast Sjaifudian considers that the opening up more to FDI damages the people's economy because it results in sharper competition for them if they are manufacturing similar type products (Sjaifudian 1996, p. 175). Indeed in the past small establishments in the weaving, sugar, rice milling, soft drink, footwear, household utensil and equipment industries have suffered from competition with large establishments (Poot et al. 1990, p. 205), which is not necessarily socially undesirable. However, because in Indonesia the social cost of unskilled labour is often less than the wage rate due to extensive unemployment especially in densely populated areas, it is possible that larger more capital-intensive producers of a product may have lower monetary costs but higher social costs of production than smaller more labour-intensive producers of the product, resulting in a socially undesirable demise of the smaller enterprises through competition. Unfortunately we know very little about where, when, and in what industries this has happened. It is desirable that this matter be investigated so that in those cases where market competition has produced socially undesirable outcomes, corrective measures can be considered.

Foreign companies in Indonesia can also benefit HMEs and SMEs. Sometimes FDI in similar type products will result in more competition for Indonesian establishments of a similar size or larger but result in increased demand for the products produced by the HMEs that are contracted to supply components to them. The use of foreign direct investment in enhancing exporting and importing can be very beneficial to domestic HMEs and SMEs. For example, it may help them develop attractive suitable products for export markets by providing them with technical assistance in design and production and sometimes with finance. Results from Jepara (Sandee et al., 2000) and Bali (Cole 1998) show that foreign direct investment by small foreign enterprises produced extensive benefits of these types for HMEs and SMEs.

It is very important that the dependence of HMEs on micro-retailers for marketing their products be realized. A survey conducted by Artiek Purnawestri in Semarang in mid-1994 found that many goods made by HMEs are hardly ever sold in stores and therefore their sales are very dependent on sales in traditional markets and by other micro-retailers such as sidewalk and itinerant traders. This is because for many of them their quality is variable and they are produced in small quantities that make them less attractive for sale in stores. The following are products made by HMEs which are almost entirely sold in markets and not in stores in Semarang, Central Java: clothing, wooden and rubber footwear, blinds/awnings, winnowing trays, fans, bamboo baskets, bamboo water dippers, wooden vegetable spoons, earthenware stoves, containers, earthenware cooking pots, water containers (*kendi*), stone mortars (*cobek batu*), bamboo flutes, tambourines, paper masks, metal toys, metal mobiles, rubber masks, and cloth dolls. The following products made by HMEs were almost entirely sold in markets and small stores but not in large stores in Semarang: biscuits, peanut and soybean appetizers, brooms from coconut fibre, rice steamers (*dandang*), pans, woks, metal frying utensils, metal stoves, flower pots, hoes, sickles, machetes/chopping knives, axes, knives, necklaces, rings and bracelets, cloth hair bands, wooden betel containers, paper kites, wooden mobiles and board games (*congkak*) (Unpublished results from a survey of markets and stores in Semarang conducted by Dra Artiek Purnawestri in mid-1994 under the guidance of Robert Rice). The AP31 survey in 1991 found that the market share of traditional markets was only 50 percent of all customers (Sjaifudian 1996, p. 175). It is critical that knowledge about the strong linkages between sales by micro-retailers and demand for many types of goods made by HMEs be disseminated to local governments including local parliaments in Indonesia so that they support the establishment and upgrading of traditional markets in order to make them more attractive to shoppers and treat fairly and be generally supportive of the activities of other micro-retailers. This will help to sustain the demand for the products of HMEs and slow down the trend of shoppers switching from micro-sellers to stores and supermarkets.

It is also very important that local government authorities understand the relationships between household and small establishments activities in different sectors. For example, pedicabs commonly supply very useful services to sellers in traditional markets. Therefore, the banning of pedicabs as in Jakarta will certainly decrease the competitiveness of sellers in traditional markets relative to stores. Small river boats are very important in carrying the products of HEs to market in Sumatra and Kalimantan (see Rice 1997, pp. 46–47).

Decentralization in 2001 has created great pressures on district (*kabupaten* and *kotamadya*) governments to increase their revenues through taxes and levies, including taxes on internal trade. Unfortunately many districts have imposed taxes and levies on commerce passing through their territories thus raising the transaction costs of commerce. Such increases in transaction costs are particularly detrimental to HMEs because they inhibit their specialization of production and therefore lower their competitiveness. Government efforts to minimize the adverse effects on decentralization of the competitiveness of household and small establishments merit strong support. (For a discussion of the effects of decentralization on the business climate see Ray 2000 and Ray and Goodpaster 2001.)

It is noted that in an economic democracy (*ekonomi kerakyatan*), as called for in the Garis-Garis Besar Haluan Negara 1999–2004, market driven activities, such as cooperatives and NGOs, must operate but in a fairer manner, and not under the hegemony of the conglomerates. The state controls all the branches of production that are important for the state and that dominate the necessities of life of the masses, because, if they are not controlled by the state, the supreme authority over production will fall into the hands of powerful people and the masses will be oppressed (Mubyarto 2000, pp. 282, 291, 298). We support Mubyarto's proposal for markets operating in a fairer manner. Indonesia's new anti-monopoly Law no. 5/1999 would help to lessen anti-competitive practices with the passage of time. Unfortunately many of the anti-competitive practices are practised by state enterprises and quasi-state establishments, making less state intervention in some instances the solution, not greater state intervention.

Summary

The Main Findings

In this chapter we have identified SIC two-digit food and drinks, textile, wood products, and nonmetallic minerals industries as being the most important HMIs and SMIs located in rural areas and discussed changes in their importance in rural areas and the whole Indonesian economy in terms of their employment and value-added in constant prices from 1986 to 1996 and 1996 to 2000. The development of these industries is very important because in the densely populated rural areas they are a leading sector along with agriculture, with the growth of the trade and services sectors tending to be pulled along behind them. The manufacturing sector has become increasingly important as an employer in rural areas as the number of farmers declined 15 percent from 1985 to 1995.

In spite of government policies favouring larger enterprises, the employment and real value-added of HMIs and SMIs grew rapidly from

1986 to 1996 but somewhat slower than the M/L manufacturing industries. However, in 1996 HMIs and SMIs continued to be of relatively minor importance in terms of value-added—accounting for only about 11 percent of total value-added of manufacturing industries, but accounted for 61 percent of total employment. Assuming that policies are not biased against them in the future, their performance is likely to improve and HMI employment in rural-areas will continue to be an importance source of survival income of otherwise near-landless labourers during the coming decade. SMIs will continue to be important both as providers of productive employment and as seedbeds from which significant numbers of SMEs grow and become M/L enterprises.

This chapter supplements various case studies of the impact of the 1997 economic crisis on individual industries by analyzing the impact of the crisis on HMIs and SMIs at the SIC two-digit level and discussing some factors affecting changes in their competitiveness. Even though some HMIs and SMEs benefited from the economic crisis starting in August 1997, overall they were hard hit as shown by a decrease in the number of their enterprises taken together, employment, and value-added in constant prices of 23 percent, 20 percent, and approximately 26 percent respectively from 1996 to 1998. Household and small manufacturing establishments in the food and drinks industry (31) were particularly hard hit compared with M/L establishments. In general industries producing tradable goods (especially exportables) using non-tradable intermediate inputs benefited from the huge depreciation of the rupiah while industries producing non-tradable goods for the local market using tradable intermediate inputs were badly damaged.[6]

Main Policy Recommendations

We now present briefly the main policy recommendations made above.

1. The changes in the financial system serving household and small establishments being undertaken by the government through the "executing" system deserve to be supported, including the further expansion of the variety of financial institutions serving these establishments into localities where these establishments are presently being underserved.
2. Efforts need to be accelerated to increase the quantity and types of collateral that can be used by small borrowers to obtain loans, including

the acceleration of land registration, the adoption by financial institutions of new forms of collateral for loans, and the development of private pawnshops. In addition decreasing the need for collateral is desirable through the facilitation of the Islamic (Shariah) financial system and companies leasing machinery and equipment to small businesses.
3. Credit guarantee schemes can contribute to the effectiveness of the financial system serving small borrowers, but the temptation must be resisted to guarantee too high a percentage of the loans in order to avoid the moral hazard of the lending institutions inadequately evaluating the creditworthiness of their prospective clients.
4. The Indonesian Marriage Law (No. 1/1974) needs to be reviewed, especially regarding its possible adverse effects on female-managed or -owned businesses.
5. With the decentralization of government functions to district level governments it is important that their capacity to formulate and implement attractive policies and programmes to facilitate the development of household and small establishments be increased. As part of this local governments including local parliaments need to be better informed about the importance of micro-retailers in marketing the products of HMEs and SMEs, so that they support the expansion and improvement of traditional markets and the "fair" treatment of micro-retailers and HMEs/SMEs.
6. Some local government subsidization of training for household and small establishments is attractive but usually the training will be more effectively delivered by the private and public sector training providers. In most cases it is desirable to charge fees for the training in order to ensure that those receiving it value it enough to invest their own time and money. We support the current emphasis on market-based approaches to the provision of financial and business services to household and small businesses because it is likely to result in more self-sustainable and efficiently provided services than delivery by government offices.

High Priority Future Research

Industries classified at the two-digit level include a wide variety of industries at the five-digit level that operate under widely varying conditions including in different localities, and therefore require varying policy and programme interventions. With the recent transfer of much policy making and programme formulation from the central government to district governments, it is very important that the capacity of these local governments to analyze the factors affecting the competitiveness of HMIs and SMIs be enhanced so that local government policies, programmes, projects and activities (PPPAs) affecting them can be improved.

Because of the extensive unemployment of unskilled labour in the densely populated regions of Indonesia—especially disguised unemployment and underemployment, the social cost of unskilled labour is less than the wage rate. Because of this the social cost of production of labour-intensive enterprises can be less than the social cost of production of usually larger capital-intensive enterprises producing the same product, but the labour-intensive enterprises' monetary cost of production will be greater. The latter usually results in the competition between the smaller and larger enterprises eliminating the smaller ones even though their social cost of production is less than the larger enterprises—an undesirable market outcome. Research is needed in Indonesia to determine what, if any, industries are experiencing this undesirable outcome, followed up by policy recommendations to improve the situation.

More research also is needed about incidences when the social productivity of different types of economic activities is less than the private productivity resulting in the market mechanism yielding a greater supply of the activity than is socially desirable. In rural areas this is a result of external diseconomies in the form of pollution and the overexploitation of a commonly-owned resource such as coastal fisheries, rivers and lakes, forests, and pastures. In urban areas it is commonly caused by excessive utilization of public space such as roads, sidewalks, markets, and parks by micro-retailers. It is also important that local government capabilities to analyze these situations and to formulate appropriate PPPAs be strengthened.

Notes

1. In this chapter the Central Statistical Agency (BPS) definition of household and small establishments is used, namely 1–4 workers including the working owner, and 5–19 workers.
2. The villages of Indonesia are classified into rural and urban in census years based on the score of each village taking into account several factors, for

example in 1990 population density, percent of agricultural households, and the availability of urban-related facilities such as school, market, hospital, roads and electricity (*Penduduk Indonesia: Hasil Survey Penduduk Antar Sensus 1995*, p. xxxvii).
3. Disguised unemployment is the number of persons who can be taken away from doing their present tasks to doing other tasks during the whole year without there being a decrease in the output from doing their present tasks. The production does not decrease because the remaining persons work longer hours or their productivity increases per hour worked. There is also extensive seasonal unemployment in rural areas. In some cases, especially when there is a commonly-owned natural resource, such as a state forest, river, lake, coastal fishing area, publicly-owned space, etc., taking away persons results in an increase in production because it results in less overexploitation of the commonly-owned resource. Hill states there are labour surplus conditions in Indonesia which worsened with the economic crisis in 1997 (Hill 2000, p. 205 and 271).
4. The GDP deflator for manufacturing industries without petroleum and gas was used to convert value-added in current prices into 1993 constant prices, with this deflator being 1.0 in 1996, 1.82521 in 1998, and 2.28781 in 2000.
5. These figures should be considered to be approximations because of low accuracy.
6. Tradable goods are goods which are imported and their domestically produced substitutes (importable goods) and goods which are exported (exportable goods).

References

Asian Development Bank. "Best Practice in Creating a Conducive Environment for SME". Policy Discussion Paper no. 1, June 2001. Asian Development Bank SME Development TA: Policy Discussion Papers 2001/2001. Available at http://www.adbtasme.or.id/docs/sme-pp01_e.pdf

Asian Development Bank. "Best Practice in Creating a Providing BDS to SME". Policy Discussion Paper No. 2, June 2001. Asian Development Bank SME Development TA: Policy Discussion Papers 2001/2001.Available at http://www.adbtasme.or.id/docs/sme-pp02_e.pdf

Asian Development Bank. Report and Recommendation of the President to the Board of Directors on Proposed Loans and Technical Assistance Grant to the Republic of Indonesia for the Community Empowerment for Rural Development Project. Manila: Asian Development Bank, September 2000. Available at http://www.adb.org/Documents/RRPs/IND/rrp-L1765.pdf

Asian Development Bank. "SME Constraints and Needs with Special Focus on Gender Issues". Policy Discussion Paper No. 5, June 2001. Asian Development Bank SME Development TA: Policy Discussion Papers 2001/2001. Available at http://www.adbtasme.or.id/docs/sme-pp05_e.pdf

Asian Development Bank. *SME Development TA: Policy Discussion Papers 2001–2002.* Available at http://www.adbtasme.or.id/docs/download_e.htm

Badan Pusat Statistik. *Statistik Indonesia 2000.* Jakarta: Badan Pusat Statistik, 2001.

Badan Pusat Statistik. *Statistik Industri Kecil 1996.* Jakarta: Badan Pusat Statistik, 2000.

Badan Pusat Statistik. *Statistik Industri Kerajinan Rumahtangga 1996.* Jakarta: Badan Pusat Statistik, 2000.

Bank Indonesia. *Annual Report 2001.* Jakarta: Bank Indonesia, 2002.

Berry, Albert and Brian Levy. "Indonesia's Small and Medium-Size Exporters and Their Support Systems". *World Bank Policy Research Working Paper 1402.* Washington, D.C.: The World Bank, 1994.

Berry, Albert, Edgard Rodriguez and Henry Sandee. "Small and Medium Enterprise Dynamics in Indonesia". *Bulletin of Indonesian Economic Studies* 37, no. 3 (2001): 363–84.

Biro Pusat Statistik, *Statistik Industri Besar dan Sedang, Kode Klasifikasi Industri.* Jakarta: Biro Pusat Statistic, 1996.

Blakely, Edward J. *Planning Local Economic Development: Theory and Practice: Second Edition.* Thousand Oaks, California: Sage Publications, 1994.

Canela, Eduardo. *Business Development Services for Small and Medium Enterprises and Cooperatives in Indonesia: Some Key Guidelines and Needs.* Report PEG 36, Jakarta, Indonesia: Partnership for Economic Growth Project, 2000. Available at http://pegasus.or.id under publications.

Center for Economic and Social Studies and The Asia Foundation (eds). *Kekuatan Kolektif Sebagai Strategi Mempercepat Pemberdayaan Usaha Kecil.* Jakarta: Center for Economic and Social Studies and The Asia Foundation, 1999.

Cole, David C., and Betty F. Slade. *Building a Modern Financial System: The Indonesian Experience.* Cambridge, UK: Cambridge U.P., 1996.

Cole, William. "Bali's Garment Export Industry". In *Indonesia's Technological Challenge*, Hal Hill and Thee Kian Wie (eds), pp. 255–78. Singapore: Institute of Southeast Asian Studies, 1998.

Departemen Koperasi, Pengusaha Kecil dan Menengah Republik Indonesia 1999. *Statistik Koperasi, Pengusaha Kecil dan Menengah.* Jakarta: Departemen Koperasi, Pengusaha Kecil dan Menengah Republic Indonesia, 1999.

Hill, Hal. "Small and Medium Enterprises in Indonesia: Old Policy Challenges for a New Administration". *Asian Survey* 41, no. 2 (2001): 248–70.

Hill, Hal. *The Indonesian Economy, 2nd edition.* Cambridge, U.K.: Cambridge University Press, 2000.

Hindrakusuma, Sentanu. "Industri Makanan Olahan Skala Kecil: Globalisasi, Iklim Usaha, dan Kebijakan Yang Berpengaruh". In *Pengembangan Ekonomi Rakyat Dalam Era Globalisasi: Masalah, Peluang, dan Strategi Praktis*, Frida Rustiani (ed.), pp. 189–99. Bandung: Yayasan AKATIGA and YAPIKA, 1996.

Kantor Menteri Negara Urusan Koperasi dan Usaha Kecil dan Menengah Republic Indonesia (MENNEGKOP). *Economic Recovery Acceleration Program Matrix: Program 8: Stimulating the Development of Micro, Small and Medium Businesses*. Prepared by MENNEGKOP for EKUIN, Jakarta: MENNEGKOP, 2000.

Liedholm, Carl and Donald C. Mead. *Small Enterprises and Economic Development: The Dynamics of Micro and Small Enterprises*. London and New York: Routledge, 1999.

Mead, Donald C. and Carl Liedholm. "The Dynamics of Micro and Small Enterprises in Developing Countries". *World Development* 26, no. 1 (1998): 61–74.

Mellor, John W. *The New Economics of Growth: A Strategy for India and the Developing World*. Ithaca, N.Y.: Cornell University Press, 1976.

Mubyarto. *Membangun Sistem Ekonomi*. Yogyakarta: BPFE, 2000.

Penduduk Indonesia: Hasil Survei antar Sensus 1995 (Population of Indonesia: Results of the 1995 Intercensal Population Survey). *Jakarta: Biro Pusat Statistik, 1996.*

Poot, Huib, Arie Kuyvenhoven and Jaap Jansen. *Industrialization and Trade in Indonesia*. Yogyakarta: Gadjah Mada U.P., 1990.

Profil Usaha Kecil dan Menengah Tidak Berbadan Hukum: Sektor Industri Kecil dan Kerajinan Rumahtangga Indonesia, Survei Usaha Terintegrasi 1998. Jakarta: Badan Pusat Statistik, 2000.

Ravicz, R. Marisol. *Searching for Sustainable Microfinance: A Review of Five Indonesian Initiatives*. World Bank Policy Research Working Paper WPS1878, Feb. 28, 1998. Available at http://www.worldbank.org/html/dec/Publications/Workpapers/WPS1800series/wps1878/wps1878.pdf

Ray, David. "National Economic Integrity and the Decentralization Process: Guidelines for Competition and Domestic Trade Policies" Report PEG 41, Jakarta, Indonesia: Partnership for Economic Growth Project, 2000. Available at http://pegasus.or.id under publications.

Ray, David and Gary Goodpaster. "Policies and Institutions to Ensure Free Internal Trade under Decentralization". Report PEG 59, Jakarta, Indonesia: Partnership for Economic Growth Project, 2001. Available at http://pegasus.or.id under publications.

Rice, Robert. "Small Enterprises as an Essential Part of the Indonesian Development Strategy". Report PEG 18, Jakarta, Indonesia: Partnership for Economic Growth Project, 2000. Available at http://pegasus.or.id under publications.

Rice, Robert and Irfan Abullah. "A Comparison of the Development of Small and Medium/Large Indonesian Manufacturing Enterprises from 1986 to 1996 by Sector".
Report PEG 23, Jakarta, Indonesia: Partnership for Economic Growth Project, 2000. Available at http://pegasus.or.id under publications.
Rice, Robert Charles. "The Indonesian Urban Informal Sector: Characteristics and Growth from 1980 to 1990". *Journal of Population* 3, no. 1 (1997), 37–65.
Rice, Robert C., Herustiati, and A. Junaidi. "Factors Affecting the Competitiveness of and Impact of the 1997–98 Monetary Crisis on Selected Small and Medium Manufacturing Industries in Central and West Java". Report PEG 72, Jakarta, Indonesia: Partnership for Economic Growth Project, 2002. Available at http://pegasus.or.id under publications.
Sandee, H, Roos K. Andadari, and Sri Sulandjari. "Small Firm Development during Good Times and Bad: The Jepara Furniture Industry". In *Indonesia in Transition: Social Aspects and Reformasi and Crisis*, Chris Manning and Peter van Diermen (eds), pp. 184–98. Singapore: Institute of Southeast Asian Studies, 2000.
Saragih, Bungaran. *Agribisnis: Paradigma Baru Pembangunan Ekonomi Berbasis Pertanian*. Bogor, Indonesia: PT Surveyor Indonesia and Lembaga Penelitian Institut Pertanian Bogor, 1998.
Sjaifudian, Hetifah. "Analisis Kebijakan Pengembangan Ekonomi Rakyat". In *Pengembangan Ekonomi Rakyat Dalam Era Globalisasi: Masalah, Peluang, dan Strategi Praktis*, Frida Rustiani (ed.), pp. 171–88. Bandung: Yayasan AKATIGA and YAPIKA, 1996.
Tambunan, Tulus. *Reformasi Industrialisasi Perdesaan*. Jakarta: Media Ekonomi Publishing, 1999.
Thee Kian Wie. "The Impact of the Economic Crisis on Indonesia's Manufacturing Sector". *The Developing Economies* 38, no. 4 (2000): 421–53.
Tim Usaha Kecil. *Studi Monitoring Dampak Krisis Terhadap Usaha Kecil (Sumatera Utara, Sulawesi Utara, Jawa Barat, Jawa Tengah, dan DI Yogyakarta*. Bandung: AKATIGA, 1999.
Timberg, Thomas. "Strategy of Financing Small and Medium Enterprises in a New Economic Environment". Report PEG 25, Jakarta, Indonesia: Partnership for Economic Growth Project, 2000. Available at http://pegasus.or.id under publications.
Urata, Shujiro. *Policy Recommendations for SME Promotion in Indonesia*. Jakarta: Japan International Cooperation Agency, 2000.
van Diermen, Peter (ed.). *SME Policy in Indonesia: Towards a New Agenda*. Papers from the National Workshop on Small and Medium Enterprise (SME) Development held in Jakarta on 8 and 9 December 1999. The workshop was convened by the Asian Development Bank, World Bank, BAPPENAS, and

the International Labour Organization, and held at the request of the Indonesian Government. Jakarta: 2000.

Weijland, Hermine. "Microenterprise Clusters in Rural Indonesia: Industrial Seedbed and Policy Target". *World Development* 27, no. 9 (1999): 1515–30.

White, Benjamin. "Economic Diversification and Agrarian Change in Rural Java, 1900–1990". In *In the Shadow of Agriculture*, Paul Alexander, Peter Boomgaard and Benjamin White (eds), pp. 41–69. Amsterdam: Royal Tropical Institute, 1991.

PART II

Entrepreneurship, Gender and Mobility Issues

5
INTERNATIONAL LABOUR MIGRATION AND RURAL DYNAMICS:
A Study of Flores, East Nusa Tenggara

Graeme Hugo

Introduction

Although international labour migration is occurring on a large scale in Indonesia with substantially more than a million workers officially deployed overseas and at least that number illegally working in other nations, its impact on the overall economy in a country of almost 200 million people, while not insignificant, is limited. However, the effects of this movement are strongly spatially concentrated within particular regions and communities, especially rural communities, from which labour migrants are disproportionately recruited. In such regions the impacts are substantial. In a context where increasing attention is being paid by policy makers in less developed economies to widening inter-regional inequalities and the need to supplement sectoral economic development strategies with regional development initiatives, such spatially focused economic impacts are of particular significance. In the meagre body of literature relating to economic effects of labour migration upon origin countries in Asia however, the bulk of analysis has been conducted at the national and individual levels of analysis while regional and community effects have been neglected.

The present paper seeks to summarize and evaluate evidence from a limited number of rural communities in the province of East Nusatenggara (NTT) in Eastern Indonesia, which have experienced significant outmigration of workers who are employed overseas on a legal, and especially illegal, basis. The regional and local economic impacts considered relate both to the 'passive' impacts of the loss of human capital on the local economy, which the emigration represents as well as the more 'active' effects of the injection of remittances into the local economy. It is found that when such a regional or community level of analysis is adopted the effects of this emigration are seen to be considerable. This is especially the case in areas which have limited local development potential or resources and which are lagging economically. Indeed, such areas are disproportionately represented among the origin areas of overseas contract workers (OCWs). There is a clear recognition of this not only within the communities affected but also among local regional officials and planners. However, nationally formulated development policies, programmes and strategies often not only do not take account of these effects but also in some cases hamper the full potential benefits to be realised. While all of the economic impacts are not beneficial to regions and communities, it is clear that international labour migration offers one of the few avenues open to lagging areas to obtain and invest capital in the local area.

This chapter explores some of these issues in one of Indonesia's poorest rural regions—the East Flores region of East Nusatenggara province. This is one of the main origins of international labour migrants leaving Indonesia for Malaysia. The chapter summarizes some of the major demographic, social and economic effects of the movement on rural communities in the region with a particular focus on a single community.[1] In this area, labour migration has become the basis of the economy of communities through the effects of remittances sent back by OCWs. Material from secondary data collections, a questionnaire survey and qualitative observation in the study area are used to examine the impacts of labour migration.

International Labour Migration in Indonesia

As one of the world's major labour surplus economies it is not surprising that Indonesia is also one of the main global suppliers of international migrant labour (Hugo 1995a). Although it was later than many other Asian labour surplus nations in entering the global market for OCWs there are over 2 million Indonesians currently working overseas (Hugo

2000a). It is difficult, however to be clear about the extent of international labour migration out of Indonesia since OCWs that officially register with the Department of Labour and Transmigration (*Depnakertrans*) represent only part (and probably a minority part) of the total movement.[2] Nevertheless, Table 5.1 shows that the official movement increased rapidly during the 1990s, especially following the onset of the crisis in 1997 (Hugo 1999).

The Middle East (especially Saudi Arabia) and Malaysia are the main destinations but in recent years the number going to Singapore, Hong Kong, Taiwan and some other destinations has become important. For each of the legal flows of workers there are also undocumented movements. In many cases undocumented movement is cheaper and quicker than going through official channels. The largest undocumented flow, indeed probably the second largest such flow in the world to that between Mexico and the United States, is between Indonesia and both Peninsular and East Malaysia (Hugo 2000b). Despite efforts to control the flow from the Malaysian end (Kassim 2002) and some regularization of illegal migrants, the undocumented flow has continued. One of the major flows of movement to Malaysia, especially East Malaysia, has been from East Nusatenggara (and especially East Flores).

Even after taking full account of clandestine migration it is clear that international migration out of Indonesia is not occurring on as large a numerical or relative scale as is the case in the Philippines. It is estimated that in 2002 some 7 million Filipinos were working overseas and in 1999 they remitted US$6.8 billion through formal channels—equivalent to a quarter of total government planned expenditure (Go 2002). Table 5.2 shows that in relation to exports and imports the total official remittances of OCWs is a much smaller proportion in Indonesia than is the case with the Philippines. However, it is interesting to note the trend in the table toward remittances increasing their absolute and relative significance.

In assessing the developmental impact of international labour migration in a large and diverse nation such as Indonesia it is of crucial importance to recognize that migrant workers are not a random representative cross section of Indonesian workers. They are selectively drawn from particular groups and areas. This is predominantly due to the significance of chain migration and the fact that once a migration network is established it facilitates and encourages further movement along that network. As a result the effects of international labour migration are concentrated in particular regions of the country and as a result are amplified in those

TABLE 5.1
Number of Indonesian Overseas Workers Processed by the Ministry of Manpower, 1969–2001

Year (Single Year)	Middle East No.	%	Malaysia/ Singapore No.	%	Other No.	%	Total No.	Percent Change Over Previous Year	Sex Ratio (Males/ 100 Females)
2001*	116,597	40	108,314	37	70,091	24	295,002	na	23
2000	128,975	30	217,407	50	88,837	20	435,219	+2	46
1999	154,327	36	204,006	48	69,286	16	427,619	na	41
1999–2000	153,890	38	187,643	46	62,990	16	404,523	−2	44
1998–99	179,521	44	173,995	42	58,153	14	411,609	+75	28
1997–98	131,734	56	71,735	30	31,806	14	235,275	−55	20
1996–97	135,336	26	328,991	64	52,942	10	517,269***	328	79
1995–96	48,298	40	46,891	39	25,707	21	120,896	−31	48
1994–95	99,661	57	57,390	33	19,136	11	176,187	10	32
1977							3,675		

Five Year Planning Periods:		Target	Total Deployed
Repelita VII:	1999–2003**	none set	943,286
Repelita VI:	1994–99	1,250,000	1,461,236
Repelita V:	1989–94	500,000	652,272
Repelita IV:	1984–89	225,000	292,262
Repelita III:	1979–84	100,000	96,410
Repelita II:	1974–79	none set	17,042
Repelita I:	1969–74	none set	5,624

* To 30 November 2001
** 1 January 1999 to 30 April 2001.
*** Year in which 300,000+ Malaysian labour migrants were regularised (194,343 males and 127,413 females).

Note: In 2000 the Indonesian government transferred to a calendar year system of accounting from previously using 1 April–31 March.

Source: Suyono 1981; Singhanetra-Renard 1986, p. 52; Pusat Penelitian Kependudukan, Universitas Gadjah Mada 1986, 2; AKAN Offices, Bandung and Jakarta; AKAN (Antar Kerja Antar Negara); Departemen Tenaga Kerja, Republic of Indonesia 1998, p. 14

TABLE 5.2
Main Southeast Asian Labour Exporting Countries: Workers' Remittances Relative to Exports and Imports (US$ million, 1980-99)

Country	Years	Workers' Remittances	Total Merchandise		R X	R M
			Exports (X)	Imports (M)		
Indonesia	1980	33	21,908	10,834	0.1	0.3
	1992	264	33,815	27,280	0.8	1.0
	1997	1,261	63,238	62,830	2.0	2.0
	1998	1,252	48,848	27,337	2.6	4.6
	1999	1,295	55,741	42,071	2.3	3.1
Philippines	1980	421	5,744	8,295	7.3	5.0
	1992	2,222	9,790	15,465	22.7	14.4
	1997	5,742	40,365	50,477	14.2	11.4
	1999	6,795	39,012	36,767	17.4	18.5

Source: Hugo 1995a; Battistella and Asis 1999; Asian *Migration News* 30 June 1999; World Bank 2000 and 2001; Soeprobo 2002, 5; Go 2002, p. 12

areas. Whereas the impact of international labour migration at the national level is limited in Indonesia, it is of significance in some regions and in many communities (Hugo 2000b).

Since the bulk of the outflow from the study area (the *kabupaten* of East Flores in the province of East Nusatenggara) is illegal, it is not possible to directly document the origins and destinations of emigrants. However, it is clear that within the province the flows tend to come not just from particular regions within the province but particular villages within those regions.

This can be demonstrated with respect to a number of 'indirect' indicators. Between the 1980 and 1990 censuses, the population of East Flores increased by only 0.31 percent per annum compared with 1.79 percent for the province as a whole and 1.98 percent for Indonesia. This differential has increased over the years with the respective population growth rates for 1961–71 being 1.71, 1.57 and 2.1 percent per annum and for 1971–80 being 1.27, 1.95 and 2.37. Between the 1990 census and the 1995 Intercensal Survey the annual population growth rate in East Flores was 0.23 compared with 1.82 percent in East Nusatenggara and 1.67

percent in Indonesia as a whole. The bulk of this difference is due to international migration. At the 1990 census there were only 78 males for every 100 females in East Flores whereas the sex ratio for the entire province was 98.4. Indeed in several *kecamatan* (subdistricts) of East Flores, sex ratios of below 50 were recorded (Hugo 2000b, p. 105). Also at the 1990 census, one third of all households in East Flores were female-headed compared with 11.8 percent for the entire province. This is a reflection of the large scale of movement out of East Flores since the movement is highly selective of men, although increasingly women are becoming involved.

Fieldwork in Flores and discussions with a number of key informants allowed the areas with large numbers of illegal overseas contract workers (mostly in Sabah) to be identified and are mapped in Figure 5.1.

In fact, analysis of population growth in each *kecamatan* in East Flores over the 1980–90 intercensal period shows that in no area did population grow at above the average for either Indonesia as a whole or NTT as a whole, indicating that all areas experienced net migration losses. This is

FIGURE 5.1
East Flores: Main Areas of Origin of
Labour Migrants to Sabah

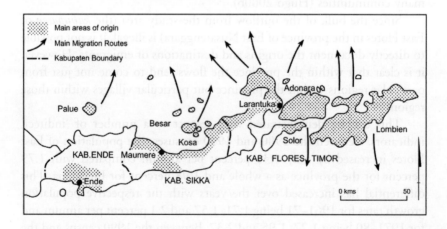

Source: Kapioru 1995 and Field Consultation

least evident in the only substantial urban area in the *kecamatan,* the capital of Larantuka. However six *kecamatan* actually recorded absolute declines in their population between 1980 and 1990—certainly a rare occurrence in Indonesia.

There is little doubt that although there is significant outmigration from East Flores to other parts of Indonesia, the bulk of the decline is due to migration to Sabah. It is indicative of two significant trends with respect to this migration. First temporary labour migration is increasing substantially in scale so that at the census large numbers of usual residents are absent. Second, the incidence of East Flores people settling permanently in Sabah and taking Malaysian citizenship is increasing. For example among a group of 118 East Flores people deported from East Malaysia in late 1995 for not having correct documents some 46 were classified as head of households and 72 as their dependents.[3] This signifies a substantial amount of family migration as compared with earlier years when the movement was overwhelmingly of young males migrating as single persons.

It is extremely difficult to arrive at an estimate of either the stock or flow of migrants in these cases. Not only because of the undocumented nature of the movement but because working in Sabah has become part of the way of life in these villages where such movement in some cases goes back to the 1940s. It has come to be expected behaviour of young men and is almost a rite of passage to adulthood for males. Moreover there is a great deal of coming and going of the migrants. In fieldwork, several villages were identified in such areas as Adonara, Tanjung Bunga and Lomblen where each household had at least one person who was or had been an OCW. While work is continuing on making estimates of the numbers involved in the migration, it would seem that a minimum figure would be around 30,000. From our fieldwork it would appear that up to 100,000 workers from the entire province of East Nusatenggara are working overseas. Of course, in terms of development impact this is considerable. This is so because the workers are from particular areas but also because the entire household of origin feels the impact. This would then entail in total more than half a million persons or 16 percent of the province's population. However while this must remain speculative, almost all households in the areas shown in Figure 5.1 are directly affected and it would seem that around a third of all households in *kabupaten* Flores Timur are also being directly affected by the migration while very large numbers are also leaving from *kabupaten* Sikka and Ende.

East Nusatenggara: The Context of Migration

From Dutch colonial times, East Nusatenggara has been depicted as a 'problem area' (Ormeling 1957, p. 5). Assessments of regional development in Indonesia's 27 provinces invariably have East Nusatenggara at or near the bottom of the rankings. The province is usually depicted in problem terms—having the highest incidence of poverty in Indonesia, the greatest incidence of low nutrition and the most frequent incidence of major natural disasters of which the 1992 Flores earthquake and tsunami are the most recent. For example an authoritative review (Barlow et al. 1990, p. 5) began as follows:

> The province of Nusatenggara has one of the smallest average incomes per head in Indonesia. It is poorly endowed with natural resources, has a low rainfall and long dry season and a population of over 3 million people pressing heavily on available land. Over-exploitation and consequent degradation of the land are widespread.

While there is debate about the measurement of poverty in Indonesia, NTT always appears at or near the bottom of provinces ranked according to prosperity. For example, the Central Bureau of Statistics in Indonesia developed an index used to identify villages, which can be designated poor and hence become eligible for a special presidential programme of assistance (Biro Pusat Statistik, 1992). In 1990, some 683 *desa* of the 1,723 in NTT (39.6 percent) were classified as being in poverty according to this index.

In an analysis of regional development in Indonesia, Hill and Weideman (1989, p. 5) point out that the least developed areas are in Eastern Indonesia, which, partly due to their remoteness from the centre of decision-making in Jakarta, have been neglected by the central government. Hence provinces of Eastern Indonesia have low levels of development and this is reflected in Regional Gross Domestic Product (RGDP) data. NTT has the lowest RGDP per capita of all provinces and it has been only 40 percent of the national figure over the last decade (Hugo 1995b, p. 47).

Table 5.3 profiles key demographic and economic features of East Nusatenggara and East Flores. In terms of development and labour surplus it is significantly worse off than the nation.

Despite its rapid rate of economic growth, GDP per capita is little more than a third of the national figure. Its workforce is growing twice as fast as the national population and the concentration of workers in the agricultural and informal sectors is much greater than in Indonesia as a

TABLE 5.3
East Nusatenggara and East Flores:
Major Demographic and Economic Characteristics

	Year	East Nusatenggara	East Flores
Total Population	1997	3,577,053	270,214
Annual Population Growth Rate (%)	1990–95	1.82	0.23
No. of Children Ever Born to Women 45–49	1997	5.02	3.79
Life Expectancy at Birth (Years)	1990	58.6	58.0
Percent Living in Urban Areas	1995	13.9	8.3
Average per Capita Income US$	1996	366	276
Annual Rate of Economic Growth (%)	1996	8.7	8.5
Economically Active Population	1997	1,802,712	133,424
Male Participation Rate	1997	75.5	73.1
Female Participation Rate	1997	57.5	56.7
Annual Rate of Growth of Welfare	1996-97	5.1	6.4
Percent Employed in Primary Industry	1997	78.3	76.0
Percent Employed in Informal Sector	1997	88.6	87.8
Percent Unemployed	1997	1.6	1.3
Percent Underemployed	1997	53.1	67.2

Source: Kantor Statistik Nusa Tenggara Timur. Nusa Tenggara Timur Dalam Angka 1997 (Nusa Tenggara Timur in Figures 1997). Nusa Tenggara Timur: Kantor Statistik, Kupang, 1998.

whole. Unemployment is low because the extent of poverty is such that people simply cannot afford to be unemployed, but more than a half of workers are underemployed.

The underdeveloped situation in NTT is evident also in the human resources situation. Despite massive improvements in education in Indonesia as a whole, 21.9 percent of the province's adults are illiterate compared with 16 percent in the nation as a whole. Overall levels of education are lower in NTT than in the rest of Indonesia, especially for males with some 18.1 percent of adult males and 27.9 percent of adult females having no schooling compared with 12.2 and 25.4 percent nationally. Some 20.7 percent of males have experienced secondary school or above education compared with 31.3 percent nationally while the comparable figures for females were 13 and 21.6 percent in 1990.

The situation in *kabupaten* East Flores is in general poorer than the province of East Nusatenggara partly due to its limited natural resources but especially to its isolation. Limited transport connections and lack of investment (both public and private) have meant that local economic development has been quite limited despite some significant possibilities for development (Hugo 1995c, Chapter 6). GDP per capita in East Flores is only four fifths the average for the province and was around US$276 per year in 1996. In every year between 1979 and 1997 economic growth was slower in East Flores than in NTT. It is apparent from an examination of the data in Table 5.3 that East Flores is one of the poorest and least developed areas within a province which is one of the poorest and least developed in the nation.

East Nusatenggara and the East Flores region within it represent a classic peripheral region in the core-periphery model of regional development. The peripheral nature of the region may also be exacerbated by the fact that they are quite different in terms of ethnicity and religion to the centre in Java. The province of NTT consistently receives less than a proportionate (in relation to its population) share of national development expenditure and private and public investment funds. For example, of the routine and development budgets substantially less than half of Eastern Indonesia's population share (15 percent) comes to the region which incidentally has 40 percent of the national land area. Java with 60 percent of the population commands 77 percent of the total budget. In addition over the 1970–90 period Indonesian banks invested only 3.5 percent of their funds in Eastern Indonesia, while less than 8 percent of foreign and domestic investment was in the region (compared with 60 percent in Jakarta alone) Sondakh (1995, pp. 141–42).

Despite Indonesia's significant economic growth in the last quarter of the century NTT has remained a lagging region. Hill (1988, p. 25) for example has pointed out:

> There are some areas however, where the high rate of growth at the national level has had little local impact especially in Eastern Indonesia and the desperately poor provinces of the Nusatenggara region east of Bali. Far from major centers of commerce and lacking any substantial resources, these mainly dry and infertile islands have been neglected by most Jakarta administrators before and after independence. The result is continued grinding poverty.

Although there have been some improvements, Hill's analysis remains largely correct.

Demographic Effects of International Labour Migration in East Flores

The demographic impact of international labour migration in East Flores has been substantial. Figure 5.2 shows that not only is the current rate of population growth in the *kabupaten* only 13.8 percent of the national level, there are six *kecamatan* which have actually experienced a population decline in the 1990s.

This is very much a result of the high level of emigration. Moreover, as was demonstrated earlier, the male selectivity of the emigration has resulted in very low sex ratios and high incidence of female-headed households in the region. Figure 5.3 shows that several *kecamatan* in East Flores have very low sex ratios as a result of the absence of male migrants. In all East Flores *kecamatan*, females substantially outnumber males. In 1997 there were four males for every five females. In East Nusatenggara males outnumber females.

FIGURE 5.2
East Flores: Population Growth by *Kecamatan*, 1990–97

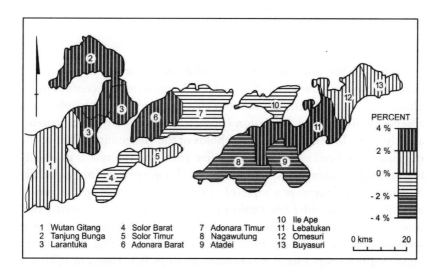

Source: Kantor Statistik Nusa Tenggara Timur. Nusa Tenggara Timur Dalam Angka 1997 (Nusa Tenggara Timur in Figures 1997). Nusa Tenggara Timur: Kantor Statistik, Kupang, 1998 and Kantor Statistik Nusa Tenggara Timur. Nusa Tenggara Timur Dalam Angka 1992 (Nusa Tenggara Timur in Figures 1992). Nusa Tenggara Timur: Kantor Statistik, Kupang, 1993.

FIGURE 5.3
East Flores: Sex Ratios by *Kecamatan*, 1997

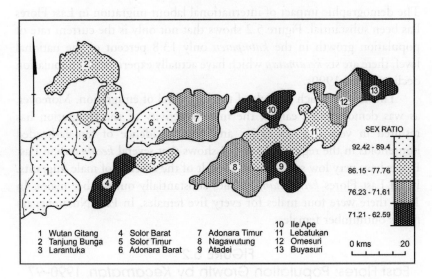

Source: Kantor Statistik Nusa Tenggara Timur 1997

What are the impacts of these imbalances? Some will be considered later in examining the social effects of migration on village communities. However, it is important to point out that most migrations involve long absences and extended separation between spouses and between parents and children. In the surveyed households of the village survey half of the migrants have been away more than five years and the rate is especially high among migrant males. The prolonged absence of migrants, especially husbands and fathers, is a topic of considerable concern in the survey area. It places considerable strain on marriages and it is reported that some men and, to lesser extent, women have taken an extra or substitute spouse in Malaysia. In the early 1990s concern over this issue was so great that there was a local government move in East Flores to initiate a transmigration scheme to resettle the wives and families of men working in Malaysia to East Kalimantan so that they could visit more frequently. This however did not gain any local acceptance because it is apparent that the local matrix of extended family, community and church support is an important source of support to the women left behind. This has been studied in some detail by Graham (1997, p. 2). In her study of a rural community of East Flores she explains:

> ...long-term labour migrants may arrive back in the village after an extended absence, but then just for a social visit. Sometimes such a man would be accompanied by his Malaysian wife and children, apparently to the surprise of his parents and siblings and even though the village woman to whom he had been betrothed when he went away was still waiting for him. Or to be more precise: perhaps, as some said, she had been obliged to wait by the man's clan brothers, who had after all contributed to the bride wealth that secured her fecundity on his behalf. Whatever its source, this loyalty may cost a woman dearly if her own child bearing years slipped away as she waited.

She further describes how some female villagers are unfaithful to absent betrothed male migrants. After saving sufficient funds to build or purchase a house, it is not uncommon for a migrant to return only to find his intended wife with another.

The families of absent migrants in the surveyed village were asked if the absence of their migrant family had a negative effect on bringing up the children and most migrant families consider that the absence of migrants has not affected bringing up the children. Nevertheless, Graham (1997, p. 3) explains:

> Formally married or not, young women in the village frequently face the experience of carrying a child to term and giving birth without the assistance, financial or otherwise, of the baby's father. Indeed as soon as the couple's first child is conceived many a young father-to-be leaves for Malaysia for a period of two to three years. Young women who lose a child in its infancy in these circumstances are sometimes doubly distressed by the fact that the father has never seen the child and by the apprehension that he may suspect they had not cared for it properly in his absence.

A report in the *Kupang Post*, the main newspaper in East Nusatenggara (23rd October 1997) reported that around 254 residents of Desa Ndetundora II in Kecamatan Ende in Flores had sought to earn their income in Malaysia over the 1995–97 three year period. Of these around 200 had left a wife and children in the village. The secretary of the village indicated that the failure of some husbands and fathers to return to the village constituted a significant problem in the village. Indeed many had not even sent back any news.

Graham (1997, p. 3) points to two sources of opposition to labour migration in the village she studied in East Flores. The Catholic Church locally has come out strongly against the migration because of the social disruption it causes. Labour migration is seen to disrupt Christian family life in Flores. The East Flores regency officials are also often against the illegal migration partly because it is out of their control but also partly because it undermines local attempts to achieve regional development.

It is apparent that the low rates of population growth in East Nusatenggara and East Flores compared with Indonesia are driven predominantly by migration. Indeed, at the time of the 1990 census, NTT had a Total Fertility Rate (TFR)[4] of 4.6 compared with 2.9 for Indonesia, indicating at that stage that NTT women on average had two more children than Indonesian women in general. However, it is interesting to consider the possible effects of labour migration on fertility. As indicated earlier, much of the labour migration out of the study involves substantial periods of separation of husbands and wives. This would seem to be an explanation for a consistent pattern of lower fertility in East Flores compared with the whole province. Table 5.4 shows that this has been a consistent pattern over 20 years.

There are a significantly smaller number of children among East Flores women than East Nusatenggara women generally from the age of 25 onwards. The use of contraceptives is much lower in East Flores than in the whole province. This would suggest that, other things being equal, East Flores fertility would be higher than the province. Hence there is little

TABLE 5.4
East Nusatenggara and East Flores: Fertility, 1976–97

	East Nusatenggara	East Flores	Difference (%)
TFR 1976–79	5.540	4.309	−22.2
TFR 1980–84	4.720	3.740	−20.8
TFR 1982–86	4.360	3.150	−27.8
No. Children Women 45–49			
1994	5.03	4.44	−11.7
1996	5.09	4.22	−17.1
1997	5.02	3.79	−24.5

Source: Kantor Statistik NTT 1989, 1995a, 1997, 1999

doubt that the prolonged absence of spouses, especially men, has resulted in a depressing of fertility levels.

A final demographic impact of labour migration is evident in age structure. Figure 5.4 shows that the East Flores age structure bears the imprint of labour migration with a cavity among males in the working age groups.

It is also interesting to note the undercutting of the age pyramid in the 0–4 age group reflecting the low level of fertility.

Migration has widened the roles of women left at home in the village. Their role in family decision-making has increased. They do household budgeting and make decisions about the schooling of children and agriculture and animal husbandry. In addition their community involvement has undoubtedly increased (Kapioru 1995). It may be that this increased independence is being asserted in the younger generation of women who are migrating independently to Sabah to seek work. While migration has an impact on family decision-making, the absence of a migrant family member led to a major change in only a quarter of the families. However there is a striking gender differential here. A third of the families with absent male migrants indicated the absence had influenced family decision-

FIGURE 5.4
East Flores: Age-Sex Structure, 1990

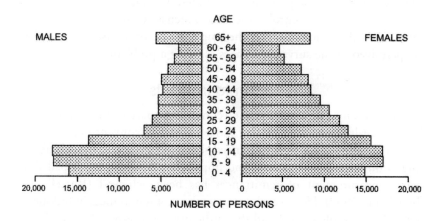

Source: Kantor Statistik Flores Timur. East Flores Dalam Angka 1994. Larantuka: Kantor Statistik, 1995.

making whereas only a single household was affected by the departure of a female migrant.

There is movement of Indonesian prostitutes in to East Malaysia to meet the demands created by Indonesian male migrants. It would seem however that the bulk of the prostitutes from Indonesia to Sabah come from Java (Jones 1996, p. 18) especially East Java. There are little data on the trafficking of Indonesian girls and women into Malaysia but Jones (1996, p. 18) maintains that there has been an increase in such trafficking. However, Graham (1997, p. 4) believes that it is chain migration which saves the bulk of such East Flores women from such a fate:

> By the time women joined the migration stream from Flores to Sabah, they were generally traveling in the company of groups of men (mostly husbands or clansmen) at least some of who had usually made the trip before and were thereby aware of its perils and pitfalls. Furthermore, women traveling from Flores to Sabah often set out to join men folk (usually brothers and husbands) already settled there.

Nevertheless it is clear that a few East Flores women fall prey to traffickers.

The role of women has changed in East Flores as a result of the heavy migration to Sabah. This has not only come about as a result of women themselves participating in migration but also because of their changed roles due to the absence of a father, brother or husband. Graham (1997, p. 6) explains that traditionally women did not work on the gardens which produce local food. However, as a result of the migration of men to Malaysia, women are required to take on these agricultural tasks. Moreover, women gain de facto control of the land of men away in Malaysia (Graham 1997, p. 8). As indicated earlier the long absences of spouses and partners are perceived in the surveyed villages as being a problem.

Economic Impacts

The key to any assessment of the economic impact of migration is the flow of wealth generated by that movement. The conventional wisdom of two decades ago that remittances generated by international labour migration were trivial in scale and impact has largely been dispelled as better measurement of remittances has been achieved (Russell and Teitelbaum 1992). However the measurement of remittances in Indonesia generally is problematical and this difficulty is exacerbated in the NTT context by the illegality of the movement, the isolation of the home area and the long history of remitting money to the area through non-formal traditional channels.

The bulk of OCWs from East Flores work in the area between Tawau and Sandakan in Sabah although they are also present in Kota Kinabalu. Most of the OCWs are manual labourers on plantations and in forestry, while there are many who are *penjaga* (guards) and police. There has obviously been a 'maturing' of the migration flow in recent years with the absolute dominance of the movement by males being reduced. Men who have settled more or less permanently in Sabah and obtained Malaysia citizenship have brought their wives and families from East Flores to Sabah. In addition, however, women are beginning to participate in the contract labour migration and obtain work in Sabah as cooks, domestic workers and in plywood factories. Timber processing factories tend to provide *asrama* (barracks) for their workers while most other OCWs live in *pondok* (rented crowded rooms shared by groups of migrants often from the same area). At the time of the survey, wages in Malaysia tended to be around RM300–400 per month[5] (around the average annual income in NTT) although in saw milling workers were paid up to RM1,000 per month. East Flores workers have gained a reputation for being diligent and hardworking in Sabah. Hence the potential for remittance sending among East Flores workers in Sabah is considerable.

An estimation of the scale of remittances associated with the largely illegal OCW migration from NTT is clearly impossible. However, a local newspaper report in 1993 quoted the BRI (Bank Rakyat Indonesia) as estimating that Rp. 8–9 billion was remitted annually through that bank in the outmigration regions. This is equivalent to around US$4 million. Moreover despite the essentially rural nature of the two major outmigration *kabupaten* (Sikka and East Flores) they account for almost a quarter of the money being deposited in BRI in the province while only having 15 percent of the total population.

There is no consolidated information on the flow of remittances into the studied region, but discussions with officials of the closest bank to the studied village revealed that the inflow of remittances has increased both rapidly and consistently since the early 1980s. The average number of such transfers received by Bank Rakyat Indonesia each day in East Flores varies between six and twelve. In addition, a rough perusal of the data for a limited time period indicates an average of RM1,000–RM2,000 or US$600 (almost twice the annual per capita income of the region) is sent each time.

Occasionally even larger amounts are sent. Migrants usually send the transfers to their wives and other family members but there are cases where individuals accumulate remittances in their own accounts. One case study for example had Rp. 42 million (US$8,100) in his account. From the above it would appear that just through one bank in one small region in NTT, there is around US$5,400 coming in from Malaysia each day or almost US$1.5 million annually. Since this is very preliminary it must be treated with caution, especially since it would represent only the very smallest tip of the iceberg of all remittances received in the East Flores region. It is perhaps put in perspective by the fact that the entire budget of the East Flores government in 1993/1994 was US$31,550.

The local Department of Labour office in Larantuka (East Flores) has a scheme with labour suppliers for official workers to remit money back to the region through the company. In 1995 the average amount remitted under this scheme was Rp. 2.5 million (US$1,200). If this is indicative, and there is every reason from discussions with other key informants to suggest that it is, it would mean that each migrant is sending back around five times the average annual income of the region each year.

If we adopt a figure of 30,000 workers from East Flores being deployed overseas and each remitting around US$1,000 per year the amount of money flowing into the province would be of the order of US$30 million per year or US$10 per head of resident population. This conservative estimate of the scale of remittances would see them represent about three quarters the size of the total receipts of the provincial government in 1993–94. Moreover if one assumes that around two thirds of the province's international migrant workers come from East Flores, the flow generated would be US$20 million per year—equivalent to twice the total budget of the *kabupaten* administration (Kantor Statistik Nusatenggara Timur 1995a). Hence, while there is a great deal of uncertainty about the precise scale of remittances it would appear that they do represent *the* major financial flow from the outside into NTT and especially into East Flores. The remittances received in the surveyed village are analyzed in detail elsewhere (Hugo 1998, pp. 88–101). It shows that migrant workers bring back more money than they send. Overall, it was found that more than a quarter of women (29.4 percent) and almost a quarter of male migrants (23.1 percent) provide more than Rp. 3 million (US$6,000) for their villages of origin and a further fifth provide between Rp. 2 and 3 million (US$4,000 and 6,000). Moreover, a further 28 percent provide between Rp. 1 and 2 million (US$2,000 and 4,000).

The impact of remittances on family and village economies is immediately apparent when one enters rural communities in NTT with large numbers of OCWs. Houses tend to be made of brick or stone rather than wood or *atap* and have glass windows, televisions and other modern appliances and there is an air of prosperity despite the often relatively poor agricultural potential of the areas of origin. Many OCWs return with valuable high cost goods. For example, 68 percent of a sample of returned OCWs in Yogyakarta, West and Central Java had brought back goods like radios, televisions, motorcycles and furniture with them (Mantra, Kasnawi and Sukamandi 1986). In East Flores the contemporary symbol of success in migration is the purchase of a *parabola* or dish to receive satellite television from Hong Kong, Malaysia and Australia, as well as Indonesia. Conventional television in these remote areas is very limited and satellite television opens up a whole new world. The cost of installation of a *parabola* is Rp. 1.35 million (US$675 or almost three times the local average annual income) but one finds them dotted all around villages with substantial numbers of migrants in Sabah.

The impact of expenditure of remittances on housing is evident. For example, whereas 18.2 percent of NTT households had houses with brick walls this applied to 40 percent in East Flores and 13.2 percent had electricity compared with 1.6 percent in the province. These indicators are all the more striking because the NTT figures include substantial urban areas like Kupang, but East Flores has only very limited urban development. The expenditure of remittances on electricity generating facilities for villages not yet included in the national grid is also evident with 13.2 percent of East Flores houses having such electricity compared with 1.6 percent province wide. Indeed groups of migrants often club together to pay for village electricity generating facilities, extension wiring etc. The high levels of television ownership also reflect the impact of remittances in these rural areas. Also, a higher proportion of householders in East Flores had cement floors than East Nusatenggara as a whole. Moreover, a substantially higher proportion of the East Flores population read newspapers and listened to the radio than was the case for the province as a whole. It is clear from the few available studies on the use of remittances in Flores that a significant amount of remittance income is spent on building or substantially renovating houses (Hugo 1995b). The results of one such study are presented in Table 5.5.

The repaying of debts is an important element since very few migrant workers (at least those going for the first time) have the necessary finances

TABLE 5.5
Desa Nelereren, East Flores: Major Use Made of Remittances in the Origin Area

Main Use	Number	Percent
Repay debts	19	15.2
Children's Schooling	25	20.0
Day to Day Expenses	39	31.2
Housing	31	24.8
Weddings, Ceremonies, Customs etc.	11	8.8
	125	100.0

Source: Goma, Mantra and Bintarto 1993, p. 407

to make the move to Sabah especially if they seek to purchase a passport, pay the 'fiscal' tax paid by people leaving the country at Nunakan on the border to Sabah and purchase a working permit in Malaysia. Together with the transport costs (the journey takes around a week), this adds up to around Rp. 300,000 (US$150). This is financed usually by loans from family members, money lenders or by the *calo* (recruiter). In the latter case the *calo* takes part of the earnings of the migrant for a specified period and provides ample scope for exploitation. Repayment of loans is important because it may be a year or so before the migrant can start to show a significant profit from their earnings in Sabah. A third of remittances sent back go to meet day to day expenses of families left behind and reflects the strong economic push exerted by the lack of opportunities in the home area, especially to earn cash as opposed to being able to produce sufficient food to feed the family.

This lack of cash factor is also reflected in a substantial amount being used for schooling of children and siblings. Bank officers report that this is a major use of money remitted from Malaysia and that an increasing amount is spent on sending teenage children to get higher education elsewhere in Indonesia (especially Java) which is better provided with higher secondary and tertiary education institutions. In some cases young adults go to work in Malaysia for a few years to earn enough to send themselves through school in Java.

The second largest expenditure of remittances from migrants in Nelereren is on the improvement of housing. This is an almost universal finding in studies of the uses of remittances and reflects the motivation of migrants to improve the level of well-being of their families. A small but significant part of the remittances are used to pay for customary obligations such as the payment of bride-price and to mount wedding ceremonies etc.

Very little of the remittances are used to purchase land because in the area of origin, traditional methods of division of land still adhere and there is little exchange of land through selling. There is some evidence of investment in transport—through purchase of minibuses which now ply the regional and rocky village roads with their vivid colors and names ('Kharisma', 'Skid Row', 'I Am Lonely', 'Rambo' etc.) and rap music blaring from a myriad of speakers. In some cases groups of returned migrants have invested in the minibuses. As yet there are few shops in the villages but increasing commercialization is evident and this is a growing avenue for investment of the earnings of migration. It is clear that the results of migration are a very important element in providing cash to the home communities. Much of the food consumed is produced by the families of origin and there are few avenues for obtaining cash apart from selling copra and cacao which, due to communications and organizational difficulties, is limited.

One of the greatest concerns expressed about international migration of LDCs is its brain-drain effects. It is argued that such mobility tends to be selective of the better educated, the more entrepreneurial, those with leadership skills etc. However one of the most distinctive features of the export of labour from Indonesia is the overwhelming dominance of unskilled workers (Hugo 1995a). This certainly is also the case in NTT and East Flores (Hugo 2000), where the male migrants overwhelmingly were agricultural workers before leaving and tended to be employed in unskilled work in Sabah—in plantation work, saw milling, construction, factory work etc. Some 57.6 percent of migrants had not gone beyond elementary school in a study of the village of Nelereren (Goma, Mantra and Bintarto 1993, p. 410). Similarly in the 60 migrant respondents interviewed by Kapioru (1995) in Adonara, none had gone beyond primary school and only 12 had actually completed primary school. All were agricultural workers before leaving for Sabah. Hence as is the case on a national level there is little evidence of the labour migration being selective of highly educated and skilled people at the regional level. Nevertheless, it is apparent that the heavy outmigration of mostly young men between the ages of 15 and 44, and to a lesser extent women, is diminishing the economically active population in the main outmigration areas. This is reflected in the lack of population growth in these areas which was demonstrated earlier. Certainly it is apparent when visiting the villages, where there are few young adult men to be seen and women, children and older men are predominant. In the main surveyed village three quarters of respondents indicated that the absence of the migrant had impacted their agricultural activities. It will be noted that this was much more the case when a male migrant (82.6 percent) was absent than was the case with females (45.8 percent). However, there does not appear to have been a reduction in food production in the villages due to the absence of the men. Women have taken on more agricultural tasks than they have done traditionally and there is a strong extended family and community tradition of mutual self-help. The major work inputs are needed when there is new land to be cleared for a new garden and it is then that the men tend to come back from Malaysia.

There is however evidence of 'brain-drain' effects in some of the villages which have been experiencing outmigration to Sabah over a long period of time, especially in parts of the island of Adonara which was where the movement began a half century ago. This is partly due to an increasing tendency for migrants to settle permanently in Sabah but is mainly due to another phenomenon. It was mentioned earlier that a substantial amount of remittances goes into meeting the expenses of educating children. While much of this applies to elementary education in the village, there is evidence of children in some areas being sent away to obtain higher secondary and tertiary education, especially in Java. These people rarely return to settle in East Flores and are scattered across the archipelago, but especially in Java. They are not only contributing to the lack of population growth but are also reducing the numbers of potential leaders, entrepreneurs and development-oriented people in the home communities. The established migration villages tend to lack young economically active people, especially men, and this may be a significant barrier to development efforts in those villages.

It is apparent that in NTT in general and in East Flores in particular, external transfers from international labour migrants in Sabah have had some major impacts upon the families of the migrants and the communities which they come from. From what has been presented so far it is clear that these transfers have had some impacts which are important from the perspective of regional development. Consumption levels have been raised substantially and the commercialization and monetisation of the local economy has increased as well. There has been an increased demand for a range of services especially in education, but also in health and other social services.

In considering regional development we need to focus on the uses made of the funds remitted to the region. The few studies (Goma, Mantra and Bintarto 1993; Kapioru 1995) made regarding this issue point out that the remittances are overwhelmingly used in consumption. However this means that there are no implications for regional development and from our preliminary investigations in the area this would not seem to be the case for a number of reasons. The first concerns the dominance of housing in the expenditure of remittances. Detailed research in Mexico has shown that the second and third round effects of expenditure of remittances on housing are considerable where they employ local people and use local materials in the construction. Careful analysis by Adelman and Taylor (1990) found that for every dollar remitted from abroad, total GNP increased by between $2.69 and $3.17 and that the largest income multipliers were in rural communities where expenditure patterns favoured purchase of locally-produced goods and services and labour-intensive production technologies. Similar findings from Bangladesh (Stahl and Habib 1991) indicate that each migrant worker overseas creates three jobs at home through remittances. Of course to the extent that housing materials, household goods and day-to-day items purchased from remittances are brought in from other parts of Indonesia it means that development elsewhere rather than in East Flores and NTT will benefit. Our studies at the moment are attempting to establish the extent to which this is the case.

In addition, it is clear that the substantial investment of remittances in schooling is making a positive development contribution. However, as was pointed out earlier, the children and siblings of migrant workers who benefited from this investment of remittances are showing a tendency to settle elsewhere in Indonesia where there are more opportunities for people with skills and higher levels of education.

Furthermore, there is some evidence of remittances being invested in productive activity such as transport and small shops. Undoubtedly the improvement in local transport is having a positive impact on the local economy. The exodus of workers is also certainly easing local underemployment problems and pressures on land resources. It is apparent from the field survey that quite different patterns of use are made of monies sent back by migrants still absent and those brought back by the migrants when they return. The former are used overwhelmingly for the daily upkeep of the origin-based family while the latter are mainly used for other investments.

Undoubtedly, there has been some leakage of funds earned by migrant workers and remitted back to East Flores out of the area, especially to Java. Bank officials in Larantuka estimate that for every $1.3 remitted, around $1.00 is remitted out of the area to meet costs such as sending children to school, purchase of large items for the household etc. Hence the leakage factor is considerable, at least, in terms of the money that comes in through the formal banking system. Also it seems likely that since there is low demand for bank funds in East Flores for lending purposes, it is likely that the surplus funds accumulated from remittances are transferred elsewhere in Indonesia.

While the impact of remittances from overseas workers has been considerable in East Flores, there have been few flow-ons from the migration which have involved investments generating local production for export to other regions or expanded local job opportunities. Although there can be little doubt that households and villages with migrant workers in Sabah have benefited, East Flores and indeed NTT remain among Indonesia's poorest areas. It is apparent that despite the high level of inflow of hard currency, regional development has remained at low levels. Why is this the case? There are a number of significant constraints upon development in East Nusatenggara generally and East Flores in particular, both in terms of physical and human resources. Among the physical constraints upon development there are a number of significant issues.

The archipelagic nature of the province and the lack of roads on the larger islands have prevented the full exploitation of the province's resources. This is exacerbated by the broken topography of the major islands. In addition, the climate and soil resources of the province are limited. Erosion is a significant problem in some areas while rainfall deficits, frequent droughts and problems of water supply plague other areas. A critical factor is the distance of the province from the main centre of decision-making in Jakarta and the nation's major urban markets in Western Indonesia. These physical constraints upon development are amplified by the limited amount of investment in the province, the low average levels of education and training, the low productivity of the workforce and the high level of ethnolinguistic diversity as well as the lack of diversity in the local agricultural-dominated economy.

On the other hand, it is clear that there are also some definite areas of development potential if these obstacles can be overcome. However it is unlikely that potential small investors such as those represented by the migrants from East Flores and their families are going to be able to overcome these barriers alone. This will only occur if a climate for small investors is created by sufficient investment in infrastructure (especially in transport) and careful planning. Some of the most promising areas of development potential are examined below

The agricultural sector, especially in Southern Flores and parts of Kupang, are over-cultivated and suffer from population pressure on farming and pastoral resources. There is scope for expansion of agriculture in some areas (North and West Flores) and improvement of methods in others. Thus there is potential for expansion of employment and export to other parts of Indonesia. In the plantation areas there is a need for greater quality control and commercialization in coffee production. The staple food locally is shifting away from corn to rice, around a third of which is still imported from other parts of Indonesia. There is a need to improve local rice production and this can be done in West Flores and West Sumba. There is potential for productivity improvements of dry land food crops. Expansion of marketing of agricultural products, especially fresh fruit and vegetables to the huge and growing urban markets in Java, is also possible if transport, processing and management can be improved.

In the fisheries sub-sector, there is enormous potential with only 25 percent of the potential sustainable capacity in the 200,000 square kilometres of the province's oceans being exploited. There is huge scope to sell fresh and processed fish to the huge markets in Java if transport, management and processing could be greatly improved.

Cattle and cattle products in NTT, can become more important given the rapidly expanding fresh meat market demand in Java as a result of income growth in urban-based middle class households. There is also opportunity for value-added contributions to locally-produced primary industry products. There are virtually no fish and meat-processing plants locally and there is a great need to develop this. Previously established meat, leather and fish processing enterprises have closed but it is clear that given a favourable environment such activities should thrive in NTT. It will however need significant investment and some local initiative to train local workers in the appropriate skills needed for these activities.

At present many consumption items such as furniture and processed foods come from Java to the province. There is need for local production of day-to-day items, especially as transport improves and makes rapidly expanding urban places like Kupang more accessible to other parts of the province.

Manufacturing is still very limited in NTT. However there are some possibilities for development. These include the development of salt production and processing as well as a cement manufacturing plant near Kupang. In addition there is the potential to develop the natural gas industry in Timor and offshore in the Timor Gap. The expansion of the handicraft industry, perhaps in association with the tourist industry, would provide the opportunity for increased production of sandalwood, weaving and other textiles. There is a need for these activities, and cloth manufacturing in particular, needs to become more commercially oriented.

Tourism is one of the most promising areas which also has significant human resource implications since it is relatively labour-intensive and has significant training requirements. The province has a wealth of natural attractions for tourists as well as marvellous beaches and a wide variety of fascinating cultural groups and a varied and rich handicraft industry especially in hand woven textiles. This is especially the case in Eastern Flores which has magnificent volcanic mountains and palm-fringed beaches. There is an opportunity to build upon the experience in Bali and Lombok and avoid the mistakes made in those areas.

In each of these areas of potential, one of the major barriers relates to the lack of investment capital. It is the argument of this paper that one of the most significant sources of such investment lies in an export industry which is well established and expanding in parts of the province—the export of workers to labour surplus countries, especially Eastern Malaysia. While the impacts of this migration have been substantial, their effects on regional development within NTT have been limited. The remittances are focused on an isolated peripheral area and the illegal status of the migrants sending the remittances is problematic as well. In addition, remittance recipients are not well integrated into regional planning efforts. There continues to be insufficient physical infrastructure, especially transport infrastructure, which is necessary to create a favourable environment for small investors. Finally, there is a deficiency of appropriate training and education programmes to assist returning migrants in making effective investment decisions.

The export of labour was explicitly incorporated into national planning efforts during the Sixth Five Year Plan in Indonesia (Hugo 1995a). Paradoxically in Flores, a province where labour migration is one of the few sources of inward fund transfers, it is not being considered at all in regional development planning.

Overseas labour migration from East Flores has benefited most of the households that have been directly involved in it. There are also some broad indications that people in East Flores have adopted more 'modern' patterns of behaviour than those in other parts of the province. For example almost two thirds (63.4 percent) of children in East Flores are fully immunised, compared with 47.1 percent across the entire province and the proportions of women marrying for the first time at age 25 or over was higher (31.5 percent) than in the province as a whole (20.7 percent). Acceptance of family planning is somewhat lower than the provincial average but this may be a function of the long absences of husbands and the late average age in marriage (Graham 1997).

Conclusions

There is no evidence of a slowdown in the growth of international labour migration out of Indonesian rural communities. Indeed, the reduction in urban opportunities within Indonesia following the 1998 crisis may be making overseas labour migration a more attractive option for rural dwellers in many parts of Indonesia. It seems inevitable that this movement will continue to increase. The extent to which the movement is divided between clandestine and legal migrations will be heavily dependent upon the policies and programmes pursued by destination governments and to a far lesser extent the Indonesian government. It is crucially important to realise that there is now a complex and well-developed network in place that will ensure the continuation and enhancement of movement into Malaysia from Indonesia, something that has been continuing for several centuries and is unlikely to be stopped completely by any policy intervention. The Indonesian government is encouraging the movement and envisages an expansion of it, although there are increasing signs of Malaysia attempting to stop it. It is likely that the movement will become more complex, probably involving more women and a wider range of types of workers and skills and it is likely that more migrants will settle in Malaysia.

There is a great need for research into these circulatory movements, especially relating to the effects in both Malaysia and Indonesia. Especially important is the construction of more sound and effective policies which will maximize their benefits and minimise costs and negative effects. In a large and complex nation like Indonesia, international labour migration is more likely to have significant impacts upon economic development in regions than it is upon the nation as a whole. This is especially the case in peripheral, poor and lagging regions such as those in Eastern Indonesia considered here. It would appear that the potential for labour migration from East Nusatenggara to Flores to contribute to the development of this lagging region is considerable. However this potential is at best only being partially realised, although the nation's overall planning strategy explicitly incorporates labour export as one of the tools of economic planning. For this potential to be fully realised in a regional context it will be necessary for national and provincial governments to be more involved. First, a mechanism should be developed to enable the migration itself to be legalized with minimal disruption to the flows of movement as they are currently occurring so that current uncertainties and chances of exploitation confronting migrants are eliminated. Second, transport and other infrastructure need to be greatly improved in the area to allow the province to sell its produce to the rapidly growing urban and middle class populations of Java. Only then will there be an investment environment which will make it possible for returning migrants and their families to have options other than house construction as a way to invest the fruits of their migration. Third, there needs to be an acceptance at all levels of government that labour migration is an important element in regional development which should be encouraged in the absence of development of other work opportunities and integrated into regional and local planning policy and programmes. While one would hope that labour migration to Sabah is not the long term solution to poverty in East Nusatenggara it is important in the short and medium terms that the benefits of this well established and successful migration system be maximised for the households directly affected by it and the region in which they live.

Notes

1. Reference is made here to a number of village-based studies of the impacts of international labour migration (Eki, forthcoming; Graham 1997; Goma, Mantra and Bintarto 1993; Kapioru 1995), but especially on a study of a single emigration village in East Timor (see Raharto et al. 1999). This involved interviewing of 125 returned migrant households and 116 households of migrant workers still away as well as a range of qualitative information collection strategies.

2. Moreover, at the time of writing the new spirit of *otonami-daerah* (regional autonomy) and freedom in Indonesia has seen many regional officers of *Depnakertrans* decide that they are no longer required to provide statistics to Jakarta. Hence the 2001 and later data are major underestimates of official OCW movement in Indonesia.
3. *Source*: Department of Labour Office, Larantruka, April 1996.
4. The Total Fertility Rate (TFR) 'indicates the number of children that will be born alive to a woman during her lifetime if she were to pass through all her child-bearing years conforming to the age specific rates of a given year' (Hugo 1986, p. 43). More simply it indicates approximately the completed total number of children women are having on average at a particular time.
5. The minimum wage levels in Malaysia for the unskilled type of work that the bulk of Flores people do in Malaysia are RM220 (US$133) for construction workers, RM300 for plantation workers and RM250 for those working in the informal sector. However especially in Sabah wages tend to be much higher reaching between RM1,000 and RM2,000 in the construction and manufacturing sectors (*Jakarta Post* 1993).

References

Asian Migrant Center. *Asian Migrant Yearbook 1999*. Hong Kong: Asian Migrant Center, 1999.

Barlow, C., Gondowarsito, R., Birowo, A.T. and Jayasuriya, S. "Development in Eastern Indonesia: The Case of Nusa Tenggara Timur". *International Development Issues* no. 13, AGPS, Canberra (1990): 110 pp.

Battistella, G. and Asis, M.B. *The Crisis and Migration in Asia*. Philippines: Scalabrini Migration Center, Quezon City, 1999.

Biro Pusat Statistik (BPS). *Statistik Kesejahteraan Rumahtangga 1991—National Economic Survey*. Jakarta: Biro Pusat Statistik, 1992.

Departemen Tenaga Kerja, Republic of Indonesia. *Strategi Penempatan Tenaga Kerja Indonesia Ke Luar Negeri*. Jakarta: Departemen Tenaga Kerja, Republic of Indonesia, 1998.

Eki, A.T. "International Labour Migration from East Flores to Sabah Malaysia: A Study of Patterns, Causes and Consequences". Unpublished PhD Thesis, Department of Geographical and Environmental Studies, Adelaide University. Forthcoming.

Go, S.P. "Recent Trends in Migration Movements and Policies: The Movement of Filipino Professionals and Managers". Paper presented at the workshop on International Migration and Labour Markets in Asia, Japan Institute of Labour: Tokyo, Japan, 4–5 February, 2002.

Goma, J.N., Mantra, I. B. and Bintarto, R. "Labour Force Mobility from East Flores to Sabah Malaysia and the Extent of the Influence in the Village

Origin: A Case Study at Nelereren Village". *BPPS-UGM* 6, no. 4A (1993): 401–12.

Graham, P. "Widows at Home, Workers Abroad: Florenese Women and Labour Migration". Mimeographed. Monash: Monash University, 1997.

Hill, H. "Ensuring Regional Growth Now the Oil Boom is Over". *Far Eastern Economic Review* 1, September (1988): 24–25.

Hill, H. and Weidemann, "A. Regional Development in Indonesia: Patterns and Issues". In *Unity and Diversity: Regional Economic Development in Indonesia Since 1970*, H. Hill (ed.), pp. 3–54. Singapore: Oxford University Press, 1989.

Hugo, G.J. *Australia's Changing Population: Trends and Implications*. Melbourne: Oxford University Press, 1986.

Hugo, G.J. "Labour Export from Indonesia: An Overview". *Asean Economic Bulletin* 12, no. 2 (1995a): 275–98.

Hugo, G.J. "Manpower and Human Resource Development in Nusa Tenggara Timur". Draft report prepared for the Regional Manpower Planning and Training Project (RMPT), Bureau of Manpower, Jakarta: National Development Planning Agency (BAPPENAS), 1995b.

Hugo, G.J. "International Migration in Eastern Indonesia". Paper prepared for East Indonesia Project, January, 1998.

Hugo, G.J. "The Impact of the Crisis on International Population Movement in Indonesia". Paper prepared for ILO Indonesian Employment Strategy Mission, May, 1999.

Hugo, G.J. "The Crisis and International Population Movements in Indonesia". *Asian and Pacific Migration Journal* 9, no. 1 (2000a): 93–129.

Hugo, G.J. "Labour Migration from East Indonesia to East Malaysia". *Revue Européene des Migrations Internationales* 16, no. 1 (2000b): 97–124.

Kantor Statistik Flores Timur. *East Flores Dalam Angka 1994*. Larantuka: Kantor Statistik, 1995.

Kantor Statistik Nusa Tenggara Timur. *Nusa Tenggara Timur Dalam Angka 1988*. Kupang: Kantor Statistik, 1989.

Kantor Statistik Nusa Tenggara Timur. *Nusa Tenggara Timur Dalam Angka 1994* (Nusa Tenggara Timur in Figures 1994). Nusa Tenggara Timur: Kantor Statistik, Kupang, 1995a.

Kantor Statistik Nusa Tenggara Timur. *Statistik Sosial dan Kependudukan Nusa Tenggara Timur 1994*. Nusa Tenggara Timur: Kantor Statistik, 1995b.

Kantor Statistik Nusa Tenggara Timur. *Nusa Tenggara Timur Dalam Angka 1996* (Nusa Tenggara Timur in Figures 1996). Nusa Tenggara Timur: Kantor Statistik, Kupang, 1997.

Kantor Statistik Nusa Tenggara Timur. *Nusa Tenggara Timur Dalam Angka 1997* (Nusa Tenggara Timur in Figures 1997). Nusa Tenggara Timur: Kantor Statistik, Kupang, 1998.

Kapioru, C. *Mobilitas Pekerja Yang Berstatus Suami, Dan Dampaknya Terhadap Perubahan Status Wanita Dan Kondisi Sosial Ekonomi Rumah Tangga*. Kupang: UNFPA, 1995.
Kassim, A. "Economic Slowdown and Its Impact on Cross-National Migration and Policy on Alien Employment in Malaysia". Paper presented at the workshop on International Migration and Labour Markets in Asia, Japan Institute of Labour, Tokyo, Japan, 4–5 February, 2002.
Mantra, I.B., Kasnawi, T.M. and Sukamandi. *Mobilitas Angkatan Kerja Indonesia Ke Timor Tengah* (Movement of Indonesian Workers to the Middle East). Final Report Book 1. Yogyakarta: Population Studies Centre, Gadjah Mada University, 1986.
Ormeling, F.J. *The Timor Problem: A Geographical Interpretation of an Underdeveloped Island*. Gronigen: J.B. Woltens. 1957.
Pusat Penelitian Kependudukan, Universitas Gadjah Mada. *Mobilitas Angkalan Kerja ke Timur Tengah*. Yogyakarta: Gadjah Mada University, 1986.
Raharto, A., Hugo, G., Romdiafi, H. and Bandiyono, S. (eds). *Migrasi dan Pembangunan di Kawasan Timur Indonesia: Isu Ketenagakerjaan*. Canberra: PPT-LIPI, ANU and Jakarta: AusAID, 1999.
Russell, S.S. and Teitelbaum, M.S. *International Migration and International Trade*. World Bank Discussion Papers 160. Washington: The World Bank. 1992.
Singhanetra-Renard, A. "The Middle East and Beyond: Dynamics of International Labour Circulation Among Southeast Asian Workers". Mimeographed. Chang Mai, Thailand: Chiang Mai University, 1986.
Soeprobo, T.B. "Recent Trends of International Migration in Indonesia". Paper presented at the workshop on International Migration and Labour Markets in Asia, Japan Institute of Labour, Tokyo, Japan, 4–5 February, 2002.
Sondakh, L. "Agricultural Development in Eastern Indonesia: Performance, Issues and Policy Options". In *Indonesia Assessment 1995: Development in Eastern Indonesia*, C. Barlow and J. Hardjono (eds), pp. 141–62. Singapore: Institute of Southeast Asian Studies, 1995.
Stahl, C. and Habib, A. "Emigration and Development in South and Southeast Asia". In *The Unsettled Relationship: Labour Migration and Economic Development*, D.G. Papademetriou and P.L. Martin (eds), pp. 163–79. New York: Greenwood Press, 1991.
Suyono, M. "Tenaga Kerja Indonesia di Timur Tengah Makin Mantap". *Suara Karya*, h.v.k., 2–6, 1981.
World Bank. *Country at a Glance Tables*. http://www.worldbank.org/data/countrydata/ countrydata.html#AAG. 2001.
World Bank. *Entering the 21st Century: World Development Report 1999/2000*. New York: Oxford University Press, 2000.

6
GENDER, SOCIO-SPATIAL NETWORKS, AND RURAL NON-FARM WORK AMONG MIGRANTS IN WEST JAVA

Rachel Silvey

Introduction

In post-1997 Indonesia, the convergence of political and macro-economic upheavals has altered the context of mobility and employment processes (Booth 2000). Structural adjustment programmes, rapid inflation, and increasing labour market flexibility have reorganized migrants' social networks and spatial behaviour patterns in ways that have had critical implications for low-income peoples' reliance on the rural non-farm sector (Manning and van Dierman 2000). Indeed, in the first years following the financial crisis (1997–99), low-income people in Indonesia relied increasingly on their social safety nets for their survival. (Cameron 1999). The operation of these safety nets in coping with crisis periods is in part a function of the gender characteristics of the networks, and is linked to the vitality of the specific rural non-farm economy (RNFE), the agricultural economy, and the urban labour market to which migrants are linked.

How have particular gender dynamics of networks, and in particular the gender-specific connections to the rural non-farm sector, facilitated or inhibited individuals' and households' access to resources during this period of economic contraction? This chapter aims to examine this question through analysis of two important issues. The first deals with how households and individuals in two villages with distinct socio-spatial networks have adopted different mobility and resource exchange patterns, and thus have relied in different ways on the rural non-farm sector during the economic crisis period. The second looks at how the gender dynamics of social networks have influenced resource access patterns linked to the rural non-farm sector under crisis. To illustrate the operation of these processes, the chapter compares the socio-spatial networks that connect two destination sites in Bekasi and Rancaekek, West Java, Indonesia with the primary origin regions of West Java and Central Java, respectively of the majority of circular migrants in each network. In these cases, both the RNFE's characteristics as well as the gender relations of the networks have shaped the ways that people have weathered resource shortages during this period of time.

At issue are two types of safety nets: household-scale and extra-household (i.e., inter-village network-scale and village-scale). While these two types of safety nets are similar and related, they are not identical, and the activities and interactions of each type provide different kinds of resources. Household safety nets, though widely critiqued within the feminist literature (see Lawson 1998), are conventionally defined as income-pooling units that may or may not include kinship relations (Smith and Wallerstein 1992; Chant 1992). From this perspective, households operate as safety nets when their members provide for each other those basic necessities that have become too expensive for individuals to afford independently. Specifically, a household serves as a safety net if its members provide shelter, food, clothing or other subsidies such as cash to members who are in need. Further, if household members carry out subsistence farm work, cooking, house cleaning, or care for the young, elderly, or infirm, these activities protect other household members from the costs of attending to these needs. The worth of such socially reproductive activities, although not generally calculated in monetary terms, is substantial in that it reduces household expenditure otherwise directed at fulfilling such needs. These workloads and resources are divided differently across households, within households, and across villages in ways that depend in part on the socio-spatial networks existing beyond the household, and the integration of these networks into specific employment sectors.

In contrast to a household safety net, a "social safety net" refers to the extra-household activities and exchanges of goods that help meet people's basic needs. As Indonesia's economic crisis intensified in 1998, initially, large numbers of urban migrants returned to their rural, origin site villages, prompted by their declining ability to afford food or rent in the cities (Manning 2000). In West Java, it was not uncommon for neighbours and extended family members living under different roofs within a village (*kampung*) to contribute to the fulfillment of one another's basic needs. Village-level safety nets included the exchange of agricultural goods via barter, charity in the form of rice for the most impoverished villagers, and village-wide contributions to the ritual food stock and preparations for major holidays and weddings. Finally, villages with strong networks of circular migrants connecting them to urban areas were involved in the regular exchange of resources that subsidized the basic needs of people in both the urban and rural nodes of the network. The rural non-farm sector played a particularly critical role in maintaining rural-urban social networks during the crisis, as women and men relied increasingly on this sector for their subsistence. Yet the role of the non-farm sector differed for the two villages under examination.

This chapter examines the interactions between the household-, village-, and network-scale exchanges of resources, and aims to identify the ways that the gender dynamics of these interactions influenced access to resources differently in the two villages since the beginning of the economic crisis. Specifically, the study focuses on the ways that two villages differ in their inter-household and network-scale divisions and exchanges of labour and resources, and how these village-scale processes interact with intra-household divisions of, and access to, particular kinds of work (income-earning or reproductive) and resources (cash and food). The project finds that the gender dynamics of social networks were important in differentiating women's and men's workloads, as well as their access to resources, and the characteristics of the sectoral ties between village and city. In sum, the project illustrates that an analysis of the gender dimensions of low-income migrants' networks can contribute to understanding the ways in which different social groups' access to resources is tied to specific networks' gendered mobility patterns, rural-urban resource linkages, and place-based differences in crisis survival patterns.

Social Networks as Safety Nets; The Role of the Rural Non-Farm Sector

Since well before 1997, low-income people in Java have relied on social networks as their safety nets (White and Wiradi 1989). Inter- and intra-village networks have facilitated the access of residents and migrants to employment, as well as their access to cash and agricultural produce. In times of economic prosperity, circular mobility and occupational multiplicity have been found to be fundamental to low-income people's subsistence and occasional prosperity in Indonesia and elsewhere (Rigg 1998; Morrison 1993). But some communities are more persistently engaged in circular mobility and more effectively involved in profitable, off-farm employment than are others. For instance, prior to 1997, income inequality in East Java was primarily produced through differences in household members' differential participation in circular or permanent migration and the associated off-farm income or lack thereof (Edmundson 1994). Those rural and semi-rural households with a large proportion of their income derived from non-farm livelihoods were profiting from their members' mobility and "occupational multiplicity" (Breman et al. 1997).

Since late 1997, according to two large-scale surveys (Sumarto et al. 1998; Beegle et al. 1998), real non-farm incomes fell because of inflation and the contraction of the modern economic sectors that were growing most rapidly prior to the crisis. Simultaneously, the agricultural sector experienced positive growth, which allowed those circulators who migrate between agricultural and non-agricultural areas to supplement their declining urban incomes with resources from the agriculture-producing nodes in their networks (Cameron 1999). Many of the poorest migrants, however, did not have the resources to continue to circulate, and their lack of access to agricultural resources and rural non-farm incomes as a safety net put them at a particular disadvantage under crisis.

The degree of strength of the rural economy, both in farm-based activities and non-farm employment, was linked to the gender dynamics in the rural regions. The network in this study that has provided the strongest resource cushion to its members (the Sunda-Rancaekek network) has also exacted gender specific costs on the women within it. It was in part due to the contributions of these women to the rural non-farm sector that their village has been able to weather the crisis relatively effectively. Yet women's workloads, both productive and reproductive, grew heavier over this period, and were particularly significant in the village with the more robust rural non-farm economy.

The two studied villages are located in the regencies of Bekasi and Rancaekek, in the province of West Java. Each of the village populations consisted of high proportions of migrants (90 percent and 63 percent of the total populations, respectively), and relied on household and extra-household safety nets and the rural non-farm sector to different degrees for their subsistence (Silvey 2003). To facilitate the discussion, the village in Bekasi and the networks linking it to the origin village of the majority of circulators, located in Central Java, will be referred to with the pseudonym of Jowo. The village in Rancaekek and the networks linking Rancaekek to its migrants' primary origin village, located in West Java, will be referred to with the pseudonym of Sunda (see Figure 6.1).

In Jowo, prior to 1997, the networks linking households to their origin sites were *denser* than those in Sunda. Specifically, there was a higher dependence on rice from the origin site in Jowo (41 percent versus 18 percent), and a greater percentage of the population sent remittances to rural origin sites on a regular basis within that network (82 percent versus 33 percent) (see Table 6.1). Prior to August of 1997, Jowo's strong network played an important role in helping migrant households survive on incomes that would have been below subsistence if they had not accessed the supplementary resources provided through the network.

In addition to the greater density of the networks linking Jowo to origin sites, Jowo's networks were more spatially extensive (see Figure 6.1). Jowo's networks were both more necessary to survival than those connected to Sunda's, *and* the nodes were less spatially accessible. So, when the period of economic decline began in late 1997, households in both villages were more in need of the resources they had once accessed through networks. But for Jowo, the cost became prohibitive of covering the distance between origin and destination sites of the network, and this made resource exchanges between rural and urban sectors more difficult. Thus, migrants in Jowo were less able than those in Sunda to access the resources previously available to them from the agricultural and non-farm sectors of their rural origins.

TABLE 6.1
Rural-Urban Resource Exchange; Network Density

	Jowo (in Bekasi)	Sunda (in Rancaekek)
Brought rice from village to city:	41 percent	18 percent
Sent remittances before crisis:	82 percent	33 percent
Since crisis:	56 percent	30 percent
N	100	85

Sources: survey by author 2000, total n = 185, and village registers

FIGURE 6.1
Locations of Jowo and Sunda villages

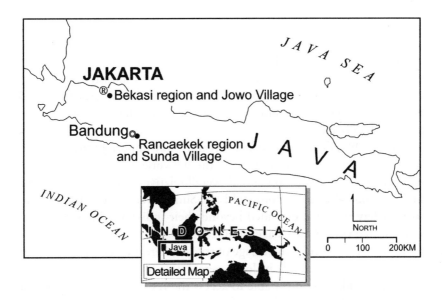

In Jowo, 66 percent of the migrants were originally from Central Java, located 8 to 15 hours away by bus, while in Sunda 75 percent came from regencies in West Java which were just 1 to 8 hours away by bus. In these cases, the distance between network nodes of the two villages was important to migrants inasmuch as it reflected the cost of transportation weighted against the benefits received for circulation. While distance itself is not a factor that universally determines access to resources in an a priori fashion, it must be overcome in order to access non-local resources, and in this way plays an important role in shaping access. The role of distance is contextually specific and forged in conjunction with other factors, such as a population's ability at a given time to pay for the cost of transportation, the compensation that migrants receive for covering the distance, or the historical perspective on migration within a particular social group. Thus, although the cost of transportation between network nodes of Jowo was approximately twice that of the cost for Sunda, prior to 1997, circular migrants in Jowo were nonetheless willing and able to bear the relatively high cost.

According to respondents, the resources, primarily rice, in the rural origin site of Jowo more than compensated for the cost of transportation between the two sites. By moving between the two sites, these low-income people managed to subsist prior to the crisis, and saved a good deal of money by not buying their rice in the city. However, their ability to continue to circulate on a regular basis was reduced when the cost of transportation rose beyond their means in 1997. Their declining mobility indicates that for these people living at the margins of subsistence, between 1997 and 2000, circular mobility became prohibitively expensive, and thus was no longer a livelihood strategy on which the migrants of Jowo could generally rely.

After 1997, the *local* safety nets became more important to household survival. Importantly, not only were the networks linking the migrants in Sunda more spatially condensed overall relative to those predominant in Jowo, but also more households in Sunda were embedded in *local* social safety nets that extended beyond their individual households yet were located within the village parameters. 37 percent of the respondents in Sunda were native to the village of study, whereas by contrast, only 10 percent of the households in Jowo were native to the village, and those few households were most able to access the resources that were shared between members of the local safety net. As the cost of transportation rose, and people's incomes declined in both villages, their reliance on local networks intensified. Because the networks in Sunda were more locally based than those in Jowo, people were able to access greater benefits from them under crisis.

Overall, while the residents of Jowo earned slightly lower nominal incomes than did people in Sunda, their real incomes were substantially lower because the cost of living was significantly higher in Jowo. Further, while individuals in Jowo were more embedded in extended exchange networks with origin households prior to 1997; their persistent exchanges were based largely on necessity. That is, the remittances they sent to Central Java were used for education, often for their own children, while the rice they brought back from their origin sites constituted part of their subsistence. Thus, when the crisis weakened their networks, the severity of the poverty in Jowo was exacerbated more than it was in Sunda. This difference between the two villages suggests that in times of shortage, the capacity to remain mobile and thereby gain access to a wide range of resources may become limited. Further, such limitations in this case were particularly acute for the lower income stratum of generally low-income people.

In part, the differences in the strength of the two networks was a reflection of the stronger rural agrarian and rural non-farm economies of Sunda's network relative to those of Jowo. In Jowo's primary rural node, rice-producing land was owned by three large landowners, all of whom had been successful urban entrepreneurs and circular migrants themselves. According to the village register, the remainder of the households in Jowo's rural origin site were composed on a de jure basis of people over 55 years old, who made up 58% of the resident population, and their grandchildren, who made up the remainder (Village Register 2000). In July, 2000, according to the village leader, 90 percent of the households in Jowo also included one working-age person, either temporarily on-leave from an urban sojourn or physically disabled in some way.

The elderly people in Jowo's rural origin village were involved in childcare and seasonal contractual agricultural labour, and relied on remittances from their adult children in the cities to pay school fees or to purchase goods beyond those needed for subsistence. They did not earn sufficient incomes to allow them to participate in generating an off-farm economy. Further, they did not view the sector as one that had room for them. Indeed, several elderly respondents mentioned in interviews that there was little point in beginning non-farm activities, because they did not see any market in the area for additional goods or services.

The working-age children of the elderly in Jowo who returned to the village on a seasonal basis to visit their children and sometimes to hand-deliver remittances, showed little interest in branching out beyond their known income-earning activities. In part, similar to their parents, the reluctance of younger people to engage in rural non-farm economic activities was a reflection of their economically marginal status. They simply lacked the resources to invest in additional activities. In addition, and also similar to their parents, they saw the rural non-farm economy as impacted. Specifically, the vegetable traders, the vendors of prepared foods (e.g., *tahu*, *tempeh*, *baso*) or traditional medicines (*jamu*), rickshaw (*becak*) drivers, and the occasional shoe repair person, toy salesman, or broom hawker all came into the village frequently enough to fulfill the demands of the people for these goods and services. Further, the trade in manufactured and processed food and goods (e.g., soap, sugar, radios, snack food, oil) at the local village market was dominated by the landed households. Although many local villagers worked during the year at the market for the wealthier families, in this capacity they were wage labourers rather than entrepreneurs in the rural market.

The weakness of the rural non-farm sector in Jowo's rural origin site made its residents all the more dependant on the incomes of the circular migrants working in the city. Indeed, the lowest income people in both destination site villages found themselves unable to continue sending remittances after the crisis began. 82 percent versus 33 percent of the people had sent remittances from Jowo prior the crisis, and more people continued to send remittances from Jowo after the crisis (56 percent vs. 30 percent). However, the decline in remittances since the crisis began was far more pronounced in Jowo than it was in Sunda (26 percent decline vs. 3 percent decline). The greater decline in Jowo, when understood in conjunction with the overall lower incomes of the Jowo network, indicates that more households faced a greater reduction in the resources available to them than did households in Sunda. All respondents who had stopped sending remittances indicated that the remittances were still needed in origin sites, but that crisis-era incomes did not permit them to continue sending cash home. This was part of what caused particular hardship in Jowo's network, and was part of the underlying weakness of the rural non-farm economy.

While this difference in the effectiveness between the two networks was partly attributable to the RNFE, it was also linked to the dynamics of the broader village economy. First, according to village leaders, Sunda's primary rural origin site had a more vital agrarian base, with all fields under production, whereas in Jowo, many fields were not in full-time use. Class differentiation was less pronounced among the part-time farmers in Sunda, as the native residents still owned plots of land which they harvested to directly support their subsistence for their survival. In addition, people in Sunda were more settled overall (i.e., 10 percent of Jowo was native, whereas 37 percent of Sunda was native, and people in Jowo mostly rented in the city (65 percent) whereas people in Sunda mostly owned their homes (52 percent) and relied less on remittances (see Table 6.1 above) than did those in Jowo's network.

These differences in agrarian structure and degree of settlement between the two villages emerged in tandem with the differences between the two rural non-farm economies. That is, Sunda's rural non-farm economy was relatively vital: 36 percent of the local residents were involved in some sort of non-farm activity during part of the year, and according to the village leader, the rural non-farm economy (RNFE) critically supplemented the agricultural base. In turn, the trade activities and small-scale enterprises spearheaded by local people were successful enough to provide working-age people with sufficient income to remain resident in the area year-round. By contrast, in Jowo's rural origin site, most young people were compelled by financial reasons to migrate, and their meager remittances left the RNFE in their origin site in a relatively weakened state. All of these processes in the two villages, linking household composition to village economies, rural to urban spheres, and agrarian to non-agrarian rural activities, meant Jowo's network was less effective as a safety net than was Sunda's.

In addition to differences in the respective agrarian economies and the RNFEs, household composition was linked to different network-scale approaches to weathering the crisis. Partly because households and networks in Jowo had fewer members on average than those in Sunda, their crisis survival strategies differed at the household scale. Specifically, in Jowo, because households had fewer members, their existing pool of potential unpaid labourers was smaller. Thus, their ability to benefit from a "reproduction squeeze" was limited by the lower number of people, and women in particular, on whose labour they could draw. While households tend to attempt to extract more unpaid labour out of their female members in order to provide a cushion in times of shortage (Arriagada 1994), this is a less effective strategy when household size is relatively small. Partly because of this difference in household composition, Sunda appears to have more households that have weathered the crisis better than those in Jowo. That is, low-income households with more members, such as those in Sunda, could provide some resources such as unpaid labour to their members that low-income households with fewer members found more difficult to extract. Further, in order to provide unpaid labour as an immediately accessible resource for other household members, spatial proximity is important. Proximity is particularly critical in periods when access to the benefits of more distant resources grows increasingly limited, such as over the years 1997 to 1999. Of the two villages, Sunda, with its denser and more localized household and extra-household networks, provided more effective safety nets than Jowo.

Up to this point, the discussion has focused on the household, network, and village scales of analysis. As discussed in the next section, a gendered analysis of these dynamics at the intra-household and intra-network scales yields a more complex picture of the RNFE and crisis survival patterns.

Engendering Social Networks: Whose Safety Net?

The empirical work that exists to date on exactly how gender influences the operation of networks suggests contradictory explanations. Preliminary evidence from Thailand (Curran 1995) suggests that the gender composition of migrants' networks may influence the strength of social ties between those migrants and their origin site communities. Specifically, in the Thai context, it appears that because young women migrants in Thailand maintain stronger ties with their parental origin site households than do young men, households may be more motivated to release a daughter than a son to migration (Curran 1995). This gendered character of migrants' networks may be intensified by the stronger pressure placed on young women than men migrants to send remittances home to their families in this context (Mills 1997). However, for Central Java, Indonesia, Diane Wolf (1992) reports that young women made their mobility and employment decisions surprisingly independently of their households' supposed labour allocation strategies. Indeed, in rural Central Java, young women often migrated to work in factories *in spite of* their parents' protestations, indicating that the gendering of household safety nets varies across places.

Wolf's (1992) study focused on rural–rural, relatively local networks, while the respondents in Curran's (1995) study were rural–urban migrants, linking endpoints that were relatively distant from one another. Taken together, these studies indicate that gender norms are place-specific, and that social networks are modified by gender *and* geography in forms that influence migration decisions and resource exchange patterns. The comparison of gender and migration in Jowo and Sunda indicates that while samples of young women migrants in both regions were indeed making migration decisions that ran counter to the wishes of their parents, inter-generational conflicts were more common and more pronounced in Sunda than Jowo. There are several possible explanations for this difference, but clearly the density, composition, and gendering of the social networks linking migrants to their origin communities were all-important factors. In particular, the greater embeddedness of women in their social networks in Sunda, and the relatively settled character of their village had implications for the gender divisions of labour. In addition it also affected the network's integration into the regional economy. The following discussion illustrates that *starting* from an analysis of gender relations within households, networks, migratory streams, and regional economic processes permits insight into the ways that gender differentiated inter-scalar processes are constituted in tandem with the characteristics of a given rural non-farm economy.

The *migrant* networks of Jowo were denser than those in Sunda, whereas Sunda's *local* networks were denser. This difference had implications for the autonomous migration of young women and for their roles and workloads within villages and households. Specifically, because there was less information circulating about female migrants in Sunda, parents were less inclined to support a daughter's independent migration than they were in Jowo. While these household tensions did not entirely inhibit the secondary mobility of young women in Sunda, the intensity of the conflicts did to slow down the "circular and cumulative causation" (Massey 1990) processes that would otherwise thicken migrants' spatially extended social networks and increase their longer distance flows of migrants. Indeed, Elmhirst (1999) has recently determined that young women's *own* dense migratory networks linking young women from Lampung, South Sumatra, with their migrant counterparts in Tangerang, West Java, may permit them some *disengagement* from parental controls and wishes, and thereby contribute to prompting their migration (also see Thomas-Slayter and Rocheleau 1995 on women's networks in Africa).

In migration studies, it is important to consider the size, composition, and density as critical dimensions of social networks that influence migrants' capacity to rely on them (Portes and Sensenbrenner 1993). Yet until recently, and with several important exceptions (Saptari 2000; Hondagneu-Sotelo 1994; Menjivar 2000; Curran and Saguy 2001), these components were examined through a largely gender-neutral lens. In the context of the crisis, low-income migrant communities in the two studied networks depended in particular on women's provision of reproductive services at low or no cost to support local community and household subsistence. Women in both villages saw their options further localized after 1997, such that longer distance circular migration and resource exchanges grew increasingly unlikely for those with low incomes. Women in Sunda, and members of their communities, with more locally embedded social networks, and greater reliance on women's unpaid family and RNFE work, were not thrust as deeply into poverty as those in Jowo.

The poverty faced by the low-income migrants in Jowo was more severe overall in part because women's networks were weaker and more spatially extended. As Cameron (1999, p. 17) argues, "One possible reason for the weaker impact of the crisis in rural areas is that informal coping mechanisms are still intact in the villages—for example, the sharing of resources across households." Yet, *within* the household, women were more seriously disadvantaged than were men in the context of the widely shared expectation that women be responsible for the majority of the domestic work and the "supplementary" income generation that has become more necessary since 1997 (Frankenberg 1999; Manning 2000; Tjandraningsih 1999). Indeed, within Sunda, while women and men had been equally involved in the RNFE prior to 1997, it was women who entered the sector, or assisted their husbands in the sector, in greater numbers after 1997 (26 percent prior to 1997, and 40 percent after 1997). Men's participation remained at an even 36 percent before and after 1997. This village-scale finding corroborates the findings of larger scale studies that noted that women's increasing labour market flexibility and women's entrance into the already crowded informal sector may have helped to shield households from the worst effects of the crisis (Frankenberg 1999; Manning 2000; Booth 2000).

In sum, in Jowo, because of a relatively weak rural agrarian base and relatively anemic RNFE, the rural-urban network had been an important resource channel for the rural area prior to 1997. But since 1997, the frequency of circular migration and longer distance resource exchanges declined as real incomes fell, and as people who were already close to the margins of subsistence found themselves unable to continue to afford circulation. In contrast, in Sunda, as a result of relatively strong and local networks, the frequency of circulation has only declined minimally, and women's intensified labour has provided a safety net for people embedded in these West Javanese social networks. This suggests that gendered social networks can either promote or discourage migration and resource exchange, depending on the various geographies of the economies and gender relationships in question. This comparison further indicates that the implications of specific network geographies are not pre-given, but rather are shaped by regional economic context and gender relations. Finally, the comparison reveals that what may be positive at the village level may have more contradictory implications for women themselves. While women in Sunda certainly benefit from the overall well-being of their households, it is their intensified labour on which that well-being depends.

In Sunda in particular, women workers provided a range of services that helped their families and communities subsist with lower expenditures. Specifically, women prepared foods from scratch rather than purchasing prepared foods, washed clothing by hand rather than paying someone else for this labour, mended clothing rather than purchasing new clothing, purchased goods from markets further afield in order to save small sums of money, walked rather than pay for a rickshaw (becak) to carry them from market to home, and prepared meals out of lower grade rice, tofu, and vegetables rather than meat. Some women migrated abroad to work as domestic servants in Singapore and Saudi Arabia, and some began participating in the RNFE by selling these services to members of their community who still had resources to purchase them, and most women carried out this work as unpaid family workers. The concluding section of this chapter discusses the implications of these findings for conceptualizing the interactions between gender dynamics, migrants' social networks, and the rural non-farm sector.

Implications for Theory

Research on Indonesia focusing on the interactions between migration decisions and household survival strategies spans over three decades and, like migration theory more generally, reflects a range of theoretical perspectives and analytical emphases. Some studies have focused on the influence of household structure in shaping the migration decisions and labour market participation of household members (cf. Guest 1989; Manning 1987; Leinbach et al. 1992; Hugo 1992). Other research has emphasized the role of power relations and hierarchies *within* households in determining who migrates and with what effects on livelihood (Hetler 1989; Williams 1990; Wolf 1992; Elmhirst 1995). A third stream of scholarship has highlighted the *inter-relatedness* of household structures and individual dynamics in producing particular mobility patterns and employment behaviour (Leinbach and Watkins 1998, Hugo 1998, Lawson 1998 on Latin America). The comparison of Sunda and Jowo builds on these streams of scholarship to examine the inter-linkages across scales of analysis, with a particular focus on gender relations, and their embeddedness in social networks (Portes and Sensenbrenner 1993). The study suggests that the social networks linking household relations with village resource exchange patterns, including productive and reproductive labour and the role of the rural non-farm economy, helps explain the capacity of particular households and villages to cope more or less effectively with the shortages associated with the most recent national economic crisis. However, the study also underscores the point that success of these localized networks has come at the expense of intensified labour among the women and girls within the households.

In Sunda's network, the RNFE played an important role in people's crisis survival, and it did so *along with* the support from the network's strong agricultural base, relatively high rates of land and home ownership, and heightened extraction of women's unpaid labour. This suggests that in conjunction with these additional village- and network-scale socio-economic advantages, a thriving RNFE can serve as part of a village safety net during a period of shortage. Both Sunda's and Jowo's networks operated differently during this period of economic downturn than they had under conditions of relative prosperity. This serves as a reminder that under crisis, low-income people may not continue to be able to access even the social resources available in their safety nets (Roschelle 1997; Menjivar 2000; Silvey forthcoming). Indeed, it appears that the lowest income people have faced particular barriers to access during this period of economic contraction, and that women have faced particularly heavy work burdens. In Jowo, the weakness of the RNFE became a particular problem under crisis. Because occupational multiplicity is the norm, and agriculture-producing sites provide an important buffer for communities in times of crisis, mixed-use development sites may provide better outcomes to villages than do industrial zones.

Positive village and household outcomes appear to be linked to women's intensified labour. While women in these villages and households certainly benefit from the coping capacities of their communities, it is important to keep in mind that they also bear much of the burden of helping their communities cope with periods of resource shortage. As researchers continue to examine socio-spatial networks in a range of locations and economic contexts, these gender dynamics should remain at the centre of the conceptual figures of geographies of subsistence and crisis survival.

References

Arriagada, I. "Changes in the Urban Female Labour Market". *CEPAL Review*, 53 (1994): 91–110.

Beegle, K., E. Frankenberg and D. Thomas. "Measuring Change in Indonesia: Preliminary Results from the Indonesian Family Life Surveys". Interim Report submitted to the World Bank, 26 October 1998.

Booth, Anne. "The Impact of the Economic Crisis on Welfare: What Do We Know Two Years On". In *Indonesia in Transition: Social Dimensions of Reformasi and Crisis*, Chris Manning and Peter van Dierman (eds), pp. 145–62. Singapore: Institute of Southeast Asian Studies, 2000.

Breman, Jan, Otto van den Muizenberg, and Ben White. "Labour Migration in

Asia". Working Papers on Asian Labour, International Research Programme on Changing Labour Relations in Asia (CLARA). Cruquiusweg, The Netherlands: International Institute of Social History, 1997.

Cameron, L. "Survey of Recent Developments". *Bulletin of Indonesian Economic Studies* 35, no. 1 (1999): 3–40.

Chant, S. (ed.). *Gender and Migration in Developing Countries*. London: Belhaven Press, 1992.

Curran, Sara. "Gender Roles and Migration: Good Sons vs. Daughters in Rural Thailand". Seattle Population Research Center Working Paper No. 95-11: University of Washington and Battelle Institute, 1995.

Curran, Sara and Abigail Saguy. "Migration and Culture: A Role for Gender and Social networks?" *Journal of International Women's Studies* 2, no. 3 (2001): 54–77.

Edmundson, W.C. "Do the Rich Get Richer, Do the Poor Get Poorer? East Java, Two Decades, Three Villages, 46 people". *Bulletin of Indonesian Economic Studies* 30, no. 2 (1994): 133–48.

Elmhirst, R. "Gender, Environment and Transmigration; Comparing Migrant and Pribumi Household Strategies in Lampung, Indonesia". Paper presented to the Third WIVS Conference on Indonesian Women in the Household and Beyond. Royal Institute of Linguistics and Anthropology, Leiden, 1995.

Elmhirst, R. "Household Moral Economies and Migration: Negotiating Gender, Kinship and Livelihood Practices in an Indonesian Transmigration Area". In *The Household and Beyond: Cultural Notions and Social Practices in the Study of Gender in Indonesia*, Koning, J., Nolten, M., Rodenburg, J. and Ratna Saptari (eds), pp. 208–34. Leiden: KITLV Press, 1999.

Frankenberg, Elizabeth, Duncan Thomas, and Kathleen Beegle. "The Real Costs of Indonesia's Economic Crisis; Preliminary Findings from the Indonesian Family Life Surveys". Santa Monica, California: RAND, 2000.

Frankenberg, Elizabeth; Thomas, Duncan; Beegle, Kathleen. "Dimensi 'Jender' dalam Krisis: Fakta dari Survei Kehidupan Keluarga Indonesia" (Gender Dimensions of the Crisis: Evidence from the Indonesian Family Life Survey). *SMERU (Monitoring the Social Crisis in Indonesia) Newsletter*, 6 (1999): 1–3.

Grootaert, C. "Social Capital, Household Welfare and Poverty in Indonesia". *Labour Allocation and Rural Development: Migration in Four Javanese Villages*. Local Level Institutions Working Paper. Washington, D.C.: The World Bank 1999.

Guest, Philip. *Labour Allocation and Rural Development: Migration in Four Javanese Villages*. Boulder, Colorado: Westview Press, 1989.

Hadiz, Vedi R. *Workers and the State in New Order Indonesia*. London and New York: Routledge, 1997.

Hetler, C. "The Impact of Circular Migration on a Village Economy". *Bulletin of Indonesian Economic Studies* 25, no. 1 (1989): 53–75.

Hondagneu-Sotelo, Pierrette. *Domèstica; Immigrant Women Cleaning and Caring in the Shadow of Affluence.* Berkeley: University of California Press, 2001.

Hugo, G. "Gender and Migration in Asian Countries". In *Women's Empowerment and Demographic Processes*, Harriet Presser and Gita Sen (eds.), pp. 287–317. International Studies in Demography Series, Oxford: Oxford University Press, 2000.

Hugo, Graeme. "Women on the Move: Changing Patterns of Movement of Women in Indonesia". In *Gender and Migration in Developing Countries*, Sylvia Chant (ed.), 174–95. London: Belhaven Press, 1992.

Lawson, Victoria A. "Hierarchical Households and Gendered Migration in Latin America". *Progress in Human Geography* 23, no. 1 (1998): 323–42.

Leinbach, T. and J. Watkins 1998. "Remittances and Circulation Behaviour in the Livelihood Process: Transmigrant Families in South Sumatra, Indonesia". *Economic Geography* 74, no. 1 (1998): 45–63.

Leinbach, T., J. Watkins, and J. Bowen. "Employment Behavior and the Family in Indonesian Transmigration". *Annals of the Association of American Geographers* 82, no. 1 (1992): 23–47.

Manning, C. "Rural Economic Change and Labour Mobility: A Case Study from West Java". *Bulletin of Indonesian Economic Studies* 23, no. 3 (1987): 52–79.

Manning, Chris. "Labour Market Adjustment to Indonesia's Economic Crisis: Context, Trends and Implications". *Bulletin of Indonesian Economic Studies* 36, no. 1 (2000): 105–36.

Manning, Chris and Peter van Dierman. "Recent Developments and Social Aspects of Reformasi and Crisis: An Overview". In *Indonesia in Transition; Social Aspects of Reformasi and Crisis*, Chris Manning and Peter van Dierman (eds), pp. 1–11. Canberra: Australian National University and Singapore: Institute of Southeast Asian Studies, 2000.

Massey, Douglas. "Social Structure, Household Strategies, and the Cumulative Causation of Migration." *Population Index* 56, no. 1 (1990): 3–26.

Menjivar, Cecilia. *Fragmented Ties: Salvadoran Immigrant Networks in American.* Berkeley and Los Angeles, California: University of California Press, 2000.

Mills, Mary Beth. "Contesting the Margins of Modernity: Women, Migration, and Consumption in Thailand". *American Ethnologist* 24, no. 1 (1997): 37–61.

Morrison, P.S. "Transitions in Rural Sarawak: Off-farm Employment in the Kamena Basin". *Pacific Viewpoint* 34 (1993): 45–68.

Portes, Alejandro and Julia Sensenbrenner. "Embeddedness and Immigration: Notes on the Social Determinants of Economic Action". *American Journal of Sociology* 98, no. 6 (1993): 1320–50.

Rigg, J. "Rural–Urban Interactions, Agriculture, and Wealth: A Southeast Asian Perspective". *Progress in Human Geography* 22, no. 4 (1998): 497–522.

Roschelle, Anne R. *No More Kin; Exploring Race, Class, and Gender in Family Networks*. London: Sage Publications, 1997.

Saptari, Ratna. "Networks of Reproduction among Cigarette Factory Women in East Java". In *Women and Households in Indonesia; Cultural Notions and Social Practices*, Juliette Koning, Marleen Nolten, Janet Rodenburg, and Ratna Saptari (eds), pp. 181–98. Richmond, Surrey: Curzon Press, 2000.

Silvey, Rachel. "Spaces of Protest: Gendered Migration, Social Networks and Labor Activism in West Java, Indonesia", *Political Geography* 22, no. 2 (2003): 129–55.

Smith, J. and I. Wallerstein. *Creating and Transforming Households: The Constraints of the World Economy*. Paris: Cambridge University Press, 1992.

Sumarto, S., A. Wetterberg and L. Pritchett. "The Social Impact of the Crisis in Indonesia: Results from a Nationwide Kecamatan Survey". Mimeographed. Preliminary draft, SMERU, Jakarta, 1998.

Thomas-Slayter, Barbara and Diane Rocheleau. *Gender, Environment, and Development in Kenya; A Grassroots Perspective*. London: Lynne Reiner, 1995.

Tjandraningsih, Indrasari. "Krisis dan Buruh Pabrik: Dampak dan Masalah 'Jender'" (The Crisis and Factory Workers: Some Gender Issues). *SMERU, Monitoring the Social Crisis in Indonesia*, World Bank 6, 1999.

Village Register for 'Jowo'. Mimeo, 2000.

Village Register for 'Sunda'. Mimeo, 2000.

White, B. "Population, Employment, and Involution in a Javanese Village". *Development and Change* 7 (1976): 267–90.

White, Benjamin and Gunawan Wiradi. "Agrarian and Non-Agrarian Bases of Inequality in Nine Javanese Villages". In *Agrarian Transformations: Local Processes and the State in Southeast Asia*, Gillian Hart, Andrew Turton and Benjamin White (eds), pp. 266–302. Berkeley: University of California Press, 1989.

Williams, L. *Development, Demography, and Family Decision Making: The Status of Women in Rural Java*. Boulder: Westview Press, 1990.

Wolf, Diane 1992. *Factory Daughters; Gender, Household Dynamics, and Rural Transformation in Java*. University of California Press: Berkeley and Los Angeles, California, 1992.

7
MICRO AND SMALL-SCALE ENTERPRISES IN JAVA, INDONESIA:
A Gender-based Comparative Analysis of Entrepreneurial Behaviour and Performance of Enterprises

Surendra P. Singh
Harsha N. Mookherjee
Safdar Muhammad

Introduction

The concept of low income people entering the economic main stream through self-employment and perhaps creating new business and jobs that can revitalize communities has considerable appeal. Also, the less than successful results of industrialization policies in densely populated areas of developing countries and the inability of the agricultural sector to absorb surplus labour and reduce poverty have prompted the need to focus on alternatives. The case of micro and small enterprises (MSE) as a source of employment and income creation reflects this reality. The potential contribution of small enterprises (fifty workers or less) in generating employment and income in developing countries has been increasingly recognized. The development of MSEs is seen as a way of targeting aid at the poor and creating job opportunities (Liedholm, McPherson and Chuta 1994; Humphrey and Schmitz 1996).

Additionally, MSEs are also important because of their geographic location and increasing participation by women in developing countries. Many, if not the majority of new women workers in developing countries have entered the labour force through the MSE sector, primarily because of ease of entry and limited access to other enterprises and employment opportunities. Small enterprises play a critical role in times of economic change by providing a buffer for both upward and downward mobility. The development of the MSE sector has also been considered as an alternative strategy to strengthen the role of small town in rural development (Downing 1990). Recognizing this, the Government of Indonesia (GOI) has long recognized the importance of small scale and cottage industries in regional and national economic development. Recent economic turbulence and concern with growing economic and social inequalities have stimulated discussions of means and objectives of government policies regarding small businesses.

Indonesia's population grew at a rate of 1.6 percent per annum over the decade from 1990 to 2000. Its population is relatively young implying that Indonesia's labour force will grow faster and the demand for new job opportunities will continue into the future. The size of the nation's labour force increased from 52.4 million in 1980 to over 101 million by the year 2000. After 33 years of virtually uninterrupted 7 percent annual growth, Indonesia's GDP slumped nearly 13 percent in 1998 and per capita income dropped from $1,200 in 1996 to $570 in 2000. An estimated 40 million people are living below the poverty line (www.USAID.gov). Despite the rapid growth in the past, the structure of economic activities is still based on informal or traditional activities in which most people are employed. Agriculture, including forestry and fishing, is an important sector, accounting for almost 20 percent of the GDP and more than 50 percent of the labour force. However, agriculture is not able to absorb the additional labour force, and the modern sector where the growth has been impressive, has not been able to slash either underemployment, or to absorb the 2.3 million workers entering the workforce annually. Because of the country's limited capacity to absorb labour, it is necessary to develop job opportunities.

The majority of the research in micro and small-scale enterprises in developing countries has focused on examining characteristics of enterprises and entrepreneurs, and measuring the growth of micro and small enterprises (Zapalska and Edwards 2001). In terms of participation, both male and female entrepreneurs are involved in operating such enterprises. There are however, not many micro studies focusing exclusively on gender-differentiated firms and comparable data.

Research on women entrepreneurs is extensive in developed countries; however, studies of women entrepreneurs in developing countries are comparatively scarce (Allen and Truman 1993; Lerner, Brush and Hisrich 1997; Mukhtar 1997). Although there is a tendency to conduct research based on "female only samples," not many comparative studies have been undertaken (Mukhtar 1997). In addition, because of the wide variation in social structures, work, family, and organized social life in developing countries (Allen and Truman 1993), studies of women entrepreneurs are needed. It is also criticized that the cumulative knowledge of female business remains limited and presents a static and therefore distorted view of the process of female business formation and growth (Carter and Cannon 1992). Developing countries including Indonesia need the full participation of women in their struggle to confront the challenges of poverty, as women constitute roughly half of the population. Given the growth of entrepreneurship among women in Indonesia and other countries, it is important to better understand women's entrepreneurship for policy programme development.

Purpose

Against this background, an attempt is made here to fill some void in the knowledge of women entrepreneurs in developing countries by examining micro and small-scale enterprises at two levels (the individual and the enterprise) in Java, Indonesia. Our effort in this chapter will be directed toward analyzing and separating differences in characteristics of enterprises, entrepreneurs, entrepreneurial behaviour (attitudes and perceptions), and performance of enterprises by female and male entrepreneurs. The chapter also examines the factors that influence performance of women entrepreneurs in Java. In the end implications of findings are discussed in the context of future policies and programmes to promote micro and small enterprises.

The specific objectives of this chapter are to determine whether Javanese women entrepreneurs differ from their male counterparts with respect to: (1) personal background; (2) business organizational characteristics, performance indicators and business growth; (3) perceived business problems and motivations; and (4) entrepreneurial behaviour. Apart from the economic significance of small businesses in the private sector, the survival of these businesses has far reaching social implications. Acquiring a comprehensive and integrated view of women entrepreneurs and their businesses, which are presumed to be unique due to culture-specific customs, values, and language should prove to be invaluable in formulating policies and programmes for entrepreneurial development.

Previous Research

Historically, the role of non-farm activities has been of increasing importance in rural economy of Java since the colonial period (Effendi 1991). Several studies in Java have indicated the increasing importance of off-farm employment, small-scale industries, and participation of women in micro and small-scale industries (Stoffer and Sutanto 1990; Evers 1991; Singh, Comer and Effendi 1994; Berry, Rodriguez and Sandee 1999).

A large number of research in entrepreneurship has been founded upon the premise that entrepreneurs can be identified by the distinctive personality characteristics that they possess (Zapalska and Edwards 2001). From the literature, a number of consistencies can be observed as to the characteristics of entrepreneurs. The entrepreneur is independent by nature, risk taking, achievement oriented, self confident, optimistic, hard working and innovative. Other characteristics of a successful entrepreneur typically include such attributes as being competitive, independent, decisive, and self confident (Zapalska 1997). The implication of this is that a person will be less successful at entrepreneurship unless he/she exhibits these characteristics.

A number of studies suggest that female-owned businesses are smaller in scale and are typically characterized by lower financial performance and slower growth rates than male-owned businesses (Hisrich and Brush 1987; Fisher, Reuber and Dyke 1993; Srinivansan, Woo and Cooper 1994; Johnson and Storey 1994). Female-owned enterprises are also more likely to employ female workers. Other studies have concluded that women are more likely to be engaged in small retail or service businesses where the growth rate is limited (Dant, Brush and Iniesta 1996). Prior studies have suggested that social structures, family, and organized social life affect the female's access to entrepreneurial opportunities and may influence performance. Recent research studies on gender differences provide mixed conclusions but tend to support gender similarities more than differences (Chaganati and Parsuraman 1996; Sonfield, Lussier, Cormen and McKinney 2001).

In the past, some studies have focused on the motivation that underlies the actions of entrepreneurs (Tinker 1987; Grown and Sebstad 1989). Much of the analysis in these studies was developed in an attempt to understand the differences in experience between female and male entrepreneurs. Cobbe (1985), Tinker (1987), and Downing (1990) suggested that women had different business objectives and strategies from men. Female entrepreneurs, they argued, tend to grow laterally, engaging in multiple income-generating activities.

Studies of the performance of women entrepreneurs are few (Brush 1992), with the majority of research not being comparative among groups of women and men. Although studies conducted in the 1990s added to our understanding of performance similarities and differences, "performances" in entrepreneurial businesses were operationalized differently making it difficult to compare across studies. Most frequently used operationalizations of performance include survival, growth in employees, and profitability (Srinivansan, Woo and Cooper 1994; Lerner, Brush and Hisrich 1997). Lerner, Brush and Hisrich (1997) developed a model based on five theoretical perspectives to explain performance of women entrepreneurs in the Israeli context.

Zapalska (1997) found significant differences between men and women with respect to the objectives for their ventures and what they perceived as critical success factors. The study concluded that women entrepreneurs in transitioning economies differed from men in: the obstacles they faced, their reasons for starting a business, their goals, and the factors they perceived as important to success. Past research also revealed that female-owned enterprises are frequently hindered by a lack of business information, advice, and access to networks and business support systems (Hisrich and Fulop 1994; Bliss and Garratt 2001). Financial problems or lack of financial experience and skills consistently pose greater problems for females than males (Aldrich 1989). Kallerberg and Leicht (1991) however, found that female businesses were just as successful as male businesses. There are problems that both men and women entrepreneurs face, but historical and social factors make it more difficult for women to organize and operate enterprises (Hisrich and Fulop 1994). Additionally, Hisrich and Fulop (1994) cite several "female only" factors: fewer mentors, the culture's lack of respect for women in business, and the insufficient business training of women. Zapalska (1997) cites lack of information and insufficient training opportunities as barriers to starting a business that may impact women more than men.

In summary, many studies have attempted to identify the similarities and differences between male and female entrepreneurs. While more similarities than differences were found, relatively consistent differences between the two gender groups in the areas of personal background, business characteristics and performance exist. This study extends these previous studies in Java, Indonesia, by proposing a gender analysis of micro and small-scale enterprises.

Research Questions

In accordance with the objectives of the study, the following research questions are delineated:

1. How are micro and small-scale enterprises distributed by type, size, age, employment, employment growth rate and by gender of the owner/operator?
2. What are the overall personal and demographic characteristics of female entrepreneurs and do they have a different background than their male counterparts in terms of education, training, age, and the length of their involvement with current business?
3. Do women entrepreneurs differ from male entrepreneurs in their perception of business problems and needs and assistance?
4. Do male and female entrepreneurs differ in their entrepreneurial behaviour (attitudes and perception), leadership qualities and behaviour?
5. What are the important factors that influence the performance of female entrepreneurs?

Study Area And Research Methodology

The Study Area, Sample and Data Collection

The sampling method of the survey was designed to obtain comparative data for relatively developed and lesser developed areas (villages), the smaller enterprises among the five major groups of industries, and male- versus female-owned/operated enterprises and entrepreneurs (Singh et al. 1999). The island of Java selected for the study, is divided into four provinces. The two Javanese provinces of Central Java and Yogyakarta, with heterogeneous qualities of small-scale enterprise development were purposely selected for the study. Two districts in each of the selected provinces were selected randomly, and from each district a village was purposely selected to represent contrasting physical as well as socio-economic characteristics and density of population. The selected villages Tamananagung and Krendatan in Central Java, and Bangunjiwo and Banjaroyo in Yogykarta Province in general, represented relatively developed and lesser-developed areas and varied in rural non-farm activities. It was postulated that the villages with more developed hinterland would have better opportunities for business and employment than the villages with lesser-developed hinterland. It was theorized that the diversity of the villages would provide a wider and comprehensive insight into the nature and factors affecting the development of small-scale enterprises in Java (Singh et al. 1999).

A stratified random sample of micro and small-scale enterprises in each of the selected villages was selected from the list of enterprises provided by the local officials and village leaders. The sample included all major types of non-farm activities (production/manufacturing, food processing, textile/garment, trade, and services) as well as a diversity of enterprises in terms of size and type. A coded questionnaire containing two major parts was formulated. The first part included questions dealing with general information about the enterprise and its history. Information was collected on: type of business activity, location and seasonality of business, number and type of workers, resources used, marketing and other activities. Included in the second part were questions to determine socio-economic characteristics of entrepreneurs, perception, attitude, problems, and outlook of entrepreneurs. The data from 200 entrepreneurs was collected through the personal interview method, using trained enumerators during the Summer and Fall of 1996.

Since the focus of this exploratory study was on delineating characteristics of female-owned/operated businesses and entrepreneurs, and how they compared to their male counterparts, bivariate analysis was used. Chi-square analysis was primarily used to examine Questions 1 and 2, and t-tests were utilized to examine Research Questions 3 and 4.

Descriptive Profile of Micro and Small-Scale Enterprises

Small is a relative concept, and what is considered small in one country may not be considered small in another. Also, there is no common agreement among studies, authors and organizations about what constitutes a small-scale firm (Singh et al. 1999). In this study, the definition used by the Central Bureau of Statistics (*Biro Pusat Statistik*) of Indonesia to classify industries is used. This classification is based on the number of workers employed. The small-scale industries are classified as industries with 5–19 workers, and micro enterprises (household/cottage establishments) are classified as workers with less than 4 workers.

All of the responding 200 businesses were identified as "small" or "micro" enterprises. 44 percent (n=88) of the sample consisted of male business operators/owners, and 56 percent (n=112) consisted of female business owners/operators. Of all the enterprises surveyed, the majority (36 percent) were in food processing, followed by production/manufacturing (29 percent) and trade (18.5 percent) (Table 7.1). Enterprises operated by male entrepreneurs were dominated by production/manufacturing sub-sectors (70.7 percent), whereas female-owned/operated enterprises were concentrated in food processing and trade sub-sectors (78.8 and 67.6 percent). The Chi-square test of significance for differences in the distribution of enterprises by types revealed that distribution in different groups (types) varied significantly by gender of entrepreneur (Table 7.1). This shows that most of the female-owned/operated enterprises are concentrated in informal or traditional sector, whereas males generally operate businesses in relatively more progressive and capital intensive sub-sectors. The typical enterprise was 12.2 years old; male enterprises on an average were in existence a little longer (12.6 yrs.) compared to female enterprises (11.9 yrs.) (Table 7.1).

Almost 94 percent of the selected small enterprises were sole proprietorships and the remaining were family or part-ownership, which is typical of MSEs (Table 7.2). A large number (90.5 percent) of the enterprises were initiated by the present owner or operator. The remaining were initiated by parents, grandparents or a close relative. This means that only few enterprises were inherited, and the majority were started or initiated by the present owner or operator. This information has positive implications for the development of new enterprises and entrepreneurship. Separation of ownership and operation generally does not exist for rural small-scale enterprises in Java. The owner is usually also the operator. Among the 200 selected enterprises, 82.5 percent of the enterprises had combined owner and operators, i.e., owners were also the operators. In some cases (17.5 percent) where the owners were not the operators, the operator was either a relative or a person close to and well-trusted by the owner.

TABLE 7.1
Distribution of Selected Enterprises by Gender of the Owner/of Operator, Enterprise Type, and Average Number of Years in Operation

Enterprise Type	Gender of Operator/Owner								All	
	Male				Female					
	N	Percent	N	Percent	N	Percent of all selected enterprises	N	Percent of all selected enterprises	Average years in operation	Max. years in operation
Production/Manufacturing	41	70.7	17	29.3	58	29.0			13.3	40.0
Food Processing	21	29.2	51	70.8	72	36.0			13.8	46.0
Garment/Textile	4	44.4	5	55.6	9	4.5			16.1	26.0
Trade	12	32.4	25	67.6	37	18.5			9.3	32
Service	9	39.1	14	60.9	23	11.5			7.5	30
Transportation	1	100	0	–	1	0.5			5.0	5.0
Total	88	44	112	56	200	100				
Mean yrs. In operation		12.6		11.9					12.2	

X² (Chi-Square) value for the sex of operator = 11.071; Significant at 0.05 level of probability.

Capacity to Create Employment and Growth of Enterprises

In densely populated areas of developing countries, small-scale enterprises are considered as important means of creating employment. Typically, the selected MSEs were quite small in terms of employment with the average number of current workers being 5.25 (inclusive of the proprietor). At the start of the business, 21 percent of the enterprises had only one worker (i.e., the proprietor), and another 50 percent had two workers. Only 3 percent of the enterprises started with more than five employees. The female-owned/operated enterprises had significantly fewer workers compared to male-owned/operated enterprises (Table 7.2). The highest number of workers employed was also significantly higher for male enterprises, 6.2 compared to 3.4 for female entrepreneurs. Consequently, the labour absorption capacity of the enterprises in the area was low. Overall almost 50 percent of the labour was hired labour, while the remaining was family or proprietors' own labour (Table 7.2). It is important to note that almost half of the labour force was unpaid family labour. This is of significance when considering the type of enterprise or providing support to enterprises.

A number of recent studies have shed light on the dynamic characteristics of small enterprises in developing countries (McPherson 1996). Many small enterprises do not grow at all and failure rates are high. But there are some that grow in dramatically rapid fashion. It is important for policy makers to know what factors cause some small enterprises to grow and why others do not grow, but continue to survive for many years. According to traditional neo-classical theory, workers are added until the value of the marginal product of the last worker is equal to the wage paid to that worker. This implies, that the firm's growth will occur as a reaction to changes in technology, the wage rate, or the price of the product. Therefore, the factors that impact on supply and demand for the product produced by the small enterprises, may affect growth rates of these enterprises.

Growth of small enterprises can be measured in several ways, including growth in sales, profits, or number of workers. Defining growth in terms of sales or profits might be preferable to a labour-based measure from an accuracy standpoint. However, small entrepreneurs in general, do not keep records and reporting of sales and profits may not be reliable (McPherson 1996). As a result, the growth in this study is measured in

TABLE 7.2
Selected Organizational and Performance Indicators of Selected Enterprises in Java, Indonesia

Characteristic	Male	Female	All
Legal Status of Business (percent)			
Sole Proprietorship	96.5	96.4	96.5
Partnership	3.5	3.6	3.5
Employment:			
Av. No. of Workers (Current)			
Owner/Operator	1.00	1.00	1.00
Family	1.24	1.31	1.28
Hired	3.01	1.12	1.96
Total ***	5.25	3.40	4.24
Highest-No. of workers Enterprise ever had***	6.21	3.43	4.50
Average Annual Growth Rate in Employment By Type of Enterprise (percent)			
Manufacturing/Production*	38.34	18.31	32.47
Food Processing	9.25	4.26	5.67
Textile/Garments	21.25	31.80	27.11
Trade	0.44	6.24	4.36
Services	13.36	13.23	13.49
Total***	22.83	9.19	15.15
Av. Total Capital Invested At the Start (Million Rp.)	1.83	1.37	1.60
Av. Net Income Last Month (Rp).**	424,978	270,684	338,573
Percent of Entrepreneurs receiving credit from organized sources	37.50	34.80	36.00
Percent engaged in farming	23.9	17.9	20.5
Percent of household income from Enterprise	79.56	62.55	70.03
Future growth of enterprises, perceived by entrepreneurs (percent)			
Increase	45.5	2935	36.5
Slight increase	27.2	33.9	31.0
No Change	19.3	25.6	22.8
Decrease	8.0	11.9	9.7

*** Significant at the 0.01 level of probability, 2 sample t-test; ** Significant at the 0.05 level of probability, 2 sample t – test, * Significant at the 0.10 level of probability, 2 sample t – test

terms of changes in the number of workers. Following McPherson (1991) growth is defined as:

$$\text{Growth} = \frac{\text{Current employment} - \text{Initial employment}}{\text{Firm age}}$$

Current employment here refers to the number employed at the time of the survey, initial employment refers to employment at the start of the firm, and firm age is the years the enterprise has been in operation. Thus, the difference between the current year (1996) and year the firm was started gives the age of the firm. Average annual growth rate in employment (Growth) by gender and type of enterprises in the sample is estimated and presented in the Table 7.2.

The selected enterprises do not show considerable degree of dynamism. The overall employment in the average enterprise grew by 15.15 percent per year from its beginning until the time the survey took place (Table 7.2). These rates seem to be in line with those reported for other countries. Liedholm (1990) reported similar rates of around 15 percent for Columbia, Nigeria, and India. The growth rate for male-operated enterprises was more than 2.5 times (22.83 percent) higher compared to (9.19 percent) for female-operated firms (Table 7.2) and the difference was significant between male and female enterprises. Calculated average annual growth rates exhibited a considerable amount of variation by type of enterprises (Table 7.2). The fastest growing sectors were manufacturing/production (32.47 percent) and textile/garments (27.11 percent), while the least dynamic sector appeared to be trade (4.36 percent), and food processing (5.67 percent). The selected enterprises also exhibited differential patterns of growth according to the gender of the operator. Overall, female-operated enterprises grew less than half the rate of male-operated enterprises. One of the fastest growing sectors, the manufacturing/production, tended to be dominated by male entrepreneurs, whereas one of the least dynamic sectors, food processing, was dominated by female entrepreneurs. This may be one of the main reasons for the much lower growth rate for female-operated enterprises. Interestingly, female-operated enterprises generally grew much slower than the male-operated enterprises with in the same sector as well. Only textile/garments enterprises, operated by female entrepreneurs, grew faster than male operated enterprises (Table 7.2).

Average Capital Investment, Income and Credit

Small-scale enterprises are often seen as easy to start due to the small capital requirement. About 5 percent of selected enterprises needed less than Rp. 10,000 to start the business. On the other hand about 6 percent of the enterprises invested Rp. 5 million or more to start a business. On an average female enterprises invested only about 75 percent of the typical male enterprise investment. Male-operated enterprises required comparatively higher average capital to start than the female operated enterprises (Table 7.2). This is partly because of the type of enterprises the males operated. But the very high standard deviation for each type of enterprise indicated considerable variation within the same type of industries.

Net income varied considerably by type of enterprise and gender of operator. The average net income was significantly lower for female-operated enterprises, and was approximately 64 percent of the income of the male-operated enterprises (Table 7.2). Also, it should be noted with concern to local developers that more than one-fourth of the enterprises fell in the lowest income category of Rp. 100,000 per month. A much higher percentage of female enterprises, 38.4 percent compared to 9.1 percent of the male enterprises, had net income per month below Rp. 100,000. Only 2.7 percent of the female entrepreneurs compared to 11.4 percent of male entrepreneurs had net income per month of above Rp. 1 million. Overall 36 percent of all the selected entrepreneurs indicated that they had ever received credit from organized sources. The percentage varied by type of enterprise and whether it was operated by a male or female entrepreneur. A large number of entrepreneurs borrowed from "family" and "friends". This indicates that relatively smaller number of enterprises, male or female, have access to or used formal credit.

Importance of Enterprises in Total Household's Income and Future Plans for Growth

Almost 21 percent of entrepreneurs responding were engaged in farming (Table 7.2). For the selected entrepreneurs (households) on an average, 70 percent of the total income was from the enterprise(s) they operated and percentage varied from a low of 9 percent to 100 percent. More male entrepreneurs were engaged in farming but a substantially higher percentage of their household's income was earned from the enterprise(s) they operated (Table 7.2). When asked about their future growth plans of the enterprise, the majority (45.5 percent) of male entrepreneurs said they planned to increase (expand) compared to only 29.5 percent of the female entrepreneurs. 8 percent of the male entrepreneurs and almost 12 percent of the female entrepreneurs expected a decrease in the future. The opinions about the future growth of the enterprise varied significantly between male and female entrepreneurs (Table 7.2). Male entrepreneurs were more optimistic about their future growth than the female entrepreneurs.

Profile and Personality Characteristics of Selected Entrepreneurs

A large percentage (56 percent) of the enterprises had female owners/operators but the percentage varied by type of enterprise. The highest percentage of female-operated enterprises was in food processing (Table 7.1). The average age of entrepreneurs was 41 years; male entrepreneurs were about 4 years older (43 years) than their female counterparts (39 years). The youngest operator was 17 years old and oldest was 75 years old. The average age was highest in services followed by transportation and manufacturing/production sub-sectors). More than 92 percent of the entrepreneurs were married, and the remaining were either divorced or widowed (Table 7.3). Entrepreneurship in rural Java, is dominated by local Javanese. A very large majority (89.5 percent) of the selected entrepreneurs were of Javanese ethnicity and belonged to the Islamic religion. The remaining (10.5 percent) were of Chinese ethnicity. The largest percentage of Chinese entrepreneurs (22.2 percent) were in textile/garments, followed by manufacturing/production (13.8 percent). More than 71.5 percent of the entrepreneurs in the study were born in the villages where they currently operate businesses.

The quality of human resources affects the development of small enterprises in rural areas. The level of education was low among the entrepreneurs selected for the study. Almost 7 percent of the selected entrepreneurs were illiterate, while another 57 percent had up to primary (6th grade) school education. Only about 3.0 percent either had few years of college or completed a college education (Table 7.3). Female operators had less education than their male counterparts. However, the educational level between male and female was not significantly different. This general lower literacy level must be considered in planning any enterprise programme aimed at female entrepreneurs. A large percentage (52.7 percent) of female entrepreneurs indicated to have had no formal training compared to 40.9 percent of male entrepreneurs. With respect to technical education, almost no entrepreneur had any formal skill training. Most (38 percent) said that their knowledge was based on "self teaching" followed by parents or family (33 percent). Only about 10.5 percent said

TABLE 7.3
Selected Characteristics of Entrepreneurs By Gender

Characteristics	Male (n=88)	Female (n=112)	All (n=200)
Sex of Entrepreneur (Percent)	44.00	56.00	100.00
Average Age (Years)	42.97	39.39	41.20
Martial Status (Percent) – Married	93.18	90.72	92.5
Not Married	6.82	9.28	7.5
Ethnicity (Percent)			
Chinese	8.00	12.5	10.5
Javanese	92.0	87.5	89.5
Education (Percent)			
No school (cannot read/write)	4.5	8.0	6.5
Primary school	50.0	63.50	57.50
Junior High School	18.2	14.30	16.0
Senior High School	18.2	11.6	13.0
College	4.5	1.8	3.0
University	4.6	.9	2.5
Operator had any training in the Business being operated (Percent)			
(yes)	59.1	47.3	52.5
(no)	40.9	52.7	47.5
Technical skill/training (Percent)			
No training	5.7	7.1	6.5
From Parents/Family	22.7	41.1	33.0
Formal Education	0	5.4	3.0
Self taught	45.5	33.0	38.5
Informal workshop/apprentice	18.2	4.5	40.5
Other	7.8	9.0	–

X^2 (Chi-square) value for the sex of entrepreneur 29.49; significant at 0.01 level of probability.

that they had attended informal workshops. The Chi-square test of significance for differences in the type of technical skill by gender of entrepreneurs revealed that skills/training varied by gender of entrepreneurs. More male entrepreneurs (45.5 percent) indicated that they were self-taught, but 41 percent of female entrepreneurs were taught by their parents/family (Table 7.3).

Motivation to Start a Business and Preference for Type of Business

The need for additional income was the motivating factor given by most entrepreneurs for starting the business. Need for additional income was followed by desire to be independent or for self-identity in 30 percent of the entrepreneurs. Other reasons given for starting the business were: the desire to be independent or creative, tradition, and flexibility (Figure 7.1). When asked why they chose a particular type of business the majority said that it fit with the family circumstances, was profitable, or both. Other reasons given were: personal factors and the area's development environment. Obviously, the motivation for starting the enterprise was generally based on income prospects. But family needs and management skills were also offered as reasons. The primary motivation for men and women to start up a business differed significantly as indicated by a highly significant chi-square value (20.03) for the difference between the genders.

FIGURE 7.1
Primary Motivation to Start a Business as Indicated by the Selected Entrepreneurs by Gender

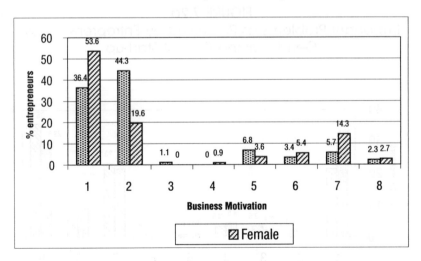

Where, 1 = Need for additional income 2 = Wanted to be independent 3 = More control 4 = Flexibility 5 = Need to be creative 6 = To preserve the tradition 7 = Combination (1&2) 8 = Combination (1&5).

X^2 (Chi-Square) value for the gender of entrepreneur = 20.3, significant at 0.01 level of significance.

Perceived Business Problems and Needs of Selected Entrepreneurs By Gender

Problems faced by small entrepreneurs may be structural or managerial. For developing policies and programmes it is necessary to know the problems/constraints faced, needs of the entrepreneurs, and whether the problems vary by type of enterprise. Entrepreneurs were asked what they thought were the main problems faced by their enterprise at two different points in time: when the enterprise was started, and at the time the survey was conducted (currently). A broad spectrum of business problems and needs that small business owners are likely to face were included. The majority of business problems were adopted from previous research (Dodge and Robbins 1992). The highest in the list of problems perceived by entrepreneurs at the start-up was lack of capital followed by poor marketing. Both males and females at the start of the enterprise ranked capital, marketing, labour, and facilities as the four main problem areas (Figure 7.2a). Furthermore, perceptions of problems appeared not to change much between the startup and the time of the survey. But the percentage

FIGURE 7.2a
Important Problems as Perceived by Entrepreneurs by Gender at the Time of Start-up

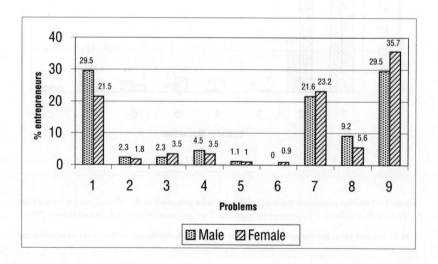

of respondents who perceived that they have these problems varied and some additional problems appeared after the start-up. Significantly almost one-third of the respondents thought there were no problem at the start and of these, female operators were more conspicuous. This may be due to the fact that these entrepreneurs did not expect much or had any plans for the future (Figure 7.2a).

Financial problems in the form of capital for the business were more frequent among female entrepreneurs than among male entrepreneurs at the time of the survey (Figure 7.2b). Labour problems were also significantly more frequent among female entrepreneurs. Capital and marketing remained from the start up through the survey period as the two most significant problems for the entrepreneurs (Figures 7.2a and 7.2b).

A total of eight problems in two major groups (marketing and basic management skills) were listed to gauge responses from entrepreneurs as to

FIGURE 7.2b
Important Problems as Perceived by Entrepreneurs by Gender at the Time of Survey (Currently)

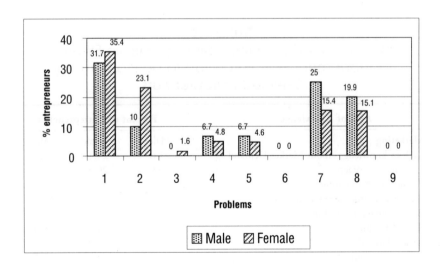

Where, 1 = Capital 2 = Labor 3 = Skilled Manpower 4 = Facilities and Tools 5 = Competition 6 = Management 7 = Marketing 8 = Other 9 = No Problem

how their lack of knowledge in these areas were perceived to be a problem. A significantly large number of female business owners/operators were perceived to have a lack of knowledge on legal matters, and inventory control compared to male operators. But record keeping was perceived to be a problem by more male operators (Table 7.4). In marketing, although both males and females faced similar problems in all areas, female operators compared to male operators perceived more problems due to lack of knowledge. These results are important when considering training programmes for entrepreneurs.

Entrepreneurship and Leadership

Entrepreneurship is an accumulation of the outlook, perception and attitude of the entrepreneurs dealing with internal as well as external factors that may influence business process and outcome. Consequently, entrepreneurship is a result of certain thought patterns rather than the setting or business itself. Not everyone can be a successful entrepreneur. There are certain qualities, however, that seem to separate those who are likely to be successful as entrepreneurs and those who may not (Zaplaska 1997; Singh et al. 1999).

TABLE 7.4
Lack of Knowledge in Marketing and Basic Enterprise Management Skills Perceived to be Problems by Selected Entrepreneurs

Area of Knowledge	Percent of Entrepreneurs		
Marketing	Male	Female	All
Lack of knowledge About Market Demand	21.6	24.1	23.0
Customer Contacts	13.6	20.5	17.5
Promotion/Advertising	51.1	58.9	55.5
Business environment conditions	46.6	51.8	49.5
Basic Management Skills			
Record Keeping	72.7	64.3	68.0
Legal Matters**	69.3	83.0	77.0
Inventory Control*	23.9	43.8	35.0
Cash Flow	45.5	44.6	45.0

* Significant at 0.01 level of significance; ** Significant at 0.05 level of probability.

Attitudes and Perceptions of Entrepreneurs (Entrepreneurial Behaviour)

A number of statements adopted from previous research (Voorhis 1980; Downing 1990) were included in the study to measure attitudes and perceptions of male, female and all entrepreneurs toward management (entrepreneurial behaviour) (Singh et al. 1999). The relative importance attached to different statements was captured using a Likert type, five-point scale (1=strongly agree, 2=agree, 3=doubt, 4=disagree, and 5=strongly disagree). Differences between male and female operators' responses were tested for various statements. In Table 7.5, selected statements and their mean scores used to measure the relative importance attached to different statements by gender are presented. Also only statements found to be significant for differences between two genders are listed (for details please

TABLE 7.5
Differences in Attitudes/Perceptions (Entrepreneurial Behaviour) of Selected Entrepreneurs by Gender of Entrepreneur

	Statements	Male	Female (Mean)	Total
A	I am generally optimistic.*	1.43	1.77	1.62
B	I enjoy associating with my co-workers after work.*	1.64	2.00	1.84
C	I like to know & seek to know what ever is happening.*	2.05	2.61	2.36
D	When I am right I can convince others to believe so.***	2.18	2.39	2.30
E	I enjoy impressing others with the things I am able to do.*	2.57	2.96	2.79

Significant at: *0.01, **0.05 percent, and ***0.10 level of probability.
The mean is calculated to measure the relative importance attained to different statements by gender using a Likert Scale 1–5, where 1= strongly agree with the statement, 2= agree, 3= doubt, 4= disagree, and 5= strongly disagree.

see Singh et al. 1999). A 't'-test for the difference between the means of two related samples showed no significant overall difference between the importance attached to various statements by males and females. A total of five statements were significant for gender differences at a 0.10 level of significance or lower. The responses (means) of males and females on various behaviours were similar, except when dealing with their employees. Results indicated that male entrepreneurs appeared to be more optimistic about their business and had more confidence in their communication abilities than female entrepreneurs. Also, male entrepreneurs liked to know or were more aware of situations that affected their business than the female entrepreneurs. More women entrepreneurs in general, did not have very strong opinions and appeared to be more flexible compared to their male counterparts (Table 7.5).

Leadership Qualities/Behaviour of Entrepreneurs

The reason for fostering leadership is to empower people to achieve some external goals, not merely to exercise leadership as an end in itself. Leaders provide meaningful direction and focus (i.e., purpose) to collective effort and in this process cause others to willingly exert effort to achieve the purpose. Leadership does not have to be imposed like authority. It is welcomed and wanted by those who are led. Leaders are most needed when the resources (human, financial, institutional, intellectual) available to achieve goals are limited.

A number of statements in this study were used to measure leadership ability and attitude that project leadership qualities and if they differ by gender of the entrepreneur. The relative importance attached to different statements was captured using Likert type format 1–5 scale. A 't'-test for the difference between the means of two genders indicates significant differences in four statements. These statements along with mean scores attached to different statements by gender are presented in Table 7.6 (For details please see Singh et al. 1999). Male entrepreneurs appeared to agree more with statements regarding advice from seniors and valued the guidance of others more than female entrepreneurs. Males appeared to listen more to their subordinates than female entrepreneurs, involve them in problem solving, and making decisions. Both male and female entrepreneurs equally believed in using team approach and credited their success to the team or to all employees rather than to an individual (Table 7.6).

TABLE 7.6
Differences in Responses to Statements Regarding Leadership Qualities and Behaviour by Gender of Entrepreneur

	Statements	Male (Mean)	Female (Mean)	Total (Mean)
A	Advice and warnings from superiors are very useful in improving my performance.***	1.98	2.18	2.09
B	To me guidance and warnings that are given by the leader are very useful for the improvement of my job performance.*	1.52	1.94	1.75
C	Leader always listens to the complaints and opinions of the subordinates and uses them to improve their performance.**	1.74	1.98	1.87
D	Involving subordinates in making decisions to solve problems is one of leadership characteristics.***	2.06	2.26	2.17

Significant at: * 0.01, ** 0.05, and *** 0.10 level of probability.
The mean is calculated to measure the relative importance attained to different statements by gender using a Likert Scale 1-5, where 1= strongly agree with the statement, 2= agree, 3= doubt, 4= disagree, and 5= strongly disagree.

Factors Affecting Performance of Enterprises

Prior studies suggest that social structures and organized social life affect the female's access to entrepreneurial opportunities and may influence performance (Aldrich 1989). Lerner, Brush and Hisrich (1997) used five theoretical perspectives to explain performance. In this study to further examine relationships between selected factors identified from previous studies, statistical analysis including Pearson's correlation and multiple regressions were used. With previous studies as a guide, the following hypotheses were formulated and examined to test relationships between six selected major groups of variables (demographic, human capital, motivation and goals, decision-making, business history, and industry grouping), and performance. The dependent variables selected to measure business performance (performance indicators) were: annual growth rate in employment, the size of employment, and the last month profit (please see Singh, Reynolds and Muhammad 2001 for details). The independent variables under six groups and three dependent variables are listed in Table 7.7 along with the t-statistics.

H1: The influence of years enterprise has been in operation (age) will be negatively associated with business performance.

H2: The influence of close family ties will be positively associated with business performance.

H3: The difference in profitability, labour intensity, entry situation, competition, training, economic motivation, and style of management will affect business performance and will differ by sub-sectors.

The following model was developed and used to determine the impact of the variables on the performance of selected female enterprises in Java, Indonesia:

$$PERFORMANCE_J = \beta_0 + \sum_{I=1}^{5}\alpha_I DEMO_{IJ} + \sum_{I=1}^{3}\gamma_I HUMCAP_{IJ} + \varphi_I MOTIVATION_J + \lambda DECISION_J +$$

$$\psi BUSHISTORY_J + \sum_{I=1}^{5}\pi_I SECTOR_{IJ} + e_I$$

$$(j = 1,2,3,.....112)$$

In regards to H1, the results confirm Jovanovic's learning theory (1982) that the age of enterprise and the growth rate are inversely related. In addition, the results indicated that the age of entrepreneurs inversely affected the performance of female enterprises implying that younger women entrepreneurs performed better compared to older entrepreneurs (Table 7.7).

In addition, the total number of family workers appeared to have a significant positive impact on the performance of women enterprises as all three performance variables (in this study) were found to be positively related to the total number of family workers. The study also revealed that presence of competitors in the area has positive influence on the performance of firms. The business history (social learning theory), measured by the family history of business, was found to be not significant in impacting the performance of female enterprises. The other variable which appeared significant in this study was the industry grouping. The enterprises belonging to textile, services, and manufacturing sectors showed better performance than the food-processing sector. On the other hand trade sector performed well when performance was measured in terms of profit, but low in terms of growth rate and size of employment.

TABLE 7.7
Regression Results of Factors Affecting Performance of Female-Operated Enterprises in Java, Indonesia

Groups of Variable	Independent Variables	Dependent Variables (Performance Parameters)		
		Growth Rate	Size of Employment	Profit
	Constant	0.165	3.442	11.858
		(1.236)	(2.706)***	(18.023)***
Demographics	Age of entrepreneurs	–0.000332	–0.00284	–0.00133
		(–1.987)**	(–1.783)*	(–1.614)*
	Marital status	–0.0056	–0.597	0.450
		(–0.627)	(–0.700)	(1.020)
	Age of enterprise	–0.00058	0.000121	–0.000658
		(–2.630)***	(0.057)	(–0.604)
	Number of family workers	0.00488	0.894	0.261
		(2.574)**	(4.928)***	(2.778)***
Human Capital	Owner as well as initiator	0.00187	–0.385	–0.306
		(0.256)	(–0.552)	(–0.848)
	Owners and operators	0.000729	–0.00192	–0.239
		(0.135)	(–0.037)	(–0.899)
	Training	0.000215	–0.837	0.00130
		(0.043)	(–1.745)*	(0.052)
Business History	Business family history	–0.00171	0.227	0.00116
		(–0.386)	(0.536)	(0.053)
Motivation & Competition	Presence of competition	0.00945	0.140	–0.0093
		(2.206)**	(0.341)	(–0.440)
	Economic motivation	0.00235	0.345	–0.00245
		(0.550)	(0.843)	(–0.116)
Decision-Making	own decision	–0.00065	–0.240	0.317
		(–0.113)	(–0.437)	(1.118)
Industry Grouping	Textile	0.275	4.716	1.301
		(2.805)***	(5.032)***	(2.685)***
	Trade	–0.00085	–0.196	0.298
		(–0.158)	(–0.380)	(1.116)
	Services	0.00806	0.975	1.141
		(1.235)	(1.563)	(3.534)***
	Manufacturing	0.126	3.250	0.700
		(2.124)**	(5.733)***	(2.387)**
	R^2	0.295	0.496	0.259
	F-Value	2.672***	6.308***	2.237***
	N	112	112	112

t-values are given in parentheses
*** Significant at 0.01;** Significant 0.05; and * Significant at 0.01 level of probability.

The analysis revealed that each of the performance measure was influenced by the same, as well as different sets of variables. Overall, the most influential variables in explaining performance of female-owned businesses were total number of family workers and industry sector. In addition, certain demographic variables such as age of enterprise and age of entrepreneurs were found to be important in this analysis.

Summary and Implications

Research on women entrepreneurs is extensive in developed countries, but there are comparatively few studies that have examined characteristics and performance of female-owned enterprises and entrepreneurs in Indonesia and other developing countries. The primary goal of this study was to profile micro and small-scale enterprises with the aim to highlight gender-based differences in the characteristics of enterprises (such as type, size, capacity to create employment, performance, problems, and needs), entrepreneurs and entrepreneurial behaviour that may impact management and growth of enterprises. The study thus, seeks to provide a better understanding of women-owned/operated enterprises and entrepreneurs and issues affecting the success of micro and small-scale enterprises in general and women enterprises in particular.

The majority (56 percent) of micro and small-scale enterprises (MSE) surveyed in the selected provinces of Java were owned/operated by women entrepreneurs. Further examination of data revealed that micro and small-scale enterprises were initiated and operated by the entrepreneurs, concentrated in more traditional/informal and less dynamic product markets. The majority (83 percent of total number) of enterprises in the MSE sector were in food processing, production/manufacturing, and trade. The dominant industries were those with low entry barriers (in term of capital and technology), and high labour content in value-added. The study suggests that MSEs have the potential to absorb labour and are able to provide income for rural households. However, the data also suggests that in the present form, the role in generating employment for the rural population is limited, as the annual growth rate in employment was relatively low. Many MSEs remained almost static and grew very little in terms of employment

The ratio of females to males among the selected entrepreneurs was 1.3 to 1. The Chi-square test of significance for differences in the distribution of enterprises by types revealed that distribution in different groups (types)

varied significantly by gender of entrepreneur. Businesses run by female entrepreneurs were typically components of the informal sector (mostly in food processing), usually small, self-financing, sole proprietorships that relied on family labour, required low skills, and sold directly to consumers. Women tend to rely on unpaid family labour more than male entrepreneurs—partly as a result of home-based locations of many of their enterprises but also because of their limited time and mobility related to their domestic responsibilities (Downing 1990). A significant difference was observed between male and female entrepreneurs as to their perception of their growth potential. This indicates that for various reasons, women do not see their enterprises growing in the near future. The traditional nature of women's as compared to men's enterprises is also suggested by the different nature of their output markets. Women's final products more often than men's are sold directly to consumers. Gender differences were found in terms of reasons given by entrepreneurs for starting a business. Majority of women entrepreneurs (53.6 percent) indicated the need for additional income as the main reason compared to that of men (36.4 percent). On the other hand the majority of men (44.3 percent) in comparison to women entrepreneurs (19.6 percent) expressed "wanted to be independent" as their primary reason.

In general, entrepreneurs had little education or training. The relationship between education level and the gender of entrepreneur was not significant. Women entrepreneurs had lower levels of education and more men than women had training in the business they were operating. But in terms of technical/skill training, differences were found by gender of entrepreneur. Although the average enterprise in the survey grew at an annual rate of 15 percent, female-operated enterprises grew less than 9 percent, and more than 56 percent of the enterprise grew at below 10 percent annual growth rate. Even within the same sub-sectors, women's enterprises grew at a much slower rate than men's did. The rate of employment growth in enterprise is inversely related to the number of years that they have been in operation. This indicates that established enterprises provide additional source of employment opportunities compared to new ones. The more important factors in explaining the performance of female enterprises were total number of family workers and industry groups. These factors are different than found in studies in other countries (Lerner, Brush and Hisrich 1997). For the majority of problems, gender was not a distinguishing factor. However, female entrepreneurs expressed slightly higher incidence of business problems in financial and marketing areas and significant differences were observed in legal matters.

Of the listed eighteen statements in the study to measure entrepreneurial behaviour (i.e., attitudes and perceptions toward management) only five showed significant differences in behaviour by gender. The responses of males and females are similar except when dealing with employee and employee relations, knowledge about the factors that may have influence on business, and style of relating with the people. Among the nine statements regarding leadership qualities and behaviour, only four were found to be significantly different indicating differences between genders about leadership behaviour. In contrast to our expected findings, women owners/operators were found to be more autocratic than men and reluctant to involve subordinates in decision-making. In addition they were reluctant to follow advice, heed warnings from superiors or leaders to improve performance, and listen to or solve complaints of employees. This is in line with the female tendency to have more centralized control over all their business operations (Mukhtar 1997).

From a programming/policy viewpoint, the findings raise a question on how best to invest in micro-enterprise development. Given that women own the majority of micro and small enterprises and these enterprises appear to be less dynamic in terms of their contribution to growth, how should the programme be designed to intervene in specific enterprises? Small-scale industries in rural areas have not received much attention from the Indonesian government in the past (Stoffer and Sutanto 1990). From policy viewpoint, the findings of this study shed doubt on one policy/programme to assist all MSEs. Given that women own the majority of MSEs and these enterprises appear to be characterized by slow or no growth, one common programme may work for all. To the extent that women do have different motivations, objectives and needs from men programmes and policies need to be gender-differentiated. At the programme level it is important to recognize that enterprises are heterogeneous groups with different opportunities, needs, constraints, and programme assistance must be tailored to reflect such differences. A better understanding of enterprises and entrepreneurs can make a major contribution to the development of improved approaches for promotion of efficient and equitable growth of MSEs. These results imply that careful attention may be paid to the differences in male and female entrepreneurs found in the study, before designing assistance policies/programmes for entrepreneurs. Programmes are needed to increase the opportunity for female entrepreneurs and creating an environment that fosters women's participation in entrepreneurship.

Notes

Surendra P. Singh, Professor of Agribusiness, Tennessee State University, Nashville; **Harsha N. Mookherjee**, Professor of Sociology, Tennessee Technological University, Cookeville; and **Safdar Muhammad**, Associate Investigator, Tennessee State University, Nashville.

The work for the study was supported by the U.S. Agency for International Development under the HBCU grant programme, research project "Entrepreneurship and the Development of Micro- and Small-Scale Enterprises in Java, Indonesia", Grant No. HNE-5053-G-00-5059-00.

The authors wish to thank administrators and staff of the Population Studies Center, Gadjah Mada University, Yogyakarta, Indonesia for their assistance in data collection and administration of the study. The authors also appreciate assistance received from Professor S. Comer, Dr. F. Tegegne, and Dr. E. Ekanem, at Tennessee State University and Mr. Agus Sutanto at Gadjah Mada University in collection and analysis of data.

References

Aldrich, H. "Net working Among Women Entrepreneurs". In *Women-owned Businesses*, O. Hagen, C. Rivchun, and D. Sexton (eds.), pp. 103–32. New York: Praeger, 1989.

Allen, S. and Truman C. (eds.) *Women in Business: Perspectives on Women Entrepreneurs*. London: Routledge Press, 1993.

Berry, Albert, Edward Rodriguez and Henry Sandee. "Firm and Group Dynamics in the Role of SME Sector in Indonesia and Philippines". A paper presented to the World Bank Project on The Role of Small and Medium Enterprises in Development, Chiang Mai, Thailand, 13–14 August 1999.

Birley, S., C. Moss, and P. Saunders. "Do Women Entrepreneurs Require Different Training"? *American Journal of Small Business* 12, no. 1 (1987): 27–35.

Bliss, Richard T. and T. Nicole. Garratt. "Supporting Women Entrepreneurs in Transitioning Economies". *Journal of Small Business Management* 39, no. 4 (2001): 336–44.

Brush, Candida G. "Research on Women Business Owners: Past Trends, A New Perspective and Future Directions". *Entrepreneurship Theory and Practice* 16, no. 4 (Summer, 1992): 5–30.

Carter S. and T. Cannon. *Women As Entrepreneurs: A Study of Female Business Owners, Their Motivations, Experience, and Strategies for Success*. London: Academic Press, 1992.

Chaganti, R. and S. Parasuraman. "A Study of the Impacts of Gender on Business Performance and Management Patterns in Small Business". *Entrepreneurship Theory and Practice* 21, no. 2 (1996): 73–73.

Cobbe, Louise Barrett. "Women's Income Generation and Informal Learning in Lesotho: A Policy-Related Ethnography". Ph.D dissertation, Florida State University, 1985.

Dant, Rajiv P., Candida G. Brush, and Francisco P. Iniesta. "Participation Patterns of Women in Franchising". *Journal of Small Business Management* 34, no. 2 (1996): 14–27.

Dodge, Robert H., and J.E. Robbins. "An Empirical Investigation of the Organizational Life Cycle Model of Small Business Development and Survival". *Journal of Small Business Management* 17, no. 4 (1992): 22–29.

Downing, Jeanne. "Gender and the Growth and Dynamics of Micro Enterprises". GEMINI working paper, no. 5, Washington, D.C., 1990.

Effendi, T.N. "The Growth of Rural Non-Farm Activities at the Local Level: A Case Study of Causes and Effects in a Sub-district of Upland Central Java". Ph.D. Thesis, Flinders University, Adelaide, Australia, 1991.

Evers, Hans-Dieter. "Trade as Off-farm Employment in Central Java". *Sojourn* 6, no. 1 (1991): 1–21.

Fisher, Eileen M., A. Rebecca Reuber and Lorraine S. Dyke. "The Theoretical Overview and Extension of Research On Sex, Gender Entrepreneurship". *Journal of Business Venturing* 8 (1993): 151–68.

Grown, C. and J. Sebstad. "Introduction: Toward a Wider Perspective on Woman's Employment". *World Development* 17, no. 17 (July 1989): 13.

Hisrich, R. and C.G. Brush. "Women Entrepreneurs: A Longitudinal Study". In *Frontiers of Entrepreneurial Research*. Cambridge, MA: Babson College (1987): 187–99.

Hisrich, Robert and Gyula Fulop. "The Role of Women Entrepreneurs in Hungary's Transition Economy". *International Studies of Management and Organizations*. Winter (1994): 100–18.

Johnson S., and D. Storey. "Male and Female Entrepreneurs and Their Business: A Comparative Study". In *Women in Business: Perspectives On Women Entrepreneurs*, S. Allen and C. Freeman (eds.), pp. 70–85. London: Routledge, 1999.

Jovanovic, Boyan. "Selection and Evaluation of Industry". *Econometrica* 50 no. 3 (1982): 649–70.

Kallerberg, A.L. and K.T. Leicht. "Gender and Organizational Performance Determinants of Small Business Survival and Success". *Academy of Management Journal* 34, no. 1 (1991): 136–61.

Lerner, Miri, Candida Brush and Robert Hisrich. "Israeli Women Entrepreneurs: An Examination of Factors Affecting Performance". *Journal of Business Venturing* 12 (1997): 315–39.

Liedholm, C., M. McPherson and E. Chuta. "Small Enterprise Employment Growth in Rural Africa". *American Journal of Agricultural Economics* 76, no. 5 (1994): 1177–82.

McPherson, M.A. "Micro and Small-Scale Enterprises in Zimbabwe: Results of a Country-Wide Survey. GEMINI, Technical Report no. 25, Washington, D.C., 1991.

McPherson, M.A. "Growth of Micro and Small Enterprises in Southern Africa". *Journal of Development Economics* 48 (1996): 253–77.

Muktar, Sayeda-Masooda. "A Gender-Based Comparative Analysis of Managerial Characteristics of Owner(s)/Manager(s)". In *Proceedings of The 1997 Conference, Association for Global Business*, Washington, DC, Nov. 21–23, 1997 pp. 400–9.

Singh, S.P., T.N. Effendi, and S. Comer. "The Role of Non-Farm Activities in Java, Indonesia". *Atlantic Economic Society Best papers Proceedings* 4, no. 2 (1994): 154–61.

Singh et al., *Micro- and Small-Scale Enterprises And Entrepreneurship in Java, Indonesia: Results of a Survey*. Department of Agricultural Sciences, and Cooperative Agricultural Research Program Nashville, Tennessee State University, 1999.

Sonfield, Matthew, R. Lussier, J. Corman, and M. McKinney. "Gender Comparisons in Strategic Decision-Making: An Empirical Analysis of the Entrepreneurial Strategy Matrix". *Journal of Small Business Management* 39, no. 2 (2001): 165–73.

Srinivasan, R., C.Y. Woo and A.C. Cooper. "Performance Determinants for Male and Female Entrepreneurs". In Babson Entrepreneurship Research Conference, Cambridge, MA., 1994.

Stoffer, Wim and Agus Sutanto. "Rural Small Scale Industries and Regional Development A Case Study From Bantul District, Special Province of Yogyakarta". *The Indonesian Journal of Geography* 20, no. 60 (December 1990): 25–39.

Tinker, Irene. "The Human Economy of Micro Entrepreneurs". A paper presented at the International Seminar on Women In Micro- and-Small Scale Enterprise Development, Ottawa, Canada, 26 October 1987.

Voorhis, K.R.V. *Entrepreneurship and Small Business Management*. New York: Allyn and Bacon, 1980.

Zapalska, Alina M. "A Profile of Women Entrepreneurs and Enterprises in Poland". *Journal of Small Business Management* 35 no. 4 (October 1997): 77–83.

Zapalska, Alina M., and Will Edwards. "Chinese Entrepreneurship in a Cultural and Economic Perspective". *Journal of Small Business Management* 39 no. 3 (July 2001): 286–92.

8
MIGRANT ENTREPRENEURS IN EAST INDONESIA

Marthen L. nDoen
Cees Gorter
Peter Nijkamp
Piet Rietveld[1]

Introduction

Self-employment has been an avenue for migrants to survive in their new environment. Like migrants elsewhere, migrants in the province of East Nusa Tenggara (located in the periphery of Indonesia) have shown a strong propensity to engage in self-employment. Although information on the migrants' type of work is unavailable, it is presumed that, as with other regions in East Indonesia, the majority of the migrants in this region are included in self-employed activities (Manning and Rumbiak 1991). Self-employment consists primarily of small businesses operated by the migrants possibly with the help of a limited number of workers.

In Indonesia the ethnical dimension in migration has always been important. Since 1998, it has become evident that ethnic and religious differences between migrants and the original population are a major source of tension in the various regions. These tensions are potentially significant when migrant entrepreneurs are faced with the decision of staying in business at the same location or leaving for a new destination. One of the objectives of this paper is to learn the role these ethnic tensions play compared with other location factors.

The engagement of the migrants in business activities is more prominent in urban than rural areas. Two explanations seem to be relevant for migrants' entrepreneurial activities. The first explanation is provided by *cultural theory* (Jenkins 1984; Light 1984) which contends that the success of the migrants in entrepreneurial activities is due to the cultural endowments embedded in their original cultural tradition. According to this theory, the alien status of migrants has placed them in a marginalized situation, where they are prone to racial, ethnic, and religious discrimination from the host society (Auster and Aldrich 1984; Light 1979). This disadvantageous situation brings the migrants together, increases solidarity and cooperation among them, and eventually gives them an edge in competition with other groups. These practices have been found among the migrants in Irian Jaya (West Papua), who have utilized ethnic solidarity and ethnic resources to establish and manage small businesses (Manning and Rumbiak 1991). Business relationships are based on kinship and regional ties by which the migrants establish and coordinate their business.

The second explanation comes from *structural theory* which accounts for the start up of new businesses by the migrants when unfavourable economic conditions bring about a failure in the labour market. A decline in the economy brings in its wake a periodic increase in unemployment in the host society, and the migrants are singled out to blame for stealing the jobs. Furthermore, the lack of education among migrants as well as inadequate skills creates additional barriers to acceptance into the market. Faced with these conditions, migrants are forced into self-employment as an alternative to wage labour and also as a strategy for survival. In the self-employment sector, the migrants are better able to avoid prejudice and resentment from the host society and avoid direct conflict with local people.

In the recipient society, the migrants act as a *middlemen minority* (a group of traders from a different ethnic background) by distributing products between the elite and the general customers (Turner and Bonacich 1980; Light 1980). The role they play in the economy as middlemen places them as collectors of surplus for the elite. Addressing the middlemen minority argument, Bonacich (1973) proposed a "sojourning" migration argument, which contends that the migrants regard themselves as sojourners apart from the local community, a group that initially had planned only a temporary stay in a particular destination and maintained a desire to return to their home place in the future. From the perspective of this argument, migrants in East Nusa Tenggara can be described as middlemen between the producer elite, mostly residing in Java, and the local customers. This role is not restricted only to migrants in East Nusa Tenggara but to migrants everywhere in the outer islands (Hugo 1997; Spaan 1999).[2]

The aim of this paper is to describe the backgrounds of ethnic migrants in East Indonesia and to investigate the importance of various factors that affect their decision to move or stay. Among these factors are market opportunities, existence of informal networks and ethnic tensions. The paper examines a case study carried out in Kupang, the capital of East Nusa Tenggara province. Migrant entrepreneurs were interviewed shortly before riots broke out in 1998.

Data and Methodology

The data for this research was obtained from a survey of 334 migrants in Kupang, Indonesia. This research is focused on migrants from three major islands: Makasar and Bugis from the island of Sulawesi, Javanese from the island of Java, and Minangkabau from West Sumatra. The questionnaire interviews were completed between early October and the middle of November 1998 just before the riots that took place at the end of November. During the interviews, we managed to establish a special rapport with several respondents, who were then able to help us as informants and provided us with diverse information about the situation of migrants in their current region. This enabled us to tap into the migrants' complaints about local attitude. The selection of informants was based on their experience and openness to the researcher.

At the outset of this study, the plan was to conduct the research utilizing random sampling, but lack of participation from the respondents compelled us to use another sampling method: snowballing sampling. In this process, the enumerators approached only a few respondents to start with, and later asked their recommendations for the next set of respondents. When they had finished interviewing the second group of respondents, the enumerators then asked their advice and recommendations for further respondents. It is clear that snowballing sampling may lead to problems connected with the randomness of the sample. However, given the circumstances, it was the only way to obtain the co-operation of a sufficient number of respondents.

Background Characteristics of Migrants in East Nusa Tenggara

Migrants in this survey are a distinct group in terms of place of origin, age, educational level, and length of residence. Looking at the geographical distribution of place of origin, the majority (55 percent) are from South Sulawesi, followed by Java (mainly East Java) (33 percent) and West Sumatra (12 percent). Migrants from South Sulawesi have the largest community; those from West Sumatra have travelled the furthest distance to this region (see Table 8.1).

The age profile of the respondents in Table 8.1 shows that age differences among these three ethnic groups are generally not significant. Young migrants are in the majority in East Nusa Tenggara; on the average they are between 34 to 35 years of age (last column of Table 8.1). Migrants from South Sulawesi are above the average age of the total, whereas those from Java and West Sumatra are below the total average age. These results also

TABLE 8.1
Means and Standard Deviations* of Characteristic Variables by Place of Origin

Variable (in years)	Place of Origin			
	South Sulawesi	Java	West Sumatra	Total
Age	35.47	32.98	30.93	34.10
	(11.25)	(9.56)	(6.51)	(10.35)
Education	6.92	8.69	11.55	8.06
	(2.96)	(3.32)	(2.84)	(3.42)
Duration of Residence	13.38	9.01	8.00	11.29
	(8.95)	(6.11)	(5.61)	(8.08)
Business Experience	14.20	9.07	9.75	11.98
	(8.92)	(6.14)	(7.11)	(8.25)
Number of cases	184	110	40	334

* Standard deviations are in parentheses.
Source: Primary data.

indicate that there are not many migrants in the older age groups living in East Nusa Tenggara. It is likely that older migrants returned to their original home areas to spend their remaining years and to look after the property they have been able to buy there during their time of migration (nDoen 2000).

The migrants in East Nusa Tenggara have an average of 8 years of education, up to and including the junior high school level. Migrants from West Sumatra have the highest number of years of education (12 years), and those from South Sulawesi have the lowest (7 years). The Javanese on average are better educated than the migrants from South Sulawesi.

Table 8.1 shows that migrants have stayed in East Nusa Tenggara for an average of just over 11 years. Those from South Sulawesi have the longest average stay (13 years) and those from West Sumatra have stayed approximately 8 years. However, some migrants from South Sulawesi have even been living in this region for more than 30 years and since they own local property, it is likely they might remain in their current location indefinitely.

Migrants in this region have around 12 years of business experience. Migrants from South Sulawesi have the highest average (14 years) and those from Java and Sumatra both have roughly 9 years of experience. Note that the pattern of duration of stay is almost identical with years of business experience, indicating that the majority of the migrants who arrived here were not previously entrepreneurs in their home areas.

Since they were not entrepreneurs in their place of origin, it is most likely that the push factor is more dominant in the migrants' decision to move. Limited job opportunities as well as class backgrounds are the main reasons driving the migrants to move away from their place of origin. As shown in Table 8.2, the majority of respondents (45 percent) were without jobs, and around 18 percent were peasants. The intriguing part of Table 8.2 is that the majority of the respondents had no business experience at all before they moved: around 60 percent of respondents (unemployed and peasant) have had little exposure to business activities. A quarter had been self-employed or owned a small business in the place of origin, and around 12 percent were professional workers or civil servants before they moved to East Nusa Tenggara. Around 45 percent of the people from each group were unemployed. However more migrants from West Sumatra have been exposed to business (38 percent) compared to Java (26 percent) and South Sulawesi (22 percent). 24 percent of the migrants from South Sulawesi and 15 percent from Java had been peasants before moving to East Nusa Tenggara and becoming entrepreneurs.

Lack of business exposure was connected with the family background. The majority of migrants come from families with peasant backgrounds. When the occupation of the migrants' parents is taken into account, we have 64 percent who worked as peasants and only 34 percent who had run a small business in their place of origin (Table 8.2), indicating that the majority of respondents did not grow up in a strong entrepreneurial environment. It is difficult to find comparable studies in Indonesia, but the work of Kim and Hurh (1985) can give us some idea: they found an absence of business experience among the majority of Korean migrants in Chicago.

When place of origin is taken into account, 77 percent of the parents of migrants from Java and 65 percent of those from South Sulawesi were peasants. This is very different from the parents of migrants from West

TABLE 8.2
Migrants' Characteristics by Occupational Status, Parents' Occupation and Reason to Migrate to East Nusatenggara

Variable	Place of Origin			
	South Sulawesi (%)	Java (%)	West Sumatra (%)	Total (%)
Occupational Status in Place of Origin				
Unemployed	45.7	44.5	45.0	42.5
Small Business Owner	21.7	25.5	37.5	24.9
Private/Civil Servant	8.7	15.5	15.0	11.7
Peasant	23.9	14.5	2.5	18.3
Parental Occupation				
Peasant	64.7	77.3	22.5	63.8
Small Business Owner	34.8	18.2	75.0	34.1
Private/Civil Servant	0.5	4.5	2.5	2.1
Reason to Migrate				
Job Opportunity	23.4	30.0	25.0	25.7
Business Opportunity	76.6	64.5	72.5	72.2
Others	–	5.5	2.1	2.5

Source: Primary data

Sumatra, where around 75 percent had already engaged in business. The findings are not surprising, for people from West Sumatra have long been known for their entrepreneurial skill, and are the most mobile group in Indonesia.

Given the fact that 45 percent were unemployed before they moved, the push factors appeared far more important than the pull factors in motivating the migrants to leave their home region. In private interviews, most migrants blamed discrimination for their failure in the job market.[3] But one should not ignore the fact that their general low educational qualifications gave them little opportunity in the labour market. Table 8.1 shows that more than 90 percent had achieved only primary and high school education, which in the current situation is not enough to compete in the labour market. Even for university graduates the labour market is very tight.[4] In that sense, structural factors have compelled the migrants with lack of business experience to search beyond their home region for other places to live.

Encouraged by the lack of entrepreneurial activities among the local people, 25 percent of the migrants who already owned small businesses moved to the current region because they perceived better opportunities there. Some migrants moved to avoid competing back home with their relatives in the same line of business (Ndoen 2000). Since their relatives were engaged in a similar product line, they felt uneasy about encroaching on their customers. Thus, for those people, moral factors were more dominant than economic factors.

Table 8.3 presents a cross-tabulation of reasons to migrate in relation to migrants' occupation in their place of origin. The majority of migrants came to this region for business opportunities. Among the unemployed, 45 percent came for employment, 53 percent for business opportunities and 2 percent for other reasons. Of those who previously owned a small business, 92 percent came for business opportunities and only 4 percent for employment; for private workers or civil servants, 69 percent came for business opportunities and around 28 percent came for jobs. This raises the question of why the majority of these migrants did not initially plan to find work in the labour market. One explanation is that they had prior information about the socio-economic conditions in East Nusa Tenggara. Since this region is considered one of the poorest regions in Indonesia, the migrants must have realised that there was little hope for finding jobs in the labour market. The modern sector is still undeveloped and 80 percent of the local population still relies on the agricultural sector as a source of income (BPS Propinsi Nusa Tenggara Timur 1997, p. 9). The most promising way to survive in East Nusa Tenggara is in the business sector because it does not require specialized knowledge.

Migration experience is not discussed because it was found that the results are parallel to that of business experience. This is because the majority of the migrants were first-time movers and the majority of them were engaging in business activities for the first time as well.

The Model

For the analysis of the role of social and economic factors in determining the decision of the migrants to stay in their current place, a regression model is used. In constructing the model, a wide range of variables is included so that as many different sources of social and economic impact as possible could be taken into account.

The regression model to be estimated can be formulated as:

$$Y_i = \alpha + \sum_{k=1}^{12} \beta_k X_{ik} + \varepsilon_i$$

With Y = Propensity to Stay; X1= Weak competition; X2 = Local Tolerance; X3 = Market Accessibility; X4 = Niche Concentration; X5 = Capital

TABLE 8.3
Cross-tabulation of Reason for Migration in Relation to Migrant's Occupation in Place of Origin

Reason for Migration	Migrants' Occupation in the Place of Origin				
	Unemployed (%)	Small Business Owner (%)	Private or Government Worker (%)	Peasant (%)	Total (%)
Job Opportunity	45.0	3.6	28.2	6.6	25.7
Business Opportunity	53.0	92.8	69.2	93.4	72.2
Others	2.0	3.6	2.6	2.1	
Total	45.2	24.9	11.7	18.3	100.0

Source: Primary data

Accessibility; X6 = Supporting Network; X7 = Duration of Residence; X8 = Age; X9 = Education; X10 Migration Experience; X11 = Business Experience; X12 = Place of Origin; e = Error Term.

The dependent variable Y (propensity to stay) is based on the entrepreneur's response whether he expects to stay in the same region within a two-year period (measured on a scale of 1 to 10). The exact formulation in the questionnaire is whether the respondent has plans to leave the place, where 10 indicates not interested at all in leaving and 1 indicates that he is very interested in leaving. This formulation can be interpreted as a continuous measurement of the discrete (1–0) willingness to stay variable that plays a large role in migration and housing market research (see for example Clark and Van Lierop 1986). Furthermore, X1, X2, X3, X4, X5, and X6 are the scores reflecting respondent's perceptions of how favourable the current location is for business. The variables are measured on a range from 1 (least favourable) to 10 (most favourable). Duration of residence, age, education, migration experience and business experience were measured at their face value in years. Only place of origin is a dummy variable, where 1 indicates that the migrant is from South Sulawesi, and 0, otherwise.

The dependent variable Y assumes integer values on a scale from 1 to 10. In a strict sense this can be interpreted as a limited dependent variable since values in between the integer values are ruled out. A possible way to address this problem would be the use of latent variables, where the dependent variable Y as it is measured is based on an underlying latent variable Y^* (see for example Maddala 1983). Thus, Y can be interpreted as the rounded value of Y^*. The relationship between the two is:

$$Y=n \text{ for all } n-0.5 < Y^* < n+0.5$$

Where n assumes values from 1 to 10. This is essentially an example of censoring. However, there is little reason to expect that this rounding procedure will seriously affect the estimation results. The reason is that the variance of the error term in this type of models is rather high so that correcting for the rounding errors implied by the use of integers will not have a substantial impact on the estimates. Therefore we decided to ignore the rounding problem in the rest of the paper and use ordinary least squares. As a technical aside, one might be tempted to use a multinomial logit model here, but that would not be appropriate, since this would ignore the fact that the responses Y=1,2,3,...,10 are ranked in a definite order. Another alternative would be to use ordered probit analysis, but this would ignore the fact that the values of Y have been defined on the interval scale: the distance between value 1 and 2 is meant to have the same size as the distance between 2 and 3.

Results of the Regression Analysis

Table 8.4 presents three variants of the regression analysis. Model 1 is the sub-model where the propensity to stay is regressed only on six core variables. Model 2 is a full model with both the six core variables and the six control variables (including the dummy variable). Finally, in Model 3 we try to trace the non-linearity relation by introducing business experience squared to the full model.[5]

Table 8.4 illustrates that all core variables are significantly related to the dependent variable propensity to stay for models 1, 2, and 3.[6] In Table

TABLE 8.4
Regression Result for Migrants' Propensity to Stay at Their Current Place as a Function of Socio-economic Factors

Variable	Model 1 β	Model 2 β	Model 3 β
Constant	−0.82	−1.81	−1.41
Weak Competition (X1)	0.13***	0.11**	0.11**
Local Tolerance (X2)	0.34***	0.39***	0.40***
Market Accessibility (X3)	0.39***	0.41***	0.42***
Niche Concentration (X4)	0.16***	0.16***	0.15***
Capital Accessibility (X5)	0.12***	0.09**	0.07*
Supporting Network (X6)	0.33***	0.31***	0.31***
Duration of Residence (X7)		0.01	0.01
Age (X8)		−0.01	−0.01
Education (X9)		0.04	0.04
Migration Experience (X10)		−0.00	−0.00
Business Experience (X11)		0.03	−0.05
Place of origin (South Sulawesi=1) (X12)		0.61***	0.60***
Business Experience Squared			0.003***
R-Squared	0.62	0.64	0.65
Number of cases	334	334	334

*** Significant at the 0.01 level
** Significant at the 0.05 level
* Significant at the 0.10 level

8.4, all perception related variables (X1–X6) are significant in these estimations. Given the fact that these perception variables have been standardized in the same way (on a scale from 1 to 10) so that it is meaningful to compare the size of the estimated coefficient, one can distinguish a group of location factors with a relatively strong impact on the propensity to stay (market accessibility, local tolerance and supporting networks) and a group of factors that have a smaller impact (niche concentration, weak competition, and capital accessibility).

In Model 3, we include the variable business experience squared, which is significant at the 0.01 level (see Table 8.4). A score of 10 indicates that a respondent has given the highest possible outcome (very much agrees) for all underlying indicators. In the case of supporting network (will you get help from relatives when there are problems, will new migrants live with their kin group, will new migrants receive facilities from their kin group before they become self-supporting), a score of 1 indicates that a respondent has given the lowest possible outcome. The variable place of origin is positively related to propensity to stay indicating that migrants from South Sulawesi have a propensity to stay in their current region of almost two points (0.6 points on a 10-point scale) higher than migrants from Java or West Sumatra. The propensity to stay is based on qualitative responses (1 – not interested at all to 10 – very much interested) to three underlying questions: plans to leave within two years, willingness to move to a hypothetical better business location and confidence that there are no better business opportunities elsewhere. Business experience squared is positively related to the dependent variable propensity to stay, indicating that as the period of migrants' experience in business activities increases, their inclination to stay in their current place increases more rapidly.

After scrutinising the effect of the full set of core variables, it appears that social factors like local tolerance and to a lesser extent supporting network are about equally important as economic factors such as market accessibility.

Discussion and Interpretation

In this section we have reclassified migrants' responses on the independent variable and the dependent variable into 3 categories: low, medium and high. The category 'low' is based on an average value of between 1 and 3.33; 'medium' is based on an average value of between 3.34 and 6.66;

and the category 'high' obtains from an average value between 6.67 and 10. The result for the variables will now be discussed in order of importance.

From Table 8.4, market accessibility is the most important variable in keeping the migrants in East Nusa Tenggara. All three models have consistently demonstrated that this variable's estimated coefficient has the highest magnitude, implying that the entrepreneurs give a heavy weight to access to the market in their current place when they consider the alternatives in other places. The regression coefficient of this variable is the highest (0.42) in Model 3, indicating that as the migrants' perception of access to the market changes 1 point on a scale of 1 to 10, it has an effect on migrants' propensity to stay of 0.42 of a point on the same scale. Given the qualitative nature of the variables involved, a precise interpretation sounds rather tedious: a one point increase on the access to market scale means that the situation improves with 1/10 of the distance between the extremes of impossible to enter the market (score 1) towards complete freedom to enter the market (score 10). The coefficients in the table can best be interpreted in relative terms: the willingness to stay is much more strongly affected by access to market than by capital accessibility (coefficients of 0.42 versus 0.07). The effect of market accessibility on propensity to stay is the highest compared with the other variables. It is shown in Table 8.5 that around 61 percent of the respondents perceive that they have high access to the current market.

One reason why the migrants wanted to stay was that there were enough consumers in the current market. 72 percent of respondents

TABLE 8.5
Proportion of Migrants' Responses to Core Variables

N=334

Variable	Low	Medium	High
Weak competition	26.0	55.4	18.6
Local Tolerance	0.6	24.6	74.9
Market Accessibility	12.3	26.6	61.1
Niche Concentration	31.1	41.9	26.9
Capital Accessibility	77.2	14.1	8.7
Supporting Network	45.5	33.8	20.7
Propensity to Stay	9.6	20.1	70.4

Source: Primary data

thought there were few obstacles to finding consumers in their current location. Another reason for staying is that monopoly status (market power of incumbent traders) was not a significant obstacle in the current market. 69 percent of the respondents thought that the degree of monopoly was low. In contrast, the migrants believed they had a problem dealing with bureaucracy in their current region. Around 68 percent thought the bureaucracy imposed too many obstacles. "Red tape" along with demands for illegal payment for licences to obtain a location in the market place impeded them from entering the market freely. In general, however, most respondents thought they still had a high chance of access to the current market.

In private interviews, some migrants admitted that business opportunities were related to the lack of interest among local people to enter such businesses. When the type of business is taken into account, migrants from South Sulawesi and Java show a diversity in their business activities; they engage in the retailing of garments, household goods and furniture. Nevertheless, despite the diversity, migrants from South Sulawesi and Java are more concentrated in certain businesses and trades. Those from South Sulawesi, for example, have control over fishing and timber trading. Migrants from Java operate food stalls and small restaurants scattered in the region. The migrants from West Sumatra are more specialised in garment trading but they also control *Minang* restaurants or ethnic food stalls.

The customers of these businesses are primarily the local middle class, whose government salaries provide their major source of income. Therefore, migrant business mainly depends on the economic condition of this class. Migrants experience a short sales boost at the beginning of the month after the civil servants receive their salaries, but start to suffer a loss of trade towards the middle of the month. Over the years, this boom-bust pattern of demand has become habitual for the entrepreneurs in this region (Ndoen 2000). Some migrants from South Sulawesi cater to their fellow migrants by providing ethnic commodities, like wedding and religious costumes (mainly for Muslims), but their number is small.

Local tolerance

For local tolerance in Table 8.4, the regression coefficient is 0.40, which indicates that as migrants perceive local tolerance to increase by 1 point on a scale of 1 to 10, the propensity to stay in their current region increases by 0.40 of a point on a similar scale. When we look at Table 8.5, around 75 percent of the migrants thought the tolerance in current region was high and actually almost no one thought that there was low tolerance towards the migrants. The migrants believed that local people were pleased to accept them and they also felt safe in their current place. Some 89 percent of the migrants considered that the degree of acceptance was high. We also have 89 percent thinking they were very safe in their current place while only 11 percent thought their safety was at risk. None of the migrants had experienced physical abuse or any other violence; one hundred percent of them believed this was due to their cultural and religious practices. While all of the groups believed ethnic tolerance to be high, 28 percent of the respondents from both South Sulawesi and West Sumatra felt they had experienced a medium degree of hostility. However, we have to be careful in interpreting these results, as it is possible the migrants did not want to offend the enumerators who were mainly from the local community. Nevertheless it is safe to conclude that the entrepreneurs had no indication that violence would erupt just weeks after the interviews were carried out.

Although, the majority of the migrants asserted they had no problem with the local people, some of them complained about "mischief" they had experienced from some young locals, "naughty boys," who had illegally taxed them. This placed a burden on the businessmen who lost their competitive edge when they were forced to raise their prices. Because of their status as outsiders, the migrants felt they were unable to challenge this taxation. To ease the conflict, migrants often hired local employees to deal with the naughty boys as well as help with public relations between the migrants and local community.[7]

Employment characteristics

To give an idea of the relationship between the migrants and the local people, Table 8.6 shows the proportion of migrants who employ other people in their business. It appears that 23 percent of the migrants from South Sulawesi, 53 percent of the migrants from Java and 25 percent of migrants from West Sumatra employ between one and eleven additional workers. The main sector where the Javanese are active (food stalls) apparently gives rise to a larger number of employees than the other sectors. In Table 8.7 we show the distribution of workers according to the relationship with their bosses. It appears that migrants from South Sulawesi

TABLE 8.6
Proportion of Migrants with and without Employees by Place of Origin
(in percentages)

N=185

	South Sulawesi	Java	West Sumatra	All Migrants
Without employee	76.6	46.6	75.0	66.5
With employee	23.4	53.4	25.0	33.5
Total	100.0	100.0	100.0	100.0

Source: Primary data

TABLE 8.7
The Relationship of Employee to Migrants' Employers by Place of Origin
(in percentages)

N=288

	South Sulawesi	Java	West Sumatra	All Migrants
Close Relative	54.8	31.8	23.7	38.2
Fellow Migrants	17.2	37.6	18.4	28.5
Friends	0.0	3.2	2.6	2.1
Local People	28.0	27.4	55.3	31.2
Total	100.0	100.0	100.0	100.0

Source: Primary data

and Java rely mainly on relatives and fellow migrants as a source of labour while the majority of employees hired by those from West Sumatra are local people. However, in general, the migrants primarily employ workers from their place of origin, which underlines the 'enclave character' of migrant's activities.

Competition for space in the market poses a potential conflict between migrant entrepreneurs and the local entrepreneurs. Migrants (mostly from South Sulawesi) occupy stores in the market and control the imported goods and wares. In contrast, local traders concentrate on local products and are only allowed to sell in the front of the stores as street vendors. Moreover, local entrepreneurs find that the rent for stores would be too expensive for them to afford (Ndoen 2000).

Supporting network

For supporting network, the results in Table 8.4 show the regression coefficient is 0.31, indicating that as migration perception on the supporting network changes by 1 point, the propensity to stay changes by 0.31 of a point. Table 8.5 demonstrates that while 46 percent of migrants thought they had low support from their fellow migrants, the majority thought the support to be medium or high. A similar proportion can be seen for each group, but, if we concentrate on the ethnic background of medium support, 53 percent of migrants from West Sumatra, 36 percent of migrants from Java and 29 percent of those from South Sulawesi thought they had medium support.

When we consider high support networking, 26 percent of migrants from South Sulawesi thought they had high support, 16 percent of migrants from Java thought so, but only 7.5 percent of those from West Sumatra fell into this category. Although migrants were willing to support their fellow migrants, the majority did not agree that new arrivals should live with previous migrants and also concurred that previous migrants had no moral obligation to look after the newcomers. 71 percent of the respondents felt it was not necessary to offer financial assistance during a time of crisis unless it was in the form of a loan to be repaid with or without interest.

Most migrants interviewed had in one way or another received some kind of support from previous migrants when they first arrived in the region. Prior ties based on ethnicity and kinship are the basis for such support. The relationship between previous migrants and the newcomers can be described as paternalistic, where the former is the patron for the latter. Each group creates its own cultural standard used to help fellow migrants. New arrivals from West Sumatra might initially stay with previous migrants, but after a time they are required to stand on their own two feet. It is not common for entrepreneurs from West Sumatra to lend money, but they do provide goods for new migrants to sell in other markets. At this point, the recipients are expected to work hard. In return, with their predecessors acting as guarantors, new migrants are provided with openings into the local wholesale market. This system encourages new migrants to become small business owners in the future.

In contrast, many new migrants from South Sulawesi are invited to join close relatives already established in the area. Some earlier migrants encouraged relatives to set up businesses of their own while others invited their relatives to actually work for them. Earlier migrants consider it a moral obligation to share their new wealth with family members and extend invitations to help relatives escape poverty in their home region. Since the new migrants are close relatives, it is common for them to remain with their hosts until they have established businesses of their own. Working with the family is a nursery process for skill formation. When the new migrants have shown their business acumen, their predecessors will lend them money to start their own businesses. Sometimes the new migrants are prone to excessive exploitation. There was one case where a new arrival received only shelter and a small payment for three years before he could start his own business (nDoen 2000).

Migrants from Java show different types of support. They tend to come in groups of at least 5 people, who then live together and share the rent for their house. Before the decision to move is made, they try to get information from previous migrants. While new migrants are encouraged to join them, they are expected to bring commercial goods with them from Java. Since most of them do not have business experience, Javanese often work first with the previous migrants. Because earlier migrants do not want to use local workers, new migrants provide a source of cheap and loyal labour for them. In contrast to migrants from South Sulawesi and West Sumatra, some Javanese migrants remain as casual labour.

Niche concentration

As shown in Table 8.4, the variable niche concentration has a regression coefficient of 0.15, indicating that as the migrants' perception on niche concentration changes by 1 point, their propensity to stay increases by 0.15 of a point. Looking at Table 8.5, we have 42 percent of the migrants perceiving niche concentration in the current region as medium, 27 percent thought it was high and 31 percent thought it was low. When the migrants were asked what they thought about the position of their group members in current business activities, 52 percent thought they had a high concentration with respect to other groups; 49 percent thought there was a low concentration of other groups in current business. Around 61 percent of the migrants also thought that the number of new migrants in the businesses of previous migrants was low. This indicates that the migrants did not believe the new migrants were likely to enter a business dealing in the same commodities as the previous migrants. One of the reasons is that they want to avoid competition within the group. When we consider ethnic background, the proportion of low, medium and high values for niche concentration are not much different among the three groups. For instance, 30 percent of migrants from Java, 27 percent from South Sulawesi and 20 percent from West Sumatra thought niche concentration in the current market was high.

Although some migrants have asserted that there is high niche concentration, this refers to horizontal integration rather than to vertical integration. Some products are totally controlled by particular ethnic groups: fish by migrants from South Sulawesi, ethnic restaurants by migrants from West Sumatra, and small food stalls by migrants from Java. All of these businesses rely on the skills brought with them when they moved. The migrants from South Sulawesi are very skilled in building fishing rafts, which are used to catch tons of fish each evening. These rafts are scattered around the bay of Kupang.

Vertical integration may occur in timber trading among the migrants from South Sulawesi and in the garment trade among people from West Sumatra. In timber, there is a well-known businessman who provides timber for other smaller merchants to sell to local consumers. This stronger niche concentration is a result of the concentration of wooden boat ownership by people from South Sulawesi. By controlling the transportation of timber, migrants from this region have an edge on any competitor from outside their ethnic group. Migrants from West Sumatra seem to achieve vertical integration in the garment trade. This is due to the fact that, in the last ten years, several entrepreneurs from West Sumatra have served as wholesalers of garments in the region. Although the wholesalers are free to sell to anyone, prices are discounted for their fellow migrants from West Sumatra, who in turn sell at lower prices as well. This pattern of relationship indirectly gives them a better edge to win their competitors. Some migrants from Java are able to survive because they brought their goods with them from Java.

Weak competition

Weak competition is our next variable of interest. In Table 8.4, migrants' perception of weak competition has a regression coefficient of 0.11, which indicates that as the perception concerning the level of weak competition increases by 1 point, the migrants' propensity to stay in their current place increases by 0.11 of a point. This demonstrates that the weaker the competition the greater the propensity to stay. Or, putting it another way, as competition becomes more intense, the migrants' propensity to stay in their current place decreases. Most migrants (55 percent) thought that weak competition in the current place was medium (Table 8.5). A large proportion of the migrants thought that the number of sellers was still low in this region, so there was a high probability that profits would be made. In addition, the majority of migrants believed that the rate of increase of new sellers was still low, so the competition was not so great. When ethnic background is taken into account, weak competition is more likely to be perceived by migrants from West Sumatra than by those from any other ethnic background. 95 percent of the migrants of West Sumatra, 87 percent of the Javanese and 75 percent of migrants from South Sulawesi, believed that they have low and medium weak competition in the current region.

Since migrants from West Sumatra carry out their businesses individually, they are therefore likely to be more sensitive to competition both within the group and outside the group (a high percentage of the respondents —72.5 percent— perceive medium levels of weak competition). Given the fact that they enter limited business types and the concentration of all business is in a limited market, there is potential for intra-ethnic competition. The presence of intra-ethnic competition can be seen if we take the spatial arrangement of shops and stalls into account. Migrants from West Sumatra tend to congregate in a particular section in the market and serve almost identical commodities to the market. Every entrepreneur competes for potential customers by lowering the price or offering the customer the opportunity to buy now and pay later (usually at the beginning of the month). Intra-ethnic competition is less prevalent among the Javanese and the migrants from South Sulawesi because of the diverse commodities sold by them.

Capital accessibility

Capital accessibility is the least important variable in the estimated models. The regression coefficient is 0.07 (Table 8.4), which indicates that as access to capital increases by 1 point, it will affect the dependent variable propensity to stay by 0.07 of a point. The small effect is due to the fact that most of these migrants have almost nothing to do with formal banks. When asked if they perceived any problems in borrowing from the bank, most of them thought the obstacles to borrow were low, and the majority felt that an under-the-table arrangement with bank officials was not required. In addition they felt it was not necessary to forge a special connection with a bank officer in order to borrow the money from the bank. In that sense, we can conclude that the banking sector is reliable in the eyes of the migrants, even though only a small number have, or even want to have, access to the bank.

Table 8.5 shows that 77 percent of the migrants thought they had poor access to the banking sector. And there was a similar proportion for each ethnic group: 86 percent of migrants from Java, 75 percent of migrants from West Sumatra, and 73 percent of migrants from South Sulawesi. A number of migrants from South Sulawesi and Java do not have access to formal banks because they do not have any collateral. Some migrants avoid banks because they think using them will create problems in the future if they cannot repay a loan. This happens to migrants with limited education who rely more on their kin groups as sources of capital, even though the interest charged is higher than that of the banks. Some migrants from Java who are able to meet collateral required by banks in their home region are not interested in access to local banks. They indicated they are able to repay their loans from the proceeds of their business in the current place. In addition there are some migrants who are able to borrow money from relatives at modest interest rates (See also Spaan 1999). There are also some devout Muslims who prefer not to borrow from the banks because they perceive the charging of bank interest is against *Shariah* (Muslim Law).

Regarding capital needs in their current place, the migrants interviewed asserted that they tended to start with small amounts of initial capital. Sponsorship from previous migrants was limited to taking loans in the form of goods from a local distributor. This has been the practice of migrants from South Sulawesi, and from West Sumatra. The practice among migrants from West Sumatra is that the previous migrants provide the goods for the new migrants, and therefore, the need for a large amount of cash for the initial business is not necessary (see the earlier discussion on supporting network). As mentioned above, some migrants from Java are not interested in having access to local banks because they have borrowed from the banks at home. This makes good sense, given fact that they are able to meet the bank's requirement on collateral in their home region. Some migrants from Java claim that they have no trouble in paying back their loan (nDoen 2000).

Conclusions

As entrepreneurs, the migrants in the East Nusa Tenggara province are comparable to other migrants in many respects. They are generally young, come from a peasant background and have average educational achievement. Only a small percentage have previous business experience. This can be observed by looking at the background of the migrants' parents and business ownership in their place of origin. Migration occurred on both an individual as well as a collective basis either through invitation or self-decision. On an individual basis, the migrants came either on their own (West Sumatra), or through sponsorship from relatives (South Sulawesi). On a collective basis, as is the practice among Javanese migrants, they arrived as a group.

The migrants come to this region and engage in entrepreneurial activities primarily as small business owners. The migrants' involvement in business is driven by both push and pull factors. Interest in their current region has been fuelled by business opportunities (pull) as well as unemployment in their original location (push). Migrants from South Sulawesi concentrate their business on fishery and timber; many Javanese have food stalls; and those from West Sumatra deal mainly in garments. Reliance on previous migrants is still a viable prospect in the process of migration. Ties of kinship and regional origin are utilized initially by migrants to find help in setting up their own businesses, but, as the period of stay extends, the reliance on fellow migrants decreases. At this point they sometimes seek assistance from outside their kin group.

The analysis of the propensity to stay in the current place provides a consistent pattern of relationships. All the economic and socio-cultural variables have a significant effect on migrants' propensity to stay in the current region. However, accessibility to the marketplace, local tolerance and supporting networks are the three most important factors in determining a favourable business climate. Migrants projected that current conditions would prevail and that they would remain in the same place for the next two years. It is clear that both economic and social factors have strong effects on the migrants' propensity to remain in their current homes. In general migrants initially, have a low dependency on formal capital sources because they are able to obtain start-up capital from relatives. Later as they become more established they do obtain financial capital from banks.

The results from the regression model should be interpreted with some caution. The data was collected through snowball sampling, which to some degree may lead to duplication of responses among the migrants. Therefore, the results from this analysis can be utilized only for limited purposes, and it is difficult to generalize the regression results for all entrepreneurial migrants. Although the life histories of some migrants have been included in the analysis, it is not enough to capture the sheer dynamism of entrepreneurial migration. This research relies on cross-sectional data, which might be insufficient to study the full dynamic aspects of entrepreneurial migration: a longitudinal data set is necessary for that.

Having discussed the migrants' business characteristics, we now relate these results to existing theories, which seek to generalize behaviour. One interesting result is that the relation between years of residence and propensity to stay is insignificant, indicating that this variable has little effect on migrants' inclination to stay in the current place. In other words, we have no evidence to suggest that the longer the years of stay in the current region, the stronger is the inclination to stay beyond two more years or permanently. We can conclude that the chances of remaining in the area are the same irregardless of the length of time the migrants have already been there. This being so, the *middlemen minority* argument seems to be an adequate explanation of migrants' business in East Nusa Tenggara (Turner and Bonacich 1980; Light 1980). The migrants in this region can be depicted as middlemen between the major entrepreneurs in Java and local consumers. Although some migrants may permanently stay in their current place, others remain only temporarily as sojourners. Except for a few West Sumatrans, most migrants rely on local Chinese as suppliers for their businesses. A large proportion of manufactured products are imported from Java and distributed by the Chinese suppliers. Thus, it is correct to say that the migrants play the role of a middlemen minority by distributing the products to remote areas in this region.

Notes

1. Department of Economics, Satya Wacana Christian University, Salatiga, Indonesia
2. The industrialisation policy during the Suharto regime in Indonesia gave Java a central position as the source of manufacturing goods in the archipelago. The goods were imported to the local economy by big wholesalers or by the migrants themselves.
3. Some of the migrants interviewed complained about bribery in the job market. The migrants could not afford to pay the amount of money asked

by the authorities to secure a job in the public sector. For that reason they had to find some way of becoming self-employed.
4. In November 1999, there were around 1,000 people competing for 27 positions in the Municipality of Kupang (*Kupang Pos* 11 November 1999).
5. We also tried other non-linearities in the duration type of variables, but it turned out that this did not help to improve the statistical "fit" of the model. (See nDoen 2000.)
6. To make the formulation simpler, we omit the term "the perception of" when discussing the various location factors.
7. One fishing merchant admitted that every day 30 percent of his catch was given away free to the surrounding community; he allowed this to happen because he wanted to maintain good relations with local people around the fishing harbour (private interview).

References

Auster, E. and Aldrich, H. "Small Business Vulnerability, Ethnic Enclaves and Ethnic Enterprise". In *Ethnic Communities in Business*, R. Ward and R. Jenkins (eds.), pp. 189–210. Cambridge: Cambridge University Press, 1984.

Bonacich, E. "A Theory of Middlemen Minorities". *American Sociological Review*, 38 (Oct, 1973): 538–94.

BPS. *Indikator Ekonomi Nusa Tenggara Timur 1997*. Kupang: BPS, Propinsi Nusa Tenggara Timur, 1997.

Hugo, G. "Changing Patterns and Processes of Population Mobility". In *Indonesian Assessment, Population and Human Resources*, G.W. Jones and T.H. Hull (eds), pp. 71–88. Canberra: Institute of Southeast Asian Studies, Research School of Pacific and Asian Studies, Australian National University, 1997.

Clark, W.A.V. and W. van Lierop, "Residential mobility and household location modeling", in P. Nijkamp (ed.) *Handbook of Regional and Urban Economics*, North Holland, Amsterdam, 1986, pp. 97–132.

Jenkins, R. "Ethnic Minorities in Business Agenda". In *Ethnic Communities in Business*, R. Ward and R. Jenkins (eds), pp. 231–38. Cambridge: Cambridge University Press, 1984.

Kim, K.C. and W.M. Hurh. "Ethnic Resources Utilization of Korean Immigrant Entrepreneurs in the Chicago Minority Area." *International Migration Review*, no. 19 (Spring 1985): 82–111.

Light, I.H. "Disadvantaged Minorities in Self-Employment". *International Journal of Comparative Sociology* no. 20 (1979): 31–45.

Light, I.H. "Asian Enterprise in America: Chinese, Japanese, and Koreans in Small Business". In *Self-Help in Urban America*, S. Cummings (ed.), pp. 35–57. Washington: Kennikat Press, 1980.

Light, I.H. "Immigrant and Ethnic Enterprise in North America". *Ethnic and Racial Studies* 7 (1984): 195–216.

Maddala, G.S. *Limited dependent and qualitative variables in econometrics,* Cambridge University Press, Cambridge, 1983.

Manning, C. and Rumbiak, M. "Irian Jaya: Economic Change, Migrants, and Indigenous Welfare". In *Unity and Diversity, Regional Economic Development in Indonesia since 1970,* H. Hill (ed.), pp. 77–106. Singapore: Oxford University Press, 1991.

Ndoen, M.L. *Migrants and Entrepreneurial Activities in Peripheral Indonesia, A Socio-economic Model of Profit-seeking Behaviour.* Amsterdam: Tinbergen Institute, 2000.

Spaan, E. *Labour Circulation and Socioeconomic Transformation: The Case Of East Java, Indonesia.* The Hague: NIDI, 1999.

Turner J.H. and E. Bonacich. "Toward a Composite Theory of Middlemen Minorities". *Ethnicity* 7 (1980): 144–58.

PART III

Indonesia's Rural Non-Farm Economy: Case Studies and Policy Development

9
SMALL ENTERPRISES, FUNGIBILITY, AND SOUTH SUMATRAN TRANSMIGRATION LIVELIHOOD STRATEGIES

Thomas R. Leinbach

Introduction

As the forces of globalization continue to expand and isolation is broken down, new opportunities and forms of employment have become reachable by rural populations. It is almost a truism that the livelihood patterns and strategies of families increasingly assume non-agricultural or non-farm employment. Despite a large literature on the rural non-farm economy there is much we do not know about its characteristics and potential (Saith 1992). One especially critical topic in this perspective is the growth and viability of small enterprises. This chapter examines several aspects of small enterprise development and its employment-generating capabilities in a particular context, Indonesia's transmigration programme, and seeks to link the findings to both the theoretical and empirical literature on the topic (see also Leinbach 2003). In addition it speaks to the latent potential of Indonesia's important but understudied rural non-farm economy.

Objectives

This chapter has several specific objectives. First, a brief review of the rural work, livelihood and enterprise literature is undertaken focusing especially on research in Indonesia. Second, the theoretical context associated with peasant household enterprises and the family mode of production is presented. Third, the patterns of enterprise activities are examined for a sample of families in nine South Sumatran transmigration schemes. Statistical modelling is used to extract generalizations and explain the activities in terms of economic, social and contextual variables. In addition qualitative analyses of business experiences are presented using a case study approach with information derived from several in-depth household interviews. In this regard the family mode of production is used as a theoretical tool to gain insight and particularly to expand upon and seek more generalization on Lipton's (1984) defined concept of 'fungibility'. Overall the ultimate goal is to achieve a deeper understanding of the ways in which small enterprises, including home industries, contribute to family livelihoods.

Rural Work, Livelihoods and Enterprises Literature

The literature on livelihood strategies and rural non-farm activities in the developing world is quite large and there is insufficient space here to give it due justice. Yet it is important to mention noteworthy pieces that are guiding the research effort. In a very general vein there are several recent works, which address the debates on rural development, differentiation, work and livelihoods in a variety of settings. The works by Deere and deJanvry (1979), Bebbington (1999), Grabowski (1995), Koppel, Hawkins and James (1994), and Saith (1992) stand out. In addition a wide ranging discussion of off-farm employment situations in Asia (Shand 1986) and an excellent review article on household strategies and rural livelihood diversification with reference to sub-Saharan Africa (Ellis 1998) must be mentioned. In regards to Africa, the work on de-agrarianization and employment (Bryceson and Jamal 1997) and more generally on peasant theories and smallholder policies in Africa, Latin America, and Asia (Bryceson, Kay and Mooi 2000) are key texts. Finally both the classic paper by Lipton (1968) and the paper by Ranis and Stewart (1993) which aim to explore the major determinants of dynamism in rural development emphasizing specifically nonagricultural activities from both a theoretical and empirical perspective are valuable.

More specifically there is an extensive and growing literature on rural industry, small enterprises, and rural capitalists-micro entrepreneurs. In this regard the various themes in the general works by Grosh and Somolekae

(1996), Prugl and Tinker (1997) and Mead and Liedholm (1999) advance our understanding of small enterprises in various contexts. This is also true of the more specific papers by Archers and Muller (2000) on Thailand, Livingstone (2000) on Vietnam, Stokke (1994) on Sri Lanka, and Rutten (1999) on India, Indonesia and Malaysia.

Finally with respect to Indonesia specifically, there is a smaller body of work that addresses rural industry and non-agricultural activities—mostly in Java—in both an historical and contemporary vein. In regards to the former, a set of case studies focusing on economic diversification in a variety of settings is well known (Alexander, Boomgaard and White 1991) and three others tracing and blending in contemporary developments of the rural non-farm economy are also useful (Breman and Wiradi 2002; Huisman and Kragten 1997; Heinen and Weijland 1989). Examples of small-scale industry and entrepreneurship issues and policies in the Indonesian setting are reflected in a variety of specific works (Berry, Rodriquez and Sandee 2001; Sugiarti 1989; Tambunan 1994; Mizuno 1996; Singh and Sutanto 1998; Weijland 1999; Hill 2001; van Diermen 1997).

The Transmigration Programme

Over time a variety of programmes have been implemented in a 'top down' fashion to expand rural incomes and development in Indonesia. One of these, the transmigration programme, has played a particularly conspicuous role in efforts to promote rural change (Davis and Garrison 1988; Leinbach 1989). The transmigration programme was initially built on the notion of alleviating the overcrowded conditions of Java, Bali, and Lombok by shifting landless agricultural people to less densely populated agriculture-based settlements in the Outer Islands. This largely government planned and financed effort was initiated by the Dutch in the early 1900s. From the outset of the programme until 1970, approximately 625,000 people were moved. Subsequently during the first two Five Year Development Plans (Repelita I 1969/74 and Repelita II 1974/79) some 450,000 people were moved, and during Repelita III (1979/84) 535,000 families were moved (Leinbach 1989). A prevailing focus in the development plans through 1984 was the establishment of agriculturally viable destination sites in which to settle the growing numbers of transmigrants. In Repelita IV (1984/89), employment generation through investment in labour-intensive enterprises was given high priority, and transmigration was seen as a major vehicle for job creation. In this objective, the programme was intensified and a target of 3.75 million people (750,000 families) was announced. The Ministry of Transmigration (MOT) eventually backed away from this goal saying that budgetary shortfalls would prevent its realization. Nonetheless the lack of funds was overcome by encouraging the participation of self-financing transmigrants.

The target for Repelita V (1989–1994) was 550,000 families (2.5 million people) requiring an estimated 4.5 million hectares of land. In fact official MOT figures estimate that only 68,413 families (294,175 people) were moved during Repelita V. Thus from 1950 through 1994 approximately 1.48 million families or 6.4 million people were moved. This total does not include those settlers, which were moved or volunteered during the Dutch period from 1904. While the above figure does presumably include spontaneous migrants who received some government support, it does not include other families who moved 'on their own' with no governmental assistance. While nearly all the settlements remain active, since the mid-1990s, the programme has been de-emphasized, in part for both financial and environmental impact reasons. In December 2000 it was announced that the programme would be terminated at the end of 2001.

The term "transmigration" encompasses three different groups of people. The dominant group comprises sponsored (*umum*) transmigrants, which receive extensive support from the government during the initial five years of settlement in the form of transport, land, housing, and social services. In addition there is a local (*lokal*) transmigrant group. Members of this group originate in or near the settlement areas to be developed and receive the same benefits as the sponsored transmigrants. The third group consists of spontaneous (*swakarsa*) transmigrants. These individuals move at their own expense and settle in a site of their choice. Spontaneous migrants may be registered; direct government support to this group is available, but the support is less than that provided to either the sponsored and local groups. Such support is provided in the form of credit rather than subsidy, although registered spontaneous migrants receive the same amount of land (2 to 5 hectares of which usually only 1.25 hectares are actually cleared) and benefit from the same socioeconomic services as do the sponsored transmigrants. Spontaneous transmigrants may also be unregistered, a group that includes those who move to a site on their own and are not entitled to government support. Criteria for selection to the sponsored, local, and registered spontaneous transmigrant groups included voluntary registration, low income, knowledge of farming or a special skill, married and under 40 years old, and good health. Unregistered spontaneous transmigrants, on the other hand, were not restricted by these criteria.

Prior Research on Non-Farm Employment in South SumatranTransmigration

Ongoing work regarding peasant livelihoods and family growth and survival in the context of the Indonesian transmigration programme has focused on several critical activities. First it is clear that off-farm employment whether on-scheme or off-scheme has been and is critical to success and survival in these environments. In addition while off-farm income is part of family survival, it also enables upward mobility. For example with additional off-farm children's schooling and higher education may be financed and consumer goods may be purchased. Off-farm employment is important in all rural Indonesian households but it is an especially pervasive activity in the transmigration schemes. Much of this activity is locally focused on the scheme of residence, and although males (household heads) are more likely to participate in off-farm employment than females (spouses), both exhibit similar locational behaviour. Jobs taken off the scheme tend to supplement wage earnings from other jobs already held on the scheme, and the occurrence of off-scheme employment is generally low. The family is a key variable in off-farm employment participation. Family characteristics determine the income necessary to achieve some nominal level of survival. Such factors as farm income, number and age of children, and number of family members working either on or off the farm were identified as being strongly associated with employment patterns, and particularly the patterns of the head of the household (Leinbach, Watkins and Bowen 1992). Therefore, decisions are made in accordance with a family survival strategy, which is based on family labour resources, an evaluation of time commitments to family and farm work, and a cognizance of physical capabilities and existing skills to participate in specific types of off-farm jobs.

Gender and age related roles in the family are especially important (Watkins, Leinbach and Falconer 1993). Women, for example, have a lower capability than men to participate in off-farm employment, and particularly employment away from the scheme, because of their socially defined responsibilities toward the home and family. This capability changes with age, however, as children mature to independence, thus lessening the demands placed on women. Concomitantly there is a reduction with age in the physical capacity to work in manual labour, which is especially pronounced among males (Leinbach, Watkins and Bowen 1992). Decisions must be made, therefore, to allocate time first between the farm and jobs taken away from the farm, and second between family members according to their capability. The latter involves the identification of appropriate types of jobs to ensure maximum benefits to the family, either through immediate income levels or through longer-term income security.

Additional findings reveal that on-scheme and off-scheme off-farm employment (OFE) is affected by the size of land holdings and variations in the family life-cycle stage. Smaller land holdings are associated with a greater level of on-scheme OFE participation for both heads and spouses. Further, households in the earlier stages of the life cycle are more likely to undertake off-farm employment as it is in this period that household labour is the most constrained. But again gender differences are present for spouses are more likely to be involved, particularly in off-scheme employment, later in the life cycle. This clearly reflects the gender division of labour in the household and the allocation of domestic labour for childcare. Critical too is the finding that processes operating at different levels influence labour allocation. This ranges from the 'historical-geographical context' at the scheme scale to the process of social differentiation at the household level and the way in which particular family demographic structures articulate with the broader social relations of the community (Leinbach and Smith 1994).

Finally the work on off-farm employment in South Sumatra has shown that circulation or *merantau* is an important aspect of off-farm employment and that remittances derived from this short-term behaviour make a fundamental contribution to family livelihoods and to local economic development. A schematic model depicts the ways in which families respond to economic conditions given the presence or absence of certain skills, as well as the structure and demographic composition of the household.

The research results point up several avenues for future research investigations. Among these one of the most potentially rich is the role of small enterprises, both on- and off-scheme, and the presence of home industries as mechanisms for generating employment and income in marginal agricultural settings. One perspective is to analyze household enterprises using the theoretical lens of the family mode of production and the concept of fungibility (Lipton 1984; Leinbach and Del Casino 1998).

Theorizing Family Enterprise

The analysis of peasant societies encompasses a vast literature that attempts to illuminate the dynamics of peasant forms of economic and social organization (Deere and de Janvry 1979; Harriss 1982; Ellis 1993). One model is based on the work of Chayanov (1966) who argues that peasant households and rural social organization resist capitalist penetration because their logic is household subsistence and simple social reproduction, not that of profit maximization. In this model, the household is conceived as a unitary productive and reproductive enterprise, which seeks to maximize total returns or utility (Chayanov 1966; Lipton 1968), not profit, subject to the opportunity costs of farm labour and the perceived "drudgery" of the work. In neo-classical economic terms, the peasant household enterprise (PHE) does not increase production to the point where marginal costs equal marginal revenue, but to where marginal utility of outputs equals marginal disutility of work (Hunt 1979, p. 75). In other words, the PHE trades-off its consumption needs against the labour required satisfying them. Further the uniqueness of household decision-making in the Chayanov model is solely attributable to the lack of a labour market. This uniqueness disappears, however, when a labour market is introduced. In addition, Chayanov's theory makes no distinction concerning the separate roles of men and women in the peasant household across the life cycle. For him, male and female labour, young or old, is perfectly substitutable in farm production, and the male household head or patriarch runs the household.

The other wider issue, which arises from the Chayanov theory of peasant economy, concerns the theoretical merits of a separate peasant mode of production distinct from the capitalist mode. The idea of a distinct peasant or household mode of production appears in various guises in the literature. The most conspicuous in non-Marxist writing are the domestic mode of production put forward by Sahlins (1972) and the family mode of production (FMP) advanced by Lipton (1984). In the former the FMP is envisaged as a special economic theory applicable to precapitalist societies. In the latter the FMP is oriented toward capturing the flexibilities of resource use in household forms of production whether in agriculture or non-farm economic activities (Ellis 1993).

For Lipton (1984) the key to understanding the family mode of production (FMP) is fungibility or "the extent to which a rise or fall in the availability of a 'resource' can be treated as if it were a change in cash funds, and thus converted swiftly, conveniently and without loss into a change in whichever input, to which activity, maximizes benefit" (Lipton 1984, p. 191). Thus the PHE as a unit of both production and reproduction, and in exercising control over both labour and capital, may easily and efficiently shift resources internally in response to changing conditions. Capital and labour resources will meet productive or consumptive needs according to priorities; say by restricting immediate consumption for investment in a petty productive enterprise, or using petty capital to meet basic household needs during a reproductive crisis. This can be done through shifts in resource allocation in time (i.e., between seasons), space (i.e., from one area of production to another), and/or within the family (i.e., between generations, siblings, etc.). Thus, in the "FMP there exists extended fungibility (EF) of resources between production, preparation of consumables...and reproduction of the family's capacity for both of these" (Lipton 1984, pp. 191–92).

In Lipton's terms, therefore, where peasant households operate simultaneously a number of income-generating activities ranging from subsistence production, petty trade and services, and petty commodity production, to agricultural and off-farm wage labour, the flexibility of resource use is considerable and allocation decisions rather complex. Distance from the political core (i.e., urban areas) also allows for the growth of the FMP in rural areas at a greater rate than in urban ones. Lipton wants to expand the definition of the 'informal sector-FMP' and blur the boundaries between it and the 'formal economy'. In essence, he sees value in examining FMPs and the flexibility present in this particular mode of production.

Lipton thus theorizes the survival of FMP, particularly in rural areas of the developing world, and the decisions people make in order to survive. He also stresses the importance of broadening the definition of FMP to include the multiple sets of tasks and activities that a family (and its members) engages in for survival. His work provides an important set of analytics, particularly the concept of fungibility and extended fungibility, which is well worth examining in an empirical context. With some notable exceptions (Potter 1977), we know far too little about decision-making within FMP enterprises and more generally the relationship between production and reproduction in the peasant household.

There are, however, limitations to Lipton's conceptual schema of FMPs. Before moving on to the analysis three weaknesses in Lipton's work should be highlighted. These include: (1) a naive bifurcation of the urban-based state and its rural other; (2) a lack of attention paid to the role of gender in the division of labour within FMP enterprises; and (3) a lack of analysis of the spatial dynamics of FMP enterprises. This chapter examines Lipton's notion of fungibility and examines the implications of his work in relation to the growth of small enterprises whether home based or external to the household. It addresses the need to understand the complex relationships between family modes of production, social differentiation within households, and external incentives and pressures on household economies.

Spatial Aspects of Fungibility

One of the key differences between FMP enterprises and capitalist ones, Lipton argues, is that an FMP enterprise "allocates costs, benefits and risks as to maximize expected utility to the household, not profits to the enterprise" (Lipton 1984, p. 192). The more resources (both human and capital) a family has, therefore, the more flexibility a FMP enterprise has for productive and reproductive tasks. This is not to say, however, that FMP enterprises never attempt to move toward the capitalist sector, they do. It is likely, however, that fungibility will be appropriated first for consumptive utility and second toward expansion of the enterprise. Key to this discussion, therefore, is the amount of disposable resources available to the household and the use of those resources, or the extended fungibility available within a given household. This includes both human and capital resources.

Lipton's concept of extended fungibility also raises important questions in relation to the gendered division of labour within FMP enterprises. But Lipton fails to examine these questions in depth. In particular, how do the shifts between productive and reproductive labour, consumption and production, differ in relation to local gender relations? They raise questions in relation to shifts in the economic capacity of the household and workloads of particular gendered social actors. In other terms, how might resource allocation be manipulated to benefit particular gendered subjects within the household?

Fungibility and extended fungibility are spatial concepts. Resource allocation is a spatial phenomenon and is dependent on, but also modified by, the spatial contexts in which social actors engage in FMP enterprises. A FMP enterprise, therefore, may choose to shift its human and capital resources spatially to deal with spatial factors, a new road or the growth or contraction of their community, for example. They may modify their behaviour in relation to the influx of state agents during particular periods of time (i.e., during growing seasons when extension agents are more active or during periods of social unrest in urban areas). The spatial extent of a FMP enterprise is thus fluid in time as it is in space.

Sample Schemes and Data Sources

South Sumatra has been one of the most important receiving provinces in the transmigration programme. Given the long history of transmigration to the province as well as its diverse environments, the province has a group of settlements of varying ages that are supported by a wide variety of agricultural bases. Thus, it is possible to examine possible differences in the incidence of OFE and other activities among settlements of widely varying characteristics. Within the setting of South Sumatra, nine individual transmigration sites were selected for study (Figure 9.1). The sites were selected to emphasize different agricultural environments, settlement histories, and access to towns and market centres that provide opportunities for employment and the sale of goods and services (Table 9.1). The schemes focus primarily on rice production, but rubber and other tree crops also play an important role in several areas. For example, rice production under irrigation is the primary activity in the villages of Karang Binangun, Sukanegara, and Hardjowinangun. Such a production system should allow double cropping and, in principal, higher incomes.

These villages are in one of the oldest settlement schemes in the transmigration programme, and tend to have the greatest variety of supplemental crops, such as corn, cassava, and peanuts. Infrastructure provision such as schools and service and trade establishments are also more highly developed. The villages are easily accessible from local market centres. For example, the towns of Gumawang and Baturaja are located approximately 30 and 90 kilometres away from the villages above. In contrast, the villages of Sumber Jaya and Makarti Jaya in the Telang and Upang schemes are based upon tidal swamp rice production, and are located in the delta of the Musi River. Conditions here are harsh. There are no roads and access is limited to a canal system, which has been carved out of the low-lying areas. In addition, the closest major market is Palembang, which is two hours away by boat. The village of Cinta Karya is based upon

FIGURE 9.1
Location of South Sumatran Transmigration Sample Sites

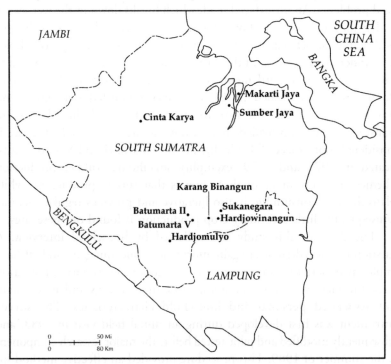

Source: Author's own data.

TABLE 9.1
Transmigration Study Sites: South Sumatra

Scheme	Sample Size	Model	Date
1. Karang Binangun	29	irrigated rice	1952
2. Sukanegara	33	irrigated rice	1952
3. Hardjowinangun	63	irrigated rice	1937
4. Hardjomulyo	108	rainfed rice	1974
5. Batumarta II	62	smallholder rubber scheme	1977
6. Batumarta V	45	smallholder rubber scheme	1979
7. Makarti Jaya (Upang)	79	tidal swamp rice	1970
8. Sumber Jaya (Telang)	79	tidal swamp rice	1979
9. Cinta Karya (Sekayu)	62	rainfed rice	1981

Note: Household sample represents an average sample proportion by scheme of approximately 10 percent.
Source: Author's own data.

rain-fed rice production and no irrigation is utilized. In addition, the soil quality is quite poor and low levels of production are worsened by pest and weed problems. An unsurfaced road, which breaks down in the wet season so that movement is very limited and more costly, only accesses the sole local market at Sekayu. As a result of these difficulties, many households have undertaken to work off the farm. In fact some families have moved to other transmigration settlements or have returned to Java. The village of Hardjomulyo, established in 1974, is also a rain-fed rice settlement. However, the soils in this area are much richer, and the Ministry of Transmigration has provided more infrastructure. As a result, the site is considered more successful. Finally, the Batumarta II and V settlements, created in 1977 and 1979, exemplify smallholder rubber production schemes. The advantage of these sites is that rubber production, while relatively time consuming, is also lucrative and provides regular income. Consequently, little secondary crop production is found on these sites.

The data for this study was collected by household interview. A questionnaire was designed to gain information concerning on- and off-farm employment activity and labour mobility, labour inputs, farm production costs, production output, revenues, marketing, savings and investment, and associated personal and household characteristics. The survey instrument was first developed during an initial field visit in 1988, and subsequently modified and pilot-tested before the major research component in the summer of 1989. This procedure provided an effective method for deriving appropriate and quality data.

A two-stage stratified sampling design was utilized at the level of each scheme. First, areal administrative subdivisions (*rukun tetangga*) were chosen. These were selected to provide uniform areal coverage of the settlements. Secondly, the head of each subdivision identified households within the sampled area to represent sponsored, spontaneous, and local transmigrants. Households were randomly chosen in each village to reflect proportions of transmigrant types. A total of 560 households across the nine schemes were identified and interviewed during the summer of 1989. In addition, in-depth interviews were undertaken in a select number (35) of households during the summers of 1989 and 1990. These were designed to provide case studies of employment histories, opportunities, personal and family economies, and decision-making strategies within the household. A follow up in-depth interview for the majority of these same 35 households was carried out in 1994 in order to chart changes in livelihood patterns since the initial interview.

Patterns of Business Ownership Among Transmigrant Households

The questionnaire focused on the existence and characteristics of business ownership among the transmigrant households. Questions posed separately to the head and the spouse in the family included: do you have a business now, what year did you begin the business, what type of business do you have, is the business located on-scheme or off-scheme, was capital required to start up the business and if so what was the capital source for the business, and finally has the business created new jobs.

Of the 560 heads interviewed over the nine transmigration schemes, 58 percent responded yes to the question, do you have a business now? The same question posed to spouses revealed that 40 percent operated a business. Thus business activities appear to be an integral part of the livelihood process in the transmigration schemes. While the above responses reveal the simple incidence of ownership among the head and spouse, even more important is the matter of whether heads alone, spouses alone or both head and spouse in a particular household have a business. In addition the location of the business whether on-scheme or off-scheme was of interest. This latter question begins to address the notion of fungibility through the mobility characteristics of entrepreneurs and their abilities to engage in commerce outside of the immediate local area. Further an aim is to identify social and economic characteristics associated with these entrepreneurial individuals and their businesses.

Of the total household businesses about 24 percent were head only owned businesses. Of these businesses, 71 percent were situated on the scheme whereas 29 percent were operated off the scheme. Significantly fewer situations occurred where the spouse alone operated a business: 6 percent. Of these nearly 80 percent were located on-scheme and the remainder were located off-scheme. Perhaps most surprising were the results of dual business households. Nearly one-third of the households were of this pattern. Further, both heads and spouses having businesses on the scheme dominated the incidence of both individuals operating businesses. Over 80 percent of dual business households were of this form.

In addition to these aggregate patterns of business, ownership and their locations were the variations by scheme. An effort was made to depict and assess variations in business activity density by scheme characteristics. For example to what extent do the economic base and age as well as location influence the incidence of businesses? An initial effort using cartographic depiction of this variation allows us to examine the patterns for some additional insight (Figures 9.2–9.4). The pattern of head-operated businesses reveals that ownership is uniformly high in nearly all the settlements (Figure 9.2). However the older settlements, with the exception of Sukanegara, appear to have higher incidence of business ownership. This is reasonably attributed to the larger populations and market potential in this settlements as well as the need for a more diverse set of activities given the potential demand. The incidence of businesses is somewhat lower as we might expect in the smallholder rubber schemes where incomes are higher and there is therefore less need to work at this activity in addition to farm (rubber) income. All of the more environmentally harsh and less accessible settlements (Makarti Jaya, Sumber Jaya, and Cinta Karya) also have on average half of the heads in the sample families

**FIGURE 9.2
Head-Operated Businesses**

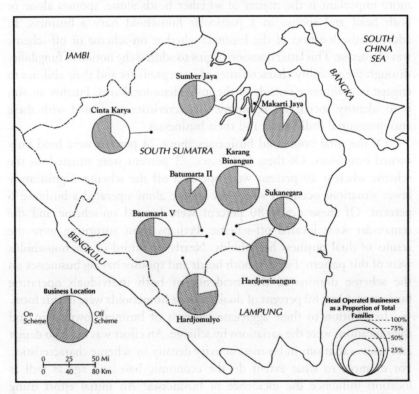

Source: Author's own data.

working at separate businesses. Nearly all of these locations, which have high proportions of heads engaged in businesses, also carry out those businesses on the scheme. The major exceptions will be where small service centres might be accessible and therefore businesses can be carried out in the town. Cinta Karya is such an example where male heads will work in the informal sector of the nearby town of Sekayu at a variety of informal sector jobs including the operation of pedicabs (*becak*).

In regards to spouse business operations, the overall proportions mirror those of the head (Figure 9.3). Of course overall spouse business participation is lower given the demands of household and farm work. In addition although some spouses do travel to market vegetables, the demands of other forms of work in the household, the care of children and at times

FIGURE 9.3
Spouse-Operated Businesses

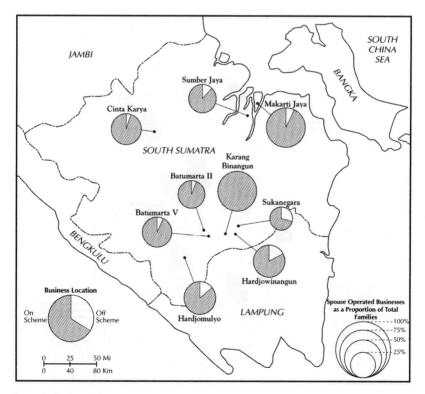

Source: Author's own data.

agricultural work on the farm means that such businesses will nearly always be located on-scheme as opposed to off-scheme.

Finally it is noteworthy to examine a map of business ownership which includes families where both head and spouse operate separate businesses in order to contribute to household income (Figure 9.4). Karang Binangun, Makarti Jaya, and Hardjomulyo stand out in this regard. Several illustrations of this joint behaviour in business ownership are given below in our case studies.

Home Industries

A not uncommon strategy for some transmigrant households is to develop a business which is home-based. Such industries are less numerous than

FIGURE 9.4
Family- (both Head and Spouse) Operated Businesses

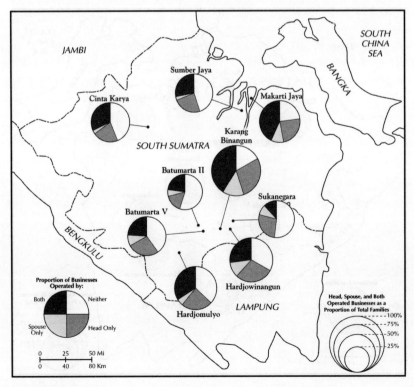

Source: Author's own data.

the other types of industries enumerated above but they are nonetheless useful as a means of gauging strategies of livelihood. Head-operated and spouse-operated businesses are nearly identical in number (Table 9.2). Among the most common home industries in which heads engage are bamboo crafts, furniture making, *tempe* and *tahu* production and cassava chips. The spouse home industries include also basket making, *tempe* and *tahu*, cassava chips, and seamstress. While the incidence of head or spouse home industries is relatively small, about 12 percent for each, there is some interesting variation in the pattern of such industries which is a function of settlement type, age and transport accessibility. Where incomes are somewhat higher, e.g., in the rubber producing schemes of Batu Marta, there is a much lower incidence of home industries. The lower incidence also is true of the tidal swamp schemes in the delta of the Musi River where difficult access, by canal, limits the household from marketing their home produced goods for cash or trade. Another relatively poor scheme, Cinta Karya, has a higher than average incidence of home industries, as does Hardjomulyo. Both of these are rain fed schemes which have difficult agricultural conditions. But because of difficult transport, and despite the proximity of the small town of Sekayu, very little of the production in Cinta Karya is marketed off-scheme whereas the better road networks around Hardjomulyo produces an opposite

TABLE 9.2
Home Industries: Head and Spouse-Operated

Scheme	N	Head-Operated	Sold Off-Scheme	Spouse-Operated	Sold Off-Scheme
Karang Binangun	(29)	7	3 (43%)	10	7 (70%)
Sukanegara	(33)	7	2 (29%)	5	1 (20%)
Hardjowinangun	(63)	7	1 (14%)	3	0 (0%)
Hardjomulyo	(108)	16	9 (56%)	19	11 (58%)
Batumarta II	(62)	3	0 (0%)	4	1 (25%)
Batumarta V	(45)	4	1 (25%)	6	2 (33%)
Makarti Jaya	(79)	9	0 (0%)	8	0 (0%)
Sumber Jaya	(79)	3	0 (0%)	2	1 (50%)
Cinta Karya	(62)	10	2 (20%)	11	0 (0%)
TOTAL	(560)	66	18 (27%)	68	23 (34%)

effect. Both Sukanegara and Karang Binangun also have a higher than average incidence of home industry. One might attribute this simply to the fact that these are older settlements with an aging population. While the younger generation may remain to carry on the agricultural activities in these irrigated environments the older generation may turn to the production of home goods to supplement the extended family's income stream. This division of labour within a household clearly illustrates Lipton's notion of extended fungibility and the ways in which households allocate labour to accomplish specific objectives.

Characteristics of Business Ownership and Operation

Previous research on off-farm employment in general reveals that male household heads are much more likely to engage in off-farm employment than the spouse and that on-scheme off-farm employment is much more common than off-scheme work (Leinbach, Watkins and Bowen 1992). These findings apply to business activity as well as we have noted above. For example, it is one and a half times more likely that a head will own and operate a business in any given family as opposed to a spouse. Thus gender and business location in off-farm employment in general are two key dimensions in the patterns of business operations.

In order to gain deeper insight into the patterns, business ownership has been modelled using a simple logistic regression approach (Hosmer and Lemeshow 1989; Menard 1995; Fox 1997).[1] A series of linear logit models each with a single covariate were estimated for head-owned businesses and separately for spouse-owned businesses. Each response term measured the presence or absence of a head-operated or spouse-operated business respectively. The covariates were chosen to reflect meaningful predictors and these were grouped into demographic, social and economic categories. The specific demographic variables included age and number of persons living in the household. The social or human capital variables included years of formal education, special training, type of transmigrant household, and number of years lived on the transmigration scheme. The economic set was comprised of land owned (in hectares), whether any land was rented out to other operator families, and amount of cash income from farm. Rather than emphasize the goodness of fit or the predictive value of the models, we sought to learn which covariates produce a relationship which suggests a greater likelihood of business ownership.

In examining the results of the separate models for the head-owned businesses, age, education, type of transmigrant household and land owned significantly increase the likelihood of business ownership (Table 9.3). Thus among heads owning businesses, with respect to age and education, we can say that older individuals are less likely to own businesses and that better educated individuals are more likely to own businesses. This latter conclusion obtains even though education beyond elementary school is quite rare among the head and spouse in transmigrant families. In addition the greater the amount of land owned by the family the less likely it will be that a head will own and operate a business (Leinbach and Smith 1995). The inference here is that larger amounts of land owned generate higher incomes and thus there is presumably less need in general to operate a business. A final covariate, type of transmigrant family, also relates significantly to business ownership.

TABLE 9.3
Logistic Regression Results: Head-Owned Business

Variable	HEAD B	S.E.	Wald	Sig.	Exp(B)	Model Chi Square	
DEMOGRAPHIC							
Age	.027	.008	12.7	.000**	1.027	13.01	(.000)
Persons	−.039	.046	.72	.396	.962	.72	(.395)
SOCIAL							
Education	−.129	.028	21.2	.000**	.879	23.4	(.000)
Special Training	.263	.266	.98	.322	1.301	.992	(.319)
Type Transmigrant						13.57	(.004)
Sponsored	−2.10	1.08	3.76	.052	.124		
Spontaneous	−2.28	1.09	4.33	.038*	.103		
Local		−3.18	1.16	7.50	.006**	.042	
Years on Scheme	.003	.009	.097	.755	1.00	.097	(.756)
ECONOMIC							
Land	.097	.044	4.87	.027*	1.101	7.71	(.005)
Rent Land	.065	.413	.024	.876	1.067	.024	(.876)
Cash Farm	.000	.000	.233	.629	1.000	.232	(.630)

* Significant .05 probability level; ** Significant .01 probability level

Although all three of the categories are significant, it is the spontaneous and local groups which are identified with the stronger likelihood of the head owning a business. While sponsored (*umum*) families receive extensive support from the government during the initial five years on the settlement in the form of transport to the scheme, land, housing and a variety of social services, the other groups do not receive the same support. Even though the land allocation is similar, direct government support to the registered spontaneous (*swakarsa*) settlers is different. In general the support to this group is less and is provided in the form of credit rather than subsidy. Unregistered spontaneous families move to a site on their own and are not entitled to government support. Unassisted families, including local settlers, have had trouble in obtaining land with some security of tenure. The implication of these facts applied to the current problem is that more pressure is put on the head in the spontaneous and local groups to derive income from more diverse sources, including owning and operating a small business. Combining these four significant covariates into a single model results in the retention of all except age. A forward stepwise logistic regression analysis using the likelihood ratio criterion for entry reveals that education is drawn into solution first followed in subsequent steps respectively by type of transmigrant family and land owned. Correct classification of the observations yields a 60 percent rate.

As with the analysis of off-farm employment, we hypothesize that substantial differences might exist between the explanation of head- and spouse-operated businesses. This is in fact the case. The analyses carried out for the head were replicated for the spouse-owned businesses. Data on age, education and training reflect characteristics of the spouse (Table 9.4). Significant covariates include age, education, special training, and whether land is rented to others. While the age variable is significant, the opposite effect is measured. That is older individuals are more likely to engage in and operate a business. This finding is consistent with off-farm employment in general and the plausible explanation is that as women age and the family life cycle advances there are fewer small children which require the care of the spouse and therefore more time is freed up for alternative reproductive activities (Table 9.4).

As with the head results, spouse education is a positive influence (Table 9.4). That is better educated spouses, however small the degree of educational attainment, are more likely to own and operate a business. This finding reinforces the importance of education and skill development and training in the development of business and entrepreneurial activities.

TABLE 9.4
Logistic Regression Results: Spouse-Owned Business

Variable	HEAD B	S.E.	Wald	Sig.	Exp(B)	Model Chi Square
DEMOGRAPHIC						
Age	–.018	.008	4.841	.028*	.982	4.87 (.027)
Persons	.012	.045	.071	.790	1.01	.07 (.790)
SOCIAL						
Education	–.058	.029	3.991	.046*	.943	4.03 (.045)
Special Training	–.813	.331	6.01	.014*	.450	5.91 (.015)
Type Transmigrant						2.66 (.446)
Sponsored	.101	.771	.017	.895	1.10	
Spontaneous	–.034	.783	.002	.965	.966	
Local	–.460	.836	.302	.582	.632	
Years on Scheme	–.007	.009	.500	.479	.993	.499 (.480)
ECONOMIC						
Land	–.013	.023	.298	.585	.988	.307 (.579)
Rent Land	1.17	.435	7.28	.007**	3.231	7.99 (.005)
Cash Farm	.000	.000	.261	.610	1.000	.262 (.609)

* Significant .05 probability level; ** Significant .01 probability level

Special training is also significant and this acknowledges the fact that women, whether on the scheme or off, have participated in skill development. This might be delivered through a variety of village efforts or social agencies in the rural areas.

Finally the association of spouse-owned businesses with land rented out to others suggests that where a family has gradually acquired sufficient land to rent out there is a trade-off that occurs in productive activities and associated work demands (Table 9.4). Work on the land is difficult so that a spouse may choose, if conditions are appropriate, to develop a small business rather than carry out physical labour particularly again as the life cycle progresses.

Combining these five significant covariates into a single model results in the retention of only special training. Each of the other variables becomes insignificant. This is also confirmed in a forward stepwise logistic regression analysis using the likelihood ratio criterion for entry. The regression results from the spouse model suggest that several variables may be working together in a combined effect to produce the results obtained and that indeed it may be appropriate to examine the ways in which the covariates produce joint effects.

Case Studies of Business Enterprise

Quantitative analyses provide a useful initial approach for exploring data relationships and allow us to begin to define more closely factors which may be associated with the propensity and rationale for individuals to engage in small enterprises to supplement agricultural activities. It is clear from the above analyses that age, education, land ownership and training are all in some way related to the development of a variety of business activities. But these findings do not allow us to penetrate the complex makeup of families and their backgrounds and the interrelationship between a variety of factors which are in many cases almost impossible to measure. We therefore turn to a case study approach where a story of livelihoods and aspirations can be pieced together from in-depth interviews. We begin with the situation of Ibu Agustina and her husband in Desa Cinta Karya, one of the more remote and difficult transmigration schemes in South Sumatra province.

Ibu Agustina and Pak Parto

Agustina, 24 years old, was born and completed primary school in Central Java. Since her parents did not have the means to pay for her education at the secondary level, she stayed at home to help them. Just after her fifteenth birthday, Agustina moved with her parents to the transmigration area in South Sumatra. When Agustina was 20 years old, she married Pak Parto, 35 years old and a mobile trader living in Desa Cinta Karya. They had two children in 1994, a three year old daughter and a two year old son.

Before marriage, Parto lived with his mother who had obtained her own land through the transmigration process (Parto's parents are divorced and his father is still living in Java). However she felt there were considerable 'social' problems at this location as a result of an ongoing conflict between the transmigrants and the local people about land ownership. Therefore, Parto's mother decided to sell her land and buy another property in a nearby locale. It was at this time when Parto met his prospective bride.

After marriage, Parto built a house on a small piece of land he received from his father-in-law. Everyday he travelled by bicycle to nearby wholesalers (a one hour journey) or to Sekayu (a one hour trip by bus) to buy chickens and rice for resale in his village. The rice, purchased for an average of Rp. 500/kg and sold for Rp. 575–600/kg, allowed him to earn about Rp. 5,000 per day.[2] His profits came primarily from rice as most of his customers could afford to purchase chickens only on special occasions. From these earnings, Parto and Agustina saved about Rp. 30,000 per month. After accumulating Rp. 250,000, they opened a small grocery store behind their house. Agustina worked here as the shopkeeper while Parto continued his trading activities.

In addition to selling commodities for cash, Parto also extended credit to his customers at a rate of 300 to 400 percent on an annual basis. Repayment was expected at the end of the rice harvesting season. If customers still lacked cash, he agreed to accept repayment in the form of gold as well as agricultural products such as chickens, soybeans and rice. Offering credit to his customers was not a problem since he usually bought on credit himself by usually providing a guarantee of seven grammes of gold or about Rp. 150,000 in cash to his supplier in Sekayu. A payment on his loan was expected each month in order to provide the lender with the cash flow necessary to maintain his own business.

Profits from Agustina's *warung* (household sundry goods store) were not nearly as great as were those in her husband's trading venture. A major impediment to greater income production was the lack of capital which would have allowed her to sell goods on credit. At the end of the harvesting season her average daily income was about Rp. 2,000, but during '*paceklik*' (before harvesting when resources and food were in short supply), her income dropped to Rp. 500 per day. Transactions dropped sharply during the rainy season when the prices of goods had to be increased 400 to 500 percent. When Agustina first opened the *warung*, her inventory included a variety of merchandise such as rice, onions, salt, sugar, tea and coffee, kitchen tools, cigarettes, matches and firewood. However after six months, it was clear that rice and cigarettes were the only goods in demand. Few of the other items sold. While the shop provided only a minimal income, Ibu Agustina considered it preferable to working as a farm labourer. In addition to providing more job security than farm work, operating her own business allowed her to have a better social standing among the women in her village.

Often families' livelihoods are constrained by the development context over which they have little control. The most significant obstacle in the Cinta Karya area was poor infrastructure and in particular a deteriorated road linking the village with Sekayu town. During dry periods, the problem was not severe because *opelets* (minibuses) were able to negotiate the road. However throughout the rainy season it was impossible for public transport to reach this area. Moreover people were often unable to use their motorbikes to transport agricultural products to market and bring manufactured goods and supplies back with them. Under these conditions, Parto had no choice but to travel to Sekayu by bicycle and was forced to spend many long hours on foot while he carried his bicycle. The return trip, when he had to carry his goods as well, was even longer.

Parto enjoyed his trading occupation and was satisfied with his earnings. At this point in time he had many steady customers in nearby villages, and because of very little competition, there was a rapid turnover of goods and profits. However, he felt that without any improvement in transport infrastructure, the journey would become increasingly more difficult for him as he grew older and his ability to continue this activity would gradually decline.

Parto's aspirations for the future included the acquisition of more land for investment purposes as land values in the region increased. While he would have to hire someone to cultivate the land while he continued his work as a trader, farming would provide supplemental income for the family. He was also interested in diversifying by purchasing cattle and was looking forward to buying a motor vehicle to help him develop his mobile trading activities. Parto was very keen to obtain credit (a loan) from *Bank Rakyat Indonesia* (BRI) but up to that point had not been able to provide the necessary collateral.

The situation of Pak Parto and Ibu Agustina revealed a number of constraints faced by transmigrant families in a remote location. First, the trading activities carried out by the family head as well as his spouse were driven by necessity but also clearly an interest in upward mobility. Unlike other families engaged in trading, they had virtually no supplemental income from farming. Although they attempted to build up savings, their profit from trading was too low to accumulate enough capital to borrow funds. Thus it was impossible for them to invest in additional land or other business ventures. Farm labour away from home was not an option for Ibu Agustina as they had two children not yet in school. Both Agustina and Parto had minimal education and were forced to rely primarily on unskilled trading activities. Finally, poor infrastructure, a factor over which they had no control, had a contradictory impact.

Difficult access to markets during the rainy season allowed Pak Parto to sell his goods at inflated prices and earn higher profits. However, he recognized that as he aged, it was unlikely he would be able to continue with his trading business. Moreover, as improvements were made to the road, his customers would have better access to nearby towns and his competition would increase.

Pak Semanti

Originally from East Java, Pak Semanti was 40 years old at the time of the survey and was married to a woman half his age. He moved to the Batu Marta transmigration area as a spontaneous transmigrant (not fully supported by the government) nine years earlier. In contrast to many of the transmigration schemes, Batu Marta was an area where the government had experimented with rubber smallholdings. While some spontaneous migrants received land, this was not the case with Semanti. When he arrived at the scheme he had no job and no land, so for the next two years he stayed with a friend of his father's in a nearby village. Since he had experience as a farm labourer in Java, Semanti found work by engaging in *merantau*, short-term circular migration. For three years he carried out seasonal work in Banding Agung, a village about 200 km away, where he collected rattan from the forests and sold it to local buyers. In addition he occasionally traveled 150 kilometres to Tarsi Lontar as well as 100 kilometres to Sumber Tani to harvest coffee. His average earnings from these activities were about Rp. 35,000 a month.

During this time Semanti managed to save nearly Rp. 300,000 which he used to buy 2 hectares of land in the scheme. He planted 380 rubber trees on one of the hectares. His house was on the second hectare where he planted 200 coffee trees, 15 orange trees and 7 coconut trees. Five years later, with savings from his farm and off farm income, he was able to buy an additional 2 hectares of land outside the village.

In addition to growing coffee, coconuts and oranges on his initial plot of land, Semanti grew dry padi. On average, he harvested 600 kilogrammes of dry field padi each year which brought in Rp. 100,000 per annum. He used these earnings as additional working capital for an off-farm business. As his rubber trees matured and he began to tap the latex, his rubber smallholding provided an additional Rp. 1,209,500 of income per year. Semanti projected that when the rubber trees were fully mature, and if he worked approximately 325 days a year, his total annual income would grow to Rp. 1,309,600. At this point in time the daily income from his land was nearly double the amount he could earn as an off-farm labourer and there was no need for him to continue this work.

In addition to farming, Semanti operated a small business selling gasoline, fertilizer, and rice. In trial and error fashion, he explored the market potential and in fact located his business in several nearby communities before he settled on his immediate village. Since this area had been settled first, the rubber was more mature and income levels were higher. Thus the landowners had more purchasing power for the goods he sold.

When asked about household expenditures, Semanti estimated that 50 percent of the income in village households was spent on rice and other consumable items. The rest was used for clothing, education, health care, cigarettes, and improvements on their homes. According to Semanti, both the household head and his spouse frequently worked in the off-farm sector when they needed cash quickly to satisfy basic needs. Thus off-farm employment clearly served as a reserve strategy to insure survival in tight economic situations. He also noted that many people found temporary work in the off-farm sector when they needed cash to pay school fees for their children's continuing education.

In this particular area, he noted, people preferred to work on-scheme rather than off-scheme because it allowed them to carry out tasks on their rubber plantations more easily. It takes about seven years until a rubber tree is mature enough to produce latex. As their rubber trees aged and more latex could be tapped, rubber small holders were required to give continuous attention to the trees. At this point, off-farm activities decreased. The pattern and intensity of tapping the rubber trees often produced a cyclical pattern to off-farm and small business activity. As latex production diminished after five or six years, there was a subsequent shift to alternative activities including small enterprises and off-farm work through *merantau*.

Semanti reported that the second stage of off-farm employment, which evolved as a result of scheme maturation and a deliberate effort of transmigration policymakers, was usually quite different from their initial activities. Because they now had a stable capital base and income source, they explored managerial or supervisory positions. Off-farm employment in this second stage included agricultural products wholesaler, contractor, supplier and other jobs supported by an urban based and managed activity. Additional economic activities included operating a transport service (with leased vehicles) to connect Batu Marta with Batu Raja, opening a *warung* or starting a handicraft manufacturing enterprise in the village.

The situation of the Semanti family is in strong contrast to that of the Partos where off-farm activity is much more critical as a means of survival. A basic difference is the remuneration received from the primary income earning activity as a rubber smallholder. Moreover the contrast between these cases allows us to gain a better understanding of the temporal sequencing of work performed off-farm and in the small enterprise sector.

Upon arrival at the scheme, initial employment may be almost any type of work that an individual can find. However once there is a regular and substantial source of income, the labourer (whether head, spouse or child) can be more selective as the immediate need for cash is not as much of an issue. In addition, individuals may use an existing business or activity as collateral for a loan or direct capital to initiate new activities. This is especially critical given the start-up needs for many small enterprises. Despite the efforts of BRI, access to loans and credit are still elusive to most people in rural areas. As *Koperasi Unit Desa* (KUD) continues to be an unreliable source of capital, small would-be entrepreneurs have no alternative but to seek start-up funds from *rentenir* or moneylenders.

Fungibility, Off-farm Employment and Small Enterprise Development

Off-farm employment in the South Sumatran transmigration context revealed that it is not only common but also critical to families' survival as well as upward mobility. On-scheme work by both the head and spouse is very conspicuous. Agricultural labour and trading activities by the head and spouse respectively represent the highest shares of employment. Yet it is clear that many families derive incomes in diverse ways. In part this is a function of success or the lack thereof in farming and the ability to save and invest funds from part-time work in land and other opportunities. Given harsh environments many families have halted the production of rice and adjusted their efforts, where possible, to accommodate other crops (e.g., rubber and coconuts) which are more lucrative and require less demanding labour inputs.

In these and other situations, there is the opportunity to complement farm activities with small business enterprises. The pattern of business activity does vary by scheme and the development context. Older settlements, with the exception of Sukanegara, appear to have a higher incidence of business ownership. This is reasonably attributed to the higher populations and market potential, which allows more diverse services and activities. A significant finding is the strong incidence of dual businesses in the households. Nearly 29 percent of the households reported that both the head and the spouse operated a business (Figure 9.4). In these situations over 80 percent of such households operated businesses on the scheme rather than away from the scheme. Environmental influences on agriculture, income needs, development situations of certain schemes and access to towns as well as business skills explain these patterns.

In terms of characteristics of the entrepreneurs, older individuals are less likely and better-educated individuals more likely to own businesses. In addition the greater the amount of land owned by the family the less likely it will be that a head will own and operate a business. Finally type of transmigrant family, also relates significantly to business ownership. While all three of the categories are significant, it is the spontaneous and local groups, which are identified with the stronger likelihood of the head of the household owning a business. The implication applied to the current study is that more pressure is put on the head in the spontaneous and local groups to derive income from more diverse sources, including owning and operating a small business.

Finally substantial differences exist between the explanation of head- and spouse-operated businesses. In regards to female-operated businesses, while the age variable is significant, the opposite effect from that of the head of the household is measured. That is older women are more likely to engage in and operate a business. This finding is consistent with off-farm employment in general and the plausible explanation is that as women age and the family life cycle advances there are fewer small children, which require their care. Therefore more time is freed up for alternative reproductive activities. As with the head results, education is a positive influence. That is a better educated woman, however small the degree of educational attainment, is more likely to own and operate a business. As noted above this finding reinforces the importance of education and skill development and training in the development of business and entrepreneurial activities and clearly provides a significant correlate of extended fungibility (Lipton 1984, p. 191).

At the outset of this paper it was argued that Lipton's concept of fungibility is an important analytic tool for understanding the differentiation of peasant economies. Resource allocation, and the flexibility present in the economies of family enterprises, can allow some peasant families to expand their holdings and business opportunities in rural areas. This is not done, however, inside a vacuum. Socio-spatial constraints are often placed on family enterprises by external forces, such as the state and more important the local development context. This is most obvious in regards to land where the constraints involve duration and nature of tenure, size of holdings and indeed land quality. As noted above the conversion of land from rice to other crops which are more lucrative and labour is less demanding illustrates one critical facet of fungibility. Theoretically, the state mandates site location of a seven-year minimum of land ownership before land title is gained and the property can be sold. As was shown in the Pak Parto case study, however, state mandates do not necessarily translate into practice. In the case of this family social problems in a particular location and conflicts with local people over land ownership have produced constraints. Parto has acquired land from his in-laws and this has severely restricted the family's income. Informal land ownership transfers or the lack thereof and the mobility of resources within a family household, therefore, can facilitate or in this particular case retard the growth of a family enterprise. The fungibility of resources and adaptation to particular circumstances is further illustrated by Parto's development of a small goods store and the nuances prevailing in the extension of credit to customers.

Similarly Ibu Agustina's participation in the family mode of production illustrates fungibility through social differentiation within the household, specifically the gendered division of labour, which is mediated by the family life cycle. In this case, farm labour for Agustina was not a viable option to enlarge the household's resources since they have two children who are not yet in school. Further her income potential is severely limited because of her lack of capital and the inability to extend credit. Seasonal constraints further reduce her profits. Yet the use of the home cum workspace for an economic activity—the *warung*—shows how fungibility extends beyond resource shifts among production activities (Lipton 1984, p. 192).

In the case of the Pak Semanti family, earnings from circular migration allowed the acquisition of land which in turn has been transformed into a lucrative rubber production business. At the same time he skillfully has engineered the construction of still another business which builds onto his current operations. As noted these extreme and contrasting family situations reveal how stages in the family mode of production transition from temporary work to land acquisition to small enterprise development. Moreover this business activity allows families to secure a loan or additional capital for further enterprise development. This application of fungibility clearly does reveal resource shifts among production activities through transfer and accumulation.

The analysis has also demonstrated how fungibility is an inherently spatial concept. Divisions of labour, land allocation and state influence, for example, are all spatially organized. Such spatial configurations act to constrain social actors' daily activities. At the same time, spatial structures can work to the advantage of certain peasant households. In the case of Ibu Agustina and Pak Parto poor infrastructure and the limited road network constrained both the supply and demand aspects of enterprise. In addition, the location of an enterprise in the home has provided a spatial advantage given mobility constraints on her work potential.

This study is a continuation of analyses which examine the conceptual utility of the notion of fungibility. It sought to produce an empirical understanding of Lipton's concept of fungibility which captures the extent to which a rise or fall in the availability of a resource (commonly in these examples—land) can be treated as if it were a change in cash funds and convertible to an activity maximizing benefit. But in addition to land, small petty enterprises may also be viewed as a converted resource which allows accumulation and greater benefit for the family according to its priorities. Both of these resources involve exercising control over labour and capital and may involve shifting resources internally in response to changing conditions. Significantly the research has extended our understanding to include the ways in which social (age, skills, education, gender, and children), economic (savings, credit extension) and physical (environment and infrastructure) characteristics may act as positive and negative constraints on the fungibility and extended fungibility process (Lipton 1984, p. 195).

Above all the work shows the implications of Lipton's notion for understanding the geographies of development surrounding peasant households. Fungibility integrated with the critiques set forth in the beginning of this paper, provide fruitful possibilities for researchers of Southeast Asian and other societies in the Pacific region. It is important to note that the concept applies to rural development very broadly and may be examined through the lenses of labour, life cycle, capital or combinations of these. Still further analyses of small enterprises that express the extended fungibility of capital and labour will be profitable as we seek to understand the complexity of development in spatial and aspatial ways.

Acknowledgements

Support for this research was provided by National Science Foundation awards INT/SES-8820423 and SBR-9323396. In addition I wish to acknowledge funding from the Committee for Research and Exploration, National Geographic Society under Grant #6928-00. Research permission was granted by the Indonesian Institute of Sciences (LIPI) and collabourative assistance was provided by Sriwijaya University (UNSRI), Palembang, South Sumatra. In addition special acknowledgement is made to M. Bakir Ali, UNSRI, for assistance in interviews and data collection. I gratefully acknowledge Mr Richard Gilbreath and the University of Kentucky's Cartographic Laboratory for the construction of the figures that appear in this paper.

Notes

1. There are a variety of uses of logistic regression modelling. Some researchers are only interested in the goodness of fit of the model. Others may be more focused on the accuracy of prediction or classification using the model in a particular problem context. Both of these purposes are most consistent with the aim of theory testing. For the immediate purpose in this paper, the interest is in theory development and therefore logistic regression is used as an exploratory tool. In this context focus is on the individual and collective contributions of independent variables and the substantive significance of their effect on the dependent variable. Similarly while stepwise approaches to regression analysis have often been criticized as ineffective or flawed such methods are often especially useful in exploratory analyses when concern is more with theory development than theory testing. This is often the case in the early stages of the study of a phenomenon, such as business ownership when neither theory nor knowledge about correlates of the activity is well developed (Menard 1995, pp. 36–38). In regards to interpretation of the results, as a function of response, variable encoding positive beta coefficients indicate that an increment in the particular covariate means that it is less likely that such a change will result in the presence of a business as opposed to negative beta coefficients which reflect the reverse.

2. The Indonesian rupiah has experienced a steady devaluation over time. In 1978 it was devalued from Rp. 415 to 620 to US$1 and in 1983, it was devalued from Rp. 620 to Rp. 1,000 to US$1. In 1994 when the most recent information was gathered from households for this study, the exchange rate was Rp. 2,140 to US$1. Thus the purchase of a kilo of rice for Rp. 500 in 1994 was the equivalent of approximately US 23 cents. The exchange rate in November, 2002 was Rp. 9,150 to US$1. Although the information presented was gathered in 1994 the case studies and other data are enduring and very much reflect existing and current situations and activities.

References

Alexander, Paul, Peter Boomgaard and Ben White (eds). *In the Shadow of Agriculture: non-farm activities in the Javanese economy, past and present.* Amsterdam: Royal Tropical Institute, 1991.

Archers, Daniel and Joanne Muller. "Thai Rural Enterprise Development Strategies in the 1990s: A Critical Appraisal". *Sojourn: A Journal of Social Issues in Southeast Asia* 15, no. 1 (2000): 153–83.

Bebbington, Anthony. "Capitals and Capabilities: A Framework For Analyzing Peasant Viability, Rural Livelihoods and Poverty". *World Development.* 27, no. 12 (1999): 2021–44.

Berry, Albert, Edgard Rodriguez and Henry Sandee. "Small and Medium Enterprise Dynamics in Indonesia". *Bulletin of Indonesian Economic Studies* 37, no. 3 (2001): 363–84.

Breman, Jan and Gunawan Wiradi. *Good Times and Bad Times in Rural Java: Case Study of Socio-Economic Dynamics in Two Villages Toward the End of the Twentieth Century.* Singapore: Institute of Southeast Asian Studies, 2002.

Bryceson, Deborah, Cristobal Kay and Jos Mooij (eds). *Disappearing Peasantries? Rural Labour in Africa, Asia and Latin America.* London: Intermediate Technology Publications, 2000.

Bryceson, Deborah and Vali Jamal (eds). *Farewell to Farms: De-Agrarianization and Employment in Africa.* Leiden: African Studies Center and Ashgate, 1997.

Chayanov, A. *The Theory of the Peasant Economy.* D. Thorner, R. Smith and B. Kerblay (eds). Homewood, IL: Irwin/American Economic Association (original 1925), 1966.

Chaves, Rodrigo A. et al. "The Design of Successful Rural Financial Intermediaries: Evidence from Indonesia". *World Development* 24 (1996): 65–78.

Davis, Gloria and Helen Garrison. *Indonesia: The Transmigration Programme in Perspective.* Washington, D.C.: The World Bank, 1998.

Deere, C., and A. de Janvry. "A Conceptual Framework for the Empirical Analysis of Peasants". *American Journal of Agricultural Economics* 61, no. 4 (1979): 601–11.

Ellis, F. *Peasant Economics: Farm Households and Agrarian Development.* 2nd ed. Cambridge: Cambridge University Press, 1993.
Ellis, Frank. Household Strategies and Rural Livelihood Diversification. *The Journal of Development Studies* 35, no. 1 (1998): 1–38.
Fox, John. *Applied Regression Analysis, Linear Models and Related Methods.* Thousand Oaks: Sage, 1997.
Grabowski, Richard. "Commercialization, Non-Agricultural Production, Agricultural Innovation, and Economic Growth". *Journal of Developing Areas.* 30 (1995): 41–62.
Grosh, Barbara and Gloria Somolekae. "Mighty Oaks from Little Acorns: Can Microenterprise Serve as the Seedbed of Industrialization?" *World Development* 24, no. 12 (1996): 1879–90.
Harriss, John (ed.). *Rural Development: Theories of Peasant Economies and Agrarian Change.* London: Hutchinson, 1982.
Heinen, Erik and Hermine Weijland. "Rural Industry in Progress". *About Fringes, Margins and Lucky Dips: The Informal Sector in Third World Countries: Recent Developments in Research and Policy,* pp. 13–33. Amsterdam: Free University Press, 1989.
Hill, Hal. "Small and Medium Enterprises in Indonesia: Old Policy Challenges for a New Administration". *Asian Survey* 41, no. 2 (2001): 248–70.
Hosmer, D. and S. Lemeshow. *Applied Logistic Regression.* New York: John Wiley & Sons, 1989.
Huisman, Henk and Marieke Kragten. "Development of the Rural Non-Farm Economy on Java: A Search for Roots and Determinative Factors". *The Indonesian Journal of Geography* 29, no. 74 (1997): 1–27.
Hunt, D. "Chayanov's Model of Household Peasant Resource Allocation and Its Relevance to Mbyere Division, Eastern Kenya". *Journal of Development Studies* 15 (1979): 59–86.
Koppel, Bruce, John Hawkins and William James (eds). *Development or Deterioration? Work in Rural Asia.* Boulder: Lynne Rienner Publishers, 1994.
Leinbach, Thomas R. "The Transmigration Programme in Indonesian National Development Strategy: Current Status and Future Requirements". *Habitat International,* Vol. 13, no. 3 (1989): 81–95.
Leinbach, Thomas R. "Small Enterprises, Fungibility, and Indonesian Rural Family Livelihood Strategies". *Asia Pacific Viewpoint* 44, no. 1 (2003): 7–34.
Leinbach, Thomas R., John Watkins and John Bowen. "Employment Behaviour and the Family in Indonesian Transmigration". *Annals, Association of American Geographers* 82, no. 1 (1992): 23–47.
Leinbach, Thomas R. and John Bowen. "Diversity in Peasant Economic Behaviour: Transmigrant Households in South Sumatra, Indonesia". *Geographical Analysis* 24, no. 4 (1992): 335–51.
Leinbach, Thomas R. and Adrian Smith. "Off-Farm Employment, Land and

Lifecycle: Transmigrant Households in South Sumatra, Indonesia". *Economic Geography* 70, no. 3 (1994): 273–96.

Leinbach, Thomas R. and John Watkins. "Remittances and Circulation Behaviour in the Livelihood Process: Transmigrant Families in South Sumatra, Indonesia". *Economic Geography* 74, no. 1 (1998): 45–63.

Leinbach, Thomas R and Vincent del Casino. "Fungibility and the Family Mode of Production in Indonesian Transmigration: The Example of Makarti Jaya, South Sumatra". *Sojourn: A Journal of Social Issues in Southeast Asia* 13, no. 2 (1998): 1–27.

Lipton, Michael. "Family, Fungibility, and Formality: Rural Advantages of Informal Non-Farm Enterprise Versus the Urban-Formal State". In *Human Resources, Employment and Development* Vol. 5, edited by S. Amin, *Developing Areas*, New York: St. Martin's Press, 1984, pp. 189–242.

Lipton, Michael. "The Theory of the Optimizing Peasant". *Journal of Development Studies* 4 (1968): 327–51.

Livingstone, Ian. "Agriculture, Small Enterprise Development and Poverty Eradication in Vietnam". *Journal of the Asia Pacific Economy* 5, no. 3 (2000): 173–89.

Mead, Donald C. and Carl Liedholm. *Small Enterprises and Economic Development: the dynamics of micro and small enterprises*. London: Routledge, 1999.

Menard, Scott. *Applied Logistic Regression Analysis*. Thousand Oaks: Sage, 1995.

Mizuno, Kosuke et al. "Rural Industrialization in Indonesia: A Case Study of Community-Based Weaving Industry in West Java". *Bulletin of Indonesian Economic Studies* 32, no. 3 (1996): 114–17.

Potter, S.H. *Family Life in a Northern Thai Village: A Study in the Structural Significance of Women*. Berkeley: University of California Press, 1977.

Prugl, E. and I. Tinker. "Microentrepreneurs and Homeworkers: Convergent Categories?" *World Development* 25 (1997): 1471–82.

Ranis, Gustav and Frances Stewart. "Rural Nonagricultural Activities in Development: Theory and Application". *Journal of Development Economics* 40 (1993): 75–101.

Rutten, Mario. "Rural Capitalists in India, Indonesia, and Malaysia: Three Cases, One Analysis?" *Sojourn: A Journal of Social Issues in Southeast Asia* 14, no. 1 (1999): 57–97.

Saith, Ashwani. *The Rural Non-farm Economy: Processes and Policies*. Geneva: ILO, 1992.

Sahlins, M. *Stone Age Economics*. London: Tavistock Publishers, 1972.

Shand, R.T. "Off-Farm Employment in the Development of Rural Asia: Issues". In *Off-Farm Employment in the Development of Rural Asia* Vol. 1, edited by R.T. Shand. Canberra: National Centre for Development Studies, Australian National University, 1986, 1–24.

Singh, Surendra and Agus Sutanto. "Entrepreneurship and the Development of

Micro and Small Scale Enterprises in Java, Indonesia". *The Indonesian Journal of Geography* 30, no. 76 (1998): 69–85.

Stokke, Kristian. "Dynamic Growth or Pauperization? Small Scale Industries in Hambantota District, Sri Lanka". *Geografiska Annaler.* 76B (1994): 187–209.

Sugiarti, et al. "Small Industry Development in the Framework of Rural Development for Broadening Employment and Business Opportunities Outside the Agricultural Sector: The Case of Small Industry Development in Tangerang, West Java". In *Rural Transformation.* Honolulu, HI: Resource Systems Institute, East-West Center, 1989, 105–24.

Tambunan, Tulus. "Rural Small Scale Industries in a Developing Region: Sign of Poverty or Progress? A Case Study in Ciamas Subdistrict, West Java Province". *Entrepreneurship and Regional Development* 6 (1994): 1–13.

van Diermen, Peter. *Small Business in Indonesia.* Sydney: Ashgate, 1997.

Watkins, J., Thomas R. Leinbach, and Karen Falconer. "Women, Family and Work in Indonesian Transmigration". *Journal of Developing Areas* 27, no. 2 (1993): 377–98.

Weijland, Hermine. "Microenterprise Clusters in Rural Indonesia: Industrial Seedbed and Policy Target". *World Development* 27, no. 9 (1999): 1515–30.

10
TRANSITIONS TO NON-FARM EMPLOYMENT AND THE GROWTH OF THE RATTAN INDUSTRY: The Example of Desa Buyut, Cirebon

Social Monitoring and
Qualitative Analysis Team[1]
The SMERU Research Institute, Jakarta

Introduction

Towards the end of year 2000, a group of researchers from the Social Monitoring and Early Response Unit (SMERU) Research Institute in Jakarta conducted a study of small-scale rural credit in a number of villages traditionally associated with wet-rice cultivation in the Cirebon area of West Java. In one of these villages, Buyut in Kecamatan Cirebon Utara, our team was struck by the dynamic economic environment within the local community. Throughout the day there was little evidence of young people chatting idly with nothing to do—a common indication of unemployment in many other village communities throughout Java. Every morning a number of vehicles collected young men and women from the village, and returned them in the evening from their work in the rattan industry. Some of those returning home carried rattan from their places of employment, apparently as models for making additional items in their own homes. At the same time, in houses throughout the village, many of the occupants—old and young, male and female—were busily occupied with rattan work. It was apparent that in Buyut, and possibly in other villages nearby, the rattan industry had become a mainstay for those people looking to obtain additional income outside the parameters of the traditional agricultural economy.

Fieldwork for this study was carried out in September 2001. The research team observed and recorded the economic activities of the village community in Buyut, and especially those associated with the rattan industry. The study aimed to concentrate on the following three areas: to examine the impact of economic activities in nearby villages on the economic life of Buyut; to assess the impact of non-farm economic pursuits on agricultural activities; and to consider briefly the influence of these non-farm economic activities on the wider dimensions of economic and social life in the village.

Information was collected from a wide range of sources during fieldwork. In addition to interviews with members of the local community involved in the entire range of economic activities within the village, valuable insights were also gathered from interviews with rattan factory staff and managers, local sub-contractors, workers at all levels of the rattan industry, industry association representatives, and government officials from various agencies.

Desa Buyut: An Overview

The village of Buyut is located in the west of Kecamatan Cirebon Utara (see Figure 10.1). It is approximately 15 kilometres from the port city of Cirebon and can be reached in approximately 30 minutes by public mini-bus (*angkot*). Buyut is part of the northern coastal agricultural region known as the Pantura, and has the most extensive area of agricultural land in Kecamatan Cirebon Utara. Approximately 103 ha of its total 153.5 ha of arable land consist of rice paddies watered by a variety of methods of irrigation: 48 ha are serviced by a technical system, 31 ha use a semi-technical system, and the remaining 24 ha employ simple irrigation methods.[2] However, some areas of rice land are less productive because the irrigation systems have not been well maintained and the permanent water sources are located some distance away. Consequently, there is frequent flooding in the wet season, while during the dry season a large proportion of the rice paddies are without water and cannot be used for other crops.

The rice fields in Buyut can be planted twice a year at most. During the wet season, which usually begins between October and December, farmers generally plant their main rice crop. In the dry season, the area under cultivation is usually far more restricted. The types of crops vary and include rice, secondary crops (primarily corn) and other food crops such as green and yellow cucumbers, watermelons and tomatoes. In general, the pattern of farming in Buyut is depicted in Table 10.1.

Usually, the farmers of Buyut do not sell their agricultural produce immediately after the harvest. Instead, following the traditional system handed down through the generations; it is stored and sold gradually according to their need for cash. Elsewhere in Central and East Java the majority of farmers no longer apply this method, preferring the *tebasan* system where their rice crops are sold while still in the field before the harvest. In Buyut, the tradition of selling agricultural produce over a

FIGURE 10.1
Map of Kecamatan Cirebon Utara

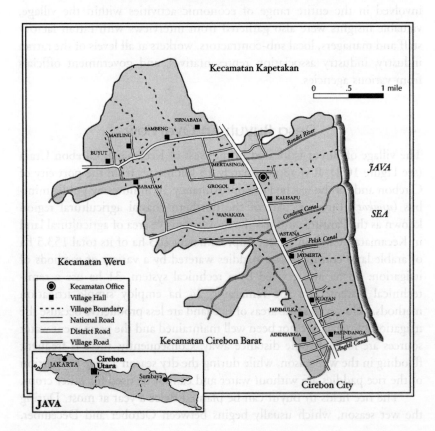

TABLE 10.1
The Pattern of Rice Farming in Buyut

Month	12	1	2	3	4	5	6	7	8	9	10	11
Planting Patterns*	Wet Season				Dry Season				Land Recuperation Period**			

Note:
* the beginning of the planting seasons can shift one or two months either way, depending on rainfall.
** the period when the land is left unplanted because there is insufficient water.

gradual period helps farmers to obtain a better price, because during the main harvest (around March or April) the price of unhusked rice tends to fall. Most farmers usually sell the bulk of their rice two months before or two months after the main harvest. However, there are also some farmers who are forced to sell just after the harvest, primarily because they require capital for the next planting season.

Like other regions along the north coast of Java, Buyut is often plagued by mice and inundated by floods. Consequently farmers cannot always rely on the produce from their rice paddies. Over the last two years, the rice harvests in the village have failed. According to the head of one farmer group, the 1998–1999 harvest failed because the rice crop was infested by pests that stunted the growth of the rice seedlings, resulting in no significant yield. Some in the village believe that the pest infestation arose because rice farmers failed to plant the recommended rice varieties uniformly throughout the area. Local agricultural officials or extension workers usually recommend the 'Digul' and IR-64 varieties, but sometimes farmers plant 'Cisadane' since it is the preferred variety in the market and can fetch a higher price.

According to local statistics collected in 1999, Buyut's total population was 5,399 or 1,282 families. Of the 1,767 people officially listed as employed in the village, 534 (or 30 percent) are farm labourers, 527 (29 percent) are farmers, 423 (25 percent) are employed in the private sector mostly in the rattan industry, 166 (9.4 percent) are government employees or pensioned civil servants, 74 (4.18 percent) are entrepreneurs, and the remainder work in a trade or in the service sector.

This official data on sources of income is, however, not strictly accurate because groups such as housewives and students, who often work in the rattan industry on a part-time basis, tend to be classified as unemployed. In addition, although no definite figures are available, an obvious shift in employment patterns is presently occurring throughout the village, since there is a strong tendency among those working in the agricultural sector to shift to the rattan industry. This trend was evident in interviews with local informants who described the limited opportunities for work as farm labourers and the advantages of working in the rattan factories.

Almost all the inhabitants of Buyut are involved in some type of income-generating activity, no matter how limited in scope. Young people in the village admit to a sense of shame and embarrassment if they are unemployed. In addition to those who cultivate their own land and those who work as farm labourers, many are employed in the rattan industry, both in rattan factories and with rattan factory sub-contractors.[3] Other economic activities include those who work in rice mills, tea factories and as unskilled labour overseas. A number of individuals produce foodstuffs for sale; others make paving blocks, bricks or wooden furniture. Many others have opened small street stalls selling a wide variety of simple household goods, basic farm supplies or foodstuffs. A few earn a living as building and construction labourers, motor vehicle or *becak* drivers, welders and hairdressers.

It is apparent that the majority of those who work in small-scale enterprises or as manual labourers receive relatively small incomes. This situation is a reflection of the generally low level of education within the local community where 41 percent have only completed primary school. Of the remainder, 32 percent are junior high school graduates, and only 20 percent have graduated from senior high school.

Non-Farm Economic Activities: Rattan

Employment in the rattan industry among the people of Buyut can be divided into the following three categories: workers who are employed in the rattan industry outside the village, especially in neighbouring kecamatan; those operating as rattan sub-contractors within the village; and the employees of these sub-contractors.

The Rattan Industry—General Background

Rattan enterprises throughout Kabupaten Cirebon originated from the home industries that were first established in the village of Tegalwangi, Kecamatan Weru. The variety of goods originally produced was quite limited and based on simple designs such as rattan sleeping mats. During the 1970s, however, these small enterprises began to attract the attention of various outside organizations, including the Department of Industry, the Directorate General of Cooperatives, Bank Rakyat Indonesia (BRI), the Indonesian Credit Association, non-government organizations such as the Research and Community Development Institute (LPPM) and the Institute of Research, Education, and Economic and Social Information (LP3ES), as well as the Department of Fine Arts at the Bandung Institute of Technology, and the West German Assistance Institute (FNS). Several of these organizations carried out research and began to support the development of rattan cottage industries in Tegalwangi. They provided technical assistance for the emerging small-scale enterprises and training for their prospective workers, as well as financing loans for prospective entrepreneurs. It was anticipated that the technical assistance would not only provide the skills required for the entrepreneurs to access the market, but also result in new designs for international exports, in particular new types of furniture. Many entrepreneurs have been producing rattan furniture since that period, and rattan products from Cirebon began to be exported after 1974. While rattan cottage industries previously only existed in Tegalwangi, they eventually began to emerge in other locations, including villages outside Kecamatan Weru. At present, the major centres for the rattan industry in Cirébon are to be found in Kecamatan Weru, Kecamatan Plumbon, and Kecamatan Cirebon Barat. In all these areas this industry has successfully absorbed workers from many villages in the surrounding hinterland. According to Hafid Setiadi et al. (2001), the rattan enterprises in Tegalwangi still employ 30 percent of all rattan workers throughout Kabupaten Cirebon.

During the 1980s, the rattan cottage industries in Tegalwangi developed rapidly with the establishment of several relatively large-scale rattan factories, which drew on both local capital and funds from outside the area to cover start-up costs. This rapid growth was largely stimulated by government policies prohibiting the export of all forms of unprocessed rattan.

In the 1990s, foreign investors from Europe, America, and Asia (Taiwan and the Philippines) began to take an interest in the rattan industry in Kabupaten Cirebon. Large-scale rattan factories were built to produce goods for the export market giving employment to hundreds of workers. Before construction of the factories was complete, the investors were already contracting out work to rattan craftsmen based in the surrounding villages.

The total number of rattan enterprises—small, medium and large-scale—has increased in number from year to year. According to data provided by the Kabupaten Cirebon Office of Industry and Trade, there were 828 such enterprises in 1996. By the year 2000 this had increased to 909 enterprises, officially employing 50,644 workers, with a total investment of Rp. 102 billion. Meanwhile, the production capacity of these enterprises had reached 604,000 tonnes, valued at Rp. 839 billion. Almost all of these rattan products (93 percent) were intended for the export market.

The growth of the rattan industry has also led to a significant increase in the volume of exports. Table 10.2 indicates that the volume of rattan exports in 1996 totalled 11,837 containers. By the year 2000 this had increased to 14,370 containers (valued at US$119 million), an average annual increase of 5.35 percent. The destination of the exports includes countries throughout Asia, Europe, America, and Africa as well as Australia and New Zealand.

Even though the rattan industry in Kabuputan Cirebon has grown significantly, it is still endeavouring to overcome a number of problems. Of primary concern is the lack of patents on designs that are often duplicated by competitors. A popular design is often reproduced by more than twenty different factories. According to the Indonesian Furniture Manufacturers' Association, before the expansion of the rattan industry, entrepreneurs and designers did not anticipate the problem of plagiarism. To help overcome this problem, a team has recently been formed to organize the registration of patents on new designs. Other problems for rattan enterprises include fluctuations in the price of raw materials and the

TABLE 10.2
Growth in the Number of Rattan Enterprises in Kabupaten Cirebon and the Volume of Exports

Year	Number of Enterprises	Volume of Exports (container)*
1996	828	11.837
1997	852	12.684
1998	864	12.757
1999	892	15.411
2000	909	14.370

Source: Kabupaten Cirebon Office of Industry and Trade, September 2001
Note: *one container is equivalent to 3.5–4 tonnes

difficulties in obtaining particular types of rattan. All the raw materials used in the industry come from Kalimantan and Sulawesi. The types of rattan that are most sought after include *mandola, manau, lambang, sega* and *fitrit*.

Box 10.1
Profiles of Two Large Rattan Factories

Company "A" (Domestic Investor)
Company "A" was established in the early 1980s in Desa Tegalwangi by a small businessman who had made the haj to Mecca, and whose father was also a rattan industry entrepreneur with strong connections in Cirebon. When first established, this new business was a limited partnership company employing sub-contractors. It produced between 80 and 100 rattan chairs per month. The raw rattan materials were shipped from Kalimantan, through a joint venture with an enterprise in Surabaya.

In 1987–88, orders from an overseas firm enabled Company "A" to expand. This firm was regarded as the 'foster-parent' of all of the rattan enterprises in Tegalwangi, and had branches in Jakarta and Yogyakarta. Consequently, Company "A" was able to increase the size of its workforce to 200 workers.

At present, Company "A" employs 400 workers (70 percent women and 30 percent men). Most of them are from the villages of Ciwaringin (Kecamatan Palimanan) and Buyut (Kecamatan Cirebon Utara). Wages received are in accordance with local minimum wage regulations. In addition, the employees are provided with transport to and from work, receive overtime payments and bonuses, social security entitlements and health insurance. The company management is aware that even though wages constitute 50 percent of production costs, the standard of living of workers and their families is strongly influenced by the state of the rattan industry. Many of the younger workers live independently of their parents, and are able to their own homes and vehicles as a result of working in the rattan factories.

> The economic crisis has actually had a positive impact on the company, because the collapse in the rupiah has made goods produced in Indonesia very attractive to foreign buyers. Consequently, workers have also been able to enjoy a share of the increased profits through monthly bonuses.
>
> Almost all production is aimed at the export market even though this is achieved through contracts with other enterprises. Supplying orders from other companies constitutes approximately 90 percent of production, while the remainder is direct sales to local and foreign buyers. The company is still encountering many obstacles in its day-to-day operations, such as how to ensure that factory production meets the specifications of the original order. Another is the problem of sub-standard work supplied by some of their sub-contractors.
>
> **Company "B" (Foreign Investor)**
> Company "B" is a rattan enterprise owned by the Taiwan Business Club. Located in the village of Lurah, Kecamatan Plumbon, it was established in 1993. Each month it produces between 5 and 10 containers of rattan products which are sent to Japan and Taiwan.
>
> This company employs approximately 600 workers from Luruh and Buyut as well as neighbouring villages from both inside and outside Kabupaten Cirebon. Similar to other rattan factories, Company B also provides transport for its workers. In addition to those employed in the factory, work is also contracted out to between 15 and 50 sub-contractors who operate in several nearby villages. Five of these sub-contractors are located in Buyut. Sub-contractors are required to use raw materials provided by the company and to carry out all stages of the furniture-making process from construction of the frames to completion of the end product.

Rattan Sub-contractors and Their Operations

Rattan sub-contractors are small-scale entrepreneurs who make rattan products according to orders received from the large rattan factories. The work is performed outside of the factories placing the orders, usually in the sub-contractors' workshops or the homes of their workers. The factories provide models or prototypes of the design to be replicated, the raw materials required (although these may be sometimes sourced by the sub-contractors themselves), and carry out quality inspections of the completed products. The sub-contractors then deliver completed orders to the factories for the finishing process. This work is always carried out in the large factories and includes stripping, sanding and lacquering, as well as the packing of the products for export. Sub-contractors are paid by the factories in accordance to the determined contract rate per unit, otherwise known as a piece-rate.

Those who establish themselves as sub-contractors have usually worked in rattan factories between 5 and 15 years before setting up their own workshops. Sub-contracting is attractive for several reasons. Large factories have always encouraged enterprising individuals to open their own businesses, and there is the potential to earn a higher income than can be achieved working as employees of the factories.

In the village of Buyut, rattan sub-contract work began around 1988. Factory owners considered it advantageous to contract out a percentage of their production to avoid the large amounts of capital required for the expansion of their factories, and to minimize the co-ordination of large numbers of workers. As a result, the number of sub-contractors began to increase in the villages near the large factories. This included Buyut, which is located only about four kilometres from the main production centre in Tegalwangi.

There are now about 15 sub-contracting businesses employing between 400 and 600 workers. On average, they hire between 6–12 male workers for their workshops and around 25 females who operate from their own homes. Apart from receiving an income that is calculated on a piece-work basis, those employed in the workshops of sub-contractors are usually provided with lunch and drinks, as well as extra food whenever they are required to work overtime. Women working from home are paid according to the amount of work that they manage to complete.

The initial capital required to establish a business ranges from Rp. 7 million to Rp. 25 million. This does not include costs associated with locating and establishing the site for the workshop. One important element in this establishment phase is a substantial cash flow so that sub-contractors are able to pay their workers prior to receiving their first payments from the rattan factories. The start-up capital required is often borrowed from the factories or from other investors. In order to avoid any lull in their business, sub-contractors normally try to secure orders from other factories through cooperative arrangements with other sub-contractors who have more work than they can manage.

Sub-contracting work is generally carried out in stages. Rattan raw materials are sorted and chosen in accordance with the product model provided by the factory and is usually carried out by the sub-contractor or a trusted representative. The next step, most often undertaken by the male workers in the subcontractors' workshops, involves cutting and heating the rattan to make it easier to shape into the required design. This is followed by frame construction, a task always carried out by males in the workshops. To complete each item, frame binding as well as rattan platting is performed by females in their homes.

By dividing the process into several stages, all workers are included in the activities of the enterprise and a teamwork environment of co-dependency is created. Any delay on the part of one worker will impede the entire work process and ultimately everyone's potential income will be reduced.

Box 10.2
Profile of a Sub-contracting Entrepreneur

Pak Udin is 31 years old and while still considered young, his face bears the evidence of extensive life experience. He is married with three small children, and he and his family live in the village of Buyut together with Pak Udin's parents who are share-farmers.

Before establishing his sub-contracting enterprise, Pak Udin worked for 15 years in a large joint-venture rattan factory in Tegalwangi that employed over 2,000 workers. Eager to start his own business and buoyed by the support of his former employers, two years ago Pak Udin decided to become a sub-contractor using raw materials provided by the factory.

Pak Udin spent Rp. 7 million from his savings on start-up capital to build a basic workshop behind his house, as well as to purchase some special equipment such as a compressor and a drill. He now employs six piece-workers in the workshop from the nearby village of Babadan. These men had previously worked for the same factory and were willing to work as contract piece-workers because the workshop is closer to their homes than the factory, and their working hours are more flexible. In addition, Pak Udin employs 25 local women who work from home, doing platting and binding. Their income is based on both the number of pieces that they manage to produce and the difficulty of the work.

While the number of workshops in Buyut is increasing, it is not difficult to find workers. The sub-contractors do not compete to hire workers because they usually have an established relationship with one particular group of workers. In fact, there is a high level of cooperation between sub-contractors so that if a workshop does not have sufficient work at any particular time, they are often called to assist other workshops to complete their own orders.

Employment in the Rattan Factories

Approximately 500 members of the Buyut community work in rattan factories in the surrounding area. In many cases, several members of the same family are engaged in this work. Information about employment opportunities is usually obtained through neighbours, friends or members of the family who are already working in a factory. Workers usually travel to and from work in vehicles provided by the factories. Every morning, approximately ten trucks leave the village each with up to 50 workers.

In general, rattan factory workers fall into one of three categories: monthly workers, daily hire workers, and those who are employed under piece-work arrangements. Only workers in the first two categories are regarded as permanent employees. Those employed as permanent monthly workers receive their wages each month, whereas the daily hire workers and piece-workers receive their wages weekly, paid every Saturday. They work an eight-hour day from Monday to Friday with an additional half-day on Saturdays.

Wages vary according to the difficulty of the work performed and the number of pieces produced. However, there is little variation in the wages paid by different factories for work of the same nature. For example, those working in the design section (cutting the rattan, making the frames for items of furniture, and constructing the models) receive an income of between Rp. 100,000 and Rp. 250,000 per week. In comparison, those in the platting, sanding, and packing sections receive somewhere between Rp. 25,000 and Rp. 120,000 per week, depending again on the complexity of the task and the total output.

Apart from their base wages, the factories provide various other benefits for their workers. These include transport to and from work and a Lebaran Bonus (in the form of cash and clothes paid at the end of the annual fasting month) given to all permanent and non-permanent workers. For permanent employees, several factories also provide other services, including additional bonuses, social security contributions (*jamsostek*), protective clothing and uniforms, as well as covering workers' medical expenses when they are ill.

Box 10.3
Profile of a Rattan Factory Worker

Tono is 26 years old and lives in Buyut. He has finished junior high school, and is married with one child. For the last seven years, he has worked for several different factories and while he always endeavours to find work with those factories paying the highest wages, he is also dependent on the factories with available work.

After hearing about the availability of work from friends, Tono was hired by one of the largest rattan factories in the village of Purbawinangun, in Kecamatan Plumbon. He is employed on a piece-work basis in the chair-platting section and is paid Rp. 6,000 per chair. By producing two to four chairs per day, he is able to earn a wage of Rp. 60,000 to Rp. 100,000 every week (By way of comparison, before the economic crisis, he was earning between Rp. 40,000 and Rp. 70,000 per week).

As a piece-worker, Tono is not paid overtime rates and does not receive any perks. However, he does receive the Lebaran Bonus which varies from year to year. His most recent bonus was Rp. 175,000.

> The factory provides transport to and from work. However, Tono often rides his motorbike to work with his wife. Tono's wife is a daily-hire employee at another rattan factory nearby where she works in the administration section. She receives a daily wage of Rp. 10,600, in accordance with the monthly minimum wage of Rp. 295,000 in Cirebon. Tono and his wife consider the income they earn working for the rattan factories to be sufficient to cover the living expenses of their extended family.
>
> Tono and his family are still living with his parents in-law, and his wife's two younger brothers who are still at school. As the family's main breadwinner, he also rents out computer playstations from his home which provide him with an additional amount of about Rp. 20,000 every week.

Employment in Rattan Sub-contracting Enterprises

Those workers who are employed by rattan industry sub-contractors appear to enjoy a number of additional benefits compared to those who work in the large factories. Since the sub-contactors' workshops are located close to their homes, workers are able to spend more time with their families. In addition, food is usually provided and workers are able to regulate their own hours by deciding when to take breaks, and choosing how much overtime they wish to take on. This is because working hours are not strictly governed. However, the continuity of work is less reliable because this depends on the sub-contractors' orders from the factories. Consequently, sub-contractors are not always able to guarantee regular daily employment which can have a significant effect on income levels of the workers.

The relative advantages and disadvantages of working with sub-contractors tend to depend on the particular workers involved. Apart from the men employed in the sub-contractors' own workshops, there are also many housewives and students whose primary interests lie outside of their employment in the industry. Students often work after school or at night, usually by doing binding or platting work and often to assist their parents who may also be employed by the same sub-contractor.

The wages received by those employed by sub-contractors vary considerably and are determined by the amount of work completed and the type of product that is being produced. Platting work usually pays between Rp. 4,000 and Rp. 6,000 for a simple model, although for a more complex piece, workers can earn up to Rp. 11,500. A platting worker usually receives somewhere between Rp. 12,500 and Rp. 25,000 per day. If the rattan work only involves binding, women working from home receive between Rp. 2,500 and Rp. 12,500 per day. Overall, workers' incomes vary widely and can range anywhere between Rp. 25,000 and Rp. 100,000 per week. Those undertaking more difficult tasks, such as making the frames for items of furniture, may earn up to Rp. 200,000 per week.

The education levels of workers employed by sub-contractors vary between those who have only finished primary school to senior high school graduates. However, years of education, especially for those who have worked for a significant time in the industry, appear to have no significant influence on wage levels.

Other Non-Farm Economic Activities

Joining Indonesia's Official Overseas Labour Contingent (TKI)

One alternative to working in the agricultural sector is to enlist as a member of Indonesia's official overseas labour contingent. In the village of Buyut there are currently about 20–30 women who are working overseas in Saudi Arabia, Malaysia and Singapore. As a result of their minimal level of education, these women have only been able to find placements as housemaids.

A number of young girls from Buyut have chosen to become overseas workers with the expectation of receiving a large salary and accumulating a significant amount of money in a reasonably short time. One worker employed in Jeddah, Saudi Arabia, for two years (1998–1999) was able to return with around Rp. 30 million, after expenses had been taken into account. Another woman who worked in Madinah for one and a half years returned home with around Rp. 16 million. It would be impossible to receive incomes as large as these working locally, including in the rattan industry.

From the capital that overseas workers are able to save, most are able to build new houses or transform their original simple bamboo structures into permanent homes. At the very least they are able to equip their houses with a range of consumer items and electrical appliances. Yet despite the perceived advantages, the level of interest in Indonesia's official overseas labour scheme remains limited because of the widely reported risks involved and the two-year contract period involved.

Brick Making

Bricks are only produced during the dry season, from around August through to October. Unplanted rice-paddies with elevated grounds are exploited for the purpose. The owners of the paddy fields deliberately set aside these areas for the brick-makers so they can use the topsoil and consequently lower the level of the paddy. This makes it easier to irrigate and ensures that the paddies are not used as a breeding ground for mice.

Approximately 50 individuals in Buyut operate small-scale brick-making enterprises. They have adjacent plots of land, each occupying around 0.3 ha, and either work alone or with assistance from their families. None of them uses additional paid labour.

No special contract is drawn up between the landowners and the brick makers. Usually, the landowners receive 500–1,000 bricks as a form of payment. Each brick maker can produce around 10,000–15,000 bricks in a season (each season is about one and a half to two months depending on when the rains begin). Red bricks are sold on location for Rp. 140 per piece. When these individuals are not making bricks, they return to their routine activities including working as farm labourers, share farmers or *becak* drivers.

Petty Retail Activities (*Warung*)

In even the most remote parts of Buyut, there is always at least one small stall (known as a *warung*) to be found selling basic everyday goods, snacks and other pre-cooked foods. Paralleling the increase in the number of workers in the rattan industry, the number of small petty retailing enterprises in the village has increased rapidly. There are now over 100 of these small stalls, all primarily operated by local women.

The daily turnover of these stalls ranges between Rp. 40,000 and 300,000 gross or Rp. 6,000–40,000 net, depending on the size of the business. Turnover increases significantly every Saturday and Sunday after the rattan workers have received their wages.

Tea Factory Workers

A small number of individuals in Buyut, mostly young women, work in the tea factories located in Kabupaten Cirebon. They are met and taken to and from work every morning and afternoon in a vehicle provided by the factories.

Their income at the tea factories is relatively small, only around Rp. 5,000–7,000 per day. By working from Monday through Saturday, they can obtain between Rp. 30,000 and Rp. 42,000 per week. Despite the low income, women continue to work in these tea enterprises, reportedly because the work is not too strenuous.

Other Activities

Other economic activities observed in the village include the making of *telur asin* (cured/salted eggs) and *lontong* (steamed rice wrapped in a banana leaf). It seems that such work produces substantial financial rewards. One family—a husband and wife and their two children—produces approximately 1,000 *telur asin* and 1,000 *lontong* every day to sell at the market in the city of Cirebon. Each *telur asin* sells for Rp. 750, making a profit of Rp. 75, and each *lontong* for Rp. 200, with a profit of Rp. 85. Another *lontong* maker produces 3,000 pieces every day, for a 100 percent return on the capital investment required.

In addition, there are several individuals who make and sell *kueh serabi* (a kind of rice flour pancake). They generally have a daily turnover of around Rp. 25,000, which provides them with a clear profit of approximately Rp. 6,000. Another individual has a small syrup enterprise employing six workers while others work as construction labourers, *becak* drivers, and welders.

The Impact of Non-Farming Activities on the Farming Sector

The large number of Buyut's inhabitants who are now working outside the farming sector—primarily in the rattan industry—has had a significant effect on the availability of agricultural labourers in the village. Fewer and fewer younger members of the community are willing to work in the farming sector, leaving older people to carry out the farming work. The economic crisis, which caused the rattan enterprises to "boom", tended to draw young people in particular away from farming activities and absorb them into the rattan industry. Male farm labourers, who previously only received Rp. 12,000 per day, since the year 2000 have had their wages increased to Rp. 20,000 for a full working day (from 7.00am to 4.30pm), or Rp. 15,000 for a half day. Apart from cash wages, farm labourers also receive food, snacks and cigarettes to the value of Rp. 5,000.

Despite this increase, the youth of the village continue to express little interest in working in the farming sector and prefer to work in the rattan industry. There are a number of reasons for this shift in choice of preferred economic activity. Agricultural labour is perceived by some to be dirty and demeaning and thus reduces a person's self respect. Farm work is also highly seasonal as well as hard and exhausting work that leaves little energy for any other income earning activities. Furthermore, employment in the rattan industry potentially offers a higher level of income, especially for those with the appropriate skills. Finally, the rattan industry offers opportunities to access credit when it is needed, as workers are able to borrow money from their sub-contractor employers before payday.

The decline in the availability of labour in the agricultural sector has not only caused farm labourers' wages to increase; it has also forced farmers to rely increasingly on tractors rather than manual labour. The manual labour that is still carried out by the local village people is limited to the harvest periods, the construction of dikes (work performed by men), and the planting and fertilizing of paddies, which is undertaken by women for around Rp. 10,000–12,000 per half day.

The combination of labour shortage and high farming costs has forced some local landowners to lease their paddies to share farmers. Rice paddies leased over a single cropping period yield returns between Rp. 800,000 and Rp. 1 million per ha, while a double cropping period brings between Rp. 1.2 million and Rp. 1.5 million per ha. By leasing out their rice paddies, landowners no longer have to concern themselves with finding the capital required to pay wages or to purchase expensive fertilizers and pesticides. In addition, they don't have to face the risks of declining rice prices or crop failure as a result of pest infestation or flooding.

Working in the farming sector is considered far less financially reliable than working in the rattan industry. Nevertheless, most farmers with small plots of land continue to manage their paddies themselves. In order to provide for their daily needs, farmers make use of their spare time away from the rice fields by working in rattan sub-contracting enterprises, by petty trading, or by working as *becak* drivers or labourers.

Meanwhile, the share farmers who lease rice paddies are generally older members of the local community who are accustomed to working as farmers. They are able to survive in the farming sector because they perform almost all the work themselves or are assisted by their families. Consequently, they do not need to spend money to employ additional labourers. Besides working in the rice paddies, they also have second jobs such as making bricks or driving *becak*.

In addition to the increased availability of work outside the farming sector, the shortage of agricultural labour and the high costs of farming have also led to a decline in the area of land devoted to farming in Buyut. The majority of farming land is now only used for crops once a year during the wet season. Meanwhile, in the dry season, although crops could still be planted, there are few landowners who are interested. This is because during the dry season the land must be attended to far more regularly and far more manual labour is required because there are no available supplies of irrigated water.

The Impact of Non-Farming Activities on Social and Economic Conditions in Buyut

According to local informants, the rattan industry began to have a strong influence in the village around 1986, when a few people from Buyut started working in a rattan factory in a neighbouring village. Nowadays, there are more than ten large factories employing workers from Buyut. Subsequently, a number of workers were encouraged by factory owners employing them to establish rattan sub-contracting enterprises in their own village. There are now more than 15 such enterprises in Buyut employing a large number of others.

The rattan industry, both the large factories and the smaller sub-contracting enterprises, has brought considerable financial benefits to the residents of Buyut. Almost all young people of working age in the village are able to find employment. School children and housewives can also find part-time work in sub-contracting enterprises. As a result, the drift to large urban centres, especially by young people, and the incidence of social conflict and petty crime have all declined. Increasing income levels and gainful employment have been important contributing factors. According to several informants, petty theft was quite common in the village before the rattan industry began to provide a stable source of employment for the local community.

In addition, rattan sub-contractors have assisted the people of Buyut with several community development programmes in the village. These have focused in particular on cleaning up the environment, Independence Day celebrations, the construction of water storage facilities and a mosque, as well as the formation of a residents' village security body.

The expansion of the rattan industry has had other positive repercussions for the people of Buyut. By increasing the purchasing power of the local community, a range of small-scale petty trading enterprises such as small shops and stalls (*warung*) have been able to flourish. One local petty trader who sells a popular kind of soup in the village can use up to 20kg of meat in a single day. Several small traders describe Saturday and Sunday as their especially busy days because that is when many of the rattan workers receive their wages. One vendor specializing in grilled chicken who operates a stall on the edge of the village is able to sell approximately 25 chickens every Saturday and Sunday.

Buyut's village head admits that the existence of the rattan industry has had a substantial impact on the local community both in direct and indirect ways. Other small-scale enterprises like brick making have also benefited from the increasing number of residents who are now building permanent houses. Previously, the walls of rattan workers' houses were made only of woven bamboo. Nowadays, however, many of them own permanent houses made of bricks and cement or they have used some of the income earned in the rattan industry to cover other costs such as purchasing wood and roof-tiles.

As far as educational attainment is concerned, the expansion of the rattan industry has had two quite different effects upon the attitude toward education within the village community. On the one hand, it has discouraged some teenagers from continuing to higher levels because students realize that they can drop out of school and still be guaranteed a steady income. On the other hand, many individuals working in the rattan industry—parents, grandparents, older brothers and sisters—are now earning sufficient income to support their children or younger siblings and are actively urging them to remain at school to pursue their education at a higher level.

Conclusions

The rapid expansion of the rattan industry from the late 1980s in several centres of production in Kabupaten Cirebon, especially in Tegalwangi, has had a substantial effect on employment and the economic life of the surrounding villages. Buyut, a village only four kilometres from Tegalwangi, is a prime example of these developments. A majority of its inhabitants—old and young, men and women—now receive at least a significant proportion of their income from the rattan industry, either as regular employees in one of the large factories, or as workers in one of the many sub-contracting workshops that have sprung up in the area, most of them owned by small entrepreneurs from the village. Housewives and students have also been absorbed into the industry as part-time piece-workers for these sub-contractors.

Another group of villagers is involved in a range of economic pursuits also outside of the agricultural sector. This includes work as petty traders selling a variety of produce and household goods, in food stalls and in brick-making enterprises, as well as wholesale food producers, drivers, tea factory workers, and in rice mills. Nevertheless, the rattan industry remains the single most important source of income for the people of Buyut.

The growing importance of the rattan industry on the economic life of the community has had a substantial impact on agriculture in Buyut, a village where 67 percent of its land area consists of wet-rice fields. Although the largest single group still claims farming or farm labour as their source of livelihood, in reality there is a growing tendency for this to be the preserve of the older members of the village community. The younger generation is now reluctant to participate in agricultural labour if they can avoid it, in part because of a shift in attitude towards farm work itself, but also because of the obvious and growing economic attraction of the rattan enterprises. As a result, there has been a significant reduction in available labour for agriculture, causing farm wages to increase sharply in the last few years, and contributing to a general decline in agricultural activity within the village.

The rattan industry has also had a significant flow-on effect on other areas of economic life within the Buyut community. Purchasing power has risen and other areas of the local economy have benefited. One clear sign of this has been the growth in the number of thriving stalls and small petty enterprises that have expanded their operations in the last few years throughout the village.

The expansion of the rattan industry has had a positive impact on communal life within the village. Almost everyone in the community is able to find gainful employment and a guaranteed source of income. As a result of a more dynamic economic environment, petty crime has been reduced and fewer young people drift away from the village to large cities.

Notes

1. Sri Kusumastuti Rahayu, Bambang Soelaksono, Sri Budiyati, Hastuti, Akhmadi, and Wawan Munawar, with editorial assistance from John Maxwell and Nuning Akhmadi. We wish to acknowledge the contribution to this study of the people of Buyut, the Village Head and his staff, the Camat of Cirebon Utara and staff, the Cirebon Regional Planning Board (Bappeda), the Industry and Trade Office in Kabupaten Cirebon, the staff and management of several rattan enterprises, and the Indonesian Furniture Manufacturer's Association (Asmindo).
2. Technical irrigation contains permanent primary, secondary and tertiary canals constructed by the government through the Local Office of Public Works. Semi-technical irrigation systems only have permanent primary and secondary canals, while simple irrigation system are those that are built entirely by the local community themselves.
3. Sub-contractors are those who make a variety of rattan products on a piece-work order basis for the large local factories.

References

Asmindo Komda Cirebon. "Company Record". Asmindo, February 2001.

Bappeda – Pemerintah Kabupaten Cirebon. "Analisis Sektor-Sektor Strategis dan Profil Keuangan Daerah untuk Menunjang Otonomi Daerah di Kabupaten Cirebon Propinsi Jawa Barat". 2001.

Bappeda – Pemerintah Kabupaten Cirebon. "Daftar Perusahaan PMA di Kabupaten Cirebon". 2000.

Desa Buyut. "Data Monografi Desa dan Kelurahan – Desa Buyut Tahun 1999". 1999.

Dinas Perindustrian dan Perdagangan Kabupaten Cirebon. "Komoditi Unggulan Kabupaten Cirebon Tahun 2000". 2001 Dinas Perindustrian dan Perdagangan Kabupaten Cirebon. "Data Potensi Industri Manufaktur". 2001

Dwiprabowo, Hariyanto, Rahayu Supriyadi and Setiasih Irawanti. "Social and Economic Aspects of Rattan in Indonesia: A Case Study in Industry and Resource in Java". XI World Forestry Congress, Analya Turkey, Vol. 3 Topic 15, October, 1997.

Hafid Setiadi, Sulaksini, Taufik Aminudin, Rita Zahara. "Laporan Studio Perencanaaan Wilayah 2001: Desa Tegalwangi Kabupaten Cirebon (Sentra Industri Kerajinan Rotan)". Program Magister Perencanaan Wilayah dan Kota Institut Tehnologi Bandung, August 2001.

Hudi Sartono, Bambang Soelaksono and Sri Kusumastuti Rahayu. "Kredit Perdesaan di Kabupaten Cirebon". SMERU, 2000.

Kantor Dinas Perindustrian dan Perdagangan, Kabupaten Cirebon. "Laporan Pelaksanaan Tugas Tahun 2000 dan Rencana Kerja Tahun 2001". 2001.

Kantor Dinas Perindustrian dan Perdagangan, Kabupaten Cirebon, Makalah Asmindo. "Sejarah Industry Kerajinan Rotan di Centra Tegalwangi Kecamatan Weru Kabupaten Cirebon". Asmindo, 2001.

Kecamatan Cirebon Utara. "Data Monografi Kecamatan Tahun 1999/2000". 2000.

11
POLICY IMPLICATIONS FOR RNFEs:
Lessons from the PARUL Project in Indonesia

Hugh Emrys Evans

Introduction

While rural non-farm enterprises (RNFEs) have long been of interest to researchers and academics, they present something of a puzzle to planners and policy makers. As this book amply testifies, researchers have found that RNFEs provide an illuminating indicator of changes taking place in rural society. The nature of goods and services produced by rural enterprises may reflect the extent of technological transformation and the degree of interaction between rural and urban markets. Their growth or decline may be seen as a measure of the impact of globalization on the rural economy and adaptation to it. The importance of RNFEs as a source of income for farm households may reveal the extent to which they are gradually becoming less dependent on agriculture and more involved in the modernizing mainstream economy.

Planners and policy makers, however, are often at a loss in knowing what to make of RNFEs and determining an appropriate policy response. Do they represent a sufficiently important part of the economy to warrant attention? Should scarce public resources be devoted to them rather than other urgent priorities? Are they likely to generate a worthwhile return on investment?

Sceptics may be inclined to answer 'no'. RNFEs are commonly perceived as micro scale operations, peripheral to agriculture and other core industries, providing only incidental employment and marginal extra income for rural households. Production methods are primitive, the quality of goods is low, and it is only a matter of time before these enterprises are swept away by larger firms using more advanced technology to produce cheaper and better goods. In sum, public investment would be largely wasted and can be used for better purposes.

These perceptions, however, are wide off the mark. It may be true that national policies for foreign investment and the decisions of multi-national corporations to come or go make big news and big impacts where they are located. It is equally true that the numerous dispersed small-scale activities of rural non-farm entrepreneurs go unsung and largely unrecorded. But while it may be difficult to measure their collective contribution to the local economy, we should not assume that it is insignificant or unimportant.

As discussed in other chapters in this book, the role played by RNFEs is often far greater than is commonly appreciated (see also Rondinelli 1993). For starters, consumers depend on them for cheap goods and services. Items sold commonly include drinks, snacks, desserts, and other prepared foods, or pots, mats, brushes, baskets and other household goods, perhaps knick-knacks, souvenirs and handicrafts for tourists. Services may take the form of small kiosks, shops, cafes, restaurants, beauty salons, and repair workshops. Here, sales are usually handled by household members themselves, and most activities are aimed at the local market.

Manufacturers depend on RNFEs for basic inputs. Typically these include bricks, blocks, roofing materials and other building supplies for the construction sector, or semi-processed agricultural commodities such as shelled nuts, dried beans or leaves, seedlings, cloth, fibre, lumber, charcoal or copra. Some of these inputs may be destined for firms and factories located nearby, but more often for markets further afield in the regional capital or other areas of the country. Here, the buyer is more concerned about quality and reliability of supplies, while the producer or trader aiming to supply more distant buyers faces problems of marketing and transport.

More subtle, and perhaps less well recognized, is the way RNFEs also contribute to the local economy by supporting agriculture. Since most of them are operated by people who are also engaged in farming, they provide a means of diversifying household income. As such, they serve two valuable functions for farm households. First, it gives a form of insurance protection against the risks of lost income due to falling prices, bad weather, plant disease and other factors causing crop failure. Second, it offers a potential source of capital for investment in agriculture. Likewise, it may be said, profits in agriculture may finance RNFEs (Evans and Pirzada 1994; Evers 1994).

By diversifying household income, RNFEs help to raise agricultural productivity. As documented in a study in Kenya (Evans and Ngau 1992), poor farmers who derive their income solely from agriculture are likely to be risk averse, and more resistant to new ideas and methods, especially if they involve increased production costs. Farmers whose household income is more diversified, have a greater tolerance for risk, and are more likely to adopt innovations, and hence become more productive producers.

In aggregate, RNFEs are still a source of jobs and incomes for a large proportion of households, especially in countries with a predominantly rural population. In terms of income, the revenue generated from an RNFE may appear small to the outsider, but it often accounts for a substantial share of total household earnings. In terms of jobs, RNFEs provide part-time or full-time employment to an even larger proportion of household members. In Indonesia, it has become widely recognized that the negative impact of the recent economic crisis on urban workers was greatly ameliorated by alternative employment opportunities to be found in rural areas, mainly in agriculture and among RNFEs.

As this implies, opportunities for employment in RNFEs are also a factor influencing the pattern of migration between rural and urban areas. The growth and proliferation of RNFEs, especially those serving local markets, is largely a function of agricultural prosperity in the surrounding area. Prosperous rural enterprises in turn help to spur the growth of smaller urban areas as service centres for rural populations, and as centres for processing and manufacturing. Thriving smaller towns contribute to a more dispersed pattern of urbanization, tempering the expansion of the largest city in the region, a common objective of many governments (Evans 1992).

If we accept that RNFEs do play an important role in the local economy, what then is the appropriate response from a policy perspective? Should they simply be left to prosper or perish in the larger scheme of things, or should special efforts be made to support them? If rural enterprises are to be supported, then what kind of policies and programmes are most likely to benefit them, enhance their sustainability, and spur their growth? Does it make sense to design programmes that aim directly to help RNFEs as a separate constituency? Would it be better to design programmes that support rural households as production units engaged in both agriculture and non-farm activities? Or should government, donors and others instead attempt to aid rural enterprises indirectly through programmes with a broader reach?

This chapter examines these issues from an operational perspective. The next section assesses a range of common approaches that directly or indirectly aim to support rural enterprises. This is followed with an account of one particular approach, currently being implemented in several regions in Indonesia. Another section takes a closer look at the impact of specific project initiatives on the performance of small-scale rural producers. The chapter closes with lessons learned from this experience.

Issues in Supporting RNFES

While there may be good arguments to support RNFEs, efforts to design and implement programmes for this purpose face numerous difficulties, both administrative and pragmatic. Reviewed in this section are a number of issues for local development programmes that aim to offer direct or indirect support to RNFEs. These have to do with jurisdiction, the characteristics of RNFEs, indirect support, and problems common to other programmes in support of economic activities. The purpose is to identify constraints that explain why past support has tended to be limited and largely ineffective.

Jurisdiction

The first issue is one of jurisdiction. Since RNFEs encompass such a diverse set of activities, they do not fall conveniently within the authority of any one government agency. This means little or no official data is collected about them, which makes them obscure and easily overlooked.

Government agencies that might help them usually have other priorities. Departments concerned with agriculture, fisheries or plantations see them as peripheral to their core activities. Those responsible for trade, industry or small and micro enterprises tend to focus primarily on urban areas. Similarly, programmes to promote farmers' cooperatives are generally organized to support agricultural production, and are ill-equipped to help non-farm enterprises. Departments for rural or community development may potentially be the most likely source of

Policy Implications for RNFEs

support, but again in practice RNFEs usually constitute only an incidental part of their broader activities.

Even when programmes for community development specifically include economic activities as eligible for support, RNFEs rarely receive it, especially when members of the community are assigned the task of selecting projects. As demonstrated for example by UNCDF programmes in Palestine and Cambodia, they tend to opt for standard infrastructure projects that benefit a large number of households, such as potable water supplies, drainage culverts, school classrooms, rural roads and village street paving. The same was largely true for many of the Social Safety Net programmes in Indonesia. For most people, proposals for economic activities are less familiar territory, harder to understand, and are seen as benefiting only select groups.

Characteristics of RNFEs

Several other characteristics of RNFEs get in the way of efforts to support them. Like farm households, they are widely dispersed geographically. This makes it costly to provide technical assistance or extension services, especially for local government agencies with tight budgets and limited resources for transport and fuel. RNFEs are also large in number, which means that even when resources are available, only a small proportion is likely to benefit. As with extension services for agriculture, public agencies tend to prefer working with larger units, which promise more cost-effective results.

RNFEs also engage in a wide range of activities. Unlike agricultural production, which involves similar inputs of tools, equipment, seeds and fertilisers, RNFEs require a myriad of different inputs. This makes it difficult to organize credit programmes for the supply of these inputs. The same holds true for efforts to provide technical assistance for production and marketing methods. But like most other small and micro businesses, RNFEs lack recognized collateral for loans from conventional commercial sources. This means loan programmes have to be custom designed, often requiring expertise and assistance from NGOs, which may be hard to find, especially in many regions of Indonesia.

Perhaps the biggest handicap of RNFEs is their amorphous profile. They don't possess a convenient label that's easily recognized by the development community. They don't correspond with conventional areas of government assistance, and they don't fall into any obvious category of donor interest that might currently be in fashion. This makes it difficult to articulate convincing objectives for a support programme, identify champions willing to sponsor it, or rally necessary resources.

Indirect Support

Indirect efforts to support RNFEs may be easier to implement and hold greater promise, since they are likely to benefit larger numbers of enterprises, but again there are limitations. The most obvious approach is through infrastructure improvements, particularly for roads, power and telecommunications. Better roads help to reduce transportation costs and make it easier for RNFEs to compete with other suppliers and to access new markets further afield. Connecting outlying areas to the electricity grid opens up all kinds of opportunities for new enterprises—discotheques in western Kenya come to mind—and for petty manufacturers to raise productivity through the use of power tools and equipment. Extending phone services to outlying villages benefits everyone.

Regulatory reforms affecting investment, production and trade can also be useful instruments for assisting RNFEs. Although the enforcement of regulations is often weak, and many small and micro enterprises consequently tend to ignore them, they can sometimes have far reaching effects, both positive and negative. Fewer rules and regulations reduce opportunities for harassment and bribery by enforcement personnel. Regulations governing street vendors may be improved by involving them in the decision making process. Certification by health authorities of food items produced by RNFEs can spur sales to supermarkets and other retailers.

Regulatory reforms having nothing to do with RNFEs may also benefit them. For example, the reduction or abolition of road tariffs on inter-district trade helps rural enterprises located far from urban markets. Simplifying planning permits and procedures for investment in new manufacturing plants not only creates new jobs, but may also open up new opportunities for rural suppliers.

It is sometimes suggested that better information on market prices can also help RNFEs in determining where and how to sell their products. The problem here is not so much in publishing the information, but in collecting it. Since this is costly, it may only be feasible for items that are widely bought and sold, chiefly agricultural commodities.

Programmes for Local Economic Development

Efforts to promote RNFEs also face other problems that are commonly encountered among programmes for local economic development. One is the lack of attention to stakeholder demands in the design of supporting programmes. In Indonesia especially, after years of top down directives from the centre, local agencies have been accustomed to following orders from above. More recently, with the advent of decentralization and greater local autonomy, local officials are exercising new found freedom to make their own decisions, but often follow the same behavioural pattern. As a result, programmes tend to be supply-driven based primarily on agency considerations, rather than the priorities of intended beneficiaries. Embedded attitudes take time to change. As yet, few mechanisms are in place to enable stakeholders to articulate their own needs and perspectives, or to empower them in the decision making process.

A related problem is the lack of market orientation. Too often, government agencies focus exclusively on the supply side, ignoring demand (Tendler 1996). Programmes stress production inputs of technical assistance, credit and materials, but pay scant attention to consumer demand, marketing, and potential buyers. One reason is that agency staff are usually recruited for their expertise in agronomy, veterinary sciences, manufacturing technology and loan programmes, rather than their business savvy or skills as entrepreneurs. Producers may learn new techniques, but hesitate to make the added investment if market conditions are uncertain. Worse yet, they may invest, then lose money due to depressed prices or lack of sales. Once bitten, twice shy.

Government agencies are also ill-equipped to assist with marketing. Their jurisdiction extends only to the boundaries of the local authority, while markets often extend much further. This makes it difficult for staff to undertake market research or recruit potential buyers in more distant locations. Public marketing enterprises and state-run cooperatives are no solution either. As in other countries, their past record in Indonesia is poor, in part due the inherent structure of the organization and the lack of appropriate staff incentives. A more promising approach is public funding for trade fairs, business promotion groups and other initiatives managed by stakeholders themselves.

A final problem to be mentioned is the limited duration of support from donor grant programmes. Despite the oft-repeated mantra of aiming to seek sustainable solutions, donors are more often concerned with breadth rather than depth, seeking to demonstrate the potentially widespread replicability of their models. In such cases, resources tend to be spread too thinly, or to be terminated prematurely before stakeholders have had a chance to internalise new ideas, methods and procedures. Once support ends, incipient structures risk collapse.

The PARUL Approach

Given this litany of potential constraints, it is rare to find a programme designed specifically to assist RNFEs per se. More common are programmes that encompass RNFEs within the scope of broader objectives. The rest of this chapter looks at one example currently ongoing in Indonesia, initially titled *Poverty Alleviation through Rural-Urban Linkages* (PARUL), and recently renamed Partnerships for Local Economic Development (in Indonesian, *Kemitraan bagi Pengembangan Ekonomi Lokal or* KPEL). Executed by Bappenas (the National Planning and Development Board), the programme is funded jointly by Bappenas and UNDP and receives technical support from UNCHS (Habitat). The programme is of interest partly because of the way it attempts to overcome many constraints just mentioned, and partly because it is being widely promoted by the Government of Indonesia as an approach in support of current policy priorities for decentralization, community empowerment and local economic development.

Launched in December 1997, PARUL has coincided with a period of unprecedented political reform in Indonesia. While the basic principles of the programme have remained constant, recent policy changes and administrative reforms have made it easier to implement and to gain wider acceptance. After an initial development phase designed to reach a consensus on the approach to adopt, implementation started early in 1999 in three regions—the provinces of North Sulawesi, South Sulawesi, and the large but sparsely populated district of Sorong in Papua. In 2001, the programme expanded to three other provinces—South-east Sulawesi, Jambi and Lampung on Sumatra Island—and now covers a total of 19 districts in the six regions.

Objectives

The programme originated partly at the instigation of UNCHS in response to Bappenas' interest in rural-urban linkages and UNDP's concern at that time with poverty alleviation. The immediate objectives of the implementation phase were:

- To enhance the capacity of central and local institutions, led by broad-based public-private-civic coalitions, to design and execute plans and strategies for strengthening rural-urban linkages as a means to promote local economic development
- To develop and implement policies, programmes and projects that support the strengthening of linkages for production and trade between rural and urban areas, with particular attention being paid to how to improve the situation of the poor, and
- To facilitate replication in other areas of the country by assisting the government and donors to adopt the PARUL approach in activities and projects concerned with poverty alleviation and regional development.

On the face of it, this doesn't sound much like a programme to support RFNEs. But as implied by the second objective, the prime beneficiaries are intended to be poorer households in more backward rural areas. As documented elsewhere in this book, many of these households engage in non-farm activity of one sort or another.

Basic Concept

The PARUL approach to local economic development derives from well-established theories supported by substantial empirical evidence. To achieve broad-based economic growth in a region, two conditions must be met. First, the region must succeed in selling its products and services to markets in other regions elsewhere in the country and abroad. Second, earnings from exports must generate additional rounds of income within the local economy through the purchase of inputs and household spending on consumer goods by those involved in export production. But for this to happen, the region must possess an efficient set of economic linkages connecting producers, traders and suppliers in rural and urban areas throughout the region and further afield.

Briefly summarized, PARUL aims to integrate lagging regions into the mainstream economy, by connecting producers to markets within the region and beyond, focusing on clusters of economic activities associated with key local export commodities. Central to this approach is an institutional component based on public-private partnerships between the government and the business community, whose function is to generate initiatives, and mobilize resources to strengthen rural-urban linkages for production and trade (Evans 2001).

Economic Strategy

Following from empirically validated theories, PARUL adopts a four-pronged strategy for economic development. The first principle is to promote local development based on exports out of the region. Here exports are taken to mean commodities and goods sold to other countries as well as to other provinces in Indonesia and larger urban markets outside the place of origin (Rondinelli 1992).

The second is to focus on clusters of economic activities associated with key export commodities that constitute a key element of the local economy. This contrasts with a more conventional approach to regional development where the focus is confined to specific geographic areas. Typically, a cluster includes large firms, small businesses, households and supporting institutions engaged in production, processing and trade associated with an export commodity. The selection of commodity-related clusters is based on four criteria that reflect

- potential external demand,
- potential for continued future growth,
- potential for involving small-scale farmers, fishermen, and non-farm businesses, raising incomes and creating productive employment opportunities for poorer households, and
- potential for multiplying initial earnings from exports into further rounds of spending and income that benefit local households.

Based on studies of the local economy in each region, PARUL stakeholders have selected a variety of clusters associated with agricultural and maritime products (see Table 11.1). While each of these clusters includes processing and manufacturing activities, a great many of them RNFEs, none of the clusters has so far focused on industrial products per se. This is to be expected given the predominance of agriculture in each of the six regions where PARUL is operating. Industrial activities here still accounts for a small proportion of regional GDP and employment, except perhaps in South Sulawesi, where it is largely confined to the main city of Makassar.

To keep the programme manageable, activities are confined initially to two or three districts in each region. Once stakeholders gain experience in

TABLE 11.1
Selected Clusters by Region

Region	Cluster(s)
South Sulawesi	Cashew nuts and shrimp farming
North Sulawesi	Coconuts and fish
Sorong district of Papua	Fish
Jambi	Melinju, coconuts
Lampung	Coffee
South-east Sulawesi	Cashews

the approach, other districts are periodically added, sometimes adopting an existing cluster, sometimes a new one. A third principle applies a "market driven" approach to local economic planning and development. The intention here is that all plans and proposed activities should start from an assessment of market demand for local products and prior identification of superior opportunities to respond to demand. This of course is conventional wisdom for any business enterprise. But while acknowledged in principle, it is all too often ignored in practice by government agencies, which tend instead to be preoccupied only with production and supply. Field experience during implementation has shown this to be one of the most difficult notions to implant firmly in the minds of agency staff and even among members of PARUL's own field teams.

Following from the previous one, a fourth principle links small-scale producers to broader markets through collaboration with bigger enterprises. One of the most commonly heard complaints from businessmen in PARUL regions is that they have potential clients aplenty, but have great difficulty obtaining adequate good quality supplies to meet their clients' needs. On the other hand, small-scale producers often grumble about the lack of information on buyers and market conditions. PARUL field staff and stakeholders are urged to start by identifying buyers first, and to involve them closely in the design of any activities for training or support to small scale producers. Buyers may include intermediaries or wholesalers who bulk and grade produce, processors, exporters, or investors looking to set up a business in the region. As with the previous element, this implies forging links to many firms and businesses located outside the region, in other provinces, even abroad.

Institutional Strategy

Unlike many earlier programmes concerned only with the economic elements of development, PARUL includes a complementary institutional component. This is designed to build and strengthen stakeholder networks that empower them to play a proactive role in decision-making and themselves to shape programme activities. This is based on the belief that those involved in each cluster and earn their livelihood from it—the farmers, traders, businessmen and other entrepreneurs—are most likely to know what the key problems are and what needs to be done to solve them. In sharp contrast to most of the earlier projects in Indonesia, the PARUL approach places primary responsibility for programme implementation not on government agencies, but on public-private partnerships.

At the time the programme started, many were sceptical that officials would adopt this idea, given the standard practice of the government—meaning mainly central government—making all the decisions. During early meetings to explain the PARUL programme, most officials would respond with polite but non-committal remarks. Later, with the fall of the Suharto regime in May 1998 and the campaign for "reformasi" that followed, audiences quickly latched onto this notion and for the most part eagerly embraced it. The institutional component includes three elements: public-private partnerships, networks of producer groups, and technical support units.

In each province and district, interested stakeholders establish public-private partnerships, with the aim of generating ideas for local economic development, mobilizing necessary resources, and implementing these initiatives. In each case, the partnership includes representatives of key actors involved in the cluster, such as producers, traders, exporters, manufacturers, local government (and earlier, line agencies of central government), research institutes, NGOs and other relevant organizations. Provincial partnerships also include representatives from district partnerships. By the end of 2001, a total of 24 partnerships had been set up, each typically with a membership of some 15–20 people. These are all officially recognized by the local government, several are considering establishing themselves as legal entities, and the one in Sorong already has.

Each district partnership is linked to sub-district networks of small-scale producer groups in those areas where the programme is active. These groups comprise farmers and/or fisher folk involved in the cluster concerned. In many areas, the network is made up of existing groups formed previously, some of which may have been dormant. In more remote areas, it is sometimes necessary to form groups from scratch, which takes time. Groups participating in the network are encouraged to come up with ideas, and the network chooses two or three people to represent its members in the district partnership. By March 2001, the latest period for which data was available, PARUL was working with some 50 producer groups in the first three regions, totalling over 1,000 members (PARUL 2001). More have since been added in newer regions.

To assist and guide the partnerships, PARUL sets up technical support teams in each region. These consist of three or four professional staff, usually based in the main city of the region, though sometimes one person may be located in a distant district. Their job is to assist in setting up the partnerships and producer networks, and to strengthen their capacity to undertake the roles envisaged for them. The level of effort needed to accomplish this task has proven greater than anticipated. The most active and effective partnerships are those that have strong committed leaders, and receive sustained support from the local government. With decentralization, an increasingly important factor is the level of interest shown by members of the local assembly.

Up until now, the cost of these support units has been paid from the programme budget, but it is intended that they should eventually be funded from local sources. Moves in this direction are already under way, but it may prove difficult to achieve in some regions. Despite recent fiscal reforms, many local governments have tight budgets and the business community is small.

Initiatives for Local Economic Development

After a slow start, PARUL partnerships have undertaken a wide variety of initiatives for economic development. Progress was slow at first, because it took a while for members to fully grasp the PARUL way of doing things. In the past, most programmes came with earmarked funds attached to them, clear instructions on what these should be used for, and the job of government officials was merely to carry out instructions. PARUL provides only token funds, partnerships are expected to decide themselves what activities to undertake, and resources have to be mobilized locally.

In the event, they have learned well how to do this. By March 2001, some Rp. 9 trillion had been raised for PARUL-related activities in the first three regions, 45 percent coming from local government sources, 42 percent from central government programmes, 8 percent from the private sector and the rest (5 percent) from PARUL itself (PARUL 2001). Partnerships there have used these funds to organize 57 field activities involving some 1,700 participants in numerous workshops, training sessions and other events. Designed largely in response to demand from stakeholders, many of whom operate RNFEs, these events aim to improve methods of fishing and cultivation, diversify production of goods from basic commodities, strengthen skills for business management, and link producers to broader markets.

In addition, partnerships have promoted numerous other initiatives and reforms. In North Sulawesi, for example, the provincial partnership commissioned a study of particular interest to RNFEs on market opportunities for products derived from coconuts, and prepared a report on the coconut sector, which has since been adopted by the governor as part of the local government's development plan for the period 2001–2004. As a result of their actions, coconut farmers have formed a province-wide association, and a local newspaper, the *Manado Post*, now publishes daily prices of selected agricultural commodities as an aid to farmers and traders.

In South Sulawesi, district and provincial partnerships have been more successful in obtaining support for their initiatives from the business community, both state and private firms. With assistance from field staff, partnerships have arranged collaborative credit agreements between farmer groups supported by PARUL and two firms in Makassar—one a secondary cooperative, the other a big distributor of farm supplies. Through these arrangements, farmers who previously were unable to do so have been able to obtain credit for fertiliser and other inputs. Through similar collaborative agreements, funds have been obtained from a large state enterprise (a cement manufacturer) and another private firm to establish demonstration plots in several districts for the cultivation and processing of cashews. But perhaps the most interesting initiative has been a joint venture between the provincial partnership and the National Cashew Processors Association based in Makassar to set up village units for initial processing of cashews (see next section).

In Sorong district, the local partnership has been particularly innovative in promoting regulatory and administrative reforms. Mainly as a result of their work, central government agreed to transfer to the district government the authority for issuing fishing licenses to large businesses, and the local council introduced regulations that restrict fishing within ten kilometres of the coastline to small-scale local operators. The local government also allocated funds totalling Rp. 1.2 billion (US$150,000) for the fishing sector in two sub-districts where PARUL operates, Teminabuan and Inanwatan. Funds from other Bappenas projects have been used for PARUL activities in the same sub-districts, and for strengthening the local government in Teminabuan. The Bank Rayat Indonesia (BRI) also opened new branches in each of these sub-districts, which previously had no banking facilities.

Case Studies of Actions to Assist RNFEs

To illustrate specific initiatives undertaken through the PARUL programme to assist RNFEs and other small-scale producers, this section presents three case studies. These include: diversifying production for coconut farmers in North Sulawesi; village processing of cashews in South Sulawesi; and expanding markets for fishermen in the Sorong district of Papua.

In each case, PARUL field staff carried out studies to assess the impact of programme support on participants' production, sales and income. The assessment is based on data collected from surveys designed to record the situation before intervention and one year later. Using limited funds and simple methods, the surveys lack full academic rigour, but they do provide an indication of trends.

Diversifying Coconut Production in North Sulawesi

Most farm households in North Sulawesi grow coconuts, which are sold mainly as fresh coconuts or copra (used for producing domestic and industrial oils). In an effort to assist farmers to increase their income, or maintain it at times when prices are low, PARUL has pursued a two-pronged strategy to expand sales by linking producers to markets and to encourage households to diversify production of items derived from coconuts. Since the programme was implemented in early 1999, several training workshops have been held to explain methods of producing fresh coconuts, copra, charcoal, seedlings, cooking oil and *nata de coco* (a local dessert). On each occasion, the training was designed to address demand from specific firms and buyers who were interested in purchasing such items.

To assess the impact of this strategy on producer incomes, the North Sulawesi field team collected information from participants at workshops held in Gorontalo and Bolaang Mongondow districts (see Figure 11.1) in February 2000, and again from the same people January 2001. The surveys covered 34 respondents in Gorontalo engaged in the production of fresh coconut and copra, and 23 respondents in Bolaang Mongondow, some of whom had also just recently started making charcoal. Each survey covered the previous coconut harvest, which occurs roughly every three months. A separate study was conducted on a group of women in Kotamabagu who have begun to produce *nata de coco* (Tuerah et al. 2001).

Fresh whole coconuts are destined mainly for the production of desiccated coconut used for confectionary purposes. The two main buyers are factories located at the eastern end of the province, one near Bitung, and the other on the north coast about an hour west of Manado. For several months prior to the second survey, both factories reduced purchases for internal reasons, the largest one because it was undertaking a complete overhaul of its equipment. Operating well below capacity, they relied mainly on suppliers close by. Reduced demand lowered average prices a modest 10 percent in nearby Bolaang Mongondow (down from Rp. 374 per unit to Rp. 336), but caused a hefty fall of 62 percent in more distant

FIGURE 11.1
North Sulawesi

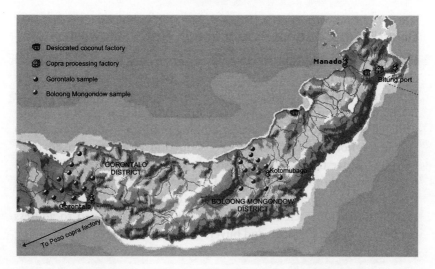

Gorontalo (from Rp. 325 to only Rp. 125) (see Table 11.2). Faced with weak demand, producers there cut back the sales of fresh coconut by 86 percent, causing average net income from sales to fall 97 percent, to virtually zero for that harvest season. In Bolaang Mongondow, producers cut back supplies by a more modest 7 percent, but a big increase in production costs reduced average net income by 41 percent.

Sale prices for copra are generally higher in Gorontalo than Bolaang Mongondow. Competition there appears to be greater. While producers in Bolaang Mongondow earlier faced what was in effect a monopsony, serving a single factory near Bitung, those in Gorontalo also supply by sea another large buyer in the district of Poso in Central Sulawesi. Over the period in

TABLE 11.2
Impact on Incomes from Diversification of Coconut Production

Item (stated as averages)	Gorontalo			Bolaang Mongondow		
	1999	2000	Change%	1999	2000	Change%
	Fresh coconut*			Fresh coconut*		
Price (Rp/kg)	325	125	−62%	374	336	−10%
Volume (units)	7,946	1,119	−86%	5,248	4,885	−7%
Revenue (Rp 000s)	2,583	140	−95%	1,964	1,642	−16%
Costs (Rp 000s)	922	94	−90%	434	735	69%
Net income (Rp 000s)	1,661	46	−97%	1,530	907	−41%
	Copra*			Copra*		
Price (Rp/kg)	1,438	1,067	−26%	931	875	−6%
Volume (kg)	6,047	4,714	−22%	1,327	4,531	241%
Revenue (Rp 000s)	8,694	5,030	−42%	1,235	3,965	221%
Costs (Rp 000s)	1,652	382	−77%	353	1,085	207%
Net income (Rp 000s)	7,042	4,649	−34%	882	2,880	227%
Combined income	**8,702**	**4,695**	**−46%**	**2,412**	**3,787**	**57%**
					Charcoal#	
Price (Rp/kg)				na	268	
Volume (kg)				na	1,154	
Revenue (Rp 000s)				na	309	
Costs (Rp 000s)				na	197	
Net income (Rp 000s)				na	112	

* Figures for one coconut harvest (3 months). # Figures per production cycle.
All figures are estimated averages per respondent

question, world demand for industrial oils weakened, impacting the price of copra in local markets. This again fell more sharply in Gorontalo, down 26 percent compared to 6 percent in Bolaang Mongondow. As a result, the price differential enjoyed by Gorontalo narrowed from more than 50 percent at the beginning of the period (Rp. 1438 compared with Rp. 931) to 22 percent one year later (Rp. 1067 versus Rp. 875).

Producers can offset weaker prices by increasing sales, but only if they can find buyers. The data revealed a very different result in the two regions. In Gorontalo, copra sales fell sharply from an average of 6047 kg to 4714 kg, resulting in a severe loss in average net income for the three-month period of 34 percent (down from Rp. 7 million to Rp. 4.6 million). In strong contrast, producers in Bolaang Mongondow were able to more than triple their volume of sales (up from 1,327 kg to 4,531 kg), reaching similar levels to producers in Gorontalo. Their revenues increased accordingly, so did costs, but average net incomes from copra also rose impressively by more than 200 percent (up from Rp. 0.9 million to Rp. 2.9 million). The expansion of copra sales in Bolaang Mongondow was in part due to several small new firms entering the market during the year.

Changing conditions in the markets for fresh coconut and copra over the one-year period combined to result in sharply different impacts in the two regions. While net average income from the two commodities fell 47 percent among respondents in Gorontalo, it rose 57 percent in Bolaang Mongondow.

Charcoal: In North Sulawesi, there is also a limited market for charcoal. This is made from the coconut shells left over from processing copra, and is used to produce activated carbon. As a result of PARUL initiatives, a growing number of farmers are producing charcoal for sale to local firms. Following one workshop in Bolaang Mongondow, 7 of 23 survey respondents have started production, yielding an average net income of Rp. 112,000 per production cycle. This represents a ratio of net income to costs of 57 percent. Since this a new activity, the volume of production is still small, and unit costs are high. But as producers become more proficient, output and income is expected to increase.

***Nata de coco*:** Another by-product in strong demand is *nata de coco*, a popular local dessert, usually produced by women. One group of 8 women in Kotamobagu in Bolaang Mongondow district typically earn a profit of

Rp. 128,000 on outlays of Rp. 40,000 per production cycle lasting 8 days. Since they currently complete 2 or 3 cycles per month, this generates additional income of around Rp. 320,000 per month, which is divided among the members of the group. While this may not sound like much, it should be remembered local people typically earn between Rp. 300,000 to Rp. 600,000 a month. Since demand is strong, groups like this could increase income substantially by increasing the number of cycles per month and the volume of production per cycle.

Processing Cashews in South Sulawesi

Since PARUL started operations in South Sulawesi in early 1999, it has been promoting a programme to encourage farmers and traders to set up small-scale village units to undertake the initial processing of cashew fruit into cashew nuts. These are then sold either directly to local stores, or to factories in Makassar, where they are processed further, graded, packaged, and exported to the United States and other countries. The aim is for village producers to add value to cashews before selling them, and hence to raise incomes and create jobs in rural areas. The programme is being promoted by district partnerships with assistance from PARUL field staff in collaboration with the National Association of Cashew Nut Processors headquartered in Makassar, three private firms and local government departments of Trade and Industry.

The processing industry in Makassar originally came up with the idea as a means to increase their supplies. They have been unable to compete with the inflated prices paid for unprocessed cashews by exporters buying for an Indian cartel. Pleas to protect the domestic industry against unfair competition by introducing export tariffs on unprocessed cashews were rejected by central government, largely under pressure from the World Bank and IMF.

To assess the impact of this programme, field staff collected information in January 2001 from 12 leaders of farmer groups from four districts, who had previously attended PARUL training workshops and who had also started village processing units after the training. Ten of these leaders are farmers, and two are traders. They provided information for two harvest seasons, before training in 1999 and afterwards in 2000. Data covered volume and costs of production, prices, sales revenues, and number of workers employed to process the cashew fruit (Ilyas et al. 2001).

The results are shown in Table 11.3. Data for 1999 relates to the sale of raw cashews and data for 2000 to the sale of processed cashews. With one minor exception, all respondents processed 100 percent of the cashews harvested or purchased in 2000. Seven of the ten farmers bought additional supplies from local growers, and all except one of the twelve respondents hired labour to process the cashews.

At an aggregate level, the data shows that this activity more than doubled average net income from cashews, up 104 percent from Rp. 8.5 million in 1999 to Rp. 17.4 million in 2000. Among the twelve respondents, results varied widely. All made a profit from cashews, but three made less income from processing than they had before by simply selling raw cashews. Profitability is closely related to price, which is roughly 35 percent higher at the factory in Makassar than in the village. Those who paid the added cost of shipping to the factory raised their earnings more than those who sold to traders in the village.

The twelve new village processing units also created 231 new jobs, or about 20 jobs per unit. Most of these units operated intermittently, one or two for the whole season, depending on supplies. Wages paid to workers varied widely from as little as Rp. 1,000/kg of peeled cashew nuts to as high as Rp. 3,000/kg. Since the lowest wages were paid by the unit that produced far and away the largest volume, the average is only Rp. 1,321/kg. Although workers there received the lowest wage, they earned more than others because they worked longer, each taking home on average Rp. 600,000 for the season, compared to the total sample average of Rp. 238,000. Although these wages and earnings are low,

TABLE 11.3
Impact on Incomes from Processing Cashews

Item (stated as averages)	1999 harvest (Unprocessed)	2000 harvest (Processed)*	Percent change
Volume sold (kg)	13,621	3,473	
Price (Rp/kg)	4,388	25,885	
Gross sales (Rp 000)	59,773	89,908	50%
Production costs (Rp 000)	51,254	72,557	42%
Net income (Rp 000)	8,519	17,351	104%
Number of workers per unit	0	22	
Earnings per worker (Rp)	0	232,278	

*With one minor exception, all respondents processed 100% of the harvest in 2000

there was no shortage of applicants for the jobs, mostly young women from local farm households.

Expanding Markets in Sorong District

Until recently, fishermen in the two sub-districts of Teminabuan and Inanwatan in the Sorong district relied on traditional methods of catching shrimp. Typically, this entailed crews of two or three people paddling longboats equipped with small nets along rivers and waters close to the shore. Fishing was restricted to 14 days a month, and sold in local markets at minimal prices. Remote and difficult to reach, the two locations were largely cut off from outside buyers.

Since mid 1999, the PARUL partnership, the local government and business enterprises in Sorong town, have collaborated in taking several steps to open up markets and raise productivity. As mentioned earlier, the local government has acquired the right to issue fishing licenses, and introduced legislation restricting fishing within ten miles of the coast to local fishermen. A number of enterprises have started buying fish from Teminabuan and to a lesser extent from Inanwatan for sale to non-local markets, mainly Singapore and Surabaya on Java Island. The PARUL partnership together with the local government department of fisheries and the business community have set up groups of fishermen in selected villages, provided them with supplies and equipment (including ice, larger nets and outboard motors), and organized several training sessions on improved fishing methods, business management, and related production activities such as using shrimp waste to fatten crabs.

To assess the impact of these activities on fishermen, PARUL field staff undertook a survey in January 2001 based on interviews with a total of 70 people, 40 in Teminabuan and 30 in Inanwatan. In each case, an equal number of people were randomly selected from among those who had attended training programmes twelve months earlier in January 2000 and those who had not. It should be kept in mind that by January 2000, some of the steps mentioned above were already under way. Data refers to a one week period in January of each year (Hasyir et al. 2001).

The data indicates clearly that average net incomes for all four groups of fishermen increased substantially over the twelve month period, rising at least 50 percent. This was due to three main factors: higher prices, expanded opportunities to sell, and improved methods of fishing (see Table 11.4).

TABLE 11.4
Impact on Incomes from Shrimp Fishing

Item (stated as averages)	January 2000 Without*	January 2000 With*	January 2001 Without*	January 2001 With*	Increase (%) Without*	Increase (%) With*	Increase (%) Both
Teminabuan							
Volume sold (kg)	15.0	41.9	11.6	47.1	–23%	13%	3%
Price (Rp 000/kg)	30	30	60	60	100%	100%	100%
Sales revenue (Rp 000)	449	1,256	693	2,828	54%	125%	107%
Costs (Rp 000)	128	343	189	693	48%	102%	87%
Net income (Rp 000)	321	913	504	2,135	57%	134%	114%
Inanwatan							
Volume sold (kg)	20.8	20.6	19.0	32.2	–9%	56%	24%
Price (Rp 000/kg)	18	18	40	40	129%	129%	129%
Sales revenue (Rp 000)	364	360	760	1,289	109%	258%	183%
Costs (Rp 000)	150	123	390	641	160%	421%	278%
Net income (Rp 000)	215	237	370	648	72%	173%	125%

* Respondents with and without support.

Local market prices in both locations moved substantially higher during the year, up 100 percent in Teminabuan and 129 percent in Inanwatan. In part, this reflects higher prices for shrimp on world markets (measured in dollars), and a 15 percent fall in the value of the rupiah against the dollar, meaning more rupiah for each dollar of sales. But an important contributing factor has been the increased presence of outside buyers from Sorong and elsewhere. Even though prices rose faster in Inanwatan, they are still only two-thirds of those in Teminabuan. The sub-district is even harder to reach, transport costs are higher, and outside buyers are not as numerous, though growing fast.

Outside buyers not only help to push up prices, they also expand opportunities for local fishermen to sell their catch. The combined average volume of sales didn't change much in Teminabuan, but rose a respectable 24 percent in Inanwatan. But a comparison between fishermen receiving support in the two locations reveals another factor at work. In Teminabuan, unlike Inanwatan, most survey respondents are members of fishermen collaboratives, which have entered into agreements with processors and exporters in Sorong town. This provides the fishermen with assured sales and the buyers with regular supplies. As a result, average volumes sold by this group has been substantially higher than the corresponding group in Inanwatan, 42 kg compared to 21 kg in the first period, and 47 kg compared to 32 kg in the later period.

The figures also reveal the impact of training and the provision of equipment. Those who received support were able to raise their catch by 13 percent in Teminabuan and 56 percent in Inanwatan, while those without support saw their catch fall (by 23 percent and 9 percent respectively). Operating costs also rose substantially, up 102 percent in Teminabuan and a massive 421 percent in Inanwatan, where a larger proportion of respondents started using more modern equipment. But the added costs clearly paid off as indicated by the increase in revenue from sales.

As a result of the combined impact of higher prices and programme support, average net income for fishermen participating in the programme increased more than twice as much as those that did not. In Teminabuan, they rose 134 percent compared to 57 percent, and in Inanwatan 173 percent compared to 72 percent.

Lessons Learned

Lessons learned from the PARUL experience suggest that any approach to local economic development, including RNFEs, must be broad based and involve local stakeholders. Market driven initiatives can achieve positive results, especially when larger firms and buyers work together with small-scale producers. However, risks are involved and revenues are highly susceptible to external factors largely outside the control of those involved.

Often, the single biggest factor influencing outcomes for producers supplying international markets is the local currency exchange rate. During the twelve month period covered by the studies discussed above, the depreciation of the rupiah worked modestly in their favour. Although not documented here, the same phenomenon yielded far greater benefits during the period following the Asian economic crisis. During 1998, the rupiah depreciated as much as 80 percent or more, and levelled off around one third of its value in 1997. While many urban workers employed in manufacturing lost their jobs as firms were bankrupted by the huge increase in the cost of servicing dollar loans, most rural workers survived and even prospered. When President Habibie visited North Sulawesi in early 1999, the governor was heard to remark, "What crisis? We're doing fine here".

Another pervasive influence on outcomes for producers of exportable commodities is prices on world markets. The governor spoke too soon, because shortly afterwards, the economic downturn in industrialized countries prompted a fall in demand for industrial derivatives from copra, causing prices to nose dive on world markets and in North Sulawesi, creating widespread concern among farmers. Fluctuations in commodity prices directly impact those involved in the chain of cultivation, processing and supply, often hurting them as was recently the case with copra and coffee products too, sometimes benefiting them as with shrimp and fish.

A third factor shown to be important in the PARUL studies is the change in the unit cost of inputs relative to the price of outputs involved in cultivation or production. Exchange rates and world markets are likely to affect the price of inputs as much as outputs, but they may work in opposite directions, squeezing profit margins or widening them. The unit cost of inputs also depends on the "lumpiness" of investments in tools and equipment and the scale of production. As may be deduced from the figures for Sorong, average unit costs for fishermen participating in the programme increased dramatically, as they invested in new technology, up 79 percent in Teminabuan and 233 percent in Inanwatan. Fortunately, this was more than offset by the rise in the sale price. But the same was not true for producers of fresh coconut in Bolaang Mongondow, where unit costs went up 86 percent while the sale price went down 10 percent, making a bad situation far worse. Economies of scale are also involved. The low profit margins of those making charcoal and *nata de coco* are largely due to the small volumes they currently produce. Cranking up the scale of production will help them once they become more proficient and find more buyers.

To the extent that RNFEs and other small-scale producers use inputs or sell outputs that are tradable internationally, they will be affected by these movements in exchange rates and world prices. Since most PARUL clusters are closely linked to international markets, stakeholders are highly sensitive to these movements, which can be beneficial but also cruelly detrimental. Other kinds of activities may be largely immune to such movements, particularly those providing goods for segmented domestic markets, or offering non-tradable services, such as food vendors, *becak* drivers, beauty salons and vehicle repair shops.

Other risks arise when local demand depends on a small number of large buyers. An attempt to promote charcoal production in Gorontalo failed, because the primary source of funds were withdrawn in light of the commercial banking crisis. The programme to promote village processing of cashews in South Sulawesi has been threatened by the collapse of two of the three key buyers in Makassar, recently driven out of business by the Indian cartel. Such disasters can have a widespread negative impact on local suppliers unless other options are available. In South Sulawesi, cashew processors have turned instead to local supermarkets.

The evidence from PARUL shows clearly that the combined impact of these external factors is far more pervasive than the limited reach of such a programme, and far outweighs anything it might achieve. But it also shows that such programmes in support of RNFEs and other small-scale producers can make a positive difference, particularly in mobilizing local resources and opening up new markets.

In North Sulawesi, at least part of the credit for increased sales of copra in Bolaang Mongondow can fairly be attributed to PARUL's efforts to link producers to new and existing buyers, and to raise the quality of produce. PARUL was less successful in Gorontalo, because most of the factories they worked with were located far away at the other end of the province. Both for copra and desiccated coconut, the main buyers preferred to draw from suppliers nearby.

In South Sulawesi, village entrepreneurs demonstrated that cashew processing is a potentially profitable activity, although much of the largest share of the cash benefits accrued to those that operated the units rather than those employed by them. The lesson here is that PARUL needs to develop and promote a model whereby this kind of business can be run by farmer groups rather than individuals, so that income can be shared more equitably among members of participating households.

In the Sorong district, PARUL and its partners have made big strides in linking remote locations to the mainstream economy. More buyers are active in local markets, prices are moving closer to world levels, fishermen are becoming far more productive, and their incomes are rising.

All this has been achieved by public-private partnerships effectively harnessing the resources of government, the private sector and local small-scale producers.

References

Bazabana, J.J. Malgloire and Paul C. Bom Konde. "New Ways of Strengthening Small Agri-foodstuff Enterprises". *Courier*, no. 166 (Nov–Dec 1997): 90–93.

Evans, Hugh Emrys. "A Virtuous Circle Model of Rural–Urban Development: Evidence from a Small Kenyan Town and Its Hinterland". *Journal of Development Studies* 28, no. 4 (July 1992): 640–67.

Evans, Hugh Emrys. "Regional Development through Rural-Urban Linkages: The PARUL Programme in Indonesia". In *New Regions: Concepts, Issues, and Practices; Vol. 3*, edited by David W. Edgington, Antonio L. Fernandez and Claudia P. Hoshino, pp. 79–94. Westport, CT: Greenwood Press, 2001.

Evans, Hugh Emrys, and Gazala Pirzada. "Rural Households as Producers: Income Diversification and the Allocation of Resources". *Conference Proceedings*. Uppsala, Sweden: Scandinavian Institute of African Studies, 1994.

Evans, Hugh Emrys, and Peter Ngau. "Rural-Urban Relations, Household Income Diversification and Agricultural Productivity". *Development and Change* 22, (July 1991): 519–45.

Evers, Hans-Dieter and Ozay Mehmet. "The Management of Risk: Informal Trade in Indonesia". *World Development* 22, no. 1 (1994): 1–9.

Hasyir, Surya Putra, et al. "Impact Assessment of PARUL Programme on Shrimp Cluster in Sorong". Jakarta: BAPPENAS, PARUL Programme, January 2001.

Hung, Le Ngoc and Dennis A. Rondinelli. "Small Business Development and Economic Transformation in Vietnam". *Journal of Asian Business* 9, no. 4 (1993): 1–23.

Ilyas, Sjarlis, et al. "Pengaruh TOT Manajemen Industri Rumah Tangga Pengkacipan Terhadap Pendapatan dan Kesempatan Kerja di Sulawesi Selatan". Jakarta: BAPPENAS, PARUL Programme, January 2001.

PARUL. "Progress Report Number 14". Jakarta: BAPPENAS, PARUL Programme, January 2001.

Rondinelli, Dennis A. and John D. Kasarda. "Foreign Trade Potential, Small Enterprise Development and Job Creation in Developing Countries". *Small Business Economics*, Quarter 4 (1992): 253–65.

Rondinelli, Dennis A. and John D. Kasarda. "Job Creation and Economic Development in Indonesia: The Critical Role of Small Business". *Journal of Asian Business* 9, no. 1 (1993): 69–85.

Tendler, Judith and Monica Alves Amorim. "Small Firms and Their Helpers: Lessons on Demand". *World Development* 24, no. 3 (1996): 407–26.

Tuerah, Noldy, et al. "Impact Assessment of Training on Products Derived from Coconuts in North Sulawesi". Jakarta: BAPPENAS, PARUL Programme, January 2001.

12
THE INDONESIAN RURAL ECONOMY: Insights and Prospects

Thomas R. Leinbach

Continuing evidence from Southeast Asia and around the globe points to the increasing rural household dependence on non-farm employment and income. Yet the rural non-farm economy is quite broad and diverse, and the specific nature of the impacts and characteristics warrant continuing investigation (Ashley and Maxwell 2001). The essays included in this volume provide a rich contemporary perspective on the nature of the non-farm rural economy in Indonesia. And in an attempt to generalize and capture the essence of the essays, it seems appropriate and useful to summarize briefly the major findings. In addition it is also beneficial to highlight future research needs and policy actions with regard to this seminal theme.

Summary of Findings

In the initial thematic essay using census data, Booth's findings suggest that over the decade from 1984 to 1993 earnings from all off-farm sources accounted for 50 percent of the total incomes of agricultural households. Yet while income diversification is taking place, agriculture is claimed as the 'main' source of income. But, it is significant to note that by the mid-1990s nearly 27 percent of rural households had no involvement in agriculture at all. This data also reveal that dependence on non-agricultural wages and salaries is skewed towards the upper income groups.

As numerous authors have reported, rural households appear to take a longer-term view of income security than merely taking advantage of immediately accessible income opportunities. Diversification in investment behaviour is crucial to families seeking to enlarge and protect incomes over a longer period (Leinbach and Bowen 1992). Investment in land and livestock is especially important in this regard (Leinbach and Watkins 1998).

An important finding in this context is that increasingly rural families appreciate the value of education (Ellis 2000, pp. 296–97). Yet in Indonesia there are significant costs associated with secondary and tertiary education. Thus only the more affluent families can afford to keep children in school to attain qualifications for employment in the manufacturing and service sectors (Booth 2000, p. 93). There are also considerable regional variations in the extent to which rural households in Indonesia have been able to diversify into non-agricultural income strategies. This appears to be particularly true in parts of eastern Indonesia such as East Nusa Tenggara, East Timor, and Irian Jaya. Yet access to off-farm employment clearly does permit even the poorest households to increase their total income and reduce the insecurity of reliance on agriculture.

Observing the rural economy through the lenses of entrepreneurship, gender and mobility produces useful insights. In the case study from Flores, Hugo concludes that there is no evidence of a slowdown in the growth of international labour migration out of Indonesian rural communities. And in the aftermath of the 1997 Asia financial crisis and reduced opportunities in the Indonesian urban areas, labour migration has become a more attractive income option for many rural dwellers. Particularly important are opportunities in Malaysia where despite that government's attempts to limit such movements, they do continue and may even become more complex by involving more women and a wider range of workers and skills. The role of labour export in the development strategies of Indonesian provinces must be addressed and recognized in light of its importance in regional development. But most important is the need to construct more effective policies, which will maximize benefits and minimize costs. The key here may be the legalization of such international labour movements.

Continuing with the theme of mobility but in intra-national context, Silvey studying migrants in West Java, emphasizes the role of gender relations and their embeddedness in social networks. Her study suggests that the social networks linking household relations with village resource exchange patterns, including productive and reproductive labour and the role of the rural non-farm economy, helps to explain the capacity of particular households to cope in the face of crises such as the most recent one in Indonesia. Empirical evidence suggests that a thriving rural non-farm economy can serve as a "safety net". Yet the lowest income households, and especially women, clearly have great difficulty gaining access to income opportunities where the RNFE is especially weak.

Singh et al. profile micro- and small-scale enterprises in an attempt to highlight gender-based differences in characteristics. Industries with low entry barriers, such as food processing and trade, were dominant and had a high content of labour in value-added. While such industries do have the potential to absorb labour, their role in generating employment appears to be limited. Women-operated businesses were usually small, self-financing, sole proprietorships that relied on family labour, low skills and direct marketing to consumers. Unfortunately women-operated businesses appear to be less dynamic and less likely to follow advice for improvement and to employ subordinates. In terms of policy, one basic issue to be resolved is the extent to which stimulative programmes need to be gender differentiated.

In contrast to the above analyses of male- or female-headed enterprises in Java, Leinbach's study of small businesses in a sample of transmigration areas in South Sumatra reveals the strong incidence of dual businesses in the households. Nearly 30 percent of the households reported that both the head and the spouse operated a business. In these situations over 80 percent of such households operated businesses on the scheme rather than away from the scheme. Home industries clearly represent one form of business and these types represent about 12 percent of the businesses reported by head and spouse. In addition there was an indirect relationship between the amount of land owned by the family and the likelihood that a head will own and operate a business. The type of transmigrant family also relates significantly to business ownership. While all three of the categories are significant, it is the spontaneous and local groups, which are identified with the stronger likelihood of the head owning a business. The implication is that more pressure is put on the head in the spontaneous and local groups to derive income from more diverse sources, including owning and operating a small business. Substantial differences exist between the explanation of head- and spouse-operated businesses. While age is significant, the opposite effect is measured. That is, older individuals are more likely to engage in and operate a business. This finding is consistent with off-farm employment in general and the plausible explanation is that as women age and the family life cycle advances, there are fewer small children who require the care of the spouse and therefore more time is freed up for alternative reproductive activities. Without doubt education has a positive influence. Better-educated spouses, however small the degree of educational attainment, are more likely to own and operate a business. As noted above this finding reinforces the importance of education and skill development and training in the development of business and entrepreneurial activities. It also ties into the discussion of education above by Booth.

But in addition this chapter seeks to produce an empirical understanding of Lipton's concept of fungibility which captures the extent to which a rise or fall in the availability of a resource (commonly in these examples—land) can be treated as if it were a change in cash funds and convertible to an activity which maximizes benefits. In addition to land, small petty enterprises may also be viewed as a converted resource which allows accumulation and greater benefit for the family according to its priorities. Both of these resources involve exercising control over labour and capital and may involve shifting resources internally in response to changing conditions. Significantly the research has extended our understanding to include the ways in which social (age, skills, education, gender, and children), economic (savings and credit extension) and physical (environment and infrastructure) characteristics may act as positive and negative constraints on the fungibility and extended fungibility process (Lipton 1984, p. 195). Above all the work shows the implications of Lipton's notion for understanding the geographies of development surrounding peasant households. Fungibility integrated with the critiques set forth in the beginning of this chapter, provide fruitful possibilities for researchers of Southeast Asian and other societies in the Pacific region. It is important to note that the concept applies to rural development very broadly and may be examined through the lenses of labour, life cycle, capital or combinations of these. Still further analyses of small enterprises that express the extended fungibility of capital and labour will be profitable as we seek to understand the complexity of development in spatial and aspatial ways.

The study of migration and entrepreneurship in East Nusa Tenggara by nDoen et al. shows that migrants' involvement in business is influenced by both push (unemployment) and pull (perceived business opportunities) factors. This work provides important confirmation that in order to set up their own businesses, migrants utilize ties of kinship and regional origin; however, this dependence is relaxed over time and some measure of independence is achieved. One interesting result is that there is no evidence to suggest that longer stays produce an inclination to stay permanently. This lends support to the middlemen minority theory, which depicts migrants as middlemen between major entrepreneurs in Java and local consumers where overwhelmingly Chinese suppliers are utilized.

These empirical studies of entrepreneurship and business operations tie into the broader and more general theme of the role of small and medium enterprises in the rural economy. Rice shows, that in spite of government policies favouring larger enterprises, the employment and value-added of household and small manufacturing industries grew rapidly from 1986 to 1996. Of note is the fact that in the latter year, 1996, the value-added was only 11 percent of total value-added for all enterprises. But in a positive vein they accounted for 61 percent of total employment. These findings also dovetail with those of Booth, which acknowledges the growth of off-farm income and especially the increase in households which report no agricultural income. Rice also shows that HMIs and SMEs benefited from the economic crisis, but overall they were hard hit as measured by a decrease in establishments between 1996 and 1998.

Van Diermen examines the macro- and micro-policy environment in Indonesia and asks how entrepreneurs of small rural enterprises have fared. He argues that several trends can be observed. First, few of the micro-policies implemented by the government have had a lasting impact on improving rural SMEs. A significant number of macro- and micro-polices placed additional costs and burdens on the compliance of rural SMEs and this has led to most enterprises operating outside of the formal economy. In addition, macro-polices that created a favourable economic environment, as reflected by consistently high growth rates in GDP, provided the best stimulus for the SME sector's growth. Along with this, growth in the agricultural sector, particularly rice, was closely connected to opportunities for, and growth of, rural SMEs. And finally policy biases towards the urban sector have exacerbated existing patterns of rural-urban migration.

The existing policy framework is neatly summarized in a separate piece in *Asian Survey* by Hill (2001, p. 251). This study notes that the key to promoting an efficient and dynamic sector is to create an environment in which these firms may prosper without long term dependence on government support. Removing major bottlenecks, e.g., financing, is essential. Hill's agenda for policy-oriented research and the high priority research suggestions of Rice provide clear directions for insightful and worthwhile investigations on this topic of small enterprises. In particular

Rice notes that the social cost of production of labour-intensive enterprises can be less than the social cost of production of usually larger capital-intensive enterprises producing the same product, but the labour-intensive enterprises' monetary cost of production is greater. The latter usually results in competition between the smaller and larger enterprises in which the smaller ones are eliminated even though their social cost of production is less than the larger enterprises. Research is needed in Indonesia to determine what, if any, industries are experiencing this undesirable market outcome. This must be followed up by policy recommendations to improve the situation. More research also is needed regarding the incidences where the social productivity of different types of economic activities is less than the private productivity resulting in the market mechanism yielding a greater supply of the activity than is socially desirable. In rural areas this is a result of external diseconomies in the form of pollution and the overexploitation of a commonly-owned resource such as coastal fisheries, rivers and lakes, forests, and pastures. Finally, Rice notes that with the recent transfer of much policy making and programme formulation from the central government to district governments, it is very important that the capacity of these local governments to analyze the factors affecting the competitiveness of HMIs and SMIs be enhanced so that related local government policies, specific programmes and projects, and activities affecting them can be improved.

The findings from two additional chapters are noteworthy. The research of the SMERU Group on the growth of the rattan industry in Kabupaten Cirebon is important for several reasons. First it examines in detail the gradual transition to a stronger dependence on non-farm income in a particular place and in a particular industry. It also examines both the economic and social impact of the ascendancy of non-farm incomes in a typical area of Java. Although the largest single group in Desa Buyut still claims farming or farm labour as their source of livelihood, in reality there is a growing tendency for this to be the preserve of the older members of the village community. The younger generation is increasingly reluctant to participate in agricultural labour, in part because of a shift in attitude towards farm work itself, but also because of the obvious and growing economic attraction of the rattan enterprises. As a result, there has been a significant reduction in available labour for agriculture, causing farm wages to increase sharply in the last few years. The general effect has been a gradual decline in agricultural activity within the village. The rattan industry has also had a significant flow-on effect to other areas of economic life within the Buyut community. Purchasing power has risen and other areas of the local economy have experienced a positive benefit.

Finally the contribution of Evans uses the case studies of diversifying production from coconuts in North Sulawesi, processing cashews in villages in South Sulawesi, and expanding markets for fishermen in remote locations of Papua to illustrate applications of the Poverty Alleviation through Rural-Urban Linkages (PARUL) programme. Recently renamed Partnerships for Local Economic Development (in Indonesian, *Kemitraan bagi Pengembangan Ekonomi Lokal or* KPEL) and executed by Bappenas (the National Planning and Development Board), the programme is funded jointly by Bappenas and UNDP and receives technical support from UNCHS (Habitat). Lessons learned from the PARUL experience suggests that any approach to local economic development, including RNFEs, must be broad based and involve local stakeholders. Market-driven initiatives can achieve positive results, especially when larger firms and buyers work together with small-scale producers. However, risks are involved and revenues are highly susceptible to external factors largely outside the control of those involved. Evans notes that often, the single biggest factor influencing outcomes for producers supplying international markets is the local currency exchange rate. Another pervasive influence on outcomes for producers of exportable commodities is prices on world markets. Fluctuations in commodity prices directly impact those involved in the chain of cultivation, processing and supply, often hurting them as was recently the case with copra and coffee products too, sometimes benefiting them as with shrimp and fish. To the extent that RNFEs and other small-scale producers use inputs or sell outputs that are tradable internationally, they will be affected by these movements in exchange rates and world prices. Since most PARUL clusters are closely linked to international markets, stakeholders are highly sensitive to these movements, which can be beneficial but also cruelly detrimental. Other kinds of activities may be largely immune to such movements, particularly those providing goods for segmented domestic markets, or offering non-tradable services, such as food vendors, *becak* drivers, beauty salons and vehicle repair shops. The evidence from PARUL shows clearly that the combined impact of these external factors is far more pervasive than the limited reach of such a programme, and far outweighs anything it might achieve. But it also shows that such programmes in support of RNFEs and other small-scale producers can make a difference, particularly in mobilizing local resources and opening up new markets. All this has been achieved by public-private partnerships effectively harnessing the resources of government, the private sector and local small-scale producers.

Insights and the Need for Further Research

Phases of the Rural Non-Farm Economy

Several additional topics dealing with the rural non-farm economy seem ripe for research. For example, recent evidence suggests that the rural non-farm economy goes through distinct phases of growth, demise and recovery (Saith 1992; Start 2001). Initially the economy is subsistence in nature while characterized by production of low value goods which are consistent with the poor purchasing power of a rural population. Subsequently in a second phase productivity increases and incomes grow. Remoteness remains high but local linkages and simple technology lead agricultural growth and fuel rural diversification. But as development proceeds into a hypothesized third phase, both increased income and reduced transport and transaction costs suggest a demise of the rural non-farm economy. Here leakages to urban areas occur as new access opens up urban markets and the locus of non-farm production is diminished under competition from urban goods and services. The protective barriers of market failure are eroded and rural leakages begin to appear. Thus rural industrial activities shed their rural linkages and locations as they modernize or are diminished via competition (Saith 2001, p. 86). This is a critical stage for policy because it is at this point that the rural non-farm sector must modernize to survive. In a final phase, where access is quite good, a new set of linkages to a congested urban-global economy develop. The locus of non-farm production shifts to the rural areas as flexible specialization is able to exploit the rural advantage. Technology and capitalization levels are elevated as simple cottage industry is transformed into a more dominant modern clustered and sub-contracted form (Start 2001). Obviously different areas may develop at different rates and many rural areas will display varying degrees of all stages concurrently. New research should aim to empirically test this theory and to explore conditions where both positive and negative deviations occur.

Linkages and the RNFE

In addition much more attention must be paid to the linkages approach to the RNFE (Saith 1992, pp. 14–16). In particular, we know too little about the interaction between rural and urban areas regarding non-farm economic activities and benefits which flow to rural residents (Leinbach 1992). For example activities may be rural located and linked to either urban or rural bases. Similarly some urban located activities may in fact have strong rural linkages and thus are critical to the rural non-farm economy. Indeed the generation of rural linkages is not contingent upon deep rural location.

The linkages between locations must also take into account that workers are increasingly mobile. Linkage patterns become more complex where with improved accessibility and transport services, many workers commute over longer and longer distances from rural to urban areas. Moreover circulation, particularly in a crisis situation, where job seekers may circulate significant distances and remain away from home for extended durations is also an important factor.

Analytically the linkage approach includes all forms of activity which retains a significant connection with income generation for rurally resident people. As the industrialization process matures, rural non-farm activities will transform their technological and production as well as locational characteristics. These adjustments affect the types and intensities of rural linkages. At an advanced stage linkages, apart from raw materials, may become restricted to remittances sent by rural origin workers (Saith 1992). The tracking of this transformation may provide analytical insights which can lead to policy developments. In addition, we need to address how systemic linkages such as those associated with financial-capital, human, labour, infrastructure and services, and social capital change as the rural non-farm economy evolves over time. Rural accessibility and the delivery of transport services play a critical role in the labour process but are only one of many themes which need further investigation.

The Value of Education

The research findings on the rural non-farm economy continue to point to the importance of education and training. Yet educational achievement is a continuing dilemma in Indonesia. Education levels in poor rural areas are especially weak. Yet the prolonged economic crisis and limited financing have forced the Indonesian government to delay the completion of its nine-year compulsory education programme for elementary and junior high school children. Under the programme, which was launched in 1994, children between seven and 15 years old are required to obtain elementary and junior high school education. Since the mandatory education programme was introduced the number of children taking part in it continued to rise to up to 70 percent of children between seven and 15 years old. The enrollment rate for elementary school was recorded at 92 percent in 1990 and rose to 95 percent in 1997, before it declined to 93 percent in 1998. For junior high school, it was recorded at 39 percent in 1990 and shot up to 56 percent in 1997 but dipped to 53 percent in 1998. The economic crisis, which also crippled other Asian economies, has effectively reduced both the government and private sectors' ability either to send children to school or to keep school education activities running (Dursin 2001). Recent data from Indonesia's Coordinating Ministry for People's Welfare and Poverty Eradication show the number of people living under the poverty line has almost doubled from 22 million people in 1997 to 40 million in 1998. The growing number of poor people in the country means, among other things, that increasingly parents can no longer afford to send their children to elementary and junior high schools. The dropout rate in both elementary and junior high schools has increased to 6 percent from the pre-crisis average of 2 percent (Dursin 2001). The continuation of social safety net programmes, where one objective is to maintain children's participation and quality of the education to at least its pre-crisis status, is imperative.

Constraint Points in Entrepreneurship and Enterprise Development

Research on small industrial enterprises, as distinguished from micro-enterprises, reveals that the success of these operations is in large part due to their cluster development which is firmly embedded in the local economy from which they derive most of their inputs (Sandee 2002). Small industries in this environment are able to collaborate to produce incremental innovations, and share information and equipment. In addition, such clustering allows joint sub-contracting and the flexible movement of workers between enterprises. Interestingly direct government support does not appear to have been very influential in Indonesia. In fact there may be some lessons here for micro-enterprise development and the successes achieved by other ventures such as in the case study of the rattan industry in Desa Buyut. Is it possible to organize similar micro-enterprises into clusters to achieve higher scaled economies, productivity and income?

At a more detailed level as we attempt to assess the reasons for success in small enterprise development a key point as noted above must be the "constraint points". That is, what particular factors explain why these enterprises fail to generate income and create employment? Obviously financing schemes, again as noted above, are critical. In fact perhaps more experimentation should be carried out utilizing small capital loans (ala the Grameen Bank) on the kabupaten or kecamatan level to well-qualified individuals who have been trained and have enterprise development plans. In spite of other strong qualifications, which may produce success, too often the entrepreneurs lack even elementary management skills.

In addition, evidence shows that access to market information and the process of integration into a wider economy are critically important for small enterprise success. Unfortunately market information—access to knowledge about market conditions and opportunities—is often poor, leading to inappropriate pricing at best and at worst, enterprise failure (Killick 2001). Coupled with this, and directly analogous to the factors which often determine success or failure in infrastructure projects, it is important to establish businesses in an environment that will be competitively sound and stimulative. An active village development committee or a carefully fostered *bapak-anak* relationship may produce this environment. Finally as we explore production possibilities in the rural economy we know too little about the role of geographical situation, proximity to small urban centres, and both forward and backward production linkages as enterprises are considered (Leinbach 1992). As noted above, in order to assess impact and encourage the most beneficial RNFEs it would be advantageous to assess to what extent an enterprise generates significant developmental linkages within the rurally resident population (Saith 1992, pp. 14–16). All of these topics it seems would warrant careful consideration and exploration in various local contexts.

Whither the RNFE under Decentralization?

We have noted that Indonesia is engaged in an unprecedented social and economic experiment. Responsibility for much government expenditure is being decentralized, largely to local (*kabupaten*) rather than to provincial governments. It is not clear at this juncture how decentralization will affect the rural non-farm economy. On the one hand contemporary evidence seems to suggest that small industries are not dramatically affected by government support. On the other it seems clear that some guidance and specific interventions will have to occur if the rural non-farm economy and especially micro-enterprises are going to becoming more effective as income and employment generators. From a policy making perspective, the state and, increasingly under decentralization, local government units face a decision: whether to step back and allow urban areas to serve as the engines of growth with perhaps little trickle down to rural areas or to intervene and invest in targeted strategies to develop rural areas in particular ways that will build incomes, allow competitiveness, and create employment.

References

Alm, James, Robert H. Aten, and Roy Bahl. "Can Indonesia Decentralize Successfully? Plans, Problems, and Prospects". *Bulletin of Indonesian Economic Studies* 37, no. 1 (April, 2001): 83–102.

Ashley, Caroline and Simon Maxwell "Rethinking Rural Development". *Development Policy Review* 19, no. 4 (2001): 395–425.

Booth, Anne. "Poverty and Inequality in the Soeharto Era: An Assessment". *Bulletin of Indonesian Economic Studies* 36, no. 1 (April 2000): 73–104.

Dursin, Kanis. "Economic Crisis Keeps Children Out of School in Indonesia". UNESCO, April 4, 2001. http://www.unesco.org/education/efa/know_sharing/grassroots_stories/indonesia.shtml.

Ellis, Frank. "The Determinants of Rural Livelihood Diversification in Developing Countries". *Journal of Agricultural Economics* 51, no. 2 (May 2000): 289–302.

Hill, Hal. "Small and Medium Enterprises in Indonesia: Old Policy Challenges for a New Administration". *Asian Survey* 41, no. 2 (2001): 248–70.

Killick, Tony. "Globalization and the Rural Poor". *Development Policy Review* 19, no. 1 (2001): 155–80.

Leinbach, Thomas R. "Small Towns, Rural Linkages, and Employment". *International Regional Science Review*. 14, no. 3 (1992): 317–23.

Leinbach, Thomas R. and John T. Bowen. "Diversity in Peasant Economic Behaviour: Transmigrant Households in South Sumatra, Indonesia". *Geographical Analysis* 24, no. 4 (1992): 335–51.

Leinbach, T.R. and John Watkins. "Remittances and Circulation Behaviour in the Livelihood Process: Transmigrant Families in South Sumatra, Indonesia". *Economic Geography* 74, no. 1 (January, 1998): 45–63.

Saith, Ashwani. *The Rural Non-Farm Economy: Processes and Policies*. Geneva: ILO, 1992.

Saith, Ashwani. "From Village Artisans to Industrial Clusters: Agendas and Policy Gaps in Indian Rural Industry". *Journal of Agrarian Change* 1, no. 1 (2001): 81–123.
Sandee, Henry. "*Industri kecil* in Indonesia: Issues in the pre- and post-crisis environments illustrated by some case studies from clusters in Central Java" in Coen Holtzappel, Martin Sanders, and Milan Titus (eds.). *Riding a Tiger: Dilemmas of Integration and Decentralization in Indonesia.* Amsterdam: Rosenberg Publishers, 2002, 211–22.
Start, Daniel "The Rise and Fall of the Rural Non-Farm Economy: Poverty Impacts and Policy Options". *Development Policy Review* 19, no. 4 (2001): 491–505.

INDEX

A

AKATIGA Foundation
  findings 75
agricultural sector
  development, emphasis on 43
  employment, source of 16, 18
  labour shortage 261, 262
  linkage with other sectors 26, 27
  low incomes 62
  role in economy 15
agricultural households
  education, investing in 30
  income, diversifying 31
  income, sources of 22, 23, 25, 32
  off-farm income 29
agricultural land
  ownership 16, 17
agricultural produce
  method of sale 246, 247

B

Bali
  agriculture, employment in 15
Bank Indonesia
  subsidized direct programme credits 82
Bank Indonesia Liquidity Credits (BILC)
  loan facility 47
Bank Perkreditan Rakyat
  loan facilities 84
Bank Rakyat Indonesia
  loan facilities 83

Bekasi
  case study 137
  circular migration, decreasing 146
  economic crisis, effect of 140, 142, 146
  household networks 138
  migrants, origin of 139
  non-farm economy, weakened 143
  rural-urban resource exchange 138
brick making
  Desa Buyut 259

C

case study on migrant entrepreneurs
  characteristics of subjects 185–9
  conclusions 202, 203
  data and methodology 184
  interpretation of findings 192–201
  model used 189, 190
  result of analysis 191
cashew processing
  PARUL initiative 285, 286
Catholic Church
  views on labour migration 116
Chayanov, A.
  theory of peasant economy 215
circular mobility
  benefits 137
  distances, effect of
  effects, study on 137

gender composition, influence
    of   144
  shortages, effect of   40
Cirebon
  rattan industry   248, 249
coconut production
  diversification   281–3
  impact on income   283–5
commerce
  impact on society   3
Common Service Facilities
  see Unit Pelayanan Teknis
conglomerates
  economic programmes,
    participating   42
cooperatives
  credit schemes   41
Cooperatives of Small-scale
    Industries
  see Koperasi Industri Kecil
corruption
  economic distortions   44
  problems   7
Credit for Small Companies
    (KUK)   42
Credit for Village Units
    (KUPEDES)   48
credit schemes
  criticisms   82
  efficiency of delivery   84, 85
  subsidized   41
  non-subsidized   42
currency
  undervaluation   5
currency exchange rates
  impact on producers   289

D

decentralization   58
  district governments, effect
    on   91
  impact on non-farm economy   303

decentralization programme
  progress   6
Desa Buyut
  agricultural produce, method of
    sale   246
  brick making   259
  case study   245
  employment   248, 260
  labour migration,
    international   258
  location   245, 246
  non-farm activities, impact
    of   260–63
  population breakdown   247
  rattan industry   248
  retail activities   259
  rice farming   247
  tea factory   260
Desa Nelereren
  expenditure of remittances   122
development banks
  loan facilities   48
Dewan Penunjang Ekspor
    (DPE)   49, 50
discriminatory practices
  women, against   88

E

East Flores
  Desa Nelereren   122
  expenditure of remittances   121
  fertility rates   116
  geographical disadvantages   126
  labour migration, impact of
    113
  population age structure   117
  population decline   113, 116
  population sex ratio   114
  women, role widened   118
East Nusatenggara
  agriculture, reliance on   31
  demography   111

Index

economic characteristics 111
economic potential 127, 128
farm holding income 20
fertility rates 116
investment capital, lacking 128
migrants, characteristics of 185, 187
migrants, self-employment of 182
national expenditure, receiving less 112
outmigration of workers 104
population decline 116
problems 110
regional gross domestic product 110
tourism potential 128
eastern Indonesia
agriculture, reliance on 18
East Timor
farm holding income 20
economic crisis
after Suharto 5
government revenue, decreasing 58
manufacturing establishments, effect on 75
rural areas, effect on 7
SMEs, effect on 57
economic distortions
corruption, caused by 44
education
expenditure of remittances 122
importance 30, 294, 301
employment
agricultural sector 15, 63
manufacturing sector 63, 73, 74
rattan industry 255
SMEs, in 56, 57
entrepreneurs
assistance 81
migrants *see* migrant entrepreneurs

entrepreneurship
effect on business outcome 170
research 154, 155
Export Support Board of Indonesia *see* Dewan Penunjang Ekspor

F
family mode of production enterprises
differences with capitalist enterprises 217
Lipton's theory 216, 217
farm holdings
income, source of 22
province, by 21
size, impact of 24
farm income
linkage with off-farm employment 28
female-operated enterprises
dynamism, less 295
factors affecting 175
family workers, impact of 174
income 164
industries involved 165
South Sumatran transmigration, in context of 236
startup capital 163, 164
fertility rates
eastern Indonesia 116
fishery
economic potential 127
market expansion 287
Flores
see also East Flores
demography 111
economic characteristics 111
labour migration 107–9
national expenditure, receiving less 112
problems 110
Sabah, migration to 109

food processing industry
  problems 80
foreign direct investment 89, 90
fuel
  price plan 6
  subsidy, reducing 5, 6

G

gender dynamics
  effect on rural economy 137
Gianyar District
  lifting of levies 56
globalization
  effects 4
government owned pawnshops
  collateral, providing 86
gross domestic product
  decrease 153

H

household manufacturing establishments (HME)
  assistance programmes 87, 88
  costs, inflated 85
  decentralization, effect of 91, 92
  economic crisis, effect of 78
  employees, number of 76, 79
  employment, growth of 73, 74
  growth 71
  income, alternative source of 61, 62
  industries 76, 79
  loan facilities 81–4
  loans, collateral for 86, 87
  policy recommendations 93, 94
  predominance in rural areas 61
  products, distribution of 90, 91
  value added 76, 79
  women, participation of 88
  workers, distribution of 70
household manufacturing industries
  changes 66

distribution 66
future research 94, 95
policies, objectives of 80
housing improvements
  expenditure of remittances 123
human trafficking
  into Malaysia 118

I

income
  agricultural households 19, 20–23, 25, 26, 32
  diversification, importance of 294
  farm holdings 22
  fishermen 287–9
  services, providing 22
  non-agricultural sources 23
  off-farm, see off-farm income
  rural dwellers 62
industrial estates
  SMEs, for 46
industrialization
  poverty, reducing 63
inter-village networks
  facilitating employment 136, 137
Islamic banking
  problem of collateral 87
ISO-9000
  SMEs, training of 48

J

Java
  agriculture, employment in 15, 18
  better schools 122, 124
  manufacturing, labour intensive 61
  off-farm income 20
  rural economic diversification 8, 9
Javanese women entrepreneurs
  research, basis of 154, 155
  see female-operated enterprises

Index

Jovanovic's learning theory
   confirmation 174

K

Kemitraan programme 46
   disadvantages 53
   obligations of conglomerates 42
KIK/KMKP credit programme
   problems 54, 55
   termination 42
Klinik Konsultasi Bisnis (KKB) 47
Koperasi Industri Kecil
   (KOPINKRA) 46
Koperasi Unit Desa (KUD) 47
KUK credit scheme 42
Kupang
   location for case study 184
KUPEDES
   micro-credit programme 48

L

labour force
   agriculture 4
   decline in availability 261, 262
   employment pattern 7
   growth rate 153
   percentage breakdown 16
labour migration
   brain drain effect 123, 124
   easing local unemployment 125
   Desa Buyut 258
   eastern Indonesia 104
   illegal 107
   impact 103
   labour exporting countries 107
   long term 114, 115
   no slowdown 294
   positive outcomes 129
   research, need for 129, 130
   sex ratio 108
land ownership
   constraints 237

Latin America
   similarities 24, 25
Lingkungan Industri Kecil (LIK) 46
Lipton, Michael
   concept of extended
      fungibility 216, 217
livelihood patterns
   changes 3
loan facilities
   see also credit schemes
   Bank Rakyat Indonesia 83
   collateral, problem of 86, 87
   government owned
      pawnshops 86
   home/small manufacturing
      establishments 81
   KUD 47
   KUEPEDES 48
   rural development banks 48
   small-scale credit (KUK) 48

M

macroeconomic imbalances
   remedies 5, 6
male entrepreneurs
   attitude and perception 171
   behaviour 172
   characteristics 166
   motivation 167
   problems, perceived 168, 169
   views on leadership qualities 173
male-operated enterprises
   net income 164
   start up capital 164
manufacturing
   growth, tracing 71
   income, source of 22
   labour intensive 61
   potential in eastern Indonesia 128
manufacturing establishments
   employment 73, 74
   value-added income 72

manufactured goods
  trading 141
market restrictions
  small-scale farmers, on 55, 56
migrant entrepreneurs
  capital accessibility 200, 201
  case study 184–6
  characteristics 187
  competition 199, 200
  employers, as 195, 196
  influences 296, 297
  local tolerance, effect of 194, 195
  location 183
  middlemen minority theory 183
  niche concentration, perception of 198, 199
  reasons for migrating 188
  South Sumatra 221–3
  support network 197, 198
migration
  circular *see* circular mobility
  labour *see* labour migration
Mid Oil Platts Singapore (MOPS) price 6
Ministry of Cooperatives and Small Businesses
  entrepreneurs, developing 50
Ministry of Industrial Development and Trade
  human resource development 49
  quality control advice 49

N
national expenditure
  regions, comparing 112
New Order
  emphasis on SMEs 38
  macro-policy changes 40–43
  policy, mixed 39
  political patronage 43
  state enterprise sector, impact on 43

non-farm economy
  Desa Buyut, effect on 262
  effect on availability of labour 260, 261
  literature 210
  perception 141
  phases 300
  research, need for 300–303
  social impact 262, 263
  supplementing agricultural base 142
  support programmes 273
non-farm enterprises
  assistance, indirect 272
  assistance from United Nations *see* Poverty Alleviation through Rural-Urban Linkages (PARUL)
  characteristics 271, 272
  contributions to economy 268, 269
  cost of inputs, effect of 290
  currency exchange rates, effect of 289
  employment, source of 269
  government assistance 270, 271
  policy planning 267, 268
  role 268
  world market prices, effect of 290
non-agricultural sector
  constituents 9
  literature 8
  migration, role in 4
  reducing unemployment 7
  role of elderly 141
  role of women 137
North Sulawesi
  coconut production, diversifying 281, 282
Nusatenggara Timor (NTT) *see* Eastern Indonesia

Index

O

off-farm employment
  holding size, affected by 214
  importance to survival 235
  income, impact on 24
  linkage with total farm
    income 28
  transmigration, effect on 9
off-farm income
  agricultural households 29, 293
  growth 27, 31
overseas contact workers
  East Flores 119
  illegal 107, 108
  level of skills 123
  registration 105
  remittances 107, 119, 120
  sex ratio 107
  source 104, 105
  target countries 106

P

Philippines
  labour migration 105
  urban-rural linkages 27
policies
  directed at rural areas 4, 5
population
  growth rate 153
  rural areas 4
poverty
  decline 30
  rate, increasing 153
  reducing, means of 63
Poverty Alleviation through Rural-
  Urban Linkages (PARUL)
  assistance to non-farm
    enterprises 274
  basic concepts 275, 276
  cashew processing 285, 286
  diversifying coconut
    production 281, 282
  failures 291
  impact on incomes 283, 284, 285
  initiatives 280, 281
  market expansion 287
  objectives 274, 275
  strategy 276–9
  technical support teams 279
pribumi entrepreneurs
  promotion 41
privatization
  progress 6, 7
programmes for economic development
  problems encountered 273, 274

R

Rancaekek
  circular migration, rate of 146
  household income 142
  migrants, origin of 139
  non-farm economy, importance
    of 148
  rural-urban resource
    exchange 138
  subject of study 137
  women, role of 146–8
rattan industry
  background 248, 249
  effect on agricultural
    labour 260–62
  employment 255, 257, 258
  enterprises, increase in 250
  factories, profiles of 251, 252
  flow-on effect 264
  impact on communal life 265
  social impact 262, 263
  sub-contractors 252–55
  worker, profile of 256, 257
Repelita
  1960s, focus in 40
  emphasis 41
  transmigration programme 211, 212

regional gross domestic product
    eastern Indonesia 110
remittances
    uses 122, 123
    impact on economy 121
    impact on regional
        development 126
    overseas contract workers 119, 120
    study on uses 125
rice farming
    pattern 247
rural households
    income, sources of 17

S
Sabah
    migrant labour 109
savings and loans cooperatives
    loans to household
        establishments 84
self-employment
    reasons 183
services
    income, source of 22
shrimp fishing
    income, increasing 288
small and medium enterprises
        (SMEs)
    avoidance of formal economy 55
    corruption, problems arising
        from 44
    credit schemes 41, 42
    economic bias 44, 45
    economic crisis, effect of 57
    employment, generation of 56,
        67
    future 58, 59
    government revenue, impact
        of 42
    policies, influences on 51, 52
    policy, mixed 39
    programmes 45–9

State Policy Guidelines, 1999–
    2004 38
systems ISO-9000 appraisal 48
trends 52
Small Business Consultancy Clinic
    see Klinik Konsultasi Bisnis
small enterprises
    economic role 153
    gender analysis 157
    growth, factors affecting 161
    growth measurement 161
    labour, quality of 165
    labour requirements 161
    performances, factors
        affecting 173
    performance indicators 162
    potential for income
        generation 176
    problems, perceived 168, 169
    research focus 153, 154, 159,
        160
    starting, motivation for 167
    startup requirements 163
small manufacturing establishments
    economic crisis, effect of 78
    employees, number of 77, 79
    employment, growth in 73, 74
    future research 94, 95
    income, source of 64, 65
    industries, distribution of 67, 68,
        77, 79
    loan facilities 81
    policies, impact of 297
    policy recommendations 93, 94
    urban-rural distribution 69
    value added 77, 79
small rural development banks 48
small-scale credit (KUK) 48
social safety net
    definition 135
    importance 140
    non-farm economy, in 295

Index

Southeast Asia
  agrarian differentiation 9
South Sulawesi
  cashew processing 285
  income, increasing 286
South Sumatran transmigration
  agricultural labour 235
  business ownership 221, 226, 227, 236
  dual business households 295
  female operated businesses 236
  home industries 224–26
  land ownership constraints 237
  long history of transmigration 218
  off-farm employment 235
  prior research 213, 214
state enterprise sector
  New Order, feature in 43
State Policy Guidelines
  focus 40
  small and medium-sized enterprises 38
studies
  entrepreneurship 155
  female entrepreneurship 157–79
  inter-household divisions 136
  social networks 147
Survey of Agricultural Household Incomes, 1993 24
surveys
  agricultural household incomes 29
  effect of crisis on income 137

T

Taiwan
  off-farm growth rate 31
  urban-rural linkages 27
technical assistance difficulties 88, 89
Technical Service Centres
  see Unit Pelayanan Teknis

Total Quality Control (PMT)
  programme 49
tourism
  eastern Indonesia, potential in 128
trading
  dominated by landed households 141
transmigration programme
  distinctive groups of people 212
  objectives 211
  South Sumatra *see* South Sumatran transmigration

U

Unit Pelayanan Teknis (UPT) 46, 47
  problems 53, 54
United Nations Centre for Human Settlements
  technical support for PARUL 274
United Nations Development Programme
  funding of PARUL 274

V

value-added income
  definition 65
  manufacturing establishments 72

W

WARSI programme
  SMEs, access to 49
West Java
  extended families, role of 136
women
  contribution, crisis survival 148
  contribution, non-farm sector 137
  economic crisis, effect of 145

migrant workers, as 144, 145
role widened 117, 118, 146
women entrepreneurs
  see also female-operated enterprises
  age, effect of 174
  attitude and perception 171
  behaviour 172
  characteristics 166
  Javanese *see* Javanese women
    entrepreneurs
  motivation 167
  problems 156, 168, 169
  research 154–7
  research findings 176–8
  training, level of 165
  views on leadership qualities 173
women workers
  employment 31
workers
  distribution between
    industries 70, 71
  unpaid 70